Johnson's
mother
&baby

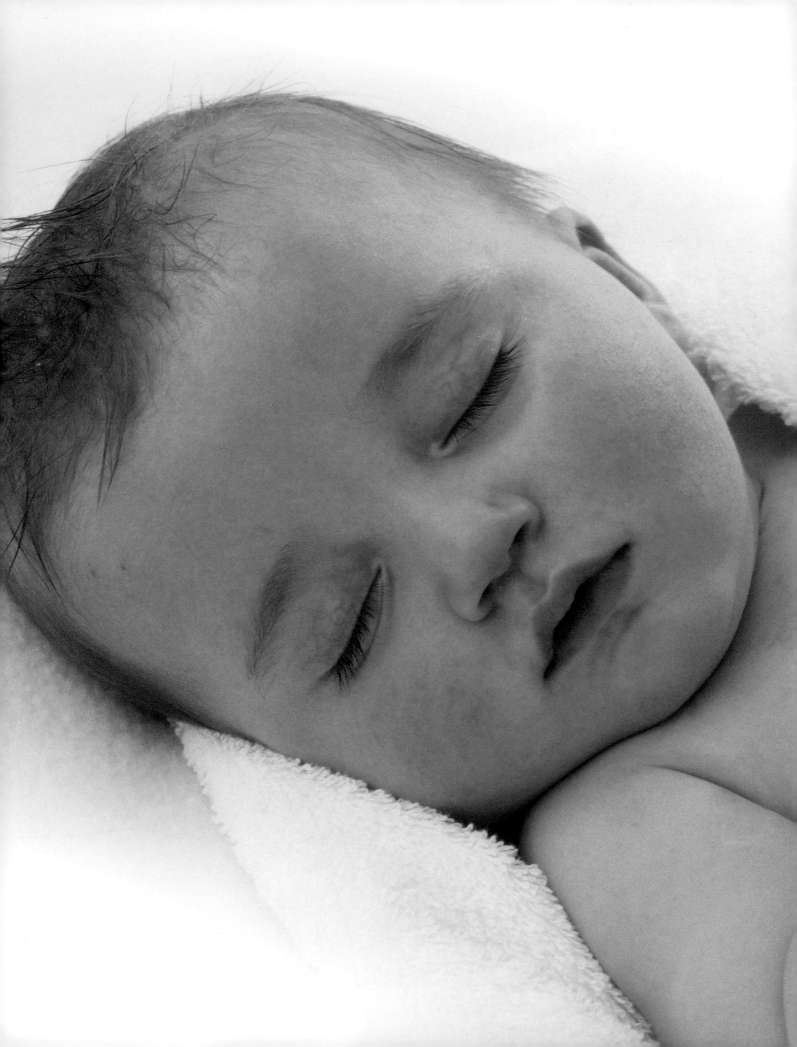

Johnson's® mother & baby

Consultant Editor

Dr Carol Cooper
MA, MB, BChir, MRCP

Photography by Ruth Jenkinson

A Dorling Kindersley Book

LONDON, NEW YORK, MUNICH, MELBOURNE, DELHI

To my mother, from her baby

Senior art editor: Glenda Fisher
Project editors: Angela Baynham,
Corinne Asghar, Anne Esden
Project art editors: Alison Tumer,
Liz Brown, Edward Kinsey
DTP designer: Karen Constanti
Production controller: Heather Hughes
Managing editor: Anna Davidson
Managing art editor: Emma Forge
Art direction: Sally Smallwood
Jacket editor: Beth Apple
Jacket designer: Nathalie Godwin

Category publisher: Corinne Roberts

First published in Great Britain in 2003 by
Dorling Kindersley, A Penguin Company
80 Strand, London, WC2R 0RL

Every effort has been made to ensure that the information contained in this book is
complete and accurate. However, neither the publisher nor the authors are engaged in rendering
professional advice or services to the individual reader. The ideas, procedures, and suggestions
contained in this book are not intended as a substitute for consulting with your healthcare
provider. All matters regarding the health of you and your baby require medical supervision.
Neither the authors nor the publisher shall be liable or responsible for any loss or damage
allegedly arising from any information or suggestion in this book.

A CIP catalogue record for this book is available from the British Library

ISBN 0 7513 1314 9

Reproduced by Colourscan Overseas Pte Ltd, Singapore
Printed by Toppan Printing Co (HK) Ltd, Hong Kong

See our complete catalogue at
www.dk.com

A Message to Parents from Johnson & Johnson

The most precious gift in the world is a new baby. To your little one, you are the centre of the universe. And by following your most basic instincts to touch, hold, and talk to your baby, you provide the best start to a happy, healthy life.

Our baby products encourage parents to care for and nurture their children through the importance of touch, developing a deep, loving bond that transcends all others.

Parenting is not an exact science, nor is it a one-size-fits-all formula. For more than a hundred years Johnson & Johnson has supported the healthcare needs of parents and healthcare professionals, and we understand that all parents feel more confident in their role when they have information they can trust.

That is why we offer this book as our commitment to you to provide scientifically sound, professionally reviewed guidance on the important topics of pregnancy, baby care and child development.

As you read through this book, the most important thing to remember is this: you know your baby better than anyone else. By watching, listening, and having confidence in your natural ability, you will know how to use the information you have in your hands, for the benefit of the baby in your arms.

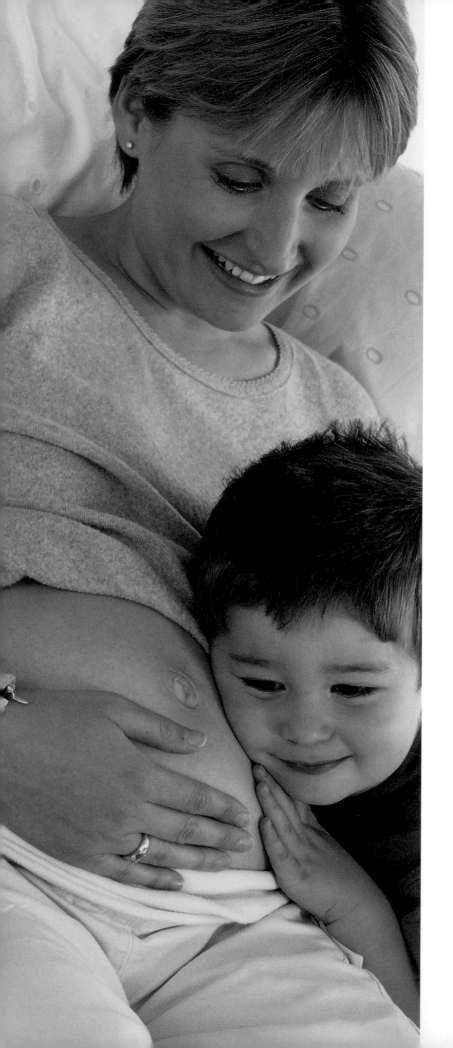

contents

baby and child care 81

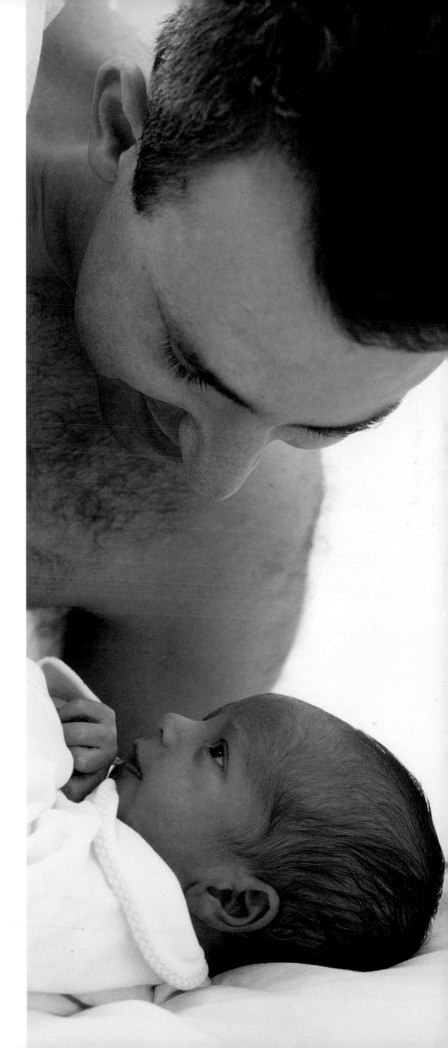

introduction

From the moment you start to think about becoming parents, you are embarking on life's most amazing adventure. People have babies every day, but when it happens to you it is the most magical experience in the world, one that alters your perspective on life. As you welcome your baby as the newest member of your family, you can look forward to deep joy – and plenty of fun.

As your baby grows into a child and then matures into an adult, there will be many different influences on him, but you are the most important of all. The relationship you forge with your child forms the pattern for every one of his relationships throughout life. At the same time, you have lots of practical matters to attend to, such as feeding and bathing your baby, and protecting him against illness.

There aren't hard-and-fast rules on how to bring up a baby, but there is a lot of information for new parents to absorb. This book aims to support and guide you on all the important issues of parenting, so that you can be confident and make the most of family life. Much of the advice represents a fusion of my professional expertise as a family doctor and my personal experience as a mother.

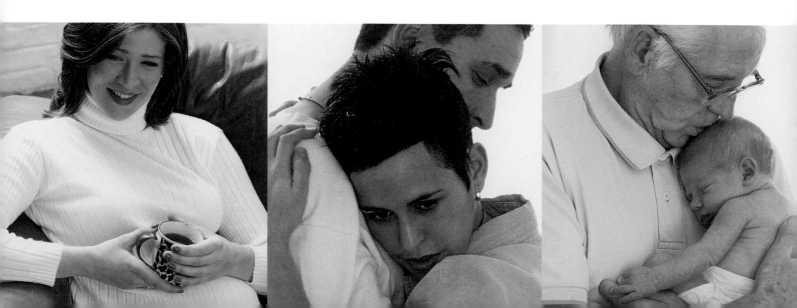

how this book works

The book is divided into four main sections.

pregnancy takes you all the way from pre-conception and planning right through to the birth and recovery afterwards. This is an exciting time and expectant women – and their partners – are fascinated by what's happening in the womb during the months of pregnancy. At each stage, words and pictures show you the changes taking place in your own body and how your baby is growing. There is plenty of helpful information on diet and exercise during pregnancy, what your antenatal care will involve, and reassuring advice on how to cope with common discomforts, and when to get medical help if conditions of concern arise.

baby and child care is fully illustrated and shows you how to look after a baby from birth until the age of three. This section, arranged chronologically to guide you as your child grows up, is where you can find information on feeding, weaning, bathing, dressing, sleeping, and the like. There's down-to-earth advice on managing a crying baby, feeding and weaning, toilet training, and other issues that we know parents can find challenging. Throughout you'll notice that the emphasis is on making the most of the time you spend with your child, even if you're carrying out only a basic task such as changing your baby's nappy.

development covers a topic that is important to parents, but can be confusing. What your child can do at each age is a barometer of his growing understanding of the world. Reaching developmental milestones also provides parents and grandparents with some glorious moments. You will get a thrill from your baby's first smile, first sounds, and first steps. We hope this section will put development into perspective and help parents appreciate the wide range of normal behaviour. Once again, the accent is on understanding a baby's and young child's development so that you can enjoy every moment, celebrate achievements, and help bring out the best in your child.

health gives valuable advice on ways to help protect your child from illnesses and accidents. Designed to be straightforward to use, it also includes a number of conditions which, though fairly common, are not always covered in childcare books – hand, foot, and mouth disease or Kawasaki syndrome, for example. While easy to assimilate, the information takes into account the latest medical thinking. Throughout, my aim is to give you the same advice and reassurance I give parents in my consulting room. I have also drawn on my own experiences as a parent to share with you my tips on caring for a baby or child who isn't feeling at his best. At the end of this section there's advice on first aid. Although we hope you never need to put these procedures into practice, it is a good idea to read through this section and keep it as a handy reference if needed.

At the very end of the book you'll find a resource list, consisting of names and addresses of support groups, charities, and other organizations. These are divided into four categories to correspond with the four main sections of the book, and internet addresses are included wherever possible.

the richness of family life

You will soon find out that parenting isn't a one-way process. Your moods and your child's moods will affect each other, and there will inevitably be highs and lows as your child grows up. This is completely normal. Becoming a parent may be natural, but it is not always a simple transition to make. This book is here to help you meet the challenges, and deal with the hopes and fears that are part of family life.

We recognize, too, that families come in all shapes and sizes, and that parents have important relationships other than the one with their child. That's why you will find there is something for everyone – whether you're a working parent, stay-at-home parent, single parent, or even a grandparent or caregiver. We hope you'll discover plenty in this book to guide you and stimulate you. As I have learned, raising children is a uniquely satisfying experience. We wish you great happiness and fulfillment as you set out on this amazing adventure.

Dr Carol Cooper MA, MB, BChir, MRCP

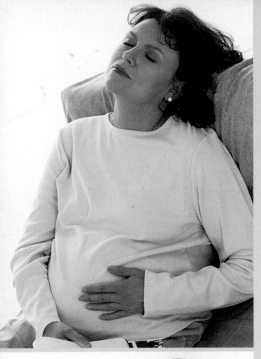

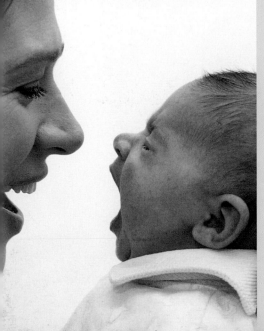

pregnancy

The next nine months or so are an extraordinary time for you and your growing baby. Your body and your emotions will change as never before, while inside you your baby is developing faster than he will at any other time in his life. Soon, your tiny embryo will become your fully developed new baby. Don't worry if you have questions. This section will give you guidance on the choices available for antenatal care and labour. Before you know it, you'll be ready for the momentous process of birth and the many joys that lie ahead.

planning a baby

How wonderful! You've decided you'd like to have a baby. It's a big decision because it's going to change your life for ever – but in the nicest possible way. Trying for a baby can be an anxious time, but most couples do not experience problems. Don't expect to become pregnant immediately, but do consider the possibility that, within a few months, you will be expecting your child.

lifestyle considerations

Before you start trying for a baby and once you are pregnant, it's worth taking a lifestyle check.

No one is expecting you to change radically, but there may be some adjustments that you and your partner can make to ensure you're doing all you can to safeguard your health and that of your child.

Diet

Healthy eating during pregnancy doesn't differ much from any other time: opt for fresh fruit and vegetables, limit processed food, biscuits and cakes, and don't eat too much fat. Once you're pregnant, avoid undercooked meat; unwashed vegetables and salads; unpasteurized foods and cheeses (see page 27). You won't be sure you're pregnant until you're at least two weeks into the pregnancy, so you might want to avoid these foods when you start trying to conceive.

It's also recommended that you take a folic acid supplement (0.4 mg) as soon as you start trying to get pregnant, as this has been shown to reduce the incidence of spina bifida and other neural tube defects.

Menstrual cycle
The menstrual cycle lasts on average 28 days, during which the uterus prepares itself for fertilization. The uterine lining (endometrium) thickens to receive a fertilized egg, then sheds if the egg is not fertilized. Follicle-stimulating hormone (FSH) causes an egg to mature, and luteinizing hormone (LH) triggers its release. Oestrogen levels peak just before ovulation and the rise in progesterone stimulates the endometrium to thicken. Ovulation takes place around day 14, and the most fertile period is approximately day 12 to day 16.

The first step towards healthy eating is to look at the foods in your daily diet. Early in pregnancy, some women find that their appetite comes and goes. Try to eat a variety of foods each day. An average non-pregnant woman needs about 2,200 calories per day. When you are pregnant, you need about 300 calories more.

Smoking

Stop smoking when you begin trying for a baby and don't resume after the birth to avoid risking your health and the health of your baby. Each puff subjects you and the fetus to harmful chemicals such as nicotine, tar, and carbon monoxide. If you or anyone else smokes around the baby,

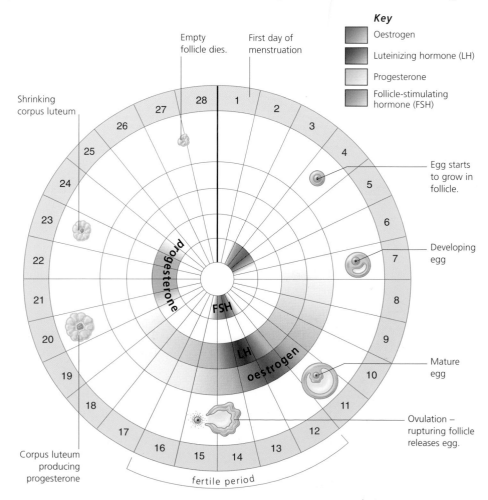

Key
- Oestrogen
- Luteinizing hormone (LH)
- Progesterone
- Follicle-stimulating hormone (FSH)

Empty follicle dies.

First day of menstruation

Shrinking corpus luteum

Egg starts to grow in follicle.

Developing egg

Mature egg

Ovulation – rupturing follicle releases egg.

fertile period

Corpus luteum producing progesterone

progesterone

FSH

LH

oestrogen

trying for a baby

♦ Don't worry too much about timing sex with the day you're ovulating – research shows that couples who make love throughout the month tend to conceive most quickly. Just enjoy your sex life.

♦ At the same time, bear in mind that you are at your most fertile and most likely to conceive in the middle of your menstrual cycle (see diagram opposite).

♦ Cut down on coffee consumption – it can take longer to conceive if you're drinking more than three cups a day.

♦ If you have a hectic lifestyle, try to take things more calmly than usual. There's no real evidence that stress interferes with conception, but it certainly can't do any harm to reduce your stress level.

---

he or she is exposed to the harmful effects of the smoke, so it is also vital that your partner and any other members of the household stop smoking.

Alcohol

It is unknown how much alcohol is too much during pregnancy, but research shows that it may cause a serious condition called Fetal Alcohol Syndrome (FAS). Heavy drinking can also increase the risk of miscarriage. To be safe, don't drink any alcohol during pregnancy.

Other considerations

When you decide you are ready to conceive, there are several important factors you should consider.

♦ Any medical condition for which you or your partner takes regular medication – talk to your GP and/or specialist.

♦ Any genetic or congenital condition in your own or your partner's family – talk to your GP and if there are grounds for concern ask for a referral to a geneticist before you start trying for a baby.

♦ Your rubella status. If you're worried you might not be protected against rubella (German measles, which if contracted during pregnancy can harm the baby), ask your doctor for a blood test. Have a vaccination at least three months before you conceive.

♦ Don't try for a second or subsequent baby until you feel sure you can cope with more responsibility.

"Over the last 18 months we've talked more about starting a family, and now it's happening it's tremendously exciting. Finding out Jenny wasn't pregnant the first three or four months was quite a surprise. Then when we did conceive we hadn't expected to. We were amazed, as well as thrilled, when the test was positive."

SIMON NORTH, 30, HUSBAND OF JENNY, 8 WEEKS PREGNANT

Becoming parents
Creating a new life together is a unique way of expressing your love. Discuss your hopes and feelings before you start trying to conceive.

fertility problems

Although fertility problems have become more common in the last few years, don't worry, you are still unlikely to be affected. Nine out of 10 couples conceive during the first year of trying, and of the remainder, about half conceive in the second year.

Age makes a difference

If you're in your 20s you're less likely to have fertility problems, so don't rush off to your doctor if it's been three months and nothing has happened. If, on the other hand, you're in your late 30s or even your 40s, and you don't conceive within six months, it's worth going for a referral – if only to get some advice.

Many couples who fear they're having fertility problems find that just seeking professional advice seems to help, and they conceive easily at that point without the need for intervention.

Having a fertility problem investigated is a tough time for any couple, especially if – as is often the case – you're surrounded by pregnant friends and siblings.

Once you have decided to try for a baby it can be tempting to tell the world because you are excited. However, if you do you will probably have lots of questions from well-meaning friends and family about whether you are expecting a baby yet, so you might want to consider keeping your decision private for a while.

Keeping life in perspective

Try not to let your attempts to have a baby become the focal point of your life. Plan treats and holidays and don't put things off "in case" you're pregnant. If you do conceive, you'll adjust your plans as you need to, and keeping a sense of perspective is very important right now.

conception

Oh my goodness – deep down you hadn't really believed it would happen to you, and the news that you have conceived might leave both you and your partner feeling a little uncertain. Finding out you're expecting a baby is an amazingly exciting moment. Of course, it happens to thousands of people every day, but right now you probably feel as though you're the only ones it has ever happened to.

discovering you are pregnant

You can't be sure yet but you strongly suspect that somewhere deep inside you there's a tiny bundle of cells that is going to change your life for ever.

Some women "know" they're pregnant, but the vast majority don't realize until about 14 days after fertilization has taken place. Noticing your period is late is the number one sign that you're probably pregnant.

However, it is possible to have bleeding when you are pregnant – although it will probably be scantier than usual. If a pregnancy test is positive and you are bleeding, see your doctor.

Pregnancy tests

Most people buy a test from the supermarket or pharmacy and do it at home. You can, if you prefer, ask to have a test at your doctor's surgery – the ones they use are often very similar to home tests. The

Pregnancy testing kit
Home testing kits are simple to use and very accurate if you follow the instructions.

basic pregnancy test checks your urine for a hormone called HCG (human chorionic gonadotrophin). You urinate onto a stick and within a short time you see a colour change in the window, indicating you are

calculating your **delivery date**

The average pregnancy lasts for 266 days, measured from conception. As it can be difficult to know exactly when conception occurred, the delivery date is usually calculated from the first day of your last menstrual period (LMP). This means that your estimated delivery date (EDD) will be 280 days from your LMP.

To calculate your EDD, find the date of your LMP in the left-hand columns of the chart opposite. The date in the adjacent right-hand column is your EDD.

Remember that this is only an estimated date, and very few babies actually arrive on the date given. The delivery date is particularly difficult to predict if you do not have regular 28-day cycles. Doctors consider anything between 38 and 42 weeks to be a normal-length pregnancy.

Jan	Oct	Feb	Nov	Mar	Dec	Apr	Jan	May	Feb	Jun	Mar	Jul	Apr	Aug	May	Sep	Jun	Oct	Jul	Nov	Aug	Dec	Sep
1	8	1	8	1	6	1	6	1	5	1	8	1	7	1	8	1	8	1	8	1	8	1	7
2	9	2	9	2	7	2	7	2	6	2	9	2	8	2	9	2	9	2	9	2	9	2	8
3	10	3	10	3	8	3	8	3	7	3	10	3	9	3	10	3	10	3	10	3	10	3	9
4	11	4	11	4	9	4	9	4	8	4	11	4	10	4	11	4	11	4	11	4	11	4	10
5	12	5	12	5	10	5	10	5	9	5	12	5	11	5	12	5	12	5	12	5	12	5	11
6	13	6	13	6	11	6	11	6	10	6	13	6	12	6	13	6	13	6	13	6	13	6	12
7	14	7	14	7	12	7	12	7	11	7	14	7	13	7	14	7	14	7	14	7	14	7	13
8	15	8	15	8	13	8	13	8	12	8	15	8	14	8	15	8	15	8	15	8	15	8	14
9	16	9	16	9	14	9	14	9	13	9	16	9	15	9	16	9	16	9	16	9	16	9	15
10	17	10	17	10	15	10	15	10	14	10	17	10	16	10	17	10	17	10	17	10	17	10	16
11	18	11	18	11	16	11	16	11	15	11	18	11	17	11	18	11	18	11	18	11	18	11	17
12	19	12	19	12	17	12	17	12	16	12	19	12	18	12	19	12	19	12	19	12	19	12	18
13	20	13	20	13	18	13	18	13	17	13	20	13	19	13	20	13	20	13	20	13	20	13	19
14	21	14	21	14	19	14	19	14	18	14	21	14	20	14	21	14	21	14	21	14	21	14	20
15	22	15	22	15	20	15	20	15	19	15	22	15	21	15	22	15	22	15	22	15	22	15	21
16	23	16	23	16	21	16	21	16	20	16	23	16	22	16	23	16	23	16	23	16	23	16	22
17	24	17	24	17	22	17	22	17	21	17	24	17	23	17	24	17	24	17	24	17	24	17	23
18	25	18	25	18	23	18	23	18	22	18	25	18	24	18	25	18	25	18	25	18	25	18	24
19	26	19	26	19	24	19	24	19	23	19	26	19	25	19	26	19	26	19	26	19	26	19	25
20	27	20	27	20	25	20	25	20	24	20	27	20	26	20	27	20	27	20	27	20	27	20	26
21	28	21	28	21	26	21	26	21	25	21	28	21	27	21	28	21	28	21	28	21	28	21	27
22	29	22	29	22	27	22	27	22	26	22	29	22	28	22	29	22	29	22	29	22	29	22	28
23	30	23	30	23	28	23	28	23	27	23	30	23	29	23	30	23	30	23	30	23	30	23	29
24	31	24	1	24	29	24	29	24	28	24	31	24	30	24	31	24	1	24	31	24	31	24	30
25	1	25	2	25	30	25	30	25	1	25	1	25	1	25	1	25	2	25	1	25	1	25	1
26	2	26	3	26	31	26	31	26	2	26	2	26	2	26	2	26	3	26	2	26	2	26	2
27	3	27	4	27	1	27	1	27	3	27	3	27	3	27	3	27	4	27	3	27	3	27	3
28	4	28	5	28	2	28	2	28	4	28	4	28	4	28	4	28	5	28	4	28	4	28	4
29	5			29	3	29	3	29	5	29	5	29	5	29	5	29	6	29	5	29	5	29	5
30	6			30	4	30	4	30	6	30	6	30	6	30	6	30	7	30	6	30	6	30	6
31	7			31	5			31	7			31	7	31	7			31	7			31	7
Jan	Nov	Feb	Dec	Mar	Jan	Apr	Feb	May	Mar	Jun	Apr	Jul	May	Aug	Jun	Sep	Jul	Oct	Aug	Nov	Sep	Dec	Oct

explaining **fertilization**

Fertilization occurs when the sperm meets the egg, usually in the fallopian tube, and penetrates it. The sperm's body and tail then break off. Next, the head of the sperm joins forces with the nucleus of the egg – each contains half the number of chromosomes normally found in a human cell, which is 46. The 23 sperm chromosomes and the 23 egg chromosomes then pair up. This minuscule cell now contains every piece of genetic information that your baby needs to develop into the child, and beyond that the adult, you will come to know and love.

How gender is determined
You and your partner are each providing half the material to create this new human being – and your genes are now being rearranged in a totally unique way. The only difference between what your genes and your partner's do concerns sex determination: every egg a woman produces contains an X chromosome, because the genetic make-up of a female is XX. But sperm come in two different types: X sperm (which, when combined with an egg, will make a baby girl) and Y sperm (which make a boy). Whether you're having a boy or a girl is therefore decided at fertilization, before you find out you're pregnant.

Twins
A twin fertilization occurs either when a fertilized egg divides into two at a very early stage, creating genetically identical twins who are the same sex, or when two separate eggs are fertilized by separate sperm, creating fraternal, or non-identical, twins, who may be the same or different sexes.

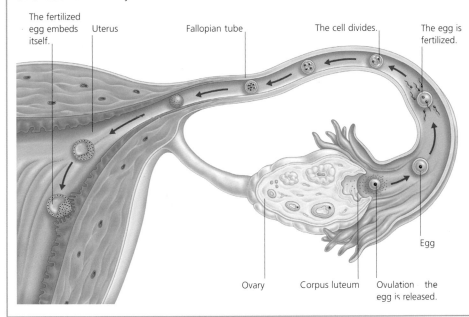

The fertilized egg embeds itself. | Uterus | Fallopian tube | The cell divides. | The egg is fertilized.

Ovary | Corpus luteum | Ovulation the egg is released. | Egg

pregnant. If no change occurs, the test is negative. Sometimes, especially if you're testing on the day your period was due, you may see just a faint colour change. It is still a positive test, although you may want to repeat it in a few days to be certain. If the test is negative but you still feel you might be pregnant, repeat the test a few days later. If there is any doubt, your doctor may perform a serum (blood) pregnancy test.

Other indications
Many women in early pregnancy don't feel any different. Some, though, do have other indications that they've conceived:
♦ needing to urinate more frequently
♦ feeling more tired by early evening
♦ a strange taste in the mouth – some women describe it as metallic
♦ feeling nauseous
♦ tender nipples that are darker than usual.

"I thought my period had started so I told my husband I wasn't pregnant. But 24 hours later there was nothing so I did a test. I was amazed when it was positive. I phoned my husband straight away and he couldn't believe it – we still can't, really. It's our secret, because we've decided we're not telling anyone else for a few weeks yet."

MARIA PEEL, 32, NEWLY PREGNANT

assisted **conception**

Fertilization fuses the genetic material of the egg and the sperm within a single cell. This is true whether your baby has been conceived entirely naturally or via an assisted reproductive technique. Often, a failure to conceive is the result of a problem in the mechanism that brings the egg and sperm together (for example, the woman may have blocked fallopian tubes, or the sperm may not be mobile enough to swim to where it's needed).

How assisted conception works
Assisted reproductive techniques such as IVF (in vitro fertilization, in which the egg and sperm are brought together outside the body) and GIFT (gamete intrafallopian transfer, in which the sperm and eggs are mixed outside the body then placed together in the fallopian tubes) allow fertilization to occur in couples whose chances of success by natural means are, for whatever reason, low.

antenatal care

What's available in terms of antenatal care differs from one region to another, and there are often a lot more options available to you if you live in a city rather than a rural area. But wherever you live you should have some choice in the type of care you receive.

types of care

Before you choose the kind of care (and birth) you want, you must understand all the possibilities. Ask your midwife for advice.

Midwives are specialists in all aspects of antenatal care, so they can advise you on what types of care are available in your area. Your doctor can also help you.

♦ **Shared care** You are looked after jointly by your GP and a midwife or team of midwives. It is the most common sort of care available in the UK. You will probably alternate your check-ups between the GP and the midwife, possibly going to the hospital once or twice for ultrasound scans and to see a consultant if the need arises.

♦ **Midwife-only care** This may be available in your region, and is the care you're most likely to have if you're hoping for a home delivery. Usually the midwives will work in a team, often of six or eight, and you'll get to know everyone on the team. The advantage of this sort of care is that you're more likely to know the midwife who's with you in labour, and who visits you at home afterwards.

♦ **Consultant care** You'll have all, or most, of your antenatal checks at the hospital, and will see the obstetrician or one of his medical staff at each visit. You will also meet hospital midwives who will carry out your routine checks. This is the care for you if there's anything to indicate any risks associated with your pregnancy, either because of a pre-existing medical condition or because of a pregnancy-related problem.

♦ **Independent midwives** These offer private antenatal care and are often used by women hoping for a home birth. They can be costly, although they're usually cheaper than a private hospital. They carry out your antenatal checks at home, and if you need a Caesarean section they'll care for you at home afterwards so you can be discharged from hospital early.

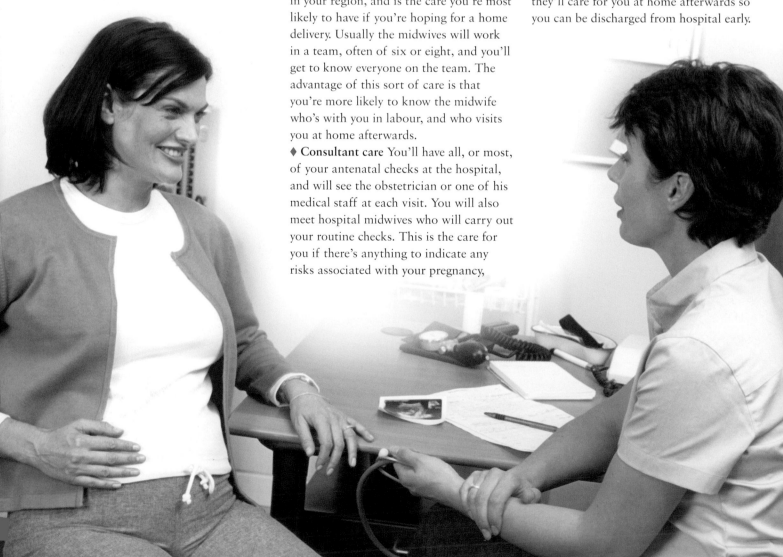

your **booking appointment**

Your first antenatal appointment is known as your "booking appointment". It's usually with a midwife, but it may also involve a chat with an obstetrician or it may be done by your GP. Where bookings are done by midwives, you may be offered the opportunity to have the midwife visit you at home – this is worth taking as it can be a lot more informal and relaxing than having to go to the clinic, and it may be more convenient if you have to travel by public transport or have other children.

What to expect
Your booking appointment will probably last about an hour. You'll be asked about your and your partner's medical history

and about your menstrual history and the date of your last period. Your blood pressure will be measured, your urine checked for protein (which could indicate pre-eclampsia) and glucose (a possible sign of gestational diabetes), and your uterus palpated to give an idea of how your baby is growing.

It's an opportunity to ask questions, and it may be worth your partner coming along too, if he is willing and able. In some areas, the booking appointment is combined with the nuchal fold scan (see below) or an early scan to date the pregnancy.

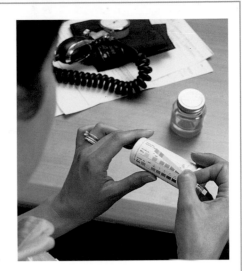

Regular checks
At each appointment your blood pressure will be tested and your urine checked for protein and glucose.

diagnostic and screening tests

In addition to the mid-term ultrasound fetal anomaly test (see page 39), you may be offered one or more of the tests listed below. The decision should be made between you, your partner, and your caregivers.

Although your caregivers may recommend certain tests, the choice about whether to have them is yours. Always ask why you are being referred for a test, so that you can make an informed decision. Bear in mind that diagnostic tests are invasive, so carry a slight risk of miscarriage.

Talk this through thoroughly with your caregivers and partner. Think about whether you would consider a termination if the test result was positive.

These tests may also reveal the sex of your unborn child, so establish beforehand whether you want this information or not.

WHICH TEST?	AT WHAT STAGE?	HOW THE TEST WORKS
Nuchal fold scan	11–14 weeks	Ultrasound check that measures a fold of skin at the back of the baby's neck: a thick fold could be an indication of Down syndrome (see page 260).
Triple or Bart's test	15–16 weeks	Uses a blood test to measure three hormones. An ultrasound is also done to date the pregnancy. Computer analysis of the hormone levels, considered with the mother's age and date of pregnancy, estimates the likelihood of Down syndrome.
Amniocentesis (diagnostic)	14–26 weeks	Involves taking a sample of amniotic fluid, and with it a few cells shed by the baby, via a needle. Results show whether your baby has Down syndrome or other chromosome disorders.
CVS (chorionic villus sampling) (diagnostic)	11 weeks onwards	Fragments of your placenta are analyzed to check for Down syndrome or other chromosome disorders.
Cordocentesis (fetal blood sampling) (diagnostic)	Used late in pregnancy – 18–22 weeks onwards	A sample of blood is taken from the umbilical cord to check whether the baby has a chromosomal abnormality, an infection, or a blood disorder such as severe rhesus disease. Not commonly done.

rights and benefits

Maternity rights in the UK have improved considerably. Mothers have been granted the right to take more time off work, although some entitlement is unpaid so not everyone can afford to take it. In general, though, rights for parents with small children are better than they've ever been in this country, and understanding your entitlements is also quite straightforward.

knowing your rights

Make sure that you look into your rights at work long before your baby is due. If you delay making your application for leave, or do not notify your employer of your intentions by a particular date, you could lose out.

Also, although no one expects to have a premature baby it is possible that it could happen to you, so it is best to be prepared well in advance. If you find out about your maternity rights by the time your baby is born it's a lot easier to get the payments you are entitled to straight away, and you will not have to worry about applying when you are busy with your new baby. You should tell your employer as soon as you know you are pregnant. The human resources officer will keep the information confidential, and you will be able to have time off for any early appointments.

your **rights**

♦ You are entitled to paid time off work for antenatal care. This can include parentcraft and relaxation classes as well as medical checks, providing your midwife or GP can confirm that you need to take these classes (they will be happy to do this).

♦ You cannot be treated unfairly at work, dismissed, or selected for redundancy because of your pregnancy.

♦ You are entitled to free prescriptions and free dental care. You may need to get an exemption certificate from your doctor or midwife.

♦ If you become ill and are unable to work you can still take sick leave, for the most part without affecting your maternity leave. For more information see www.tiger.gov.uk/index.htm

Working while you are pregnant

Working through a pregnancy, especially your first, can be a strange experience. When you're expecting a baby everything is different, and your priorities have obviously shifted: at the same time, you may feel very strongly that you're as committed to your work as ever, and no one should think otherwise.

You may feel compromised now that your colleagues know that you're about to change your life by becoming a mother. They will take their lead from you to some extent, so if you don't want to spend a long time at work talking about your happy event, resist the temptation to discuss your pregnancy, unless you have to. However, be aware that you may need to make some adjustments to your life at work.

Keeping active helps your circulation, and as you get bigger regular exercise makes you feel less weighed-down (psychologically at least) by your pregnancy.

Throughout your pregnancy, always listen to what your body tells you: this isn't the time to go for any medals for round-the-clock working, whatever you do for a living.

Taking a break
Even if you usually work through your lunch hour, try to find the time to go for a walk or even a swim one or two days a week.

registering the birth

♦ Once your baby is born you are legally required to register the birth within six weeks if you live in England, Ireland, or Wales, and within three weeks in Scotland. Go to the registry office nearest to where she was born, as that is where her details will have been sent.

♦ If you are married, only one of you need attend. If you are not married, you should attend together if the father's details are to be registered.

♦ You will be given a birth certificate and a form to enable you to get a medical card with a National Health Service number.

♦ After the baby is registered you will not be able to change the name more than once, even the spelling, and you will have to pay for a new certificate if you do this.

your maternity leave

You have statutory entitlements to time off and remuneration. These are your rights by law, and every employer must grant you these. If you have any problems, speak to your caregivers (see page 20) as they should be able to advise you.

♦ **Ordinary Maternity Leave** Regardless of the length of service you've had with your employer, or the hours you've worked, you have the right to 26 weeks' Ordinary Maternity Leave.

♦ **Statutory Maternity Pay** You are entitled to this for the 26 weeks of your Ordinary Maternity Leave, paid at a rate of 90 per cent of your average earnings for six weeks. It is then paid at a flat rate of £100 a week for the remaining 20 weeks.

♦ **Additional Maternity Leave** If you have worked for your employer for at least 26 weeks to the 15th week before your due date, you are entitled to an extra 26 weeks of unpaid leave to be added onto your Ordinary Maternity Leave, making a total of 52 weeks' leave in total.

♦ **Maternity Allowance** If you are self-employed, you may be entitled to Maternity Allowance, a government benefit, paid for 18 weeks.

Giving notice of your leave

You must give your employer at least four weeks' notice of your intention to take maternity leave, so don't leave it too long.

You may plan to work until the last few weeks, but be prepared to be flexible: you cannot predict how you will feel.

Giving notice of your return

You should give at least four weeks' notice of your intention to return to work and your starting date whether or not you are taking your full entitlement.

paternity leave

♦ Fathers are entitled to two weeks' leave after the birth of their baby. They are usually entitled to be paid at a rate of £100 a week for these weeks.

♦ Both parents are also entitled to parental leave, which is 13 weeks' unpaid leave for each parent to be taken by the child's fifth birthday.

♦ All the information given here refers to statutory obligations (the minimum entitlements available in law). Whether you're a father or a mother, always find out what the company you work for offers in terms of leave and pay: it may be considerably better than the law requires.

FIRST TRIMESTER												SECOND TRIMESTER															THIRD TRIMESTER													
1	2	3	4	5	6	7	8	9	10	11	12	13	14	15	16	17	18	19	20	21	22	23	24	25	26	27	28	29	30	31	32	33	34	35	36	37	38	39	40

weeks 0-8

It has just about sunk in that you're having a baby – and it's amazing how much is going on inside your body. By week eight, it's about four weeks since your period would have been due, but you're already two-thirds through the first trimester – even if you don't feel it.

your body changes

Lots of women don't feel or look any different at this stage – if that applies to you, don't worry, there IS a lot going on.

You are producing a lot of hormones to help establish the baby's life support system, and your breasts are already beginning to prepare for feeding your baby.

Classic symptoms

If you do feel different, it's likely to be tiredness and perhaps nausea that affect you most. The tiredness can be more draining than any you've ever experienced before: even women who are used to staying up late at night or working shifts are often surprised by having to go to bed much earlier than usual. Some say they even wake up feeling totally exhausted, and a few confess to needing a nap during the day. Nausea is the other classic early pregnancy symptom, commonly known as "morning sickness" (see opposite).

FACTS ABOUT **YOU**

♦ Your heart rate is increasing – possibly by about 10 beats per minute.

♦ Your breasts are getting bigger, and may feel a lot more sensitive than usual.

♦ Your metabolic rate is increasing by between 10 and 25 per cent.

♦ You may have put on 900g–1.4kg (2–3lb). Only a tiny percentage of this is the baby; the rest is the weight of your growing uterus and its contents, and the forming placenta.

easing your **symptoms**

Dealing with fatigue

Don't try to beat tiredness – the only thing to do is listen to your body and, if possible, change your schedule so you can rest more.

If you are commuting to work, try to change your travel times so you're not in the car or on the train at the busiest times of the day, which is stressful and can really wear you out.

Nausea

Some women find dry toast and crackers help with nausea (for more tips see *managing morning sickness* opposite).

Mood changes

If you find you are experiencing lots of mood changes and swings, talk it through with your partner so he understands how you're feeling. Don't shut him out, keep communicating.

YOUR CHANGES YOUR BREATHING RATE INCREASES • YOUR STOMACH FEELS BLOATED • YOU SOMETIMES FEEL FAINT • YOU MAY SUFFER FROM CONSTIPATION • YOU WILL NEED TO URINATE FREQUENTLY

your emotions

The first weeks of pregnancy are often a time of conflicting emotions. Although you may have longed for a baby, worries about the future, plus the hormonal changes going on inside your body, can be unsettling.

Adjusting to being pregnant

On the one hand, you're hugely excited – your life is about to be changed for ever by the arrival of a baby. You may have longed for a baby, or maybe your pregnancy is a complete surprise. Either way, you are now looking forward to becoming a mother. You know this change is going to throw you and your partner into a new world – and it's a world you can't fully know until you're actually there. So there are also worries – about how it's going to change your life, your relationship, and your career.

Hormonal changes can make you prone to mood swings, irritability, and weepiness – some women compare this time to a prolonged period of premenstrual tension!

Common concerns

♦ **Am I really pregnant at all?** If you're not experiencing many physical symptoms this is often a worry, but you are not the only woman who has thought this!

♦ **Am I putting on too much weight?** Nausea can make a lot of women eat more than usual in the early weeks, and you might not want to pile on extra pounds. Try to eat healthy snacks.

♦ **Am I going to miscarry?** Miscarriage is most common in the first trimester, but with each day and week that goes by your pregnancy is more established. If you've had any bleeding, or have any other reason to be especially worried, report your concerns to your doctor. An ultrasound may be performed.

What you can do

Talk through you concerns with your partner, but try to relax and be confident that, whatever challenges you may face as a family, your lives will be enriched by the creation of this new life.

case history

SARAH WILLIAMS, 34
8 WEEKS PREGNANT

"I've been a lot more careful about what I eat and drink over the last few weeks – fortunately I haven't felt like drinking alcohol, so I've been able to cut it out without problems. I avoid undercooked meat and unpasteurized food such as cheeses, too, because of the risks of toxoplasmosis and listeria, both of which could damage the baby, especially in the early weeks and months of pregnancy. I try not to get too paranoid about it all, but on the whole it seems sensible to play safe."

managing **morning sickness**

Pregnancy nausea is like no sickness you've ever experienced before – often it's a kind of gnawing emptiness and you feel you just have to have something to eat. The trouble is, eating doesn't necessarily help (or not for long) and may even make you vomit.

The term "morning sickness" is misleading. As many women experience nausea or vomiting in the evening as in the morning, and for the very unlucky it can go on throughout the day.

The positive side is that nausea is due to the increased amount of hormones circulating in your system – which is usually a sign of a healthy pregnancy.

A common concern is "Am I going to feel this awful for another seven and a half months?" If you're suffering badly from tiredness and sickness you may worry about this – but the answer, happily, is almost certainly no, and you should feel a lot better by week 13 or 14.

Diet and nutrition

Eat little and often to help balance blood-sugar levels. Look for foods that are rich in vitamin B6 and zinc, as nausea is linked with deficiencies in these nutrients. Try wholemeal bread, or ginger in any form. You may find it helpful to eat something before you get out of bed, such as a dry cracker or a ginger biscuit. Keep snacks to hand throughout the day. Even if you are vomiting, try to eat as healthily as you can.

Eating well
Bananas are rich in vitamin B6 and will help to prevent your blood-sugar levels from dropping.

"I've felt sick a lot, but distracting myself seems to help. If I keep busy, and I'm enjoying what I'm doing, I can keep the nauseous feelings at bay. Having plenty of snacks throughout the day also seems to help. I try always to have an apple in my bag, and a bottle of water, too."

KAREN SERGEANT, 26,
8 WEEKS PREGNANT

SEE ALSO ANTENATAL CARE pages 20–21 ● EATING WELL page 27 ● HAVING A SCAN page 29 ● DENTAL CARE page 37 ● A WORKING PREGNANCY page 41

your baby at 8 weeks

Although it's only six weeks since your baby was actually conceived (because pregnancy is dated from the start of your last menstrual period – see page 18), all the main internal organs are already in place. Of course, there's a lot of development left to happen, but the rudiments of all the vital body parts are now present and correct.

Your baby's appearance

Although your baby is tiny (just under 2.5cm/1in long), he already has the beginnings of a recognizably human face, with nostrils, lips, and a mouth with a tongue. His head and face begin as the largest part and curve inward towards the tail, or bottom – at this stage, your baby looks a bit like a tadpole. Buds have already appeared and are beginning to develop into arms and legs – there are also nodules which are growing into hands and feet.

Your baby is covered in a thin layer of skin cells, but is still translucent. He weighs about the same as a grape, and has already started moving around inside your uterus – although, of course, it will be some weeks before you'll be able to feel the movements yourself.

Development

In the early weeks of life, your baby's body parts and internal organs are forming. Over the months ahead, they will become more specialized and complicated. Initially, there are three layers of cells which go on to create the different systems of his body.

The innermost layer develops into the heart, lungs, liver, thyroid gland, pancreas, and bladder. The middle layer becomes the skeleton, muscles, sex organs, blood cells, and kidneys. The outer layer becomes the skin, sweat glands, hair, nails, and tooth enamel. At eight weeks, all these cell types are busy creating the systems they will be responsible for, so deep inside you there is an incredible amount of activity going on.

As your baby is so busy developing, you can see why it is important to look after yourself, and why you may feel very tired and rather nauseous at times during these early weeks.

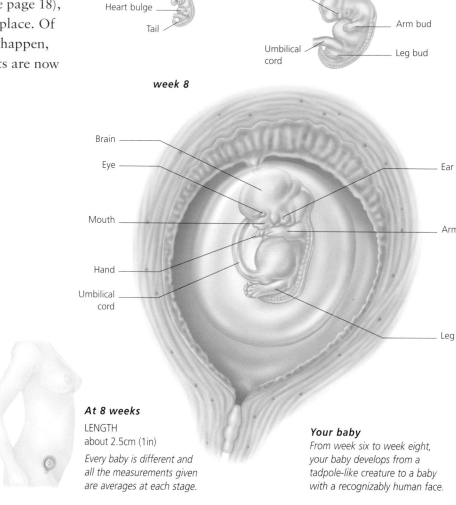

week 6
Head
Heart bulge
Tail

week 7
Eye
Arm bud
Umbilical cord
Leg bud

week 8
Brain
Eye
Mouth
Hand
Umbilical cord
Ear
Arm
Leg

At 8 weeks
LENGTH
about 2.5cm (1in)
Every baby is different and all the measurements given are averages at each stage.

Your baby
From week six to week eight, your baby develops from a tadpole-like creature to a baby with a recognizably human face.

your **growing** baby

♦ From week eight, your baby officially graduates from being an embryo to being described as a fetus. This literally means "little one".

♦ The little tail has almost completely disappeared by this stage.

♦ His heart has already started to beat, and this can now be seen on an ultrasound.

♦ This means his blood is already circulating around his little body, thanks to the pumping action of his own heart.

♦ His heart has four chambers, and beats at approximately 180 beats per minute, which is about double the speed of an adult's heart.

♦ The placenta, which will form the baby's life-support system, is developing fast and is becoming concentrated in one area of the uterine wall.

♦ The uterus, in which the baby is growing, is still only about the size of a tennis ball.

♦ Your baby's fingers and toes are beginning to develop, but these are still slightly webbed at week eight.

♦ Initially, the arms develop faster than the legs – just as later, after birth, your baby will develop hand and arm control faster than leg control.

♦ Ten dental buds have formed in each jaw. These will become baby teeth.

eating well

A good diet will benefit both you and your baby throughout pregnancy. Your baby relies on you for all of his nutrients, and so it is important that you provide your body with the right foods to sustain you both.

Basic rules

A balanced diet is a major part of good health at all times in your life. During pregnancy, diet is even more important. When you are pregnant, you need about 300 calories more a day than you usually eat. You shouldn't need supplements, but it is recommended that you take folic acid throughout the first trimester (see page 16).

Eat lots of fresh fruit and foods rich in fibre, as constipation is often a problem in pregnancy. Cut down on processed foods, as these are often high in fat and sugar and low in nutrients.

Cravings

It is common to develop a taste for certain foods during pregnancy. If you do, listen to your body and indulge yourself, as long as you stick to the safety guidelines and don't eat excessively.

Foods to avoid

Although the chances of contracting an infection from food are low, it is best to avoid the following foods:
♦ unpasteurized dairy produce, especially soft and blue-veined cheeses
♦ undercooked eggs and poultry
♦ offal and offal-based produce
♦ undercooked meats and pâtés
♦ pre-prepared meals, unless heated thoroughly.
In addition, limit your intake of caffeine and alcohol (see below) and wash all fruit and vegetables before eating or cooking.

Vegetarian diets

These can be just as healthy as diets that include meat, and the extra vegetables will be beneficial. However, you may need iron and vitamin B12 supplements. Ask your caregiver (midwife or GP) for advice.

Eating between meals

Keep healthy snacks, such as pieces of fruit, to hand so that you do not get too hungry throughout the day. Eating regular small meals keeps your blood sugar stable and can help prevent indigestion.

questions & answers

q Is it safe for me to carry on drinking alcohol?

a Frequent, heavy, or binge drinking could seriously harm the development of your baby. The safest course of action is to avoid alcohol during pregnancy.

q Should I avoid caffeine?

a Caffeine, found in tea, coffee, carbonated drinks, and chocolate, can have a detrimental effect on the digestive system, and inhibits the absorption of iron. Cut down to one cup a day, or cut it out.

Camomile tea
Try this instead of caffeinated drinks. Camomile will also help you relax.

q Are any drugs safe to take during pregnancy?

a If you have a medical condition that requires drug treatment, discuss the situation with your doctor – ideally before you are pregnant, and certainly once you are. Drugs for some conditions may be continued. It's a question of weighing up the risks to you if the drug is stopped, compared with the risk to the baby if drugs continue to be taken. Sometimes, a different drug is safer.

Street drugs aren't a good idea at any time but there are additional hazards if you're having a baby – some consequences, such as birth defects, premature birth, and placental bleeding, are very serious.

q Surely the occasional cigarette won't harm my baby?

a The evidence for not smoking during pregnancy is overwhelming. When you smoke, carbon monoxide and nicotine pass into your lungs and bloodstream. As a result, your baby receives a reduced amount of oxygen, and his heart beats faster.

If you smoke, or spend time in a smoky atmosphere (if your partner smokes, for instance), your baby is more likely to have a low birthweight, to be miscarried, or to be born prematurely, and is at greater risk of Sudden Infant Death Syndrome (see page 225). Children of smokers are also more likely to suffer from illnesses such as asthma.

Cigarette smoke makes many women feel queasy in the early weeks of pregnancy. If your partner smokes too, make a pact to give up together. Giving up smoking is the first positive thing that you and your partner can do for your new baby.

FIRST TRIMESTER											SECOND TRIMESTER																THIRD TRIMESTER													
1	2	3	4	5	6	7	8	9	10	11	12	13	14	15	16	17	18	19	20	21	22	23	24	25	26	27	28	29	30	31	32	33	34	35	36	37	38	39	40

week 12

Congratulations – you're officially pregnant! Not that nothing has been happening until now, of course – but this is the stage when a lot of couples decide to "make it official", to spread the good news and to celebrate with family and friends that there is a new baby on the way.

your body changes

You may have been looking forward to reaching this point in your pregnancy, as getting this far dramatically increases the chances of everything going well. Your clothes may be beginning to feel slightly tight, but you probably still won't look pregnant and it could be several weeks before you'll need maternity clothes.

Feeling better

If you have been suffering from tiredness and pregnancy sickness, the good news is that from this week onwards both are likely to diminish. Don't expect everything to be perfect from tomorrow, but in the next week or two, if you're lucky, you may find that two or three hours have gone by and you haven't felt sick. It's a breakthrough, and who knows, before long you might even be able to watch the late news without falling asleep!

By this stage you may have put on about 10 per cent of your total pregnancy weight gain (about 1.2kg/ 4½lb), although if you have lost weight from morning sickness, your gain may be less. Don't worry if this applies to you. You should be feeling better soon, and you will catch up by eating a healthy diet. Speak to your caregivers if you are concerned.

FACTS ABOUT YOU

♦ Your placenta has taken over production of the hormones that are supporting the baby's growth. As a result, your risk of miscarriage drops.

♦ You may develop a hormone-related dark line, called the linea nigra, on your abdomen – this will fade after the birth.

♦ You may develop dark marks on your face called chloasma, or the "mask of pregnancy". These should fade after birth.

♦ Your uterus is the size of a grapefruit.

easing your symptoms

Bleeding gums
This is due to a hormonal change. Try not to brush too vigorously, but be very careful not to neglect your dental hygiene. Make the most of your free dental care and go for regular check-ups.

Frequent urination
Lean forward when you urinate to empty the bladder fully as this may help reduce the number of times you need to go. Don't drink less water; you need more, not less, when you're pregnant.

Increased breast size
Buy a good-quality bra, and have it professionally fitted (see page 33).

Skin problems
Increased hormones may result in acne. Cleanse more often and increase your intake of fresh fruit, vegetables, and water.

YOUR CHANGES   YOU MAY DEVELOP A DARK LINE CALLED THE LINEA NIGRA ON YOUR ABDOMEN • ANY NAUSEA MAY BE JUST STARTING TO WEAR OFF • YOU MAY NEED TO URINATE FREQUENTLY

your emotions

You're probably feeling very relieved now you've reached 12 weeks and the risk of miscarriage has dropped dramatically. But you may find yourself worrying about the prospect of screening tests.

What you can do

Some women welcome an early scan as the chance to see the baby for the first time, but for others, the possible results are a source of anxiety. The fact is, every pregnant woman worries whether her baby is going to be healthy, but the chances are very high that all will be well.

Talk through the various tests that are recommended by your doctor with your caregiver, and ensure you understand what the ones you are opting for involve (see page 21).

If you and your partner do not want to have any of the screening tests that you are offered you may refuse.

case history

SARAH ELLIS, 27
12 WEEKS PREGNANT

"I had my antenatal booking appointment with a midwife this week. The whole thing took about an hour, and the midwife came to visit me at home which was a lot nicer than having to go to the hospital or clinic. We had a good chat and got on well, and it all seemed really easy-going.

"I'll need to get some blood samples tested so she gave me lots of forms to fill in, to take with me when I do go to the antenatal clinic. She tested a urine specimen there and then, and that was fine.

"The midwife asked me whether I'd thought about where to have the baby. When I replied that I thought you had to have your first baby in hospital she told me that wasn't the case – I could go for a home delivery if I felt it would be right for me. It's an exciting idea, and I do feel very drawn to it. I'm going to find out as much as I can and discuss it with my partner and then talk to the midwife when I go for my next check-up in a month's time."

having a scan

You will probably be offered an ultrasound scan some time between the 11th and 13th weeks of your pregnancy. The aim of this is to date your pregnancy accurately and check the location of the placenta, in case it is lying low. A measurement may also be made of the nuchal fold at the back of your baby's neck to help determine the likelihood of Down syndrome (see page 21). This scan can also detect whether you are expecting more than one baby.

At this stage of pregnancy ultrasound scans are usually carried out via a transvaginal probe, which gives the operator the clearest possible view inside your uterus. If you do have a external scan, you will be asked to drink lots of water to help provide a clear picture of the baby.

Having a scan is not painful, and one of the benefits is that this is your first chance to see your baby. This is an unforgettable, moving moment for both parents. You may also be given a picture, for which there might be a small charge.

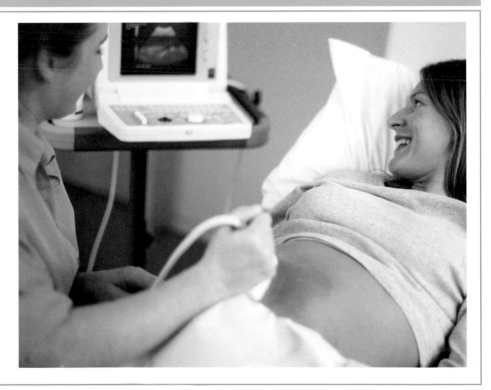

SEE ALSO   ANTENATAL CARE pages 20–21 • RIGHTS AND BENEFITS pages 22–23 • MANAGING MORNING SICKNESS page 25 • EATING WELL page 27 • MATERNITY CLOTHES page 33 • DENTAL CARE page 37

your baby at 12 weeks

It's an extraordinary thing to contemplate, but by week 12 your baby is already a fully formed human being. From now on she will get bigger and the various body systems will mature, but the most amazing developments have already taken place, and there is a tiny, kicking baby deep inside you.

Your baby's appearance

The face you will see in a few months' time is taking shape rapidly. At just 12 weeks your baby has a chin, a high forehead, and a tiny nose. Her eyes have moved to the front of her head from their earlier position at the sides, although they are shut and still spaced a long way apart.

Your baby's ears have moved higher on her head and the external ears are well developed. Improved muscular control means that she can purse her lips and wrinkle her forehead to form a frown.

The umbilical cord, which connects mother and baby, delivers vital supplies of oxygen-rich blood and nutrients. As her hands, which are already well developed, begin to unfurl, the cord will become her first plaything as she reaches out and grasps it.

Development

The weeks from eight to 12 have been a particularly busy stage in your baby's development. The main organs are all present inside this tiny fetus, although they are not yet fully functional. The heart is pumping blood around the body; the stomach is forming and is linked to the mouth and the intestines.

The cells that will form the brain are multiplying rapidly and moving to the correct areas. At the same time, the baby's head is enlarging to accommodate her developing brain.

If you could take a peek into your uterus right now, there would be no denying there was a baby in there. Even at this stage, the fetus is recognizably human – an awesome thought. She's still absolutely tiny, of course – about 6cm (2½in) long, which is about the size of a plum.

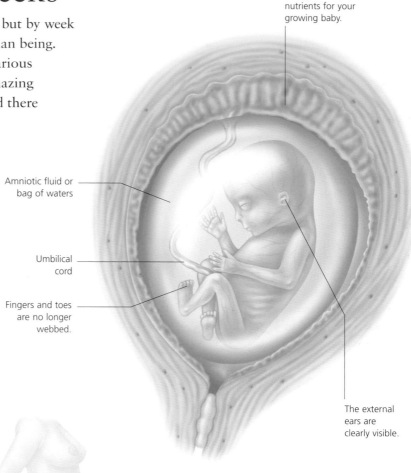

The placenta provides nutrients for your growing baby.

Amniotic fluid or bag of waters

Umbilical cord

Fingers and toes are no longer webbed.

The external ears are clearly visible.

At 12 weeks
LENGTH about 6cm (2½in) crown to rump
WEIGHT about 15g (½oz)

Your baby
Her developing muscles enable her to move around in the uterus, kicking and curling her newly formed fingers and toes.

your **growing** baby

♦ Although you can't yet feel it, your baby is quite active – she kicks and stretches within the uterus.

♦ Her immediate environment is the amniotic fluid, and your baby is already swallowing minute amounts of it in preparation for swallowing milk once she is born.

♦ She can also pass urine, which becomes the amniotic fluid.

♦ Her arms are quite well developed and can already bend at the elbows.

♦ She has wrists and ankles.

♦ She has tiny fingernails.

♦ Her head is still very large, about half the length of her entire body.

♦ Her fingers and toes have now separated and are distinct.

♦ The external genitals are developing, although it is not yet possible to tell the sex of a baby visually on a scan. Testes or ovaries have formed inside your baby's body.

♦ Eyelids have formed over the eyes, although they cannot open yet.

♦ She has earlobes.

♦ She can flex her fingers and toes and make a fist.

the placenta

By the time you reach week 12 the placenta has formed properly and is able to take over the all-important job of supporting the pregnancy. This is why the risk of miscarriage diminishes, and the tiredness and nausea you may have experienced will begin to ease.

What is the placenta?

At this stage of pregnancy the placenta is actually a lot bigger than your baby. It is a thick, disc-shaped organ which is attached to one part of the uterus, usually in the upper half.

In the early weeks the placenta grows at a much faster rate than your baby, to ensure that she is adequately nourished. From now on that changes, and by the time your baby is born, the placenta will weigh about a sixth of her weight and will be about the size of a dinner plate.

The placenta will be delivered after your baby at the birth. Have a look at it if you're given the opportunity, because it really is fascinating to see the organ that has quite literally sustained the life of your child (see page 73 for more on third-stage labour).

How the placenta works

The placenta enables you to supply all your baby's needs from now until she is born. It produces the hormones necessary to support the pregnancy, maintain the health of the uterus, and even prepare the breasts for lactation. It is a sophisticated filtering system, using your blood to deliver nutrients and oxygen to your growing baby. It also removes your baby's waste products.

What you can do

The placenta protects your baby from many toxins, but certain medicines and alcohol can still cross it, so it's important to limit your exposure to potentially harmful substances. Cigarette smoking diminishes the placenta's effectiveness and exposes your baby to toxins.

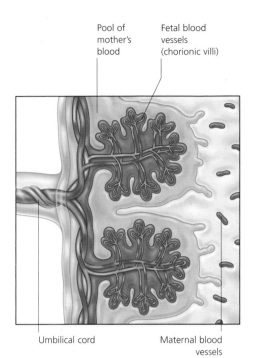

Pool of mother's blood

Fetal blood vessels (chorionic villi)

Umbilical cord

Maternal blood vessels

The structure of the placenta
The placenta allows the mother and baby to exchange fluids, nutrients, and gases, but does not mix maternal and fetal blood. Exchange takes place where the placenta adheres to the uterine wall.

---

questions & answers

q Will the midwife be able to hear my baby's heart when I go for my first check-up?

a Yes, if it is done at about 12 weeks or later. The midwife can use a hand-held ultrasound device, which uses high-frequency sound waves to check the baby's heartbeat. You will be able to hear it clearly, too. This device doesn't harm the baby, and you'll find it tremendously reassuring, and probably very moving, to hear your baby's heart beating healthily.

Hand-held Doppler device
This hand-held device is a non-invasive method of checking the baby's heartbeat.

q I'm going for a scan this week – will the scan operator be able to tell me at this stage whether I'm having a boy or a girl?

a Although the genitals are developing, it will almost certainly be too early to tell if it's a boy or a girl. A scan at this stage is really to date the pregnancy accurately; to check whether you're having one baby or more; to see that the heart is beating properly; and maybe to look at the nuchal fold (see page 29).

q I'm wondering whether to have screening tests. Are the chances high that I might be expecting a Down syndrome baby?

a The probability depends mostly on the age of the mother. A baby with Down syndrome can be born to a mother of any age, but the risk becomes greater the older

q Can my baby sense the outside world?

a She is beginning to respond to the world outside the uterus. If the mother's abdomen is pressed she may try to move away.

a woman is. In your 20s you have about a 1 in 1,000 chance; by 35 it's 1 in 350; by 40 it's 1 in 100; and by 45, it's 1 in 25. Think about what you would do if you found your individual risk was high. Would you want an invasive test (see page 21), and would you consider terminating the pregnancy? If the answer is no, you may not want to put yourself through the possible worry of a scan. However, if you would prefer to know your risk it is worth having the scan.

week 16

The fact that you're expecting a baby has really sunk in now, and hopefully the nausea and tiredness of early pregnancy have receded or even disappeared. What's more, you probably look pregnant now. This is the blooming phase of your pregnancy – enjoy it!

your body changes

This is when things start to increase rapidly – your appetite and your bump! Having said goodbye to the nausea of the first trimester, you may feel ravenous a lot of the time and your clothes may be a little tight. Pay attention to your body's needs.

Visibly pregnant

As your bump gets bigger you are going to need a few larger items of clothing, and you'll get your money's worth if you start wearing them now (see opposite). Snack on fresh fruit and wholegrain cereals – these are more nutritious than processed food and sweets and will help alleviate the constipation you may be experiencing as a result of your digestive system being more sluggish. Dried fruit is an excellent source of iron, and also helps alleviate constipation, which can be aggravated by iron supplements.

Your skin may become more deeply pigmented. Your nipples and the surrounding areolae may also become darker.

FACTS ABOUT **YOU**

♦ Your uterus is getting five times the amount of blood pumped to it as it did before the pregnancy, to support your growing baby.

♦ Your kidneys are processing 25 per cent more blood than usual.

♦ Your heart rate has increased, and its output is 30–50 per cent above its pre-pregnancy level.

♦ You've probably gained about 2.25–4.5kg (5–10lb) in weight.

easing your **symptoms**

Tight clothing
Don't ignore any feelings of tightness in your clothing or underwear – invest in looser outfits now (see opposite).

Keeping active
Getting into an exercise routine now, if you have not already, will help you keep fit as you get bigger. Look for a pregnancy exercise class, where the action will move at the right pace.

Constipation
Drink lots of water and eat plenty of fresh fruit snacks throughout the day.

Recording your symptoms
Make a note of any symptoms you experience so you remember to discuss them with your midwife when you go for your antenatal check – it's all too easy to forget if you don't write them down.

YOUR CHANGES   YOU'RE PROBABLY MORE ENERGETIC THAN IN THE EARLY WEEKS • YOUR BUMP MAY BE JUST ABOUT VISIBLE • YOU MAY HAVE CONSTIPATION

your emotions

This is often the most exciting stage of pregnancy, as you may have the pleasure of feeling your baby move inside you for the first time – a moment you will never forget.

Feeling your baby move

You may feel your baby move any time now, especially if this is your second or subsequent child. Initially you won't be sure whether what you feel is a tummy rumble or a genuine baby flutter, but over the next few weeks the sensation will get stronger and you'll soon be in no doubt at all! First-time mothers often don't notice movement until about 20 weeks or later.

Work worries

Telling people outside of your immediate circle of close friends and family can be exciting and you may be enjoying all the attention. However, making the pregnancy public can be a time of mixed feelings. At work you may fear that colleagues will think you're not so serious about your job any more, and you may wonder how you will cope if you plan to return to work after the birth. Talk to other women with children about how they managed, and you'll see that strategies to cope with being a working mother (if that's what you want, or will have to do) do emerge (see pages 114–115).

Thinking about antenatal classes

Popular classes get booked up quickly, so if you're interested in taking them, talk to your midwife at your next appointment about parenting education available at the maternity unit, if you haven't already.

"My midwife wondered whether I was having twins. I'd had a lot of sickness in the early weeks, and she thought my uterus was quite big. My husband and I went for a scan at week 15, and discovered that we were indeed expecting two babies! I feel a bit daunted, but it's very exciting."

SARAH-JANE SIMPSON, 25, 16 WEEKS PREGNANT

maternity **clothes**

Maternity clothes don't have to be expensive. If you're working you may need to invest in a significant outfit or two. Some boutiques offer up-to-the-minute styles, but think before you invest in an expensive outfit – you won't be wearing these clothes for long. If you are hoping to have more children, look for classics you can bring out in a couple of years' time. Second-hand maternity clothes outlets can be very useful; parenting organizations can often give you details of what is available in your area.

Creating your own style

It is important to feel comfortable in your clothes, not just physically but emotionally as well. Choose clothes that make you feel attractive throughout your pregnancy. Fitted bump-enhancing clothes are often more flattering to your new body shape than loose dresses and baggy jumpers, although you should choose maternity clothes that suit your own personal style and taste.

Underwear

You will need a comfortable bra that gives you good support. As your breasts will be changing size throughout your pregnancy, it is a good idea to be measured professionally. Buy two at first, then more as your breasts grow. Look for a bra with a deep band under the cups, broad shoulder straps, and an adjustable back. You may find cotton bras most comfortable. Later in pregnancy you may want to wear a light-weight bra for support while you sleep.

If you are planning to breastfeed, you will need to buy at least two nursing bras, but you should wait until week 36 of your pregnancy before you are measured for these to be sure to get the right size (see page 53).

SEE ALSO RIGHTS AND BENEFITS pages 22–23 • EATING WELL page 27 • A WORKING PREGNANCY page 41 • EXERCISE AND POSTURE page 45 • ANTENATAL CLASSES page 49 • A SENSUAL PREGNANCY page 53

your baby at 16 weeks

You may not be able to feel it yet, but your baby is already moving around quite vigorously in your uterus. His eyelids are still closed, but this week or next he might hear his first sounds – which will be sounds from inside and outside your body.

Your baby's appearance

His limbs and features are formed, his legs are now longer than his arms, and he looks more in proportion than at 12 weeks. But he still looks very thin, with transparent skin through which the blood vessels are visible: the layer of fat under his skin hasn't been laid down yet, so he has yet to become the chubby baby you'll hold after the birth.

His external genital organs are now formed, and if you had an ultrasound scan at this stage the operator might be able to tell you whether you were having a boy or a girl (although this would depend partly on your baby's position in the uterus at the time).

Development

Although he's so tiny, your baby is already quite adept at movement. He can flex and extend his limbs and fingers, and he kicks and somersaults in the amniotic fluid. This is partly so he can tone his muscles and practise the movements he'll need to make to develop his coordination after he's born.

He is also trying out facial expressions, as his facial muscles are already developed – although since the nervous system is still developing, these aren't fully under his control yet. The tiny bones in his ears are hardening, enabling him to hear your voice, your heart, and even your digestive system.

Amniotic fluid

Your baby's immediate environment is the amniotic fluid – for him, it's like being immersed in a warm swimming pool and trying out underwater movements. The umbilical cord is like a diver's breathing apparatus, because it delivers essential oxygen via the blood cells. The amniotic fluid cushions your baby from any knocks from outside the uterus.

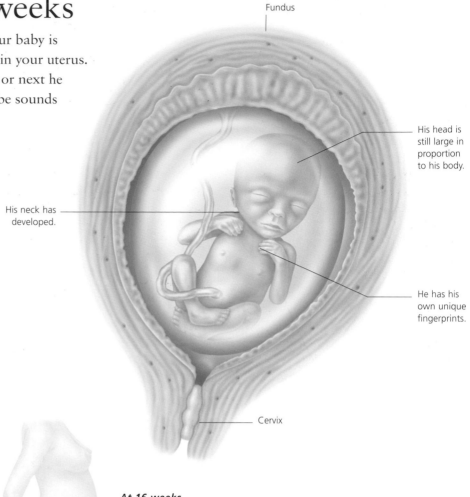

Fundus

His head is still large in proportion to his body.

His neck has developed.

He has his own unique fingerprints.

Cervix

At 16 weeks
LENGTH about 12cm (4³/₄in) crown to rump
WEIGHT about 130g (4¹/₂oz)

Your baby
His facial features continue to develop as the facial bones form, and tiny fingers and toes can be seen.

your **growing** baby

♦ This is a period of rapid growth. In the last four weeks your baby will have almost doubled in length, and his weight will have increased to about 130g (4¹/₂oz).

♦ His finger- and toenails are well formed. Some babies' nails grow so much in the uterus they need to be trimmed soon after birth.

♦ A girl baby has about two million eggs in her ovaries by this stage – the number first increases and then diminishes during pregnancy so that by birth she has about one million, compared with 200,000 at age 17.

♦ His ears have moved from his neck, where they started to develop, to their correct position on the sides of his head.

♦ Your baby swallows some amniotic fluid, and his kidneys turn this fluid into urine – he empties his bladder approximately every hour into the amniotic sac.

♦ He yawns and stretches in the uterus from time to time.

♦ He has very small eyebrows and eyelashes.

♦ Fine, downy hair has formed over his face and body (lanugo).

♦ He may suck his thumb.

♦ His skeleton is beginning to develop, first in the form of flexible cartilage, then hard bones.

♦ Small respiratory movements can be seen.

twins

If you're carrying twins you will be feeling a lot bigger at this stage than a woman who's having a singleton. Although you've got two babies in there, each might be similar in size to a single baby.

Twin growth and development

Your babies may lie the same way up, or one might be head up while the other is head down. By this stage, they will be aware of each other's presence in the uterus. You'll receive extra antenatal care if you're having twins, and your caregivers will be keen to check that each baby is growing properly.

There are some rare conditions in which one twin is a lot bigger than the other, and both babies can develop problems if this happens. Twins and multiples develop at the same rate as singletons until about 26 weeks of pregnancy, but are often not as large at birth, especially as they are usually born earlier (see page 55).

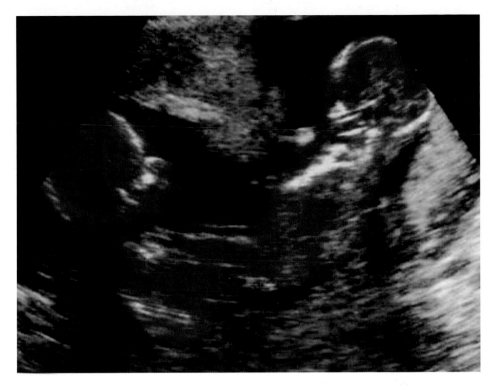

Ultrasound scan showing twins
A twin or multiple pregnancy is confirmed using an ultrasound scan. The babies may be identical, formed from one fertilized egg that then divides, or fraternal, developing from two separately fertilized eggs.

questions & answers

q Can my baby control his movements?

a The development of the nervous system means that by week 16 he can flex and extend his limbs and fingers. All the connections between your baby's brain, nervous system, and muscles are established by this stage.

q Do all babies develop at the same rate in the womb?

a No, they don't. In the early days and weeks development is at a very similar rate, but after 12 weeks there are a lot of differences, proving that every baby is unique. Try not to compare the size of your bump or your baby with that of other mothers. Your baby's growth, and the size he is when he is born, depends on a whole host of factors including his genes; whether he's your first baby or not (first ones tend to be smaller); whether you have any underlying medical condition such as pre-eclampsia; what you're eating and drinking; and whether or not you smoke (see page 47).

q If my baby's organ systems are already formed, do I still have to be careful about avoiding certain foods?

a Yes. Some of the foods considered dangerous carry the risk of passing on bacterial infections such as toxoplasmosis and listeriosis, and there are potential dangers to your baby even in the latest weeks of pregnancy. Keep to the same food code as before: wash all fruit, vegetables, and salad ingredients especially well; avoid raw and undercooked meat and unpasteurized dairy produce (see page 27).

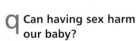

q Can having sex harm our baby?

a Your baby is well protected by the amniotic fluid, and so will not be harmed. When you have an orgasm your uterus contracts and becomes harder, as it sometimes does at other times, too. The baby will be aware of this, but it won't be a problem. These contractions may feel like hugs to the baby. However, if you've had any bleeding or a history of miscarriages or premature labours you may be advised to avoid sex (see page 53).

FIRST TRIMESTER												SECOND TRIMESTER															THIRD TRIMESTER												
1	2	3	4	5	6	7	8	9	10	11	12	13	14	15	16	17	18	19	20	21	22	23	24	25	26	27	28	29	30	31	32	33	34	35	36	37	38	39	40

week 20

There's no mistaking your pregnancy now – and congratulations, because you're half way there! Over the next few weeks your bump will continue to grow and your baby will become more active. As your baby grows, so will your unique bond with her.

your body changes

You're getting bigger, and you may be feeling a little breathless sometimes, but this is still the "blooming" phase. You are looking forward to the birth, but are still not too weighed down by the extra person you've got on board.

Gaining weight

You may notice that it's not just your tummy that's getting bigger this month – the tops of your thighs and your buttocks may be larger, too. Don't worry about this: it's an entirely natural change, as your body is laying down extra fat in pregnancy to call on when it's needed for breastfeeding.

Of course, you should stick to a healthy diet and not binge on processed or sweet food or you'll put on excess weight. Don't worry about being a bit larger all round. You should not diet at any point in pregnancy. You will lose the extra fat after the baby is born.

FACTS ABOUT YOU

♦ The top of your uterus, or fundus, reaches to about your navel, and will continue to grow about 1cm ($\frac{1}{2}$in) a week.

♦ The pressure of the growing baby might make your belly button pop out and stay that way until after the birth.

♦ The weight of the baby might make you feel a bit off balance.

♦ You may develop stretch marks.

easing your symptoms

Feeling breathless
Take things easy. Ask your midwife if you need a blood test for anaemia.

Stuffy nose and nose bleeds
Ease stuffiness with a little petroleum jelly in each nostril.

Heartburn
Avoid large meals, alcohol, and spicy food. Stretch your hands above your head to alleviate the symptoms. Antacid medication is useful and is generally safe to take in pregnancy. Talk to your GP about which antacid might be right for you.

Itchiness
Try foods rich in vitamin B. Speak to your caregiver if symptoms persist.

Increased vaginal secretions
This is normal – however if the discharge is very profuse, has an odour, or irritates, discuss it with your doctor.

YOUR CHANGES — YOUR BUMP IS GETTING STEADILY BIGGER NOW • THE BABY IS INCREASINGLY ACTIVE • YOU'LL PROBABLY BE INVITED FOR A MID-TERM SCAN AROUND THIS TIME

your emotions

As your body shape changes, it's normal to become a bit anxious about putting on weight, even though there's an entirely positive and natural reason for that right now.

Your new shape

We're conditioned from childhood to see "putting on weight" as a negative thing, and it's hard to shake off that feeling now.

Try to build a few treats into your life to make you feel more positive about your changing shape. A new haircut can be a great psychological boost; so can a make-up lesson, especially as your skin type may have altered since you got pregnant. If you can, have a pampering day out or weekend away: some salons, health farms, and spas offer special mother-to-be packages, which can be a good pick-me-up. Your bump may be obscuring your view of your feet, so a pedicure is a practical, as well as pampering, treat!

Massage
A massage can be wonderfully relaxing. Choose a practitioner who has experience of working with pregnant women. Opt for unscented oils as some aromatherapy oils should not be used in pregnancy.

dental **care**

You need to take special care of your teeth and gums while you are pregnant. Tell your dentist as soon as you know you are expecting a baby as you should avoid x-rays unless absolutely necessary. Have your teeth checked regularly. Your dentist will advise you on the best way to take care of your teeth, and check for any signs of disease or infection.

Changes to your teeth and gums

Your increased blood supply during pregnancy and the higher-than-normal level of the hormone progesterone combine to soften all the tissues in your body, including your gums. This makes them spongy and more susceptible to infection.

The increased blood supply also puts pressure on the capillaries positioned around the gum line, making them more likely to bleed, especially while brushing or flossing.

What you can do

The best way to protect your teeth and gums is to be scrupulous about dental hygiene and to follow a healthy, balanced diet. Make sure you get plenty of calcium, protein, and vitamins B, C, and D. Dairy products and plenty of fresh fruit and vegetables will supply the required nutrients. Of course, you need to avoid sugary foods, so this is yet another reason not to indulge in too many cakes, biscuits, and fizzy drinks!

Have your teeth cleaned professionally by the dentist at least once during your pregnancy to help prevent gum disease and infections. Using an electric toothbrush with a pressure sensor may prevent damage. Talk to your dentist if you have any concerns.

Flossing

Cleaning between your teeth with dental floss helps to keep them healthy, but be very gentle as your gums are softer than before you were pregnant, and will bleed more easily.

SEE ALSO   RIGHTS AND BENEFITS pages 22–23 • EATING WELL page 27 • MATERNITY CLOTHES page 33 • RELAXATION TECHNIQUES pages 48–49 • SLEEP page 57 • COMMON COMPLAINTS pages 60–61

your baby at 20 weeks

Your baby's senses are developing fast, and she's becoming much more aware of her immediate surroundings. She's starting to move around more in the uterus, and is hearing the voices of those around her, through the uterine wall.

Your baby's appearance

She now measures about 15cm (6in) crown to rump, almost half the length she will be at birth. There's been a growth spurt during the last few days, but although she's lengthened, your baby is still quite tiny – about 270g (9oz) in weight. From now on her growth rate will be less dramatic, although it will be steady as she puts on weight slowly and surely. She is covered with lanugo, a layer of ultra-fine, downy hair, which will have all but disappeared by the time she is born. The exact function of lanugo is not well understood – it could be to help regulate her body temperature, or it could be to keep the protective vernix (a thick, white, waxy coating) in place on her skin.

Development

Your baby now has the same number of nerve cells as an adult, and is increasingly sensitive and aware of what's going on around her. The sensory areas of her brain are developing quickly at the moment, and the nerves are being covered in a protective coating called myelin. Now messages can be passed from the brain to different parts of the body, which means that, increasingly, your baby's limbs are under her own control.

Tastebuds have developed on her tongue, and she will soon be able to distinguish a sweet from a bitter taste. Her skin is becoming sensitive to touch, and if you touch her through your abdomen you will find she is aware of the sensation and may respond.

When she's born she'll soon start to play and explore, and that process is already starting within your uterus: she sometimes holds onto the umbilical cord or grasps her other hand as they brush together – these are her first playthings.

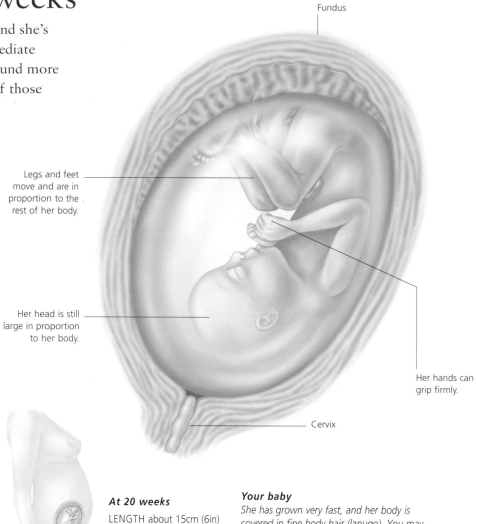

Fundus

Legs and feet move and are in proportion to the rest of her body.

Her head is still large in proportion to her body.

Her hands can grip firmly.

Cervix

At 20 weeks
LENGTH about 15cm (6in) crown to rump
WEIGHT about 270g (9oz)

Your baby
She has grown very fast, and her body is covered in fine body hair (lanugo). You may be able to feel her movements, even if this is your first pregnancy.

your **growing** baby

- ♦ Hair has started to grow on her scalp.
- ♦ She inhales amniotic fluid and practises shallow breathing movements.
- ♦ Her permanent teeth buds are developing behind her baby teeth buds.
- ♦ She has a primitive immune system and can already fight off some infections.
- ♦ A protective layer of "brown" fat, which helps in temperature regulation, is now starting to be laid down.
- ♦ If your baby is a girl, her vagina is beginning to develop at this stage; if a boy, the scrotum is still forming.
- ♦ In both girls and boys, the nipples and mammary glands appear.

- ♦ She can grasp one hand with the other, and can also form fists.
- ♦ Her eyes are still shut but she can move her eyes slowly from side to side.
- ♦ She has much more control over her movements due to the development of her muscles and nervous system.
- ♦ The nervous system is beginning to produce the myelin sheath, which coats the nerves that link muscles to the brain, allowing messages to be passed along.
- ♦ Her first teeth have formed in her gums.
- ♦ The bones in her ears are hardening, allowing her to hear the world outside the uterus.

what your baby can hear

Your baby's hearing is now well developed; she's getting to know your voice and that of your partner and anyone else in your household.

Sounds from outside the uterus

If there's a bang or a loud noise your baby might jump. She will also be aware of other noises outside the uterus, and some evidence suggests she may respond to certain types of music. Studies have shown that Vivaldi and Mozart tend to be the preferred composers for the as-yet-unborn. Mothers have reported that the memory of music stays with their baby in the early weeks of life, and sometimes a crying baby can be comforted by the sound of music that was played to her before birth – it seems to "remind" her of her time in the uterus. You can enjoy talking and singing to your baby as you relax or have a bath, in the knowledge that your sounds really are getting through to her.

Your baby's response to sounds
Your baby responds to sounds by moving, or her heartbeat may alter momentarily. As your baby develops, and you become more aware of her movements, you may find she responds to your voice or certain pieces of music.

questions & answers

q What happens during my mid-term scan?

a The mid-term, or anomaly, scan is used to check on the baby's general development and the development of the major organs. The scan operator – who may be a radiographer, an ultrasonographer, an obstetrician, or a midwife – will look in particular at your baby's heart, kidneys, brain, and spine, and will measure the baby's head circumference and length of the limbs. She'll also check that the placenta is high up within the uterus, and isn't in danger of lying over the cervix at the time when you give birth.

q I'm worried by reports that ultrasound scans can cause brain damage in babies. Should I have one?

a Scanning has been routine in pregnancy for more than 15 years, so it's unlikely there are any serious problems that haven't been detected by now. Generally, doctors regard ultrasound as safe and a good way to detect fetal abnormalities. However, having these tests does not guarantee your baby will not have any problems.

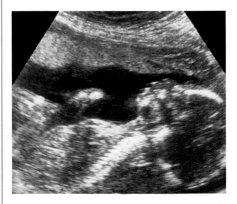

Seeing your baby
Since you discovered you were pregnant you have been getting to know your baby, but seeing her on the screen during a scan brings her closer to you than ever before.

q What will happen if my scan shows something unusual?

a If there's even a suspicion that something is in any way unusual, you'll be referred for more tests. These might be a more in-depth ultrasound check, possibly carried out at another centre with more specialized equipment and a more highly trained operator. Make sure that you understand precisely what the scan operator has seen and is concerned about.

week 24

Pregnancy is great right now. You're not so big that getting around is difficult, and you've got a lot more energy than you had in the early weeks. And although sometimes the birth still seems ages away, at other times you're starting to feel really excited.

your body changes

This is the stage when people you don't know will start to guess you might be having a baby. Around this time you may have a growth spurt, so your bump becomes more noticeable.

Getting ready

Meanwhile, your uterus is making practice or Braxton Hicks contractions, getting ready for labour. When this happens your abdomen may become hard for a few seconds. The uterus often contracts, whether you're pregnant or not, but now you are more likely to be aware of the muscles working.

Iron-rich foods are essential for the blood supply of the fetus and for you. Get as much iron as you can from your diet. Eat lean red meat, poultry, lentils, legumes, spinach and other dark, leafy vegetables, and iron-rich cereals. Vitamin C helps to increase the absorption of iron.

FACTS ABOUT YOU

♦ The fundus (top of the uterus) is above your belly button.

♦ When the baby moves you may be able to make out a little foot or leg through the abdominal wall.

♦ Your breasts may be feeling very tender due to the hormonal changes in preparation for breastfeeding.

♦ Your body is retaining water, putting weight on your thighs and upper body.

♦ You may feel hot more often.

easing your symptoms

Urinary tract infections
These are more common during pregnancy. To keep them at bay, drink lots of water every day – at least eight to 10 glasses. Water dilutes the urine, flushing out your urinary system and making infections less likely.

Indigestion
Progesterone makes the digestive system sluggish: food sits in the stomach longer and can make you uncomfortable. Avoid heavy meals – eat little and often.

Dry eyes
Dry eyes are common from about half way through pregnancy. You may notice that your eyes have less moisture and are sensitive to light, particularly if you wear contact lenses. Ask your pharmacist to recommend a solution to add moisture, and do mention that you are pregnant.

YOUR CHANGES   YOU PROBABLY DON'T NEED TO URINATE AS OFTEN • YOUR WAISTLINE HAS ALL BUT DISAPPEARED • YOU MAY FIND YOU PERSPIRE MORE THAN USUAL

your emotions

Having an obvious bump so that the world can see you are pregnant can be rather pleasant. After all, having a baby is something to be very proud of.

Dealing with other people

Not everyone sees it that way, though, and even if you sometimes enjoy having a stranger ask you about your pregnancy, you might not always want to have a half-hour chat with someone you don't know. When you're obviously pregnant lots of things you'd usually keep to yourself are clear to anyone you happen to chance upon. One, you're sexually active; two, you have (or recently had) a partner; three, you're going to be a mother in the not-too-distant future.

Some women find all this discussion rather annoying, and find it difficult to be polite to strangers who ask personal questions (was it planned? are you hoping for a boy or a girl? was it a natural or an assisted conception?) as though you were wearing a sign proclaiming: "Ask me anything you want". You may also find that people want to tell you lots of popular myths about pregnancy and birth or reminisce about their own, or other women's, experiences of labour. Some people may even want to touch your bump, including those you don't know very well.

What you can do

This can be infuriating, especially if you are feeling very tired, or are attempting to cope with any uncomfortable physical symptoms, but try not to lose your temper with people. Remind yourself that people mean well: often, it's a case of the world rejoicing with you when you're pregnant. Take pride in the fact that people are interested in the new life inside you – soon everyone will be admiring your new baby, and you will be thrilled with the attention. Just think of the extra interest as early admiration of your baby. You already think your baby is wonderful, and so do they.

a working **pregnancy**

Managing a job and a pregnancy presents quite a challenge, and while many organizations are very supportive of mothers-to-be, it is vital to listen to your body, understand your rights, and to establish a balance that is right for you. Don't be tempted to keep going just because another pregnant woman seems to be fine doing the same amount, or because of anecdotes from friends about how hard they worked when pregnant. Do what is right for you and your baby.

Know your rights

Try not to overdo things – listen to your body, pace yourself at work, and make sure your work station is comfortable.

Striking a balance
A comfortable working environment is essential. Drink plenty of water throughout the day and be sure to stretch and walk about at regular intervals.

Travelling to and from work can be exhausting when you are pregnant, especially if you have to contend with heavy traffic or crowded public transport. If you can, travel at less busy times or work from home for a couple of days each week. By working with your doctor and your employer, you should be able to avoid undue risk while you are working. In many countries, employers are legally obliged to ensure that work does not endanger the health of the mother-to-be or her baby.

Antenatal appointments
Remember that time off for antenatal care is everyone's right, no matter how long you've worked for your employer (see pages 22–23).

Planning your future
Try not to get too hung up on decisions about what you will do once the baby is born: keeping an open mind is probably best at this stage. Concentrate on now and discuss future plans once the baby is born.

SEE ALSO   RIGHTS AND BENEFITS pages 22–23 • EATING WELL page 27 • YOUR NEW SHAPE page 37
• RELAXATION TECHNIQUES page 49 • COMMON COMPLAINTS pages 60–61

your baby at 24 weeks

We think of babies as being chubby, but for most of the time your baby is developing in the uterus he's actually long and thin. But from about 24 weeks he starts to fill out, and looks more solid and baby-like.

Your baby's appearance

Part of the reason for his more solid appearance is that his skin is no longer translucent, and he is losing the fragile look that has so far characterized his time in the uterus. The brown fat, which will be crucial in helping him to regulate his body temperature after birth, is still developing – as more of it appears your baby's bottom will fill out and become more rounded.

His facial features are fully formed so that, if you could look inside and see him, he would already look like the baby you'll get to know in about another 16 weeks, although his lean face means that his eyes bulge at this stage.

Development

Most of your baby's body systems are now fully formed and starting to function. The main organs are all working, apart from the lungs, which he won't use until he is born. They are still filled with amniotic fluid, although the alveoli (air sacs) are beginning to form.

The brain and nervous system are developing fast, and the cells that control conscious thought are forming, so your baby is becoming much more aware of his surroundings and of sounds and movement in the world outside your uterus.

The main aim of the rest of his time in your uterus will be to fine-tune his systems and to lay down more fat ready for the outside world. Even though you probably feel your pregnancy still has a long time to go, your baby would have at least a chance of survival if he were born this early, and this is an indication of how well developed he really is at this stage.

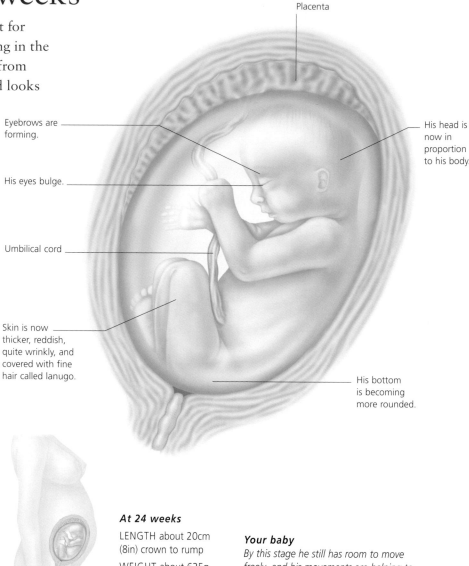

Placenta

Eyebrows are forming.

His eyes bulge.

Umbilical cord

Skin is now thicker, reddish, quite wrinkly, and covered with fine hair called lanugo.

His head is now in proportion to his body.

His bottom is becoming more rounded.

At 24 weeks
LENGTH about 20cm (8in) crown to rump
WEIGHT about 625g (1lb 6oz)

Your baby
By this stage he still has room to move freely, and his movements are helping to build strength and dexterity.

your **growing** baby

♦ At the end of 24 weeks, your baby's eyes will have opened for the first time.

♦ His heart rate has dropped to about 140–150 beats a minute.

♦ He has fingers and toes, but these are still slightly webbed.

♦ He is still constantly swallowing and then excreting the amniotic fluid as urine.

♦ Within his bowel, the meconium, which will make up his first stool, is already beginning to form.

♦ Within his lungs the small air sacs, or alveoli, are forming.

♦ Sweat glands are forming in your baby's skin.

♦ He is now able to cough and hiccup.

♦ The lanugo (downy layer of body hair) darkens. Beneath it your baby's skin is reddish in colour rather than translucent as before.

♦ He has a cycle of sleeping and waking, which you might become aware of over the next few weeks.

♦ As your baby grows, the placental blood vessels will respond by supplying him with more of the nutrients he needs.

are you carrying a boy or a girl?

You may not have wanted to find out at the scan which sex your baby is, but many parents-to-be enjoy trying to figure it out through other means. It's natural for you and your partner to wonder what this new little baby will be like.

Guessing the gender

Here are a few traditional tales about discovering the gender. They are not scientific, but you and your partner can have lots of fun trying them out.

♦ If the heartbeat is persistently above 140 it's a girl; below, you are carrying a boy.

♦ If you're carrying the extra weight out front, it's a boy; round the sides, it's a girl.

♦ Hang a needle on a thread over your abdomen – if it moves in circles, it's a boy; side to side, it's a girl.

♦ If your belly is shaped like a basketball, it's a boy; like a watermelon, it's a girl.

Getting to know your baby
Thinking about and talking to this new baby inside will help you make the transition to parenthood, and may bring you and your partner closer together.

questions & answers

q How do I know if my baby is moving around enough?

a You'll soon get to know your baby's pattern. Some babies seem more passive than others but no one knows whether babies vary in the amount they move, or if some women detect the baby's activity more than others. You may notice movements more when you are resting. The most important thing is that you feel some movements from now, if not earlier.

Getting to know the baby
Feeling the baby move is exciting for the whole family, and may help older children form a bond with the new sibling.

q Why is my bump so much smaller than my friend's, even though our babies are due at the same time?

a Your baby is almost certainly roughly the same size as your friend's baby at this stage, but the size of your bump depends on more than the size of your baby. Don't forget your bump also contains the amniotic fluid, and some pregnancies have more of this than others. Also, the amount of space inside your abdomen is governed by your physical structure and overall size. In general, bumps tend to be bigger in women who are petite than in women of a bigger build who have more space widthways. If it's not your first baby your bump may get bigger more quickly, because the uterus and abdomen have stretched in the past.

FIRST TRIMESTER												SECOND TRIMESTER															THIRD TRIMESTER												
1	2	3	4	5	6	7	8	9	10	11	12	13	14	15	16	17	18	19	20	21	22	23	24	25	26	27	28	29	30	31	32	33	34	35	36	37	38	39	40

week 28

This week marks the official start of the third trimester, so you're on the home stretch now! Revel in your pregnancy as much as you can, because when you look back you'll find it amazing how quickly it all slipped by. In about three months' time you will meet your new baby.

your body changes

Week 28 is often the stage at which being pregnant starts to make a difference to your everyday life, as you become accustomed to manoeuvring yourself with your increasing bump.

Looking good

Many women spend hours at the mirror admiring their bump – and now your breasts are so much bigger than usual, you've probably got a cleavage to be proud of.

Make the most of your new look – try wearing close-fitting maternity outfits, rather than tent-like garments, because you'll feel slimmer (honestly!), and emphasizing the bump makes you feel sexy rather than simply sack-like. Good buys if you're looking for ways to lift your spirits are earrings, scarves, necklaces, and a great haircut. Borrowing maternity clothes from a friend is a practical way to have clothes for the last few weeks of your pregnancy.

FACTS ABOUT **YOU**

♦ From now on, you'll see your caregiver (midwife, GP, or obstetrician) every two weeks then weekly from 36 weeks.

♦ Your breasts may leak colostrum (see page 86), although some women don't produce this until the baby is born.

♦ You may be short of breath when you exert yourself due to the upward pressure of the uterus on your lungs and diaphragm.

♦ You may develop varicose veins, due to the pressure on your legs.

easing your **symptoms**

Piles (haemorrhoids)
Drink lots of water and eat lots of fruit. If iron supplements are making you constipated, which increases the risk of piles, ask your caregiver for advice.

Leg cramps
These are common, especially at night. Straighten your leg, bend the ankle, and massage your calf.

Puffy hands and feet
Wear comfortable shoes, especially during the afternoon and evening when swelling in your feet is likely to be at its worst. You may have to remove any rings you wear before they become too tight.

Varicose veins
For some relief put your legs up when you can and lie down with your feet raised. Support stockings may be helpful.

YOUR CHANGES YOU MAY HAVE RIB PAIN CAUSED BY THE PRESSURE OF YOUR BABY • YOU MAY GET A STITCH-LIKE PAIN DOWN THE SIDE OF YOUR ABDOMEN AS YOU WALK • YOU'RE GAINING MORE WEIGHT

your emotions

Almost all women have anxieties and worries about having a baby, but these tend to stay below the surface most of the time. For many mothers-to-be it can be difficult to talk openly about their concerns.

Pregnancy dreams

Not surprisingly, it's often only when we're asleep that our fears are unleashed. Vivid dreams are very common in late pregnancy. Here are some of the most common pregnancy anxiety dreams.

♦ The baby is born with a handicap or deformity – this is a worry every pregnant woman has at some stage.

♦ The baby is born when you're not ready and in desperation you try to put it back – the fear here is that you won't get everything finished before the birth.

♦ You go into labour but there isn't a baby, or the baby doesn't survive – this isn't an omen that things won't go well, it's a sign that you have normal worries about the birth and becoming a parent.

"I'm doing pregnancy yoga. You meet other mothers-to-be and it's all tailored to suit women hoping for an active, natural birth, which I certainly am. There's a lot of talk about positions for first- and second-stage labour, for example. And the relaxation techniques are fabulous. I go swimming twice a week, which is really energizing."

GEMMA STONE, 23,
28 WEEKS PREGNANT

exercise and **posture**

It's not a good idea to take up strenuous exercise for the first time when you're pregnant. But these exercises are excellent whether you've done them before or not – although you should always listen to your body, and stop when you feel you've done enough. Speak to your caregiver before embarking on any exercise programme.

Exercises to try

♦ Swimming is a great all-round exercise at any time of life, and when you're pregnant it's refreshing to feel weightless and unencumbered in the water.

♦ Walking is great. In the third trimester it's also good for positioning the baby ready for birth.

♦ Yoga is an excellent form of exercise and relaxation. Choose a class that's designed for mothers-to-be.

Pelvic floor exercises

During pregnancy, increased progesterone levels soften the pelvic floor muscles. These muscles run around the urethra, vagina, and anus and are thickest at the perineum. The softening of the muscles and the pressure of the uterus can cause leaks of urine. Practise every day and resume as soon as possible after the birth (see page 79).

Good pregnancy posture

Stand tall with your back straight and your bottom tucked in, so your baby is supported by your thighs, buttocks, and stomach muscles. Well-toned muscles regain their shape more quickly after birth. Good posture will also aid digestion.

Pelvic tilt

This exercise is an excellent preparation for labour, strengthening the stomach and making the back and pelvis more flexible.

1 Kneel on all fours, making sure your back is flat. Keep your shoulders still.

2 Pull in your stomach and bottom. Gently tilt your pelvis forwards while breathing out, so that your back arches upwards. Hold for a few seconds but keep breathing. Inhale and release. Repeat several times.

SEE ALSO EATING WELL page 27 • MATERNITY CLOTHES page 33 • RELAXATION TECHNIQUES page 49 • COMMON COMPLAINTS pages 60–61

your baby at 28 weeks

If she were born now, your baby would stand an excellent chance of survival, and might even be able to breathe unaided, at least some of the time, as her lungs have become a lot more mature. She's very active right now, and you are probably aware of her movements much of the time.

Your baby's appearance

Your baby's head is much more in proportion to her body now, and she looks very much as she will when she's born. She's getting plumper all the time, and greasy vernix is now covering her body. This is to protect her skin, which is immersed the whole time in the amniotic fluid. When she is born she may still have some of this creamy substance on her body. Her skin continues to be wrinkled, as she still has a lot of fat to lay down before she is fully developed. Her eyes open and close, and the colour of the iris is now visible, although the colour may change after birth.

Development

Your baby's lungs have developed greatly during the last few weeks. The alveoli (air sacs) are now almost completely formed, and a substance called surfactant is being produced by the lung cells. This is essential to keep the lungs open when breath is exhaled.

A lack of surfactant can cause respiratory symptoms in a premature baby. If a mother goes into premature labour an injection of steroids is often given to hasten surfactant production; this can reduce the chance of the baby needing mechanical breathing assistance after delivery in a birth before 34 weeks.

Her kidneys are fully working now, producing about a pint of urine each day, and your baby's bone marrow is responsible for the manufacture of her red blood cells.

Now she is bigger, there is less fluid cushioning her from the outside world so you may be more aware of her moving. You might even see the outline of a hand or foot through your bump. This is a wonderful thing to share with your partner, as it will be his first direct contact with his baby.

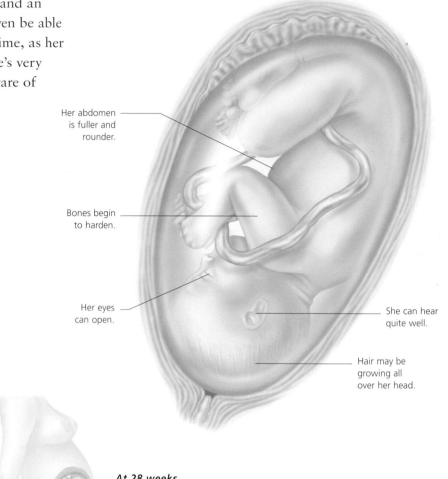

Her abdomen is fuller and rounder.

Bones begin to harden.

Her eyes can open.

She can hear quite well.

Hair may be growing all over her head.

At 28 weeks
LENGTH about 25cm (10in) crown to rump
WEIGHT about 1.1kg (2lb 7oz)

Your baby
The extra fat deposits mean that she looks like a small newborn. She can still change position easily and will be very active at this stage.

your **growing** baby

♦ Your baby gets hiccups from time to time, and you may be aware of them too. These are probably caused by the baby "practising" breathing movements.

♦ If he's a boy, his testes are descending.

♦ She may suck her finger or thumb some of the time.

♦ The placenta receives about 400ml (14fl oz) of blood from the mother's circulation every minute.

♦ Her muscles are now well toned and in proportion to her body size.

♦ Her limbs are sometimes visible moving about underneath the skin of your bump.

♦ Her skin is still wrinkled, but fat is continuing to develop underneath, giving her a less lean appearance.

♦ She has an acute sense of taste, which is greater than it will be when she is born.

♦ Her brain is growing at a very rapid rate and the nervous system is developing so that messages can be passed from the brain to different parts of the body.

♦ She has a well-developed sense of touch.

♦ She is developing the ability to orientate herself within her space.

♦ She responds to stimuli, including pain, light, and sound.

how big will your baby be?

Most women are concerned about the size of their baby. You want her to grow healthily, but late in pregnancy you may worry about giving birth to a very large baby.

What affects your baby's size?

This is determined by a number of factors. The first consideration is genetics, so if you are small, the chances are that your baby will be as well. And if your first baby is particularly large or small, it's likely that subsequent babies will follow this trend. Your own size at birth can also be an indication of how big your baby will be. First babies are often smaller than their siblings, and boys tend to be heavier at birth than girls.

If you have a medical condition such as diabetes or pre-eclampsia, this can affect the size of your baby; your pregnancy will be closely monitored if this is the case. Babies born to parents who smoke are often of a lower birthweight than those born to non-smokers. Your nutritional status can affect your baby's size, but unless you are malnourished your baby should continue to grow. If there is any cause for concern, you may be referred for an ultrasound scan.

What you can do

Listen to your caregivers' advice, but don't become too obsessed with trying to guess how big your baby will be. All babies grow at their own pace.

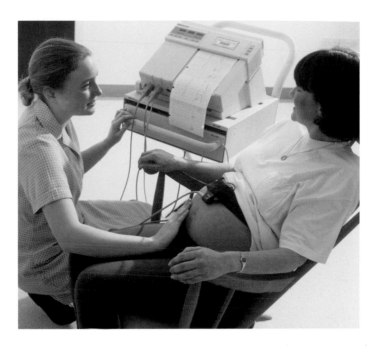

Checking your baby's progress
Your midwife will regularly check how your baby is growing and can also measure the fetal heartbeat using a hand-held device or electronic fetal monitoring (EFM).

questions & answers

q **Is my baby aware that my midwife is touching my tummy and listening to her heartbeat?**

a Yes, your baby will be aware of your midwife's checks. Usually this will be noticeable when the heartbeat is checked, because it will be faster than normal. You'll probably feel your baby move about in response to the midwife's palpations. The use of the ultrasound or Doppler listening device, which will probably be used to check the heartbeat, may disturb the baby a little. Some midwives say babies tend to squirm more when the sound of the heartbeat is listened to.

q **I've been told my baby seems small for dates, what does that mean?**

a It means your baby is smaller than would be expected at the stage of pregnancy you're at. Hearing your child is small for dates is worrying, but in the majority of cases, there's nothing to be overly concerned about. Obviously, healthcare professionals are dealing with averages when they say something like this, and it's quite possible that your baby is simply not meant to be as big as other babies of the same age. Another possible reason is that your dates are slightly inaccurate, and your pregnancy isn't as advanced as your estimated delivery date (EDD) suggests. The main concern about a small-for-dates baby is that the placenta may not be functioning optimally, so your caregiver will take extra steps to watch the baby's growth. This is generally done using ultrasound scans, which are performed at intervals throughout the pregnancy.

q **If I eat more will my baby put on more weight?**

a Probably not, unless your diet is severely short of vital nutrients. If you eat too much you will put on excess fat and will be at increased risk of gestational diabetes. On average, a non-pregnant woman requires 2,200 calories a day. When you are pregnant, you need about 300 calories more each day to stay healthy and help the fetus grow.

FIRST TRIMESTER												SECOND TRIMESTER															THIRD TRIMESTER											
1	2	3	4	5	6	7	8	9	10	11	12	13	14	15	16	17	18	19	20	21	22	23	24	25	26	27	28	29	30	31	32	33	34	35	36	37	38	39	40

week 32

There's no getting away from the bump now, and although you feel it's already enormous it is going to grow quite a bit more over the weeks ahead. The final weeks tend to fly by – soon, it's going to be week 40 and you'll be wishing you had more time to get everything finished!

your body changes

Your advanced state of pregnancy affects everything you do, from getting up in the morning to going to bed at night. Take things slowly and listen to your body.

Adjusting to late pregnancy

You're probably feeling tired again, due to all the extra demands on your body. Rest when you can – put your feet up for an hour or two each day if possible.

Your pelvic joints are expanding now in preparation for the birth. This means that you may experience some aches and pains so that you feel a bit like a disjointed doll. Avoid sudden movements. When you get out of bed in the morning, keep your legs together to swing them round and onto the floor – this reduces the chance of damage to your pelvis.

Your baby is still moving around a lot, but you can tell his space is more limited now – his movements are more like whole-body shifts and jerks rather than the rippling movements you felt when he could still do complete somersaults in the uterus a few weeks ago.

FACTS ABOUT YOU

♦ You may not be sleeping very well at night, which in turn makes you feel even more tired during the day.

♦ Pressure on your bladder means you may need to get up at least once each night to urinate. You may also leak a little urine when you run, cough, sneeze, or laugh.

♦ Your pelvis may ache, especially when you have to stand or when you've been sitting with your legs crossed, because of the weight of the baby.

easing your symptoms

Stitch
Don't rush around; sudden movements increase the chance of stitch-like pains and you'll become breathless quite easily.

Stretch marks
These will fade after the birth, but until then an unperfumed body lotion will help to ease any itching and keep the skin moisturized. Do not scratch the marks.

Backache
This is often a problem in the later weeks. Stand tall, with your pelvis tucked under and your weight distributed between your heel and the ball of your foot.

Heartburn and indigestion
Eat several small meals a day, with lots of fruit. If you can, avoid meals that are high in carbohydrates, sugars, and fats. Have your biggest meal earlier in the day.

YOUR CHANGES THE BABY IS MOVING AROUND A LOT • YOU MAY ALSO BE AWARE OF HIS HICCUPING INSIDE YOU • YOU MAY NEED TO URINATE FREQUENTLY

your emotions

Make sure you indulge yourself, just a little, by spending at least 20 minutes each day lying down, being in touch with your baby.

Bonding

"Bonding" isn't an event that happens after you've given birth, it starts from the moment you know you've got a baby inside you. Turning your attention to that baby, especially in the last few weeks, is a way of feeling close to him even before you've held him in your arms. If you have older children, it is easy to keep the focus on them, so making time for the baby is doubly important.

Relaxation techniques

Make sure the room you are in is warm enough for you to relax comfortably.

♦ Play some gentle music.
♦ If you're sitting up, concentrate on dropping your shoulders at the same time as breathing out slowly. This is also an excellent exercise to do before each breastfeed.
♦ Try lying on your left side, with your right leg supported by a large cushion – stretch out your bottom leg and bend your top one.
♦ Focus on your breathing, especially on breathing out, keeping it even and controlled.
♦ Think about the baby inside you – imagine him curled up in your uterus, waiting to be born and welcomed into your arms.

antenatal classes

By now you will be thinking more about the birth, so antenatal classes provide a great opportunity for you and your partner to learn more and discuss ideas and worries with your caregivers and other parents-to-be.

Talking it over

In some areas antenatal classes start earlier than this – some health authorities have "early bird" classes for women who are about 14 weeks. But it's generally believed that about 30–36 weeks is a good time to pass on information through a course about the birth process and life thereafter.

You'll need to have already booked onto a course to get a place by this stage (see page 33). Providers include the NHS (your midwife will give you details), the National Childbirth Trust, and the Active Birth Movement, as well as private antenatal teachers. Most classes are for

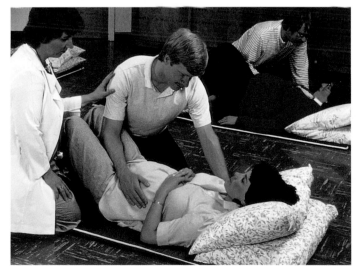

partners as well as mothers, and concentrate on passing on information about labour and delivery, options for the kind of delivery you might want, and opportunities for group

Sharing the experience
Classes can provide an oasis of time in which you and your partner can really focus on the pregnancy.

sharing. Antenatal courses are an excellent way of meeting other women in your area who are in a similar situation, so try to join a course in your own neighourhood.

SEE ALSO EATING WELL page 27 • EXERCISE AND POSTURE page 45 • THINKING ABOUT THE BIRTH page 53 • COMMON COMPLAINTS pages 60–61 • PREPARING FOR THE BIRTH pages 64–67

your baby at 32 weeks

By week 32 your baby's facial features are well developed, and his face is a lot more filled out and wrinkle-free. He's possibly head-down in your uterus, and if he is he'll probably stay that way until the birth.

Your baby's appearance

Your baby's skin, which used to be red, is now normal flesh-colour and less transparent, and he's looking very like the baby he'll be after the birth. This is due to the deposits of white fat he is continuing to lay down under his skin. Once he is born, these fat deposits will provide him with energy and enable him to regulate his temperature.

His arms and legs are now in proportion and he spends most of his time with his legs pulled up towards his chest. This is the most comfortable way for him to sit in your uterus, since he doesn't have as much space to move around as he did earlier.

Your baby will continue to kick and move his arms, so you should feel some movements, but as his space decreases over the next few weeks, they will feel less dramatic than before, which may make you feel more comfortable.

He's covered in a waxy vernix at this stage, which protects his skin, and hair is continuing to cover his head.

Development

Your baby's organs are continuing to mature, and many are already almost fully developed. The lungs are continuing to develop, although if he were born now a ventilator might still be needed to assist his breathing.

His brain and central nervous system are developing at a fast rate, but they still have a few weeks of fine-tuning to go. This is one reason why premature babies tend to have a poor sucking reflex.

As his eyes become more mature, his irises can dilate and contract, so he is able to react to, and differentiate between, light and dark.

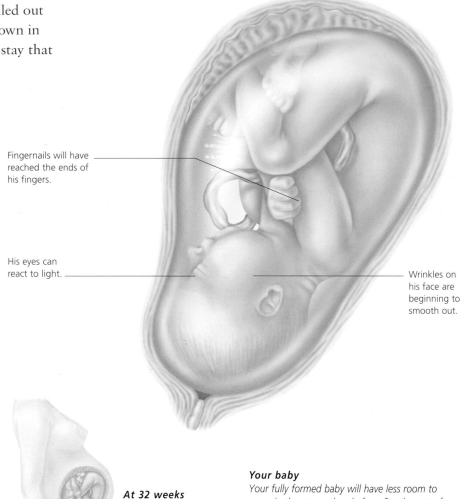

Fingernails will have reached the ends of his fingers.

His eyes can react to light.

Wrinkles on his face are beginning to smooth out.

At 32 weeks
LENGTH about 30cm (12in) crown to rump
WEIGHT about 1.8kg (4lb)

Your baby
Your fully formed baby will have less room to move in the uterus than before. For the rest of the pregnancy he will be developing fat supplies and preparing for the birth. This baby has moved into a good position, ready for birth.

your **growing** baby

♦ His movements peak around this week, so expect to have a lot of disturbed nights! From now on your baby may seem to move less because he is growing quickly, and space will be at a premium.

♦ His brain is growing a lot at this time.

♦ His bones are hardening, but in his skull the bones will remain unjoined so they can fit over one another during the journey through the narrow birth canal.

♦ His fingernails may be fully grown.

♦ His fine body hair disappears.

♦ The irises in his eyes can now dilate and contract in response to light.

♦ He's aware of the practice Braxton Hicks contractions that occur in your uterus, even if you don't notice them.

♦ He weighs about 1.8kg (4lb), but his growth from now on will be considerable, and he may double in size in the next month or six weeks.

♦ Scans of unborn babies from this stage show they sometimes have periods of "dream sleep", although it's hard to imagine what they're dreaming about!

♦ He's surrounded by about 750ml (1½ pints) of amniotic fluid, but this will reduce over the next few weeks as he grows.

your baby's position

By now your baby may be getting into position for the birth. It can be reassuring to know that your baby is head-down, although he may move again before the birth. Don't worry if your baby is positioned head-up (known as breech), the chances are that he will turn before the big day.

Is he head-down?

By this stage of pregnancy many babies are already head-down, and will remain there until they're born. The "normal" presentation is known as cephalic, and means the baby's head is pointing down into the pelvis, with his bottom up under your diaphragm and his limbs curled up in front of his chest and tummy.

If, when you go for an antenatal check, your caregiver finds that your baby is still head-up in the womb, don't worry; many babies remain head-up until a couple of weeks, or even days, before the birth, and only about four per cent of babies are breech, or bottom-down, by the due date.

What you can do

If your baby does stay breech, some exercises may be offered that could encourage your baby to turn to the cephalic position. Lots of walking may also help. An obstetrician can try to turn the baby externally, known as external cephalic version (ECV). This technique can be very successful, although babies can turn back to the breech position afterwards. Ask your caregivers whether it would be appropriate for you and your baby and whether this is available. If it is not available you can ask to be referred to a hospital that does offer this service.

Discussing the options

If your baby is in a breech position when you're 39 or 40 weeks, the decision on whether to try for a vaginal delivery or whether to have a Caesarean section should be discussed carefully with your caregivers – and you should heed their advice.

Encouraging a breech baby to turn
Resting with your head below your hips can encourage a baby in the breech position to turn. You may also like to visualize your baby turning.

questions & answers

q **I've heard it's a good idea to start counting the baby's movements about now – is this right?**

a You're thinking of something called a fetal kick chart, which is a way a mum can satisfy herself that her baby is moving often enough. There are various different methods of doing this – some require you to check for a certain number of movements in a certain period of time, and then to write them down. But it's important to get the method you're using right before you start, so talk to your caregiver about whether it's a good idea to start yet, and exactly what you're looking out for.

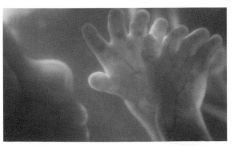

Protecting your baby
The uterus is a safe environment, but remember that some harmful substances can reach your baby via the umbilical cord, so avoid potential toxins.

q **I get breathless a lot, especially when I'm climbing up stairs. Does this mean my baby isn't getting enough oxygen?**

a Breathlessness is very common at this stage of pregnancy due to the demands of carrying the baby and his position in the uterus. Don't worry. Whether you are feeling breathless or not, oxygen will continue to be delivered to your baby efficiently via the placenta.

q **Does the placenta stop harmful substances from passing through to my baby?**

a The placenta is very selective about what it does and doesn't let across to your baby. However, some potentially harmful substances can cross the placenta. Avoid drinking alcohol, as this passes through the placenta virtually unchanged. Some drugs cross the placenta, so check with your caregiver before taking any medicines.

FIRST TRIMESTER												SECOND TRIMESTER															THIRD TRIMESTER												
1	2	3	4	5	6	7	8	9	10	11	12	13	14	15	16	17	18	19	20	21	22	23	24	25	26	27	28	29	30	31	32	33	34	35	36	37	38	39	40

week 36

You probably feel you have been pregnant for ever, and can't wait to meet the little person who is growing inside you. Many women begin to wonder what sort of labour they will have and start to make preparations for the big day. Rest and relax as much as you can.

your body changes

Put your feet up and enjoy these last few weeks. You may feel fine, but your bump is now so large that it affects all your bodily functions, and your lower abdomen and back may ache if you walk a lot. Your hands and feet might be puffy, especially at the end of the day.

Engagement

From 36 weeks, your baby's head will drop lower into your pelvis. It is "engaged" when its largest diameter is lower than the brim of your pelvis. This may make your upper abdomen more comfortable, so you have less heartburn and indigestion, but you may have the urge to urinate more often. This is completely normal at this stage, but if you also feel burning when passing water, contact your midwife or doctor, in case you have an infection.

FACTS ABOUT **YOU**

♦ The "nesting instinct" is often strong; you may feel the urge to spring-clean, but don't overdo it.

♦ If this is your first baby, heartburn, indigestion, and breathlessness should lessen once the head drops in the pelvis.

♦ Your bladder is under pressure, so you may want to urinate more often.

♦ You may tire easily, because of poor sleep and the extra weight of the baby.

♦ Braxton Hicks contractions may become more frequent and more intense.

easing your **symptoms**

Discomfort from kicking
Feeling your baby move is reassuring and exhilarating but if you find that she is kicking repeatedly in one place and making you uncomfortable, changing your position frequently can help.

Tiredness
Rest every day with your feet up, preferably on your left side. This will help build your stamina as well as increasing the blood flow to the placenta. Don't try to be too active at this stage.

Carpal tunnel syndrome
Symptoms are tingling, numb fingers caused by swollen tissues in your wrist as a result of pregnancy, creating pressure on a nerve. This usually resolves after delivery. Wearing a wrist splint and taking vitamin B6 daily may help.

YOUR CHANGES HEARTBURN, INDIGESTION, AND BREATHLESSNESS SHOULD LESSEN • YOU WILL NEED TO URINATE FREQUENTLY • HANDS AND FEET MAY BE PUFFY • YOU WILL FEEL TIRED

your emotions

Your world revolves around the birth and thinking about the changes that being a parent will make to your life. Such thoughts are normal, but can be disconcerting.

Talking it over

Remember that every woman experiences childbirth differently. Your midwife is the best person to advise you. If you feel impatient, pass the time reading or listening to music. Do things that will be difficult once the baby is born – plan an evening out with friends or your partner, go to a concert, or see a film.

Buying a nursing bra
You can now be measured for your nursing bras. A bra with cups that can be opened individually at the front is essential. Some have cups that unzip, others unhook from the strap.

What you can do

♦ Think about parenting styles and discuss them with your partner. Don't worry about problems over which you have no control.
♦ Make all your practical arrangements for the birth so that you can relax. Pack your labour bag and make your birth plan (see page 67).
♦ Stock up on some instant meals for after the birth.
♦ Take things slowly. You will become tired and breathless more easily and your ligaments are more relaxed now.
♦ Treat yourself to a haircut or a pedicure.
♦ Don't listen to scare stories about birth. Remember that people often exaggerate.

a sensual **pregnancy**

Pregnancy affects different couples in different ways. The important thing is to communicate and show affection.

Is sex safe?

Unless your doctor has warned you otherwise, you should be able to enjoy an active sex life throughout your pregnancy, if that is what you want. If you have a history of miscarriage or premature labour, talk to your caregiver. If you have any bleeding, or if you have placenta praevia, sex should be avoided. Abstain from sex once your waters have broken.

How you'll feel

This may be the first time you've had sex without worrying about getting pregnant or not getting pregnant, so some women find they really enjoy it. Also, the increased hormones and blood flow to your genitals can send your libido soaring. Conversely, some women are not interested at all.

There's no such thing as a "normal" pattern, but tiredness in the early weeks can limit your interest. Finding comfortable positions with a big bump can be quite a challenge – or a spur to your imagination. Avoid man-on-top positions, and try making love with the woman on top or side by side. The middle months are often quite a sexy time for a woman. If your partner doesn't seem that keen on sex, don't take it as a sign that you are not attractive any more. Worries about providing for the new family and concern for you often lessen the libido of expectant fathers. The important thing is to talk through how you both feel.

Making time for each other

Try to make your pregnancy a time when you relish every moment you have together and show affection whenever you can. Take every opportunity for cuddling and enjoying each other's company because when you have a new baby, finding time to be together won't be as easy as it is now.

SEE ALSO URINARY TRACT INFECTIONS page 40 • EXERCISE AND POSTURE page 45 • RELAXATION TECHNIQUES page 49 • ANTENATAL CLASSES page 49 • COMMON COMPLAINTS pages 60–61 • PREPARING FOR THE BIRTH pages 64–67

your baby at 36 weeks

Just two weeks from now, your baby would be officially "on time" if she were to be born. Although we usually count a pregnancy as 40 weeks, in fact anything from 38 to 42 weeks is considered normal.

Your baby's appearance

She's still a little bit on the thin side compared to a full-term baby, but otherwise she is identical to any other newborn you might encounter. She's got hair on her head – although not necessarily the same colour as yours or your partner's, as hair colour is notoriously difficult to predict. Her skin is beginning to smooth, and her face is losing its wrinkled appearance. Her eyes are opening and closing a lot, and she can sense light changes through your abdomen.

The lanugo, or fine hair covering her body, is disappearing now – when she's born you might notice some of it on her shoulders, but it will mostly be gone. The lanugo and her top skin layer are shed into the amniotic fluid before birth. They are then ingested by the baby and form the solid mass of her first bowel movement, known as meconium.

Development

Her lungs are now almost fully developed, and in preparation for a lifetime of breathing, she's started to "practise" breathing in and out, which involves inhaling small amounts of amniotic fluid into her lungs. Her kidneys are fully developed and her liver is able to process some waste products. The layers of the placenta are beginning to thin now.

She's developed a cycle of activity and sleep that you're probably aware of. Unborn babies often sleep during the day while you're up and about, then wake up and move around when you lie in bed at night. This may predict sleep patterns when your baby is first brought home. The movements have a different feel now as there's less space and she will not be able to move around as freely as before.

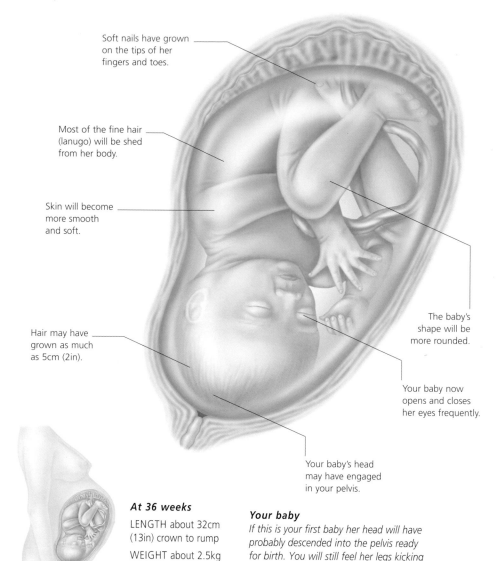

Soft nails have grown on the tips of her fingers and toes.

Most of the fine hair (lanugo) will be shed from her body.

Skin will become more smooth and soft.

Hair may have grown as much as 5cm (2in).

The baby's shape will be more rounded.

Your baby now opens and closes her eyes frequently.

Your baby's head may have engaged in your pelvis.

At 36 weeks
LENGTH about 32cm (13in) crown to rump
WEIGHT about 2.5kg (5lb 8oz)

Your baby
If this is your first baby her head will have probably descended into the pelvis ready for birth. You will still feel her legs kicking and her arms moving.

your **growing** baby

◆ There's less amniotic fluid in the womb now your baby is so much bigger.

◆ The uterus has grown to 1,000 times its normal size to accommodate the pregnancy by this point.

◆ The placenta is producing a hormone to stimulate your breasts to make milk for when the baby is born.

◆ The placenta is mature and the supply of nutrients from the placenta to the baby is at its greatest.

◆ The central nervous system is still maturing, with the baby's reflexes improving day by day.

◆ Ninety-nine per cent of babies born at this stage of pregnancy survive, almost all without ill effects.

◆ Your baby is developing her fat supplies and putting on weight more quickly now, gaining about 140g (5oz) each week.

◆ By this stage, if she's awake her eyes will be open.

◆ If your baby is a boy, his testes will have dropped down into the scrotum.

◆ If you move around a lot or press gently on your abdomen your baby may wake. Eating a meal rich in carbohydrates may have the same effect.

getting ready for birth

If this is your first baby she's likely to engage, or move down into your pelvis for the birth, any time from now on.

Has she engaged?

Engagement occurs when the presenting part of your baby – usually the head – moves lower and slips into your pelvis. You may notice your baby is engaged as the pressure on your diaphragm may ease, making it easier to breathe, or you may need to urinate more often, as the baby presses on your bladder. Your midwife will check whether she is engaged in your pelvis.

Once your baby is engaged, your midwife will check how far down into the pelvis

she is by feeling how much of her head she can palpate. It's then written on your notes as, for example, "three-fifths palpable", meaning two-fifths of the head is down in the pelvis. If the baby isn't engaged, you'll see the midwife has written the word "free" in your notes to describe this.

Late engagement

In a second or subsequent pregnancy, the uterine muscles do not exert as much pressure on the baby as in a first pregnancy, so later engagement is not unusual. If this is your first pregnancy and the baby has not engaged, your doctor may want to check that your baby's head is not too large to fit into your pelvis. You lie on your back, and the doctor will feel your baby's head

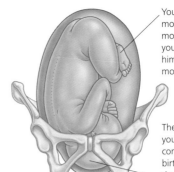

Your baby's movements are more restricted but you will still feel him kicking and moving his arms.

The soft bones of your baby's skull will compress during birth to fit through the birth canal.

Your baby's position in the pelvis
Once your baby's head is low down inside the hollow of the pelvis, it is engaged, ready for birth.

resting on the pelvic brim. Then you prop yourself on your elbows, so that the head slips down, and the doctor can feel that there is room for the head to engage.

twins

Twins are often considered "term" at 37 weeks, although it's not uncommon for them to be born as late as 40 weeks.

Giving birth to twins

♦ Exactly how labour is triggered isn't fully understood, but the size of the uterus does have a role to play and because it's been so stretched by a twin pregnancy, labour often starts earlier than 40 weeks.
♦ The type of delivery you have will in part be influenced by the babies' position

in the womb. If they're both head-down you may go for a natural delivery, but if one or both are breech you might decide to go for a surgical delivery as there's a risk you'll need one to deliver the second baby even after one vaginal delivery. Occasionally, one of the babies may be lying in a transverse position, across the uterus. If this is the case, you will need a Caesarean section.
♦ A twin birth, whether surgical or vaginal, almost always involves an obstetrician, and often a paediatrician, as well as a midwife, even though many multiple births proceed without complications.

questions & answers

q **Is it possible for a baby to lie across the uterus?**

a It is rare for a baby to lie sideways (known as transverse), or diagonally (oblique). If your baby remains in this position when you go into labour, it's more likely you'll need a Caesarean section to deliver her safely.

q **How will I know if the head has engaged?**

a Your bump may look lower than it did, and you might not be kicked in the ribs so often as you were before. You may need to urinate more frequently. Engagement is also known as "lightening". Your midwife will confirm engagement by an external examination.

q **Do my twins share the same umbilical cord and amniotic fluid?**

a Twins almost always have their own cords, even identical twins (these are formed from an early split in a fertilized egg and are genetically absolutely the same). Usually, twins (including identical ones) have their own amniotic sacs, too, so their amniotic fluid is separate. This means there is a thin membrane between them in the uterus. They may, however, share a placenta.

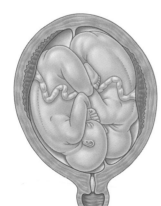

Cephalic twins
This is the most straightforward presentation.

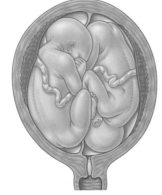

Cephalic/breech
You may need a Caesarean delivery for the breech baby.

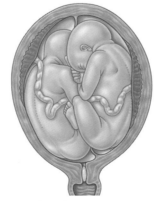

Breech twins
Your obstetrician may recommend a Caesarean section.

FIRST TRIMESTER												SECOND TRIMESTER															THIRD TRIMESTER												
1	2	3	4	5	6	7	8	9	10	11	12	13	14	15	16	17	18	19	20	21	22	23	24	25	26	27	28	29	30	31	32	33	34	35	36	37	38	39	40

week 40

A few months ago you thought this day would never arrive. In the next few days, your baby will finally be out in the big wide world and, more importantly, in your arms. It is a moment to cherish and the start of a whole new way of life, for you as well as the little person you're about to meet.

your body changes

The final few weeks of pregnancy see the greatest strain on your body, so it is important to get plenty of rest before the baby arrives.

The last few days

Your bump is impressively large and you're also probably very tired. This is entirely normal, you are carrying a ready-to-be-born person, so take it easy.

Good posture is vital. Ease the pressure by standing tall and tucking your pelvis under as much as you can. This can help alleviate the backache and pelvic pressure you feel. Many women give birth between weeks 40 and 41, but if you're still pregnant next week you'll probably see your caregiver and at least discuss the possibility of inducing your labour, although many practitioners don't advise it until about week 42 unless there are signs that the baby needs to be born (see page 75).

FACTS ABOUT YOU

♦ You'll now be having your antenatal checks weekly, or even more frequently if there's any cause for concern.

♦ Your weight gain has slowed or stopped since about week 37. In fact, you may lose about 900g–1.4kg (2–3lb) in the last couple of weeks.

♦ The weight of the baby may be causing you to leak urine. Keep doing your pelvic floor exercises (see page 45) right up to the birth, and start again as soon as you can afterwards. They really do help.

easing your symptoms

Impatience
This is arguably the main complaint at this point. Try not to become too obsessed with your estimated delivery date (EDD), it is just that, an estimate. As many as 40 per cent of babies arrive more than a week after their EDD. Make the most of the time before the birth and get plenty of rest.

Anxiety
As the birth of your baby is now imminent, it is natural to experience some anxiety. Try to relax (see page 49) and focus on the new life that you are about to bring into the world.

Shortness of breath
This is pretty normal at this stage due to the size of the baby, especially when you exert yourself. You may have to limit some of your activities, but you can still swim and do pelvic floor exercises. Keep feet and ankles moving when you can.

YOUR CHANGES YOU MAY HAVE SOME SIGNS OF ONSET OF LABOUR, SUCH AS: • A SHOW – THE LOSS OF THE MUCOUS PLUG • SLIGHT DIARRHOEA • CONTRACTIONS. REPORT THESE TO YOUR MIDWIFE

your emotions

Excitement, nervousness, fear, anticipation, longing – you go through so many different mood swings in these last few days of a pregnancy.

Coping with concerns

You and your partner may be very close, aware of this big change you're about to go through together – or you may be so nervous that you're keeping your distance emotionally. Don't shut each other out at this vital time. Try to enjoy being just the two of you, because it's going to be a long time before it's like this again.

Build in a few treats that are going to be more difficult to arrange in the weeks and months ahead – a trip to the cinema, perhaps, or a night out at a restaurant or taking walks together.

♦ Your main concern at this point is probably impatience that it's all taking so long. Try to enjoy the final days of your pregnancy without getting too uptight about being "late" – in fact, don't think of yourself as late at all. Many babies arrive after their due date, and this is especially true of first babies.

♦ Making love at this time may encourage the onset of labour. The prostaglandins in semen are thought to ripen the cervix for labour.

♦ Go through your birth plan (see page 67) and make sure you are happy with all your arrangements. The more confident you are, and the more you understand what is likely to happen, the less apprehensive you will feel.

♦ Everyone has concerns about the birth and about being parents. Try the relaxation techniques suggested (see page 49), and banish negative thoughts from your mind.

♦ Make sure you know the signs of labour (see page 68). If you are having contractions every 5–10 minutes, are in a lot of pain, having any vaginal bleeding, or think your waters may be leaking or broken, call your caregiver.

a good night's sleep

It is common to have trouble sleeping in the last four weeks of pregnancy, partly due to the size of your bump and partly because of the hormonal changes that are taking place. A good night's sleep may seem like an impossible dream, but there are steps you can take to improve your chances. A warm bath (not hot) before bed will relax you, as will a milky drink or a bowl of cereal. There are a number of self help methods you can try. Always consult a qualified practitioner and inform your doctor before trying any alternative therapies.

Diet and nutrition

A deficiency in B vitamins may contribute to your insomnia. If your blood-sugar levels fall during the night, you may wake because of hunger or nausea. Try foods rich in calcium, such as yogurt, a milky drink, almonds, or sesame seeds, as evening snacks. Foods rich in vitamin B6, such as green leafy vegetables and wholegrains, may help you sleep.

Finding a good position

Avoid lying on your back once your pregnancy is advanced as this position will compress the main artery; this may make you feel faint, as well as reducing the blood flow to the baby through the placenta. Sleeping on your left side takes the weight off your back and allows an unrestricted blood supply to the placenta and the baby. Lie on your left side and support yourself with pillows under your top leg. You may also find it comfortable to place a pillow under your bump.

Sleeping comfortably
Lie on your side and support yourself with pillows. Avoid sleeping on your back as you may feel faint.

SEE ALSO   EATING WELL page 27 ● EXERCISE page 45 ● RELAXATION TECHNIQUES page 49 ● COMMON COMPLAINTS pages 60–61 ● PREPARING FOR THE BIRTH pages 64–67 ● BIRTH PROCEDURES pages 74–75

your baby at 40 weeks

The big day is almost here (if it hasn't happened already) and your baby is about to get his first taste of life in a world he has glimpsed through the sounds and lights that have penetrated through to your uterus. From the moment he's born, he'll begin to start making sense of it all.

Your baby's appearance

The average weight of a newborn baby at term is 3.4kg (7lb 8oz), although anything between 2.5kg (5lb 8oz) and 4kg (9lb) is considered a normal weight. He's probably fairly plump by now, because in the last few weeks the fat deposits have built up under his skin, and consequently he's also less wrinkly. The lanugo has disappeared from his skin, although when he is born, you may still see some of the waxy vernix.

Your baby will have grey, brown, or blue eyes at birth. His true eye colour will be evident as he gets a few weeks older.

Development

By 40 weeks your baby's body is in full working order, and his lungs and nervous system, which matured more slowly than other body systems, are functioning properly. His brain, of course, is the organ that has the most developing still to do – but there's always babyhood and childhood, not to mention the rest of his life, to take care of that.

His immune system is not fully mature yet. During your pregnancy the placenta has provided your baby with some of the antibodies he needs. Breast milk also provides him with antibodies to protect him once he is born. His immune system will develop slowly over the first few years of his life. The myelin sheath that coats the nervous system also has some maturing to do, and will be complete when your child is about two years old.

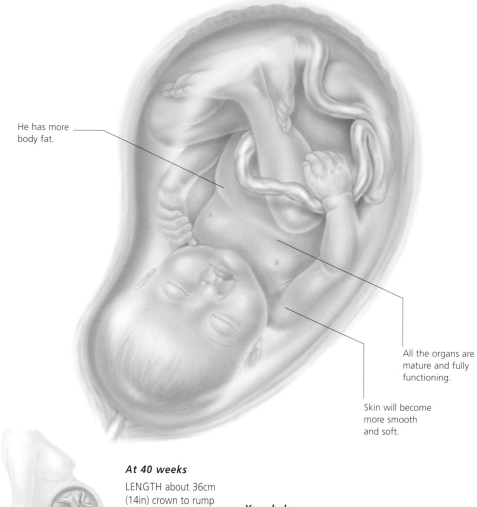

He has more body fat.

All the organs are mature and fully functioning.

Skin will become more smooth and soft.

At 40 weeks

LENGTH about 36cm (14in) crown to rump

TOTAL LENGTH about 50cm (20in)

WEIGHT about 3.4kg (7lb 8oz)

Your baby

He is now ready to be born, and much more chubby than he was before. Over the last 40 weeks, he has grown from a tiny bundle of cells into the fully formed human being now inside you.

your **growing** baby

♦ At 40 weeks 97 per cent of babies are head-down in the uterus and will be born this way.

♦ The placenta at birth is roughly one-sixth of the size of the baby.

♦ The umbilical cord is about the same length as the baby.

♦ From about 37 or 38 weeks he may not have gained weight. In fact, you may have lost a little weight in the final couple of weeks.

♦ In boy babies, the testes should have descended. In girls, the ovaries stay above the pelvic brim until after birth.

♦ Only about six per cent of babies are born on what was calculated to have been their due date. The majority are born after 40 weeks.

♦ It's now a very tight fit in the womb and he has to curl into a tight ball.

♦ The amniotic fluid, which surrounds the baby until hours or even minutes before he emerges, has changed from a colourless liquid into a pale, milky consistency because of the lanugo that has been shed into it.

♦ There is about one litre (two pints) of amniotic fluid surrounding your baby.

choosing a name

Choosing your baby's name is another exciting job for you and your partner while you await the birth. Remember that you are choosing something that will be with your baby throughout his life.

Points to consider

♦ You need to think about how the name sits with your family name, and check to see if the initials will make a word when placed together.

♦ In some families it is traditional to pass on a name. If you are not happy with this, you could perhaps make it a middle name.

♦ An unusual spelling gives your child a name that is almost exclusively his, but think how annoying it could be for him to have his name misspelt or mispronounced throughout his life.

♦ Remember that a name that suits your tiny newborn baby needs to suit a fully grown adult as well.

♦ Choosing a name that reflects the country of origin of one of the parents or another member of the family has become very popular in recent years.

♦ You may find that you and your partner just cannot decide. If this is the case, wait until he's born and then see what he looks like! Even if you have chosen a name, sometimes it just doesn't seem right when you actually meet your baby.

♦ You might want to think about a name that in some way links the baby to the circumstances of his birth, such as a name that is local to the area in which he was born.

A joint decision
Fathers-to-be can feel a little left out in the final weeks, but deciding what to call the new member of your family is something you can both do for your baby before he is born. However, be prepared in case you want to change your minds once he arrives!

---

questions & answers

q What is the nesting instinct?

a Many women get a sudden surge of energy from about week 36, when they feel they just have to clean the house or reorganize the nursery. This desire to make sure everything is ready is entirely natural, but limit yourself to arranging your baby's toys or checking your labour bag (see page 66).

q Can I be the first person to touch my baby after he is born?

a Talk your wishes through with your caregiver and your partner, and incorporate them into your birth plan (see page 67). Whether you will be the first person to make physical contact with the baby will depend on a number of issues, including your delivery position, and whether there are any concerns over the baby's health. If everything is straightforward, and especially if you are upright when you give birth, it should be possible for you to lean down immediately afterwards and take your baby into your arms.

q When will the cord be cut after the birth?

a Again, this depends on the method and circumstances of the delivery. If it's a surgical or assisted birth, the cord will be clamped and cut straight away. If you have a natural, vaginal delivery you may want to ask the midwife if the cord can be left intact until it stops pulsating. Some people believe that the baby continues to benefit from the nutrients he receives from the placenta after the birth, and if you feel you would prefer this talk to the midwife beforehand.

common discomforts

A few lucky women sail through pregnancy without so much as a stretch mark, but the majority do experience the occasional problem. Most are not serious but they can be uncomfortable and unpleasant. You will want to avoid taking drugs during pregnancy, and, fortunately, for most of the minor discomforts there are different remedies or therapies available that may help ease the symptoms.

dealing with minor ailments

Talking to other pregnant women, and women who've been pregnant recently, can be enormously helpful. Your midwife will also be an important source of useful ideas.

If something is bothering you, don't wait until your next scheduled appointment to ask for advice.

General advice

Most women are wary of taking drugs while they are pregnant, but this does not mean suffering in silence. Minor ailments of pregnancy can often be eased by a small adjustment to your diet or lifestyle. Complementary therapies are increasingly popular with mothers-to-be, and some women have reported great success in treating their ailments. However, just because something is natural does not necessarily make it safe to use in pregnancy. For example, many herbs and some aromatherapy oils should not be used by pregnant women. Always consult a qualified practitioner with experience of dealing with pregnant women, and tell your caregiver before beginning any treatments.

Vaginal infections

Infections and increased vaginal secretions are quite common in pregnancy. Always consult your doctor or midwife if you have an unusual or heavy discharge, or if you are itching. It is important to check whether your symptoms are caused by a simple case of thrush or if you have another infection. The nearer you are to term the quicker you should seek help, as some infections, such as Group B streptococcus (GBS), can be contracted by your baby during delivery.

Eating well
A diet rich in fruit and vegetables is excellent for your general health, and that of your baby. It is also a good way of avoiding constipation.

Anaemia

Anaemia is a possible, but uncommon, cause of tiredness. It's caused by a reduced amount of haemoglobin in your red blood cells. This is the result either of a diet that doesn't contain enough iron, or the heavy demands of your pregnancy. If you think your tiredness could be caused by insufficient iron it's worth asking your GP or midwife for a blood test to check your haemoglobin levels (this will be done at least once during your pregnancy as a matter of routine). Iron supplements can cause constipation, so if this is a problem a different brand or prescription may be better for you.

Backache

Carrying a baby places considerable stress on your frame, which is why backache is so common. It isn't inevitable, though, and the best way to keep it at bay is to be very aware of your posture (see page 45).

Keeping up your fluid levels
Throughout pregnancy drink plenty of fresh water to avoid dehydration and improve your digestion.

Don't make the classic pregnancy mistake of arching your back and sticking out your abdomen: this taxes your back, and it's far better for your spine if you can pull your tummy in. Balance your body weight between your heels and the balls of your feet, and sit, when you can, with both feet on the floor, rather than cross-legged.

If you do develop backache, seek help from a specialist. Your GP can point you in the direction of someone useful: it might be a physiotherapist, an obstetric physiotherapist, or an osteopath. Whoever you consult about your backache should be able to show you special exercises to help alleviate the discomfort.

Constipation

Again, this isn't an inevitable consequence of pregnancy so don't just assume you have to put up with it. Your digestive system does become more sluggish during pregnancy, but you can counteract the effects by increasing the amount of water you drink (aim for eight glasses a day), and your intake of fresh fruit and vegetables (aim for at least five or six portions a day). Dried fruit is also good (it provides extra iron, too). Homeopathic preparations may help (seek advice at the homeopathic counter at a pharmacy), and some mothers-to-be have reported good results from reflexology and acupuncture.

Heartburn

This unpleasant condition is often worst in the evening: it's caused by pregnancy hormones relaxing the valve at the top of your stomach so that the acid contents are released upwards, combined with physical pressure due to the enlarging uterus pushing the gastrointestinal tract towards the upper abdomen. You feel bloated and have a burning sensation in your upper chest. Standing tall, with your arms raised above your head, can offer a bit of immediate relief, since it increases

the amount of chest space. Eat small meals throughout the day rather than one or two large ones. Avoiding alcohol, spicy foods, fatty food, and coffee can also help. Some people find a glass of milk beneficial; for others, milk can actually bring on an attack. Eat slowly, and avoid eating just before you go to bed. Try sipping warm (not hot) mint or ginger tea after a meal.

Haemorrhoids (piles)

These are varicose veins around the rectum and anus. They're made worse by straining (so constipation can cause or aggravate them), and they can make your life a misery with itching and pain. Avoiding constipation is vital if you're at risk of piles; be sure to eat plenty of fresh fruit and vegetables. Various creams are available for piles, but make sure any pharmacist you consult knows you are pregnant, or ask your doctor for advice. There are also some herbal and homeopathic remedies available.

Varicose veins

These can be the result of the extra strain on your legs. They usually appear as bulging, bluish veins under the skin. Support tights can help, as can lots of walking, since it helps the blood return to your heart. Sit with your legs higher than your head for at least half an hour a day, or lie on the floor with your bottom against a wall and your legs up on the wall.

Finding some time for you
Many minor niggles can be eased by taking it easy and listening to your body's needs. Remember that even early in pregnancy, when you have little or no bump, your body is working much harder than usual to help your baby develop and grow.

conditions of concern

While the majority of women enjoy pregnancy without any serious problems, for a small percentage expecting a baby does trigger a cause for concern. Antenatal care is designed to identify women at risk of serious conditions before problems arise. The good news is that even if you are one of the few who may be at higher risk, it's more than likely that with specialist medical help you and your baby will both be fine.

rare and serious conditions

This highlights the importance of never ignoring your antenatal appointments. Also, if you have an inkling that things may not be fine, don't wait: always act straight away, so if there is a problem it can be dealt with as soon as possible.

There are a number of conditions that can cause potentially serious problems. These are the most common, although remember that even these are relatively rare. Always speak to your caregivers if you're worried you might be at risk.

Pre-eclampsia/toxaemia

A lot of the antenatal care you receive is aimed at watching out for the first signs of pre-eclampsia. It's most common in first-time mothers, although it's also a risk for women who had it in their previous pregnancy. Fortunately pre-eclampsia, also known as toxaemia or pregnancy-induced hypertension (PIH), is uncommon. If you include its mildest forms it occurs in 5 to 10 per cent of pregnancies – some women who

when to **call the doctor**

If you develop any of the following symptoms, act quickly – call your doctor, midwife, or the labour ward at your hospital, or get yourself to a hospital:

♦ bleeding that is bright red and/or profuse

♦ severe abdominal pain

♦ nausea or vomiting combined with blurred vision or headaches

♦ a sudden drop in the number of times you notice your baby move over a period of several hours

♦ pain below the ribs, especially at night

♦ you think your bag of waters may have ruptured or is leaking.

Managing pre-eclampsia
If you are diagnosed with slow-onset pre-eclampsia, you will need lots of rest, but if your symptoms are mild you may be able to stay at home. Your blood pressure and urine will be monitored frequently.

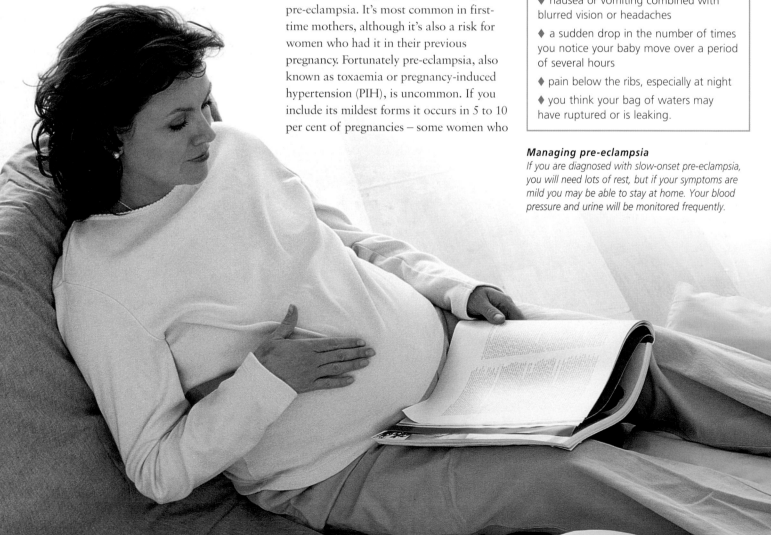

develop pre-eclampsia may have had high blood pressure before their pregnancy.

Pre-eclampsia isn't fully understood, but basically the mother's body systems become increasingly unable to cope with the pregnancy. It usually develops after 20 weeks, and may be sudden- or slow-onset. It's characterized by a rise in blood pressure; protein in the urine; and oedema, which causes swelling in the ankles, feet, and hands. Although you should have any worrying signs checked, there are other reasons why you might have swollen ankles or protein in your urine; but occurring together, two or three of the above will be taken seriously.

You'll be monitored closely, and if the situation seems to worsen, your baby may need to be delivered. This is done to prevent pre-eclampsia from progressing to eclampsia, in which the mother has seizures. Advances in the care of premature newborns mean that today many more babies survive pre-eclamptic pregnancies. The pregnancy can't be continued once pre-eclampsia becomes severe because it puts mother and baby at risk. But slow-onset, or mild, pre-eclampsia may be managed for up to several weeks.

Diabetes

If you have pre-existing diabetes you'll have been considered "high risk" since the start of your pregnancy; however, about one to two per cent (some estimates even say

Monitoring your pregnancy
If you are found to have a condition which is potentially serious, your pregnancy will be closely monitored, often with frequent ultrasound scans.

10 per cent) of women develop "gestational diabetes" during pregnancy. Diabetes means your body isn't producing enough insulin to regulate your blood sugar. Insulin is a hormone that helps the body use sugar, the body's main source of fuel. Women with diabetes have too much sugar in their blood. Gestational diabetes usually goes away after delivery.

Symptoms may include feeling thirsty and weak, although diabetes can occur without symptoms. Your midwife will check your blood sugar level or check a urine sample for glucose, which can indicate diabetes. If you have gestational diabetes your pregnancy will be closely monitored and you'll follow a special diet or take insulin.

Placenta praevia

This means the placenta is attached to the lower uterine wall and partially or totally covers the cervix. When you go into labour, the placenta will be expelled before the baby, endangering his life. If you have placenta praevia, you'll need a Caesarean section. This condition is usually picked up during routine ultrasound scans, but it may be indicated by bleeding during your pregnancy.

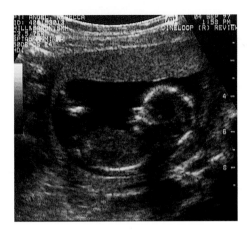

"I had sudden-onset pre-eclampsia in my first pregnancy. Over the space of a couple of days my ankles became elephantine, my hands were swollen, and I was hardly passing any urine. I called the midwife and she sent me straight to the hospital. My blood pressure was high, and through that night it climbed even higher: at dawn the doctor said the baby had to be delivered. I was only 29 weeks pregnant, and my tiny daughter was born a couple of hours later. She was in the special care unit for eight weeks, but she's fine now. My second pregnancy was problem-free, and I had a vaginal delivery despite a Caesarean with my first."

PHILIPPA CASEMAN, 33, MUM TO JADE AGED 3 YEARS AND MATTHEW AGED 8 MONTHS

coping with **miscarriage**

If you have bleeding, call your GP straight away. Sometimes, sadly, it is a sign that your pregnancy is in trouble. (This isn't always the case – if you have bleeding but a scan shows a fetal heartbeat, you have a good chance everything will be fine.)

If your have a miscarriage, it's a devastating blow for both you and your partner. Your caregiver will discuss with you whether to go home and wait for the baby to miscarry naturally, which may involve cramps and blood loss, or to have a D&C, which means surgically emptying the uterus under anaesthesia. You may get over the physical pain quite quickly, but the psychological scars take longer to heal. Miscarriage is above all a terrible shock, followed by weeks or maybe months

of wondering why it happened. You will need time to grieve.

Usually there are no answers to why your baby has died, although some babies die because they were not developing normally. If this was your first attempt to have a child, you will have worries about whether the next pregnancy will end the same way. This is unlikely; having one miscarriage doesn't mean you'll have another next time. If you do have a series of miscarriages, you can be referred to a specialist for tests into the cause.

Although it's hard, don't blame yourself for what happened. Feelings of guilt and anger are common, but it is very unlikely that there is anything you could have done to prevent what happened.

your birth choices

Every birth is a unique event, a huge turning point, and a time to celebrate. The little person you know so well, and yet don't yet know at all, will be in your arms at last. If this is your first baby, the birth will also mark the end of your old way of life and the beginning of a new phase: there's no going back, and it won't always be easy, but it will be enormously enriching and lots of fun.

understanding the options

Talk to your caregiver about how you can best prepare for the sort of experience you'd like birth to be. Spend time focusing on the birth itself – thinking about how you'd like it to go.

Of course, what happens during your labour will, to some extent, be determined by events on the day: there's nothing set in stone about labour and childbirth, so it is important to keep an open mind. However, being as prepared as possible, and finding out about the options beforehand, can really help you make the most of the birth of your child.

You probably have your own ideas about the type of birth you want, but equally you know that labour isn't a process it's possible to predict, and you have to be open-minded about the need for medical intervention if it becomes necessary.

Plan for the best-case scenario: try to be optimistic about how things will go, while accepting that if you do need medical help and therefore don't get quite the experience you'd hoped for, you will at least all emerge safe and healthy. Discuss your hopes and ideas with your birth partner, and make sure you are both comfortable with the plans.

Write your thoughts down in a birth plan, and make sure you have it with you when you go into labour (see page 67). Here are some of the options you might like to consider:

Active delivery

Active childbirth is the term used to describe a delivery in which the mother is upright, usually away from a bed, and in which she has freedom of movement throughout or through most of her labour. From a physical point of view it's the most efficient way of giving birth, because it enables you to use gravity to maximum effect. Active birth also allows a woman to remain more "in control" of events; she's less likely to feel like a "patient" if she's not on a bed and can move her body as she feels necessary.

Most UK maternity units are very sympathetic to women who want an active birth these days. They have aids such as bean bags and inflated balls for use during labour, and a few even have active birthing rooms, which have no hospital bed, just a sofa and lots of floor cushions and bean bags on which to rest between contractions. Almost all home deliveries are active births, and an increasing number of hospital deliveries are active as well.

Traditional delivery

The tradition in Western societies during the past 30 or so years has been to give birth lying on a hospital bed, possibly using foot rests to aid pushing the baby out, or lying on your left side with your right leg raised. This sort of birth is still

home **birth**

Home birth is on the increase in the UK, but it still makes up only about three per cent of the total number of births, although figures vary widely between areas.

The experience can be more intimate, more comfortable, and less pressurized: you won't have to make the decision about when to move into the maternity unit. Your caregiver, usually a midwife, will come to you when you go into labour, you won't be separated from your partner at any point during the delivery or afterwards, and studies show that you're likely to need less pain relief and to have a shorter labour, probably because you're in your own environment.

But home birth isn't for everyone: some women feel they need to be close to the technology of a hospital just in case they need intervention (although, of course, moving into hospital is always an option if you choose to give birth at home). Hospital is also the best place if you have had a complicated or high-risk pregnancy, or if there are any indications that you might have a difficult birth or a postpartum haemorrhage.

favoured by some midwives, and by obstetricians if the birth is assisted (see below), or if you've needed continuous fetal monitoring to chart the baby's heartbeat during contractions. Some women find fetal monitoring reassuring (see page 74), and prefer to opt for this kind of birth.

Assisted delivery

If you need assistance you'll definitely be lying on a hospital bed when you deliver, probably with your feet in stirrups. This isn't the sort of birth anyone would choose, but occasionally it becomes necessary due to the slowness of the second, or pushing, stage of the labour or to aid a breech delivery.

Forceps or ventouse deliveries (in which a suction cup is fitted to the baby's head and used to help ease it from the uterus) both come into this category, and are carried out by obstetricians, usually after labour has gone on for a long period of time (see page 75). These procedures have a good safety record for both you and your baby.

water **birth**

Being in water during labour, and even delivering the baby in water, has become increasingly popular during the past 25 years. Water can help reduce pain, and may reduce your chances of tearing because it helps you relax. Although delivery in water is still quite unusual, many women use water to help them manage pain during the first stage.

Many maternity units now have water birthing rooms. However, it can be difficult to "book" these in advance, and you may have to hope one is free on the day. Another option is to hire a pool and give birth at home, or to see if your hospital will allow you to take a pool in with you.

The Royal College of Obstetricians and Gynaecologists recommends that ideally the water should be at body temperature (37°C/98.6°F). If the water is hotter the mother may be at risk of dehydration and high blood pressure. A study of the use of water in labour has indicated that labour is more efficient if the mother enters the water only once she has reached 5cm dilatation (see page 70).

Current guidelines advise that you leave the pool for the third stage as the relaxing effects of water could theoretically increase bleeding after delivery or encourage retention of the placenta.

Caesarean section

This is a surgical delivery in which your baby is born through an incision in your uterine wall. A Caesarean may be elective (planned) or it may be an emergency, in which case you'll have been in labour first and something will indicate the need for a surgical delivery. During the past few years

the Caesarean section rate has increased dramatically, and more than one in five deliveries in the UK is now surgical. It is a major operation, and, as with all abdominal surgery, you will need time to recover after the birth. This means that you will not be able to perform certain activities, including driving, for a few weeks.

Deciding where to give birth
Before making a decision, visit the delivery rooms with your partner and make sure you feel comfortable with the arrangements. The staff will be pleased to answer your questions, and you will find it reassuring to know what to expect when you actually go into labour.

who's who at **the birth**

The midwife
Whatever sort of birth you have, you will have a midwife with you. He or she may be with you throughout your labour, or may pop in and out of the delivery room. If you need to have a surgical delivery, your midwife will accompany you to the operating theatre.

The obstetrician
This is a specialist in deliveries that are less straightforward. He or she will take charge if you need special care during your labour, such as an assisted delivery or a Caesarean section.

The paediatrician
A paediatrician will be present to check on the baby's health if there's any reason to expect any difficulties, or if the birth is premature.

preparing for birth

It's worth thinking about what you'll need to have ready for the birth well in advance – although you've got an EDD (estimated delivery date), there are about five weeks during which it would be entirely normal for your baby to be born. That's because from 37 weeks' gestation is considered "term", and up to 42 weeks is quite common.

a unique event

Now is the time to make your detailed plans for the birth. Taking care over these arrangements will help you to feel more calm when you do go into labour.

There are several points you should consider when making your plans.
♦ How to contact your birth partner (and/or the baby's father, if they're not the same) when you go into labour.
♦ Keep the telephone number of your midwife and/or the labour ward of your maternity unit close at hand so you can call if you have any problems, or to let them know you're on your way. Keep the number pinned up in several places around the house, so that you don't have to go up or downstairs to find the number.
♦ If you've been given your antenatal notes to look after yourself make sure they are in your bag or somewhere prominent, as you will need to take them to hospital with you.
♦ Pack what you need to take into hospital.
♦ Make sure you know how you'll travel to the hospital, and how long the journey will take.

♦ Check if you will need to pay for the car park and what change you will need.
♦ You will need to make arrangements well in advance for your older child or children to be looked after while you're both at the hospital. Make sure your child understands what will happen, who will be looking after him, and when he will see you again.

Preparing for birth at home
If you're planning a home birth your midwife will go through what you'll need. In fact, the requirements are minimal, although it's worth spending time beforehand working out which room you'd probably like to use to give birth: somewhere private, with easy access to a bathroom and hot water, is probably best. Two or three weeks before your due date the midwife will bring round a sterile

---

your **labour bag**

You will need to pack a basic kit for the birth and afterwards.

For you:
♦ nightdresses – an old nightdress or baggy T-shirt, preferably front opening, for labour, plus two or three nightdresses and a dressing gown for the next few days
♦ two or three maternity bras
♦ breast pads
♦ super-absorbent sanitary towels
♦ several pairs of pants, either cotton or disposable
♦ toiletries: toothbrush and toothpaste, flannel, towel, brush and comb, face cream, shower gel, shampoo, make-up, small mirror, perfume
♦ plastic bags for dirty washing
♦ clothes to come home in
♦ two copies of your birth plan.

For your baby:
♦ nappies
♦ stretchsuits and suitable nightwear
♦ vest
♦ cardigan or coat and a hat to come home in, depending on the weather
♦ blanket.

Do not forget that you must fit a suitable baby seat to the car in which you are bringing the baby home.

pack with the things she'll need for the birth. Keep them in a safe place, and don't interfere with them, until the delivery day.

You will still find the checklist for the labour bag useful if you are planning a home birth. It is convenient to have everything you need packed in one place, and if you do need to transfer to hospital for any reason, everything will be ready for you.

Dealing with your concerns

Even for women having their third or fourth child, there are always moments when the journey ahead seems daunting. Everyone has concerns before their baby is born – what's important is that you are able to share them with someone: your partner, a friend, or your midwife.

♦ Talk your worries through with your partner, and ask him about his. It's a good idea for him to come with you to some of your antenatal classes (see page 49) so he is as well informed as possible about the birth process, and to at least one third-trimester antenatal check so he can raise any issues with the midwife or obstetrician.

♦ You'll inevitably talk to friends and family members who've had babies recently. Their experiences can be helpful, but remember that every birth is different. Don't assume that what happens to other people will necessarily be similar to what happens to you, your partner, and baby.

birth plan

Writing a birth plan is a great way to consider your options and ideas before the big day. By stating your preferences now, you can let your caregivers and birth partner know what kind of birth you want for you and your baby.

A birth plan should not be a description of your ideal birth – everyone would like a natural, virtually pain-free labour – but a discussion of how you would like the birth to progress and your feelings about certain procedures. Be realistic. If you produce a birth plan that states that you do not wish to have any interventions at all, you will be terribly disappointed if this cannot happen. It is better to consider all the possibilities, and look for the best outcomes in all cases.

Birth Plan

I am looking forward to the birth of my first child, and I have written down a few of my ideas on how I hope my labour will progress.

1. **Support person** – My partner Dan will be with me throughout the birth.

2. **Monitoring** – I understand that you routinely do a 20-minute electronic fetal monitoring session, and I am happy for this to go ahead. If all is well, I would like the baby to be monitored from then with a sonic aid.

3. **Positions** – I don't think I will want to be restricted to the bed, and would welcome the use of bean bags and other active birth aids.

4. **Pain relief** – I will use a TENS machine I will provide myself, and if necessary may request gas and air. I hope not to need pethidine or an epidural, although in the event of needing a Caesarean section I would like to have epidural anaesthesia so I can be awake for the birth.

5. **Amniotomy** – I would prefer not to have my waters broken artificially.

6. **Episiotomy** – I would prefer to tear naturally than be cut.

Maria Peters

Your birth plan
Make sure you have two copies of your birth plan with you when you go into labour. Give one to the midwife and keep one for your reference.

---

comfort aids **for labour**

In addition to the basic items in your labour bag, you may like to have some other things for your comfort. If you are going into hospital, check with the midwife when you visit the maternity unit that you can bring extra items. These might include:

♦ alternative therapies for use in labour, such as aromatherapy oils, a massage roller, or homeopathic remedies

♦ TENS (Transcutaneous Electrical Nerve Stimulation) machine (see page 69)

♦ an extra pillow or pillows

♦ a CD player and CDs of relaxing music, plus spare batteries

♦ a thick pair of socks

♦ a hot water bottle for pain relief

♦ two face flannels

♦ massage oil

♦ a big box of tissues

♦ lip salve

♦ a spray bottle, filled with cool water to spray your face

♦ a natural sponge to suck on

♦ drinks and snacks.

what your **partner needs**

Your partner will need:

♦ a change of clothing

♦ drinks and snacks

♦ lots of change for the public telephone or a phone card – you must not use your mobile telephone inside the hospital as it can interfere with equipment

♦ telephone numbers for friends and family to let them know the good news

♦ camera and film, or video camera (check if video cameras are permitted)

♦ wipes to refresh hands and face

♦ a sponge bag with basic toiletries.

labour

This is the culmination of the last precious months. Going into labour is exciting – once it's underway you know it can't be long before you hold your baby. On the following pages you will find some suggestions of positions for labour which you might like to discuss with your caregiver.

going into labour

Many couples worry they won't recognize the early stages of labour, and will end up with a rush to the hospital or an unplanned home delivery. This does happen, but it is very rare.

It is far more common for couples to arrive at the delivery ward thinking their birth is minutes away only to find there are hours to go.

Knowing the signs

If you are tuned in to your body in the days and weeks leading up to the time your baby is due to be born, you'll probably be able to spot some of the signs that your body is preparing for labour. However, be warned, this pre-labour stage can last for two, three, or even more weeks, so don't be surprised if things don't happen quickly.

♦ A nesting instinct – the urge to rush around getting your house in order before the baby puts in his appearance.

♦ The baby moves less. This is because there's now less space in your uterus, but also the baby does seem to get a bit quieter just before you go into labour. Talk to your midwife if you're concerned that your baby is moving a lot less than usual.

♦ In the days before the birth it is normal to lose 900g–1.4kg (2–3lb).

♦ You may experience slight diarrhoea. This is your body's way of clearing out the bowel so it doesn't impede the birth.

♦ You might have a show. The plug of mucus and blood which has blocked the cervix through your pregnancy is expelled now the cervix is opening to let the baby through. You may notice it on your knickers or when you go to the toilet. If you are bleeding a lot, enough to need a pad, tell your midwife.

♦ When you see a fictional birth on television or in a film it always seems to start with a woman's waters breaking, but in real life this is a less common start to labour. If it happens tell your midwife, because most caregivers prefer the baby to be born within 24–48 hours of the water sac being ruptured, as the baby can be at risk of infection without his protective amniotic sac.

♦ You may have weeks of pre-labour, or Braxton Hicks, contractions. They tend to be quite variable, sometimes coming every 20 to 30 minutes, or even at five- to

Timing your contractions
When your contractions start, time them from the beginning of one contraction to the beginning of the next.

10-minute intervals for a short time, then stopping abruptly. Contractions of actual labour often start like severe cramps, with pains radiating down your legs as well as in your back and abdomen. Real labour contractions get stronger, last longer, and become more closely spaced.

When to go to the hospital

Once you know you are in labour you need to decide when to move into hospital. However, it can be disappointing to arrive at the hospital thinking you're about to give birth only to discover your cervix is just a little way dilated. A first labour can last up to 12 hours or more, and it is often better to spend several hours of this time at home. The following pointers might help you decide when to make the move:
♦ if your contractions are coming five minutes apart or closer
♦ if you feel you need help to get through the pain of the contractions
♦ if your waters break or you are bleeding.
   If you're in any doubt, call the duty midwife and explain your symptoms.

Arriving at the hospital

If you can, call the midwife before you leave home to let the hospital know that you are on your way. In many areas the midwife will come to you and accompany you to the hospital. Once you arrive at the hospital, your midwife will discuss your symptoms and your birth plan (see page 67). Your temperature, blood pressure, and pulse will be taken, and your urine will be tested for blood, protein, and sugar.

   Hospitals routinely monitor the baby's heart rate using a cardiotocograph for about 20 minutes when you arrive. During this you will need to lie still on the bed. If all is well you should be able to be active for the rest of the birth, but monitored intermittently.

   Continuous monitoring may be needed for breech births, multiple births, or if there is anything else of concern. Your midwife will then give you an internal examination to check how your cervix is progressing, and you can ask how far you are dilated. If you are concerned about anything or unsure about any procedures, let your caregivers know as soon as possible.

pain **relief**

Don't assume you'll necessarily need a lot of pain relief when you're in labour; some women do, some don't, and it's partly dependent on whether you've given birth before and on the position your baby is in for the delivery. But here are the options you'll want to consider:

♦ **Massage** This can be done by your partner and/or midwife. Massage of the lower back in particular can be a big help. Make sure you're very specific about what you want and when.

♦ **Moving around and distraction techniques** Keeping going and moving around, both at home and once you reach the hospital, can take your mind off the pain of the contractions and also helps your body to use them to maximum effect. Distraction means using some device to try to blot out the pain. Count backwards from 100 at each contraction.

♦ **A TENS machine** Transcutaneous Electrical Nerve Stimulation (TENS) involves a battery-operated box with wires that are attached to your body. It works by passing a tiny electrical current which reduces the pain messages to your brain. Check with your hospital beforehand if you want to use a TENS machine. Some hospitals provide them, but if not you will need to hire your own. They are usually not very expensive.

♦ **Entonox (gas and air)** Entonox is a mixture of nitrous oxide gas and oxygen, which you inhale at the start of a contraction and which takes the edge off the pain at the height of the contraction.

♦ **Pethidine** This is a morphine-like, injected drug which inhibits your brain's registering of pain. It shouldn't be given too close to the birth as it can make the baby sleepy.

the first stage

During the first stage of labour, the cervix opens up to allow the baby's head out into the birth canal. This stage is usually the longest. The contractions you feel are the muscles of the uterus thinning and pulling back the cervix.

If this is your first baby, this stage will probably take about 10 to 12 hours. Subsequent labours are often quicker, although every labour is different. Near the end of this stage, contractions become longer and stronger.

How you'll feel

No matter how confident you may feel in advance, don't be surprised if you feel a little scared at some point. The power of the uterus is truly awesome, and it can be quite daunting to feel you have been taken over by a process you can't control. Don't try to fight your labour. Allow your body to do its work, but don't be afraid to ask for support or pain relief if you need it.

Sitting forwards
This is a good way to stay upright while resting. Rest on plenty of pillows so that you are comfortable. This is especially useful if you become very tired.

epidural **anaesthesia**

This numbs the nerves in your spine to block out the pain of labour. This sort of pain relief can be restricting, in that it can stop you moving around, and it may also increase your chance of needing an assisted delivery and/or episiotomy, but it is a very effective pain reliever, and can be used for a Caesarean section as well as during a vaginal delivery.

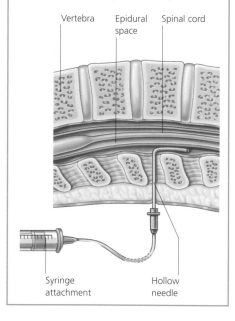

Vertebra   Epidural space   Spinal cord

Syringe attachment   Hollow needle

"I went into labour in the evening. I was considering going to hospital at 10pm at night, but in fact we didn't actually go there until about 6am the following morning – and the baby was eventually born at 3pm! I was delighted to hear that I was already half way to being fully dilated when I arrived, but then it all slowed down for a while. I think that was because I was adjusting to being in a new place."

JANET SIMPSON, 26,
MUM TO ALEX AGED 5 WEEKS

Your birth partner and the staff are there to help you and your baby. If you do decide you need pain relief, try waiting 10–15 minutes before you actually request it. Things can change quickly in labour, and you may be more comfortable by then. You may be surprised by how much you rely on your birth partner for support during the birth, no matter how independent you usually are.

Your midwife will give you regular internal examinations. Ask how things are progressing. It can be reassuring to know that labour is moving forward.

Positions for first-stage labour

During the first stage, try a variety of positions to see what feels comfortable.
♦ Try to stay upright, as this presses the baby's head against the cervix, making your contractions more effective.
♦ Move around between contractions to ease the pain, but try to stay relaxed.
♦ Use the breathing techniques you learned at antenatal classes.
♦ Do not feel inhibited about making lots of noise if that helps you.
♦ Deal with each contraction one at a time, as each happens.

Back massage
You may find this helps alleviate backache, especially if your baby is facing towards your abdomen. Talcum powder will help prevent friction if you are being massaged straight onto your skin. This position can also be comfortable for transition (see opposite).

Leaning
Your partner can support your body weight and massage your lower back if you wish. This position is ideal if you are walking around between contractions.

dilatation of **the cervix**

The muscles of the uterus contract, pulling the cervix back and stretching it to allow the baby's head to pass through. Once no more cervical "lip" can be felt, the first stage of labour is complete; you have reached "full dilatation".

Hormone changes soften the cervix, which is still closed.

The cervix thins (effaces) and begins to stretch and open.

The cervix is fully dilated when it is 10cm (4in) open.

the second stage

Once the cervix is fully dilated, you move into what's known as second-stage labour, when your body will push your baby out into the world.

Contractions in second-stage labour feel different from the first stage, because they're the feelings that compel you to bear down, or push, to help your baby out. This stage is longer for a first baby.

Transition

Moving from first- to second-stage labour is known as "transition". It can last for anything from a few minutes to an hour or more. For a lot of women it's a time of confusion. Suddenly, having felt aware of what you were doing, you may feel unsure whether you can complete the task.

Kneeling
Squatting or kneeling positions allow the pelvis to open wide and use gravity to help you push the baby out. Kneeling on all fours can also be comfortable.

Sitting upright
Ask for extra pillows to prop you up if you wish. This position allows you to relax back onto the pillows between contractions.

"Like a lot of first-time dads I had little knowledge of what to expect. I was worried for my wife, and was afraid she was in too much pain, although when we talked about it afterwards she said it was never more than she could cope with. I tried to focus on her and her needs and give her my attention."

MALCOLM STONE, 34,
DAD TO EWAN AGED 6 MONTHS

role of the **birth partner**

Transition can be a tough time for you as the birth partner, especially if this is your first baby. This is the time when both you and the mother need the support of an experienced caregiver. Whether or not you've been helping the mother physically during first-stage labour, your help may be required now to get her into a comfortable position for the second stage. If you suffer from any kind of back problem do take care not to injure yourself supporting her. She may like you to have cool flannels ready for her head between contractions, or a face spray. The second stage is hard, physical work. It's really encouraging to be told when the head is visible, so keep an eye out for the first glimpse of your tiny daughter or son!

Or it may be that your labour so far has been long and difficult, and you can't believe even more is expected of you. There may be slightly unpleasant physical symptoms during transition, too. Some mothers-to-be feel nauseous or even vomit, and others are shivery. This is the stage at which huge amounts of support are often needed. You may want to be held by your partner, or you may want to be left alone, but it usually helps if there's someone there to remind you that you're doing really well.

Supported leg
Prop yourself on cushions, then get your partner to support your leg while you push, this enables you to lie down without working against gravity.

Kneeling on all fours
Keep your hips below your shoulders and your legs wide apart. Rocking your hips from side to side may ease backache.

episiotomy

Episiotomies are no longer routine for first-time mothers, but they are not uncommon. A cut is made at the entrance to the vagina as your baby is being born so that you can push your baby out without tearing. There is a wide range of opinions on whether it's best to have an episiotomy or tear naturally: some experts claim that a tear heals more effectively. You should discuss the possibility of an episiotomy beforehand with your caregiver. One may be necessary if, for example, you need an assisted delivery. The best way to avoid either an episiotomy or a tear is to talk to your midwife about positions for delivery, and follow her instructions as the baby's head crowns.

your baby's descent **through the pelvis**

During the second stage, your baby is pushed through the bony structure of your pelvis and your birth canal.

♦ The baby's heartbeat may slow intermittently as you push during contractions, but this isn't a problem. Your midwife will check on the heartbeat between contractions using an electronic stethoscope.

♦ As her head becomes level with your perineum she'll be visible for the first time to your partner and the midwife, even if not to you. Ask for a mirror if you don't want to miss this moment yourself.

♦ She'll then disappear back into the birth canal between contractions for a while.

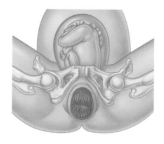

Eventually her head will remain at the edge of your vagina between contractions. This is "crowning". The midwife will tell you not to push to allow the tissues to stretch enough to avoid a tear.

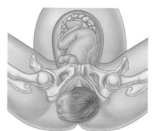

The head is born face down. The midwife will check the umbilical cord isn't looped around her neck. The baby turns her head to the side instinctively to take her first breath.

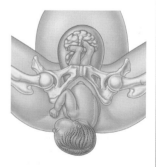

With the next two or three contractions her shoulders will be born, and in another push her legs and bottom will be out, too. The midwife will probably deliver her onto your stomach.

meeting **your baby**

Once your baby is born the midwife will be watching to check that she breathes quite quickly, and if she also cries or moves around that's an extra sign that all's well. But if you've given birth in an upright or active position you're the first person who'll be able to touch and hold her; often the feel of your hand on her back will stimulate her into taking her first few breaths and filling her lungs with oxygen for the first time.

You may be a bit shocked by her appearance. She may still be covered in vernix, the greasy, cream-like substance that coated her skin in the womb, or she may be bloody. Her face may be bright red or even blue, or it may look bruised from the delivery. A newborn baby doesn't look much like a baby of a few weeks old, so be prepared.

You may well be filled with love for this little person that you have waited to meet for so long, or you may simply feel overwhelmed by the whole experience. Lie back with your baby and congratulate yourself. You deserve it.

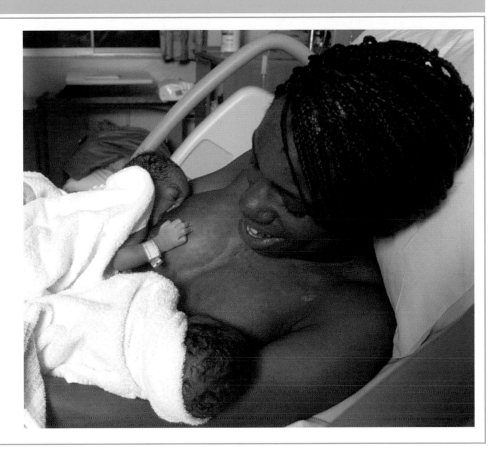

Your first family moments
For you and your partner, it's like taking part in a real-life miracle: the baby you've given life to is here, and the adventure of parenthood has begun after all those months of waiting. The midwife will probably leave you and your partner alone for a while after the birth so that you can get to know your new baby. At a distance of about 20–25cm (8–10in) she can see your face quite clearly and she will soon recognize your voice from the sounds she heard inside your uterus. Make sure your partner has a chance to hold her as well as you.

the third stage

The baby's arrival marks the end of the second stage of labour, but there's a third – the delivery of the placenta. Once the baby has been born, the midwife will place a hand on your abdomen and gently pull on the cord to ease the placenta out – she may ask you to push at the same time, but the hard work of delivery has now passed.

The placenta may slip effortlessly out of the vagina very soon after the baby. This third stage will either be left to occur naturally, or it will be aided by an injection of Syntometrine given to you by your midwife as your baby's head was born.

Managed or natural?

Syntometrine is a combination of a drug called ergometrine and the hormone oxytocin, and together they cause the uterus to contract quickly after the birth of the baby. This means that the third stage will be over quicker than if it occurs naturally. This stage may last from just a few minutes to 15–20 minutes.

Syntometrine is widely used, but not everyone wants a "managed" third stage.

If you'd rather give birth to the placenta naturally, waiting for the uterus to contract on its own, do talk to your midwife beforehand and tell her that's what you'd like. Things probably won't happen quite as quickly as if you have Syntometrine, and it may take some minutes or even up to an hour before the placenta arrives. You can help speed things up by breastfeeding your baby, as the sucking action stimulates your uterus to contract (if the baby isn't ready to suck, stimulating your nipples with your fingers will have the same effect).

birth procedures

During your labour you may require some medical help to bring your baby safely into the world. This ranges from routine procedures that give your caregivers the best possible insight into your baby's progress, to specialist treatments to give you both a little extra help if you need it. As part of your preparations for labour, make sure you understand what these procedures are and why they are performed.

types of medical help

Find out in advance what the routine is where you will be giving birth, and talk through all the possibilities with your caregivers.

No one can predict exactly what will happen when you go into labour, so learn as much about it as you can now.

Fetal monitoring

Fetal monitoring is routine for hospital deliveries, although how you are monitored, and for how long, does vary. Often fetal monitoring is intermittent, especially if you're not being given drugs, so you may find that you are connected to a monitor for just 15 or 20 minutes after you first arrive at the hospital.

You will be asked to sit or lie on the bed, and a belt will be placed around your abdomen. This records your baby's heartbeat via a printout, allowing your caregiver to monitor your baby's reaction to labour. Once your waters have broken, the heartbeat can be monitored by attaching an electrode directly to the baby's scalp. This gives a very accurate reading, but it does mean that you will not be able to move about during labour. You may be offered continual monitoring if:
♦ your labour is induced
♦ you have an epidural
♦ you have had a high-risk pregnancy
♦ the baby is premature
♦ your baby appears to be stressed.
Ask why continual monitoring has been recommended. It could be because your caregivers have reason to be concerned, or simply a matter of routine.

During the second stage of labour your midwife or doctor can use a hand-held sonic aid to check the baby's heartbeat.

Episiotomy

An episiotomy (see page 72) is a surgical cut that is made to help the baby emerge from the vagina at the birth. You may need an episiotomy if:
♦ your baby is breech or has a large head
♦ your baby is premature
♦ you have an assisted delivery (although it is not always necessary for a ventouse delivery)
♦ you cannot control your pushing or the tissues have not stretched enough.

If you have strong feelings against this, talk to your caregivers beforehand.

breech **babies**

The majority of babies (about 97 per cent) are head-down in the uterus by week 34 or 35. But a small proportion of babies are bottom-down, or breech, and remain that way. The obstetrician may try to turn the baby externally (see page 51). You may be advised to spend time in the knee-chest position, or on all fours, to encourage the baby to turn naturally.

If this hasn't happened by the time labour is imminent, you'll probably find your caregivers suggest you strongly consider opting for a Caesarean section. A recent study showed that, particularly in the West where many doctors and midwives aren't experienced in the vaginal delivery of breech babies, a Caesarean section is the safest option.

Flexed breech
The legs are flexed against the body and the buttocks are the presenting part.

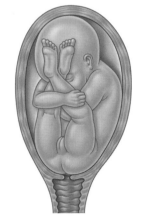

Extended breech
The baby's buttocks are presenting and the arms may be wrapped around the legs.

Footling breech
The feet are resting on the cervix. They will drop down once the membranes have ruptured.

An assisted delivery

This involves the assistance of medical instruments, such as forceps or a ventouse vacuum cup. Forceps are like tongs that fit around the baby's head and enable the obstetrician to ease the baby out of the birth canal. A ventouse vacuum cup fits onto the baby's head, a tube from the cup builds up a vacuum, and the doctor can then pull as you push to help speed up the delivery. An assisted delivery is more likely if you have an epidural, or if labour has been induced because you are less able to move around.

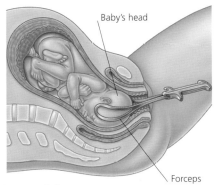

Baby's head

Forceps

Forceps delivery
Forceps resemble large, separate tongs. They fit snugly over the baby's head, and protect it as it progresses through the birth canal. Once the head has been delivered, the forceps are removed and the rest of the delivery can progress as normal. Forceps delivery requires some form of local anaesthetic (e.g. epidural).

induction

If you have not given birth by 41 weeks you will probably have a consultation, and induction may be mentioned. This means your labour will be started artificially.

There shouldn't be any need for an immediate induction, unless your caregiver fears that your placenta isn't functioning properly; you can have an ultrasound scan to check that your baby is thriving. Induction is usually urged in a firmer tone at 42 weeks because there is evidence that some babies are at risk after this stage, due to a gradual fall-off in the efficiency of the placenta.

Vaginal sweep

You may be offered this at your week 41 appointment. You'll be given an internal examination during which your caregiver will assess whether your cervix is softening in readiness for labour. The midwife or doctor will then gently push back the membranes adjacent to the cervix in the hope that this will stimulate the uterus to start contracting in the next few hours or days.

Amniotomy

This is also known as ARM (artificial rupture of the membranes). A long, thin hook is brushed against the membranes just inside your cervix. Once the waters have been ruptured the baby's head will move down onto the cervix, which usually means contractions become stronger and more powerful. Amniotomy is often carried out to speed up a labour, as well as to start it. Although it may shorten the labour, it may also make it more painful.

Starting labour with drugs

Prostaglandin inserted directly into the vagina, using tablets or a gel, is usually tried first. Prostaglandin is found naturally in your body (and in semen, which is why sex can be recommended as a way of starting labour) and it helps stimulate contractions. The gel or tablets can be used to ripen the cervix for several days. If this doesn't work, you'll probably be advised to have Syntocinon, a synthetic substance similar to the hormone oxytocin which stimulates the uterus to contract. You will have an intravenous drip, and your movement may be curtailed as a result. Contractions can be very strong.

caesarean **section**

If you have a planned, or "elective", Caesarean section you will have had time to adjust to the idea. However, if you need an emergency Caesarean you may feel disappointed, or even cheated of the birth you had planned. Remember that the most important thing is the safety of you and your baby. Ask why you are being offered a surgical delivery, as this can help to minimize any negative feelings.

A Caesarean section can be carried out under epidural or general anaesthetic, although for some unplanned operations a general anaesthetic may be necessary. Ask if your partner can be with you throughout.

If you have an epidural, a screen is set up between you and the surgeon. The birth of your baby takes about five minutes and you can hold your baby while the placenta is delivered and you are being stitched.

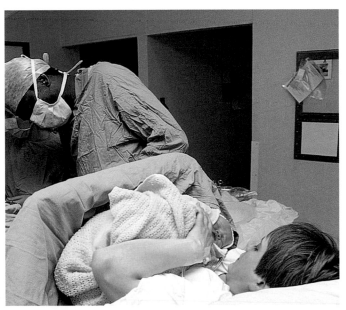

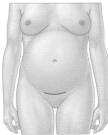

The bikini incision
If you have a surgical delivery, the incision will be made just above the line of your pubic hair. When the incision heals the scar is very discreet.

after the birth

The moment you and your partner have longed for is finally here, and your baby is in your arms at last. How do you feel? There's no right or wrong way to feel immediately after the birth. This is a time of transition, and your life has just changed in a huge way. It's going to take you and your partner a while to work through the maze of emotions that will have been unleashed.

how you'll feel

You might be exhilarated, excited, joyful, and delighted, and if so that's wonderful. However, not everyone has that response immediately, and you may find your feelings swing wildly in the next few days.

You may feel exhausted and want to just lie down and sleep, or you may feel a surge of energy and stay up all night, despite having had several hours of labour.

Becoming parents

The emotional response to having a baby is complicated in the hours and days after the birth. Many parents swing from feeling on top of the world one minute, to feeling low the next. You may feel a twinge of disappointment that you've had a boy when you wanted a girl, or vice versa, or you may feel a bit sad that the pregnancy is over and the real responsibility of parenting now weighs upon you.

You and your partner may feel closer than you've ever been, or you may both feel scared by the awesome change that this tiny new person has brought into your lives and your relationship. The important thing is to communicate with each other and to take each moment as it comes.

Your baby's first hours

♦ All your baby has ever known is the inside of your uterus, so birth certainly marks a huge change in life for him. What he'll need in the first minutes and hours of life is lots of close contact with

apgar **score**

Immediately after he's born, and if necessary again five minutes later, five simple tests are done to ascertain how healthy your baby is. The tests measure:

♦ heart rate

♦ breathing

♦ muscle tone

♦ skin colour

♦ reflex response.

For each test a score of 2, 1, or 0 is recorded, with 2 being entirely healthy and 0 an absence of response. Most babies score between 7 and 10 out of 10. If necessary, the tests are repeated five minutes later to see if the baby's responses have improved.

newborn tests

Shortly after the birth, your baby will have a number of routine tests in addition to the Apgar tests (see above). He will be weighed, the circumference of his head will be measured, and his genitals will be checked for abnormalities. Although it can be upsetting to have your new baby taken away from you, this preliminary examination takes only a few minutes, and your baby will be in the hands of an experienced midwife or doctor.

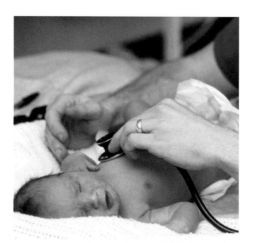

Listening to the heart and lungs
It is not uncommon for newborn babies to have a heart murmur, and this does not necessarily indicate that your baby will have a problem.

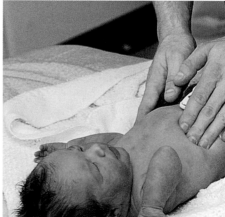

Feeling the abdomen
The doctor checks that all the internal organs are the correct size. He will also feel the pulses in your baby's groin.

special care **baby unit**

About one in 10 newborn babies has a spell in the special care baby unit (SCBU). Many of these babies have been born prematurely, before 37 weeks of pregnancy, but SCBUs aren't just for small or premature newborns. Sometimes babies born to diabetic mothers, for example, who may be quite large, are admitted to the unit for observation or because they need help. A spell in the SCBU is always a worry for parents, but it's often not a long-term situation; a baby may be admitted for just a few hours.

If your baby is transferred to the special care unit after the delivery you'll be taken there to see him as soon as is practical. Your partner may be able to go to see the baby straight away, and can return to you with information about what's going on and maybe a photograph. Information about

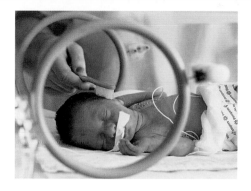

your baby's health will be extremely important to you both, and the hospital will do all it can to keep you up to date on your baby's progress.

If your baby has a stay of a few days or even weeks in the SCBU you'll be encouraged to spend time there with him as soon as you're well enough yourself. You may be

discharged from the hospital's postnatal ward, so you'll be going home without your baby. This is a heartwrenching situation, but try to remember that your baby is in the best possible place.

You'll be shown how to do as much as possible for your baby. You should be able to help wash and dress him, hold his hands, and, depending on how well he is and whether he's on a ventilator (breathing machine) or not, you may be able to take him out of his incubator to give him cuddles. You'll also be encouraged to express breast milk, probably using an electric breast pump, so he can be given your milk by tube or maybe a bottle. If he's not on a ventilator, you should also have opportunities to hold him close to you and your breast so he gets used to the idea of feeding direct from the breast.

you. Just as you will realize that you know this little person absolutely, so he will realize he knows you, too. Now he needs to get to know your scent, your face, your skin, your touch. He'll relish every moment he can spend close to you, so give him lots of cuddles and hold him to you.

♦ Immediately after the birth is an important time to get to know your baby, so unless there are health concerns you'll probably find yourselves left alone for a while to spend time together as a family.

♦ After the delivery of the placenta, and after you and your partner have been given time alone with the baby, your caregiver will examine your perineum to see if you need stitches. If you do need stitches make sure you ask for pain relief.

♦ You'll be encouraged to introduce your baby to your breast in the first half hour or hour after the birth. Research shows that the earlier you breastfeed, the better the chances of the baby latching on easily and breastfeeding going well.

♦ Don't worry if the baby doesn't show a lot of interest yet in the breast. If you had any drugs during labour these may make him drowsy, or the effort of being born may mean he is sleepy. Many babies who go on to breastfeed happily for many months take a while to get started.

♦ The birthing room should be warm enough that you don't have to put clothes on either of you straight away. Skin-to-skin contact is a great way to welcome your baby into the world.

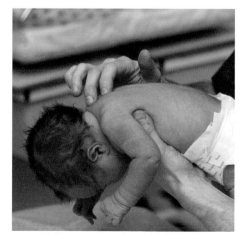

Moving the hips and limbs
The legs and arms are moved to check alignment and length, and the doctor will also make sure the hips are not dislocated.

Checking the spine
The doctor or midwife will run a finger along the baby's back to see if the vertebrae are all in place.

stillbirth

The loss of a baby just before or at birth is one of the hardest things a parent has to deal with. It's very rare, thankfully, but if it does happen to you, you'll need lots of time and space to talk things through with sympathetic people. Get to know other people who have been through the same thing. Most maternity units have trained midwife bereavement counsellors who will be on hand to give you support. You'll be encouraged to see and hold the baby, and to do as much as you can to build up a store of memories. There's no "right" or "wrong" way to grieve, and it may take a long time before you'll feel you can work through all the emotions you will experience.

the postnatal period

How you feel depends on a lot of things, but the most important is how the birth went. In the days after the birth you and your partner will get to know your baby, and you will need to begin to recover from the effort of pregnancy and birth.

starting family life

Women who've sailed through labour often feel elated, while for those whose experiences were not so straightforward, it can take longer to recover from the birth. But remember, in time you will be feeling good and enjoying your new life as a mother.

Recovery isn't just about getting over the birth physically (although that is obviously very important). It's also about working through often quite complex psychological issues brought up by labour and delivery. Your first step to dealing with both the physical and the psychological recovery is to have the support of a midwife you know and trust: this is a new mother's basic right, and hopefully you have it right now.

Communicating
Talk to your midwife about anything that's bothering you, and go through the details of your baby's birth with the midwife, and maybe also the obstetrician who was with you at the time, if you can. Talking things through with your birth partner is also important.

Adjusting to your new life
The hours and weeks after a baby is born are a time of big hormonal changes within a woman's body, and these can impact on how you're feeling. But it's a lot more than "your hormones" that are responsible for how you feel. Don't underestimate the huge upheaval your life is going through, and not just your life but that of your partner as well. Changes in your life may seem exciting, or daunting, or horrifying: whichever way you view them, though, they're certainly significant.

Building a routine
Put a framework into your day as soon as possible. For many new mothers the first few weeks are eased by the presence of a partner on paternity leave, and perhaps a mother, sister, or friend. Eventually, though, you'll be on your own with the baby, and you will need the support of local friends who are in a similar situation to your own. Contact women from your antenatal course, or join a postnatal exercise or yoga group, or a mother and child group. You could also visit the park and chat to other mothers.

postnatal **depression**

♦ One in 10 new mothers is affected by postnatal depression, as opposed to "baby blues", which affects about 90 per cent.

♦ It can make you feel low, unsure of yourself, exhausted, vulnerable, extra-sensitive, and unable to make decisions.

♦ Depression can be difficult to recognize in yourself. Talk to your partner, your midwife, and anyone else who's supporting you. Don't "be brave" if you need to open up about your feelings.

♦ Talking to other mothers, especially those who have experienced some form of depression themselves, can often be the key to recovery.

postnatal care

In the hours and days after the birth, your midwife will go through a list of checks on a regular basis. You can also help your body recover by doing some gentle exercise.

The midwife's visits
You'll be asked about how your perineum feels; the amount of lochia, or vaginal bleeding, you're experiencing; whether you're urinating and about bowel movements. Take steps to avoid becoming constipated (see page 61). You'll be asked how your breasts feel and whether they're engorged, and whether your nipples are painful when the baby feeds or after feeding.

If you experience a heavy blood clot or heavy bleeding; if you have any bleeding that smells odd; if you have any difficulty passing water; or if you have chest pains, swollen legs, or a temperature, call your midwife even if she's already been to see you that day.

getting back your figure

If you practise your exercises daily, your figure will gradually return. It is very important to take things gently to begin with.

Do not attempt any vigorous exercise until your bleeding has stopped. Exercise a little and often, and always stop if you feel any pain. If you had a Caesarean section, do not attempt any exercise (apart from pelvic floor exercises and foot pedalling) until after you have had your check-up six weeks after the birth. Ask your midwife for advice if you have any queries about which exercises are suitable for you at what stage.

Pelvic floor

You can do these exercises from day one after the birth. Your pelvic floor muscles will have been stretched, and possibly weakened, by the birth. You will have been doing these exercises during pregnancy. Start them again as soon as you can. You can also do these if you had a Caesarean section.

Pull in and tense your pelvic floor muscles, as if you were holding back urine. Hold for as long as you comfortably can, then relax gradually. Repeat 10 times.

Gentle stomach toner
For the first week, just gently pull in your abdominal muscles as you breathe out, hold for a few seconds, then relax.

After this, if you feel well enough, lie on the floor with your head and shoulders supported and your knees bent. Lift your head and shoulders as you breathe out. Hold for a few seconds, then relax. Repeat three times. Practise twice a day.

Foot pedalling
Bend your feet up and down from the ankle to improve your circulation and guard against swelling. Practise hourly. Do this from day one.

Diagonal reach
Lift your head and shoulder and reach across to the opposite ankle. Lie back and rest, then repeat on the other side.

Side bend
Keep your hips facing forwards and reach down as far as you comfortably can, moving slowly and smoothly. Rest your hand on the side of your leg.

Side leg lift
Keeping both legs in line with your hip and shoulder, raise the upper leg to shoulder height then lower. This tones the hips and thighs.

Cat stretch
This will help to strengthen your back. Begin with your back straight, then arch your back slowly upwards, like a cat. Stop if you feel any discomfort.

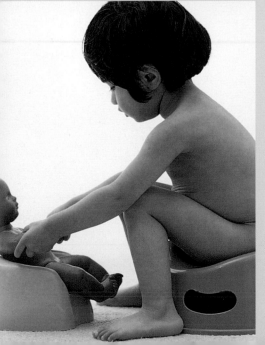

baby and child care

Looking after a baby or child is demanding, and routine tasks can be downright baffling to begin with. This section contains reassuring advice on how to handle and care for your new baby, so that soon you will gain the confidence to look after her in a way that's safe and enjoyable for you both. There is also advice on how to handle your child's emerging independence, as well as discussion of childcare choices, should you be returning to work.

caring for your newborn
birth to 6 weeks

You will spend many hours delighting in your newborn. Every baby has her very own unique characteristics and knowing what to expect – from the shape of her head to the colour of her skin – will help you feel confident about caring for her.

Meeting your baby

If you had a straightforward labour and delivery, you will be given your baby to hold as soon as she is born. One of your first questions will probably be "Is she all right?", and within the first 24 hours, medical staff will give her a thorough examination to reassure you that all is fine. Before your baby leaves the delivery room, ID bands will be placed on both you and your baby.

What to expect

Healthy newborns come in all shapes and sizes but share certain characteristics:

♦ **Head** Your baby's head may look slightly misshapen – especially if she was delivered by ventouse or forceps. This is because the soft bones that make up the skull are designed to give under pressure in order to pass through the birth canal. You may also notice a pulse beating under the fontanelles (soft patches of your baby's skull).

♦ **Skin** Your baby may be covered in a greasy substance called vernix which acts as a protective barrier. She may also look slightly blue until her breathing becomes more regular and her circulation improves.

♦ **Hair** At birth, some babies are still covered in a fine layer of downy hair, known as lanugo. This rubs off during the first week.

♦ **Body** Your baby's breasts and genitals may look swollen because of the hormones you have passed on via the placenta before birth. The swelling will go down after a few days.

checking **her reflexes**

From the moment she is born, your newborn has an incredible range of skills and reflexes which will help her survive. A number of these reflexes will be tested by your paediatrician to check that your baby's central nervous system is functioning well.

♦ **Sucking, rooting, and swallowing reflex** Your baby's most basic reflexes include sucking, which she will have practised in the womb. She will also instinctively turn her head towards the touch of a breast or finger on her cheek near her mouth as she searches for food – this is known as rooting. Swallowing is also a reflex action.

♦ **Startle reflex** This is also known as the Moro reflex. If your baby's head is not supported when she is held she will throw out her arms and legs with her fingers extended. This reflex usually disappears at about two months.

♦ **Stepping reflex** If your baby is held upright with her feet touching a firm surface, she will automatically make stepping movements. This reflex usually disappears at about one month.

♦ **Protective reflexes** Although your baby may appear to be utterly defenceless, she actually has several protective reflexes. For example, if a blanket or pillow falls over her eyes, nose, or mouth, she'll shake her head from side to side and flail her arms to push it away so she can breathe and see. Or if an object comes straight towards her, she'll turn her head and try to squirm out of its way.

♦ **Tonic neck reflex** You may notice that when your baby's head turns to one side, her arm on that side will straighten, with the opposite arm bent as if she is fencing. Do not be surprised if you don't see this response, however. It is subtle, and if your baby is disturbed or crying, she may not perform it. This reflex disappears at five to seven months of age.

♦ **Grasping reflex** (see left) Place a finger in her palm and your baby will automatically grab hold of it.

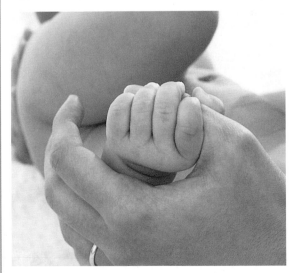

getting to know your newborn

He looks tiny and fragile, but your baby is sturdier than you think. Learning to handle him safely and confidently will help you enjoy close physical contact – one of the most powerful ways you can get to know your newborn.

the first few days

After months of carrying your baby and wondering about him, he's finally here, cradled in your arms.

The first few days with him will be an emotional time for both you and your partner. Your feelings will be many and varied, and may include the following:

♦ an incredible sense of wonder and pride at what you've produced

♦ overwhelming exhaustion as a result of labour and sleepless nights

♦ a feeling of connection so close that when your baby cries you feel like crying too

♦ tearfulness and confusion because of the huge hormonal shift occurring in your body.

As you get to know your newborn, your emotions will start to settle down. And one of the most rewarding ways of feeling close to your baby and bonding with him is through physical contact – by touching your baby, holding him, cuddling him, stroking his skin, and feeling his skin against yours.

Holding and handling

Always approach your baby slowly and quietly. Before you even touch him, make your presence known through voice and/or eye contact. The gentle and caring way in which you handle your newborn will communicate your love to him – he adores nestling in your arms.

He has barely any head control, and his head will flop uncomfortably if it's not held up. If it does flop back, your baby will feel as if he's going to fall and his whole body will jerk in fright. This is known as the startle, or Moro, reflex. Supporting your baby's head properly

when you hold him will help him feel safe and secure. Never jiggle or shake your baby's head.

♦ When picking up your baby, either slip one hand under his neck and head and the other under his bottom before lifting him gently towards you, or lift him under the arms, using your fingers at the back of his neck to cradle his head.

♦ When carrying him, either cradle him in the crook of one arm with your free arm supporting his back and bottom, or hold him against your chest with his head on your shoulder and your free arm supporting his back and head. Once you feel confident, and while he is small, you can carry him using one hand.

new **dads**

For dads, the experience of becoming a parent is different but just as intense as it is for mums.

New fathers may feel overwhelming tenderness towards their baby, as well as an enormous sense of responsibility and anxiety about keeping this tiny person safe and secure. They may also feel excluded – and jealous of all the attention given to their baby.

Spending time with their new baby – whether it involves soothing, dressing, changing nappies, carrying, or just cuddling – is very important for new fathers, helping them increase the feelings of closeness and intimacy, and calming their natural fears and worries.

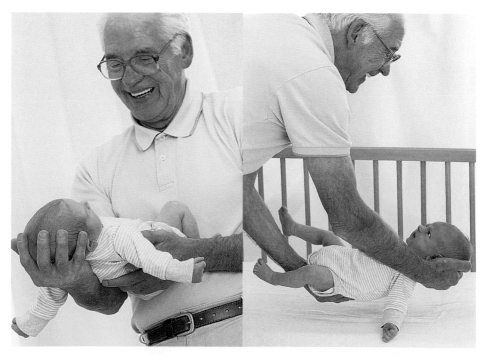

Holding a newborn
This grandfather picks up his new grandchild, slipping one hand under her neck and head and the other under her lower back and bottom, then lifting the baby towards him. When laying the baby in her cot, he makes sure he is supporting the baby's head with one hand and the lower part of her body with the other.

Safe handling
Make sure your hands are clean before changing your baby and remember to wash them after changing her nappy.

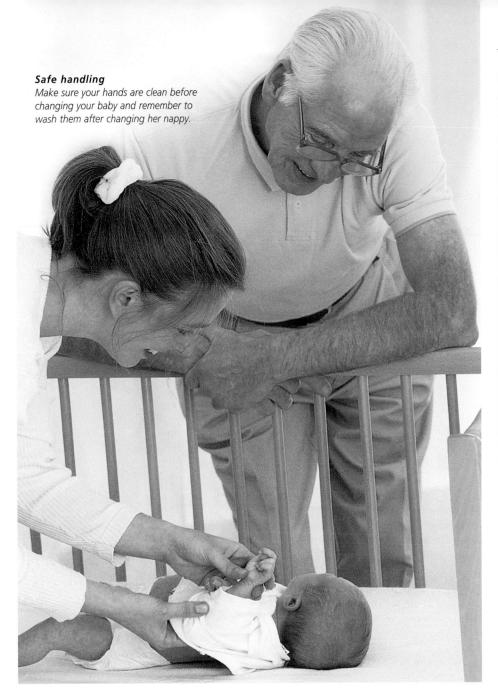

Your baby loves being close to you and will be happiest when he can feel your warmth and hear your heart beat. Carrying your baby in a sling will help you comfort him, rock him to sleep, or just keep him close, as well as leaving your hands free while you are shopping or doing the chores. Choose a sling that's easy to put on and take off, comfortable to wear and suitable for your partner, too.

Dressing your baby

Putting clothes on a tiny baby without pulling and tugging is quite an art, but one you will quickly become adept at. Try not to rush, and talk soothingly to him – if you are calm, he'll feel calm too.

♦ Place your baby on a soft towel on a flat surface. Never leave your baby unattended, especially if the changing surface is higher than the floor. Select clothes with easy-on and easy-off features.

♦ Stretch open the neck of his vest before gently easing it over his head.

♦ Reach into the sleeves to find your baby's arm then pull the sleeve back over it rather than tugging his arm through.

Out and about

As soon as you feel physically ready, you can take your new baby out and about in a sling, a buggy (if the seat reclines flat), or a pram. If you are taking him out in a car, by law you are required to have your baby harnessed in a rear-facing infant car seat that has been correctly fitted. Don't use this in the front of a car with a safety airbag on the passenger side – if the airbag inflates it could seriously injure your baby.

Meeting friends
As soon as you feel up to it, enjoy getting out to meet other mums with babies of a similar age: this can quickly develop into a useful support network.

breastfeeding your baby

Breastfeeding can be a deeply fulfilling experience, creating a strong bond between you and your baby. However, learning how to breastfeed takes practice – for both of you. The more you do it, the easier it gets.

a good start

When she is breastfeeding, your baby loves the closeness and warmth of skin-to-skin contact, seeing your face and hearing your heart beat.

Breastfeeding is good for your baby because your milk gives her the best possible nourishment. Breast milk is tailor-made for your growing baby, with all the nutrients she needs in exactly the right amounts. It also contains antibodies, which will help protect her against illness and infection, and it offers added protection against respiratory problems and allergy-related conditions, such as eczema and asthma.

Getting underway

To begin with, your breasts will produce colostrum – a clear, golden-yellow fluid which starts your baby's digestive system working and protects against infection. After a few days, your milk will come in.

♦ **Choose a comfortable position** You can feed your baby sitting or lying down. Use pillows and cushions to support your back

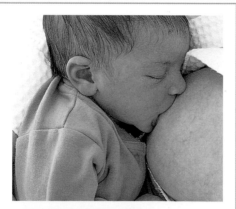

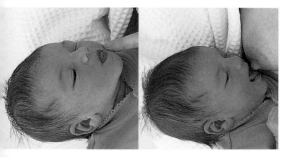

Preparing to feed
Stroking your baby's cheek with your finger, close to her mouth, will encourage her to open her mouth wide ready to feed.

latching **on**

Helping your baby latch on to your breast correctly is the key to successful breastfeeding. Stroke her cheek with your finger so she opens her mouth wide. Move her towards your breast, aiming your nipple at the roof of her mouth. When she has a good mouthful she will close her mouth, forming a tight seal. She should have all of the nipple and as much of the areola (the pigmented ring around the nipple) as possible in her mouth – otherwise she may tug on the nipple and make it sore. If you are unsure about her position, ease her off the breast (see opposite) and try again.

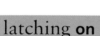

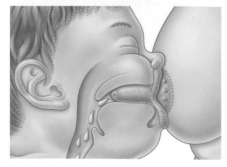

Feeding action
Your baby draws milk out of your breast by squeezing the nipple against the roof of her mouth and sucking.

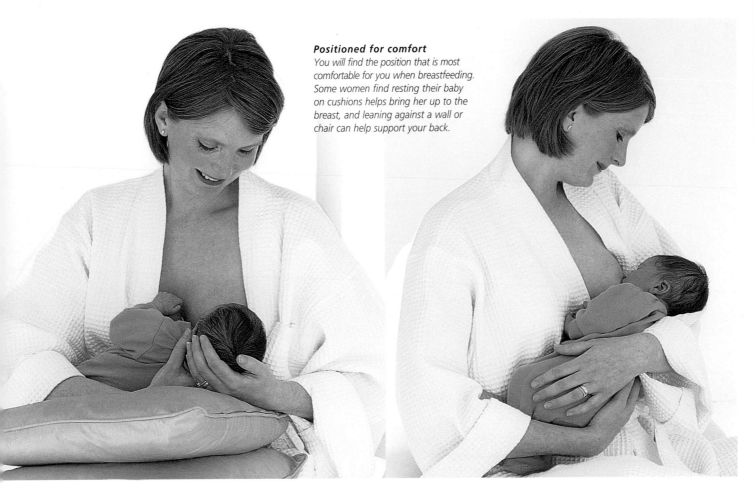

Positioned for comfort
You will find the position that is most comfortable for you when breastfeeding. Some women find resting their baby on cushions helps bring her up to the breast, and leaning against a wall or chair can help support your back.

and arms, and to support your baby's head, back, and hips. If you are sitting, use a footstool to support your feet.

♦ **Hold your baby correctly** You and your baby should be tummy to tummy, with her nose opposite your nipple and her head and body in line with each other.

♦ **Help her latch on** Check her position – start again if you don't think she is latched on correctly (see opposite).

♦ **Watch for feeding** Your baby's sucking will stimulate your let-down reflex – the release of a hormone called oxytocin which causes the milk glands in your breasts to release milk. When this happens you will hear your baby swallowing. You may also feel a tingling sensation, contractions of your uterus, or you may leak milk from the opposite breast.

♦ **Ease her off the breast** Your baby may fall asleep once she's full and naturally come off your breast. Otherwise, don't pull her off the nipple. Instead slide your little finger into the corner of her mouth to break the suction.

How many feeds?

For the first few weeks, your baby will want to be fed every few hours or so, spending between 10 and 20 minutes at each breast. She will let you know when she is hungry: feeding her on demand will keep her happy and help establish your milk supply. If possible, let her empty each breast before switching to the other (if you take her off too soon she'll feed only on the watery foremilk and miss out on the rich hindmilk) and alternate which breast you start on to help keep up your milk supply.

Look after yourself

As you get the hang of breastfeeding you will realize you can do it any time, anywhere – it's easy to be discreet if you wear loose tops or drape a scarf over your shoulder.

Don't forget to look after yourself. Get plenty of rest – accept all offers of help and try to sleep whenever your baby sleeps. Eat well-balanced meals regularly during the day – it is essential to keep up your food and fluid intake.

after a **caesarean**

If you had a Caesarean birth, your baby may feel drowsy as a result of the anaesthesia and not be very interested in feeding straight away. But encouraging her to breastfeed as she grows more alert will give her a good reason to wake up! Initially you may find it more comfortable to breastfeed lying down.

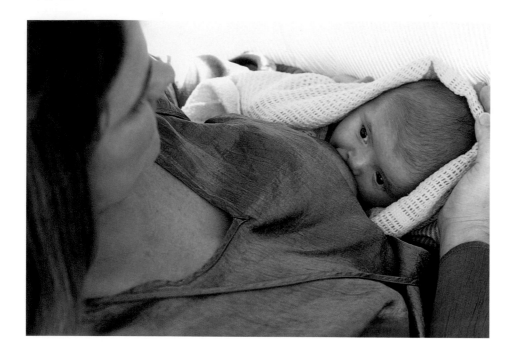

"Our first day at home Elsie fed every hour. She sucked really hard, and my nipples became sore. My midwife was wonderful: she showed me how to make sure Elsie was latching on properly which made all the difference. Within a few days I could feed her comfortably and began to really enjoy the experience."

LINDA MORRELL, MUM TO ELSIE
AGED 8 WEEKS

tips for success

When breastfeeding is going well you will feel like the proudest mum on earth, but don't worry if you come across a few problems first.

Remember that both you and your baby are learning a new skill – perfecting the art of breastfeeding can take time and patience.

Your emotions

In the first few weeks after birth you may be tired and emotional, making common problems seem overwhelming. You may feel as if all you do is feed your new baby, as he demands food every couple of hours.

Try to persevere – as your baby learns how to suck more efficiently he'll go longer between feeds, until by two months he'll need feeding only every four hours or so. Meanwhile, the hours spent feeding provide an ideal opportunity for you to get to know your baby and develop a deep connection.

Refusing the breast

There are many reasons why babies refuse the breast and most can be easily resolved.

♦ Your breasts may become so engorged (overfull, painful, and hard) that your baby has difficulty latching on. Relieve their fullness by putting a warm flannel on

them or soaking them in a warm bath. You could also try expressing some milk.
♦ Your milk may be flowing so fast it causes him to gag. Express some milk to take the pressure off and reduce the flow.
♦ Your breast may be covering his nostrils, making breathing difficult – gently pull the breast back from his face.

♦ His nose may be blocked, making breathing difficult. Ask your GP for some nose drops.

Sleeping through feeds

An experienced feeder can take most of his feed during the first three to five minutes, and once full may doze off at the breast in

protecting **your breasts**

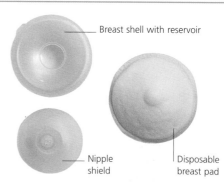

Breast shell with reservoir

Nipple shield

Disposable breast pad

If your breasts leak milk between feeds, you can protect your clothes and keep your nipples dry (which will help prevent soreness) by using absorbent breast pads which fit neatly into your bra. Plastic breast shells can also be used – these have a reservoir to catch leaking milk. Nipple shields may be used temporarily while your baby is feeding to help protect sore or cracked nipples.

expressing milk

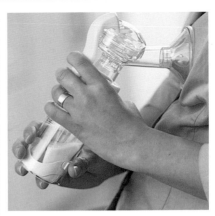

You may be breastfeeding, but that doesn't mean your partner or another caregiver can't feed your baby, too. After the first month or so you should be producing enough milk to express some into a bottle. You can store it in the fridge or freezer and use it when you need to have a break from feeding. There are two ways to express: by hand or with a breast pump. Expressing milk by hand can take longer than using a pump. If you choose to use a pump, there is a variety available to buy or hire, ranging from hand- and battery-operated to electric pumps. Whichever method you opt for:

♦ wash your hands and nails before expressing

♦ help stimulate the flow by applying a warm flannel to your breasts before you pump – looking at your baby or pictures of him may also help

♦ store the expressed milk in a fridge for up to 24 hours, or if you are away from home in a cooler with ice packs.

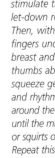

Expressing by hand
Place a warm flannel on your breast to help stimulate the let-down reflex. Then, with your fingers under your breast and your thumbs above, squeeze gently and rhythmically around the areola until the milk flows or squirts out. Repeat this action all around the breast.

a state of blissful contentment! If, however, he hasn't emptied your breast you could gently wake him up after half an hour or so (changing his nappy will wake him) and offer him some more. If he's still hungry, he'll rouse himself and finish off his feed.

Unsettled feeding

If your baby seems fretful during feeding and unable to settle into a gentle rhythm, he may be frustrated because he's not getting enough milk. This can happen if your baby isn't latched on properly. Take him off the breast, soothe him so he is calm, and then try latching him on again (see page 86).

Sore nipples

If your baby is not latching on to your breast properly or he pulls at your breast when he comes off, your nipples may

become sore or cracked. There are several steps you can take to prevent sore nipples.
♦ Check your baby's position at every feed – he should have the nipple and much of the areola in his mouth.
♦ Ease him off the breast gently when he's emptied each one.
♦ Make sure your nipples are dry before putting your bra back on, and keep them dry between feeds – use breast pads to soak up leaking milk or, if you leak a lot, use a plastic breast shell with a reservoir to collect the milk (see opposite). This milk can then be frozen or refrigerated, and given to your baby in a bottle, if you wish.

If one of your nipples becomes sore, rest the affected breast for a day by expressing milk and feeding from your other breast. You can prevent sore nipples from becoming cracked by applying nipple cream specially designed for breastfeeding mums.

bottles and bottle-feeding

Whatever your reasons for choosing to bottle-feed, it's reassuring to know that today's formula milk is produced to resemble breast milk as closely as possible. Getting organized and keeping safety in mind will help make bottle-feeding an enjoyable experience.

happy feeding

Holding your baby close, gazing into her eyes, and talking soothingly to her while she feeds from a bottle will help you to feel close and bond with her.

Keep bottle-feeding a loving occasion by:
♦ getting close – you can enjoy skin-to-skin contact if you open or lift your top and hold your baby close to your chest
♦ never leaving her with a bottle propped up in her mouth – not only could your baby choke, but she needs your affection as much as she needs feeding
♦ stopping when she has had enough – your baby knows when to stop, so you shouldn't force her to finish a bottle.

Feeding techniques

♦ Warm up the milk before offering it to your baby: run the bottle under warm tap water or sit it in a pan of warm water. Do not use a microwave. Always test several drops of the formula on the back of your wrist to be sure it is warm but not too hot.

making up a **bottle feed**

When you are making up bottles of formula, always follow the manufacturer's instructions: the ratio of powder to water is carefully calculated to give your baby the optimum nutrition. You can make up one bottle or a batch of bottles at a time. Keep the made-up milk in the back of the fridge until needed (discard after 24 hours if it is not used).

♦ Gather together everything you need: bottles, teats and caps, plastic knife, measuring scoop from formula tin, funnel, jug.

♦ Use cooled, freshly boiled water (refill the kettle each time you make up a new batch of bottles) and pour the correct amount into a sterilized feeding bottle.

♦ Measure the exact amount of formula powder with the scoop provided, levelling off with a knife.

♦ Add the powder to the water.

♦ Put the top on the bottle and shake thoroughly until all the powder has dissolved. Cool quickly by putting towards the back of the fridge (not the door) while still hot.

♦ Keep the bottle tilted so that milk covers the teat and she doesn't draw in air.
♦ Tilt your baby slightly in your arms – if she's lying flat she'll find it difficult to swallow and may gag on the milk.
♦ Wind her when she's had enough (put her on your shoulder or sit her on your lap and pat her back gently to help her release swallowed air).

How many feeds?

The best way to make sure your baby has enough is to treat bottle-feeding just like breastfeeding. Offer her the bottle whenever she seems hungry and don't worry about how much she takes. Your formula-fed baby will be satisfied for longer than a baby fed on breast milk – so she may be happy to feed every three to four hours. Some babies, however, will take less more often.

Your breast milk

Even just a few days of sole breastfeeding after your baby is born will give her a great start: colostrum – the first milk that your body produces – is packed with important nutrients

which will help protect your baby against infection during her first 72 hours of life.

Whether or not you are breastfeeding, after the second or third day of giving birth your breasts will become full of milk. This can be uncomfortable, but it is only temporary. If you don't breastfeed the milk will dry up within a few days. Meanwhile, to help ease any discomfort:
♦ take hot showers or soak your breasts in a hot bath
♦ ease the pressure by squeezing out a few drops of milk
♦ put an ice pack on your breasts
♦ wear a well-fitting, supportive bra.

Breast and bottle

It is possible to alternate breast- and bottle-feeding successfully once your milk supply is established – some mums choose to introduce formula at this point, while others express their breast milk for their baby to be fed from a bottle (see page 89). There are a number of reasons why you may want to combine breast- and bottle-feeding:
♦ you may be planning to return to work and need a caregiver to feed your baby while you are away

♦ giving a bottle means your partner can share in the feeding

♦ you may have a blocked duct or sore nipple and want to rest your breast for a while.

The best time to introduce a bottle to your breastfed baby is after six weeks. By then your milk supply is properly established and your baby is less likely to suffer from "nipple confusion" – nipples and teats require different sucking techniques. Try not to leave it later than three months: introducing a bottle to an older baby can be difficult as by this age most babies prefer a soft, warm breast to a rubbery teat!

Some mums breastfeed first thing in the morning as it involves no preparation. And an evening breastfeed, after your baby's bath and before bedtime, can make you feel close. Bottle-feeding often works well during the day. Another option is to alternate between breast and bottle feeds.

When you first introduce a bottle, your breasts may feel very full until they adjust their supply to your new feeding routine. The process will be gradual, but after a few days you will feel more comfortable.

cleaning **bottles**

To prevent your baby getting ill, you need to clean and sterilize your baby's bottles after each feed to kill any bacteria from old milk. Rinse and then wash the bottle and teat separately – use a brush to make sure any deposits in the bottle have been removed. Turn the teat inside out to check the hole isn't blocked. Rinse again in fresh water, then sterilize the bottle and teat using one of the following methods.

♦ **Boiling** Put feeding equipment in a large saucepan, cover with water, and boil for 10 minutes.

♦ **Sterilizing tablets or fluid** Put feeding equipment in a large container, cover with water, and add sterilizing tablets or fluid. Leave for 30 minutes.

♦ **Steam sterilizer** This is an electric machine that, with the addition of water, creates enough steam to sterilize feeding equipment. It takes about 10 minutes.

♦ **Microwave sterilizing unit** A specially designed steam unit which can be put in the microwave. It takes about five minutes. Check the feeding equipment is suitable for microwaves.

Sharing the joy
Introducing your baby to bottles allows your partner to share in the joy and closeness of feeding.

taking care of your baby

Your newborn may seem so fragile that even a task such as changing a nappy can seem overwhelming at first. But don't worry, you will quickly become confident when it comes to taking care of the practical needs of your baby.

changing nappies

With up to 10 nappy changes a day, you'll quickly become an expert at keeping your baby comfortable and dry with the minimum of fuss.

Most mums find disposable nappies easiest – they are convenient and super-absorbent. However, today's reusable cotton nappies also have advantages. You can buy or hire ready-shaped cotton nappies that can be fastened with Velcro tabs or poppers. Some incorporate a wrap so there's no need for waterproof pants, and laundering services are widely available. And, in the long run, they are cheaper than disposables.

What's in his nappy?
During the first day or so after birth your baby will pass greenish-black, sticky stools known as meconium – a substance that lined his gut while he was in the womb. If you are breastfeeding, within a few days his poo will be yellow and soft. If you are formula feeding, his poo will be pale brown, more formed, and more smelly.

Your newborn's first wees may look slightly red – this is because of harmless substances called "urates" which look red on the nappy. Once the urine flow is established, he will wee frequently because his immature bladder is unable to hold urine for any length of time.

If you have a baby girl you may notice a tiny amount of vaginal bleeding in your newborn. This is normal in the first week, and is caused by the hormones passed into your baby from you before birth. A clear or whitish vaginal discharge is also normal and will stop after a few days.

YOU WILL NEED   CHANGING MAT • COTTON TOWEL • COTTON WOOL • WARM WATER • FRESH NAPPY • NAPPY SACK

caring for
the environment

Concern about the environment may make you think twice before buying disposable nappies for your baby. Disposables are not biodegradable and the 4,000 your baby will need in his lifetime will sit in landfill sites for up to 200 years. In contrast, cloth nappies are manufactured from a renewable source and can be reused. Bear in mind, however, their manufacture and cleaning – especially if you are using a laundering service – also has an impact on the environment.

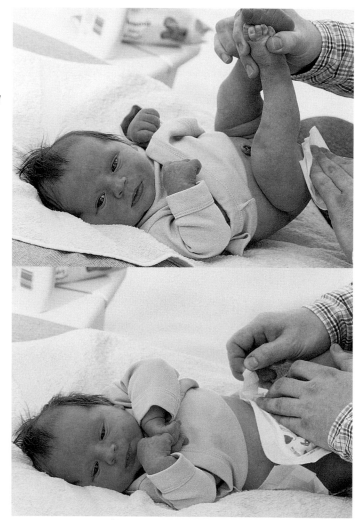

1 Use warm water and cotton wool to wipe between your baby's leg creases and around the genitals. With girls, wipe from front to back. Dry with a soft towel to avoid nappy rash (see page 218). Never leave your baby out of arm's reach.

2 Slide the clean nappy under your baby so the top is in line with his waist. Bring the front up between his legs, and hold it across his tummy. Fold the sides into the centre and fasten the tabs. Always wash your hands after changing a nappy.

topping and tailing

In the early days, when your baby comes home, you can keep him clean by simply washing the body parts that really need it.

Apart from dribbling milk and needing nappy changes, newborn babies don't get very dirty. As many newborns don't like getting wet or being naked for too long, concentrating on the parts of your baby that really do need washing will help keep crying to a minimum.

Be prepared

Get everything ready beforehand. If your baby is on a surface that is above the floor, use a safety strap or keep one hand on him at all times to make sure he does not fall. Put the bowl of warm water out of his arm or leg reach to avoid it being knocked over.

The key to keeping your baby happy is to work as quickly and calmly as possible. This will get easier as you become more practised. Meanwhile:

♦ chat and sing to your baby – the sound of your voice will help soothe him

♦ a wrist rattle or overhead mobile may also help keep a fretful baby calm.

looking after **the cord**

After four or five days your baby's cord will probably drop off – although it can take two weeks – leaving a small wound that may take a few days to heal. To prevent infection and speed up healing, remember to:

♦ clean the area every day with cotton wool and cooled, boiled water

♦ dry gently but thoroughly with cotton wool or a soft towel

♦ turn the top of your baby's nappy down to keep the cord exposed to the air and clear of urine.

Never be tempted to pull the cord – it will come off when it's ready. A few drops of old blood may appear as the cord starts to separate. If the navel becomes sticky, weepy or looks red, speak to your midwife.

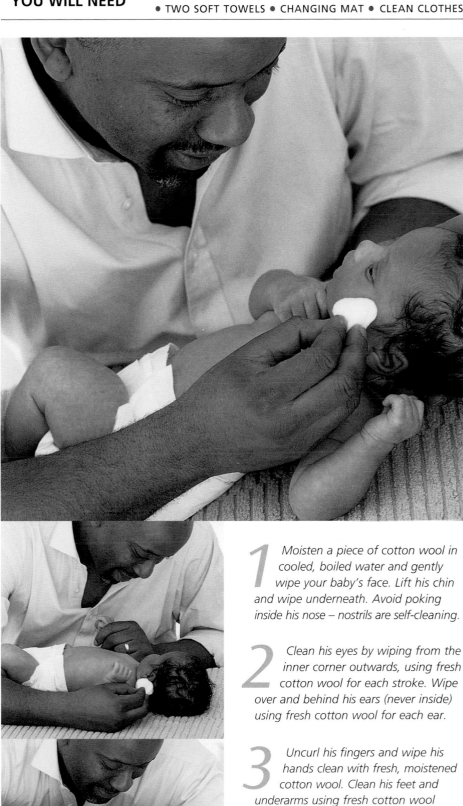

1 Moisten a piece of cotton wool in cooled, boiled water and gently wipe your baby's face. Lift his chin and wipe underneath. Avoid poking inside his nose – nostrils are self-cleaning.

2 Clean his eyes by wiping from the inner corner outwards, using fresh cotton wool for each stroke. Wipe over and behind his ears (never inside) using fresh cotton wool for each ear.

3 Uncurl his fingers and wipe his hands clean with fresh, moistened cotton wool. Clean his feet and underarms using fresh cotton wool for each new area and pat him dry after cleaning.

your baby's skin

Your newborn's skin feels soft and supple but it's also very fragile and needs extra special attention. Taking care of her skin – whether as part of your normal cleansing routine or as part of a baby massage – will have benefits for you both.

caring for her skin

Your newborn's skin is very delicate, and unlike a child's or adult's it can be easily damaged. It is prone to dryness, chafing, and irritation.

In addition, your baby's pores are not yet working efficiently, which means she will possibly develop spots. Although they may spoil your baby's complexion, most are harmless and don't require treatment.

What to expect

Most newborns develop minor spots and rashes in their first few days and weeks.

♦ **Milia** These are small white spots which usually appear on the face, especially the nose and chin. They aren't itchy and won't bother your baby. They are just the result of immature sweat glands. They will vanish with time and don't require treatment.

♦ **Heat rash** If your baby's skin becomes too warm she may get small red spots on her face and upper body. Check the room temperature and make sure she isn't sleeping under too many blankets.

♦ **Urticaria** This is a rash of red spots with raised white centres appearing on different parts of a baby's body. They will vanish with time without treatment. However, urticaria can be confused with more serious spots, so check with your GP or health visitor.

♦ **Peeling** You may notice during the first few days that your newborn's skin peels slightly – especially on the palms of her hands, soles of her feet, and her ankles. This is perfectly normal, especially if your baby was overdue. After a few days the peeling will vanish.

Caring and bonding
Caring for your new baby's skin gives you both the opportunity to experience the benefits of touch, helping you form a strong emotional bond with each other.

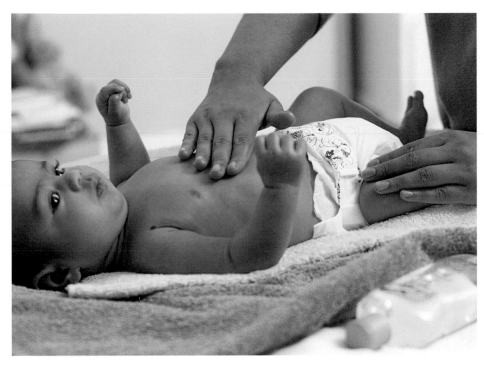

Smooth, soft skin
Lotion and oil can help keep your baby's skin smooth and soft. Use a moisturizer specially formulated for babies to help alleviate dry skin.

Different skin types
Your newborn's skin is delicate and sensitive. All babies have different skin types with a wide variety of textures and levels of dryness.

♦ **Cradle cap** Many babies between the ages of two weeks and one year develop crusty flakes of skin on their scalp which can spread to the eyebrows and behind the ears. Massaging a tiny amount of baby oil into your baby's skin at night will help soften the flakes. Wash her hair with a mild baby shampoo the following morning and most of the flakes should wash away.

♦ **Nappy rash** This can occur because ammonia and other chemicals in urine irritate your baby's skin. Be sure to apply a thin layer of barrier cream to her bottom at the first sight of soreness (see page 218).

♦ **Dry skin** Help prevent your baby's skin becoming too dry by making sure the temperature and humidity in your home aren't too extreme and keeping her out of the wind when you are out and about. If she has very dry skin, apply a specially formulated moisturizing cream to extra-dry areas when necessary.

Your baby's skin may be more prone to dryness in winter when central heating dries the air. Putting a damp towel over the radiator in her room at night is one way to help humidify the room and moisturize dry skin.

Best for baby
There is a large selection of infant skincare products available to choose from. Only use ones that are gentle to both skin and eyes. This is especially important for newborns who do not have fully developed blink reflexes or tear secretions. Adult products are best avoided as they may contain perfumes and other chemicals that could irritate your newborn baby's skin.

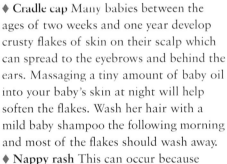

the importance **of touch**

Touch is important for healthy emotional development and communication between parents and babies. In addition, your loving touch does more than just comfort your newborn; it can actually help her grow.

The effect of touch on growth was first discovered in premature infants. These tiny babies are often separated from their parents and isolated in incubators, and are touched and cuddled much less than full-term babies. A study carried out at the Touch Research Institute in Miami, Florida, compared a group of premature babies who were massaged with a group who were

not. It was found that the massaged infants gained weight faster and were ready to go home with their parents an average of six days earlier than other infants. When they were eight months old, massaged babies had gained more weight and were more fully developed than babies who were not massaged.

Your loving touch is vital to your baby's growth. Touching occurs during everyday activities such as feeding, bathing, and rocking and through baby massage. See pages 96–97 to find out how to massage your baby.

massaging your baby

Massage is a wonderful way to show your baby that you love him, as well as helping calm him when he's unsettled. It has lots of health benefits, too, including boosting the immune system, improving circulation, and toning muscles.

WHAT YOU NEED   BABY OIL OR LOTION • SOFT TOWEL FOR YOUR BABY TO LIE ON • CALMING MUSIC

how to massage

You can massage your baby from about two weeks. Choose a time when he is not sleepy and do it in a warm room with warm hands.

A good time to massage is last thing at night, after your baby's bath, when he is calm and relaxed. It's also best to do it between feeds: if he has just been fed he may be too full to be comfortable; similarly if he is hungry he may quickly become unsettled.

If your baby doesn't like being undressed, leave his vest on and just work on his legs and arms. Otherwise, work from the head down with light strokes, massaging both sides symmetrically. Be very gentle at first, increasing the pressure only when and if your baby is obviously happy. When you have massaged his front, turn your baby over and begin massaging his back, working from the head down.

If your baby does become fretful, it's best to stop and try again another day.

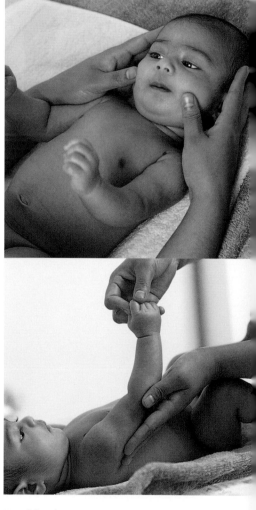

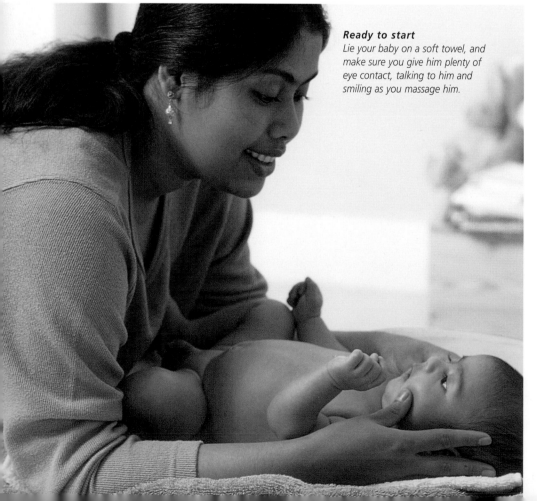

Ready to start
Lie your baby on a soft towel, and make sure you give him plenty of eye contact, talking to him and smiling as you massage him.

Head (top)
Lightly massage the crown of his head using circular strokes (avoiding his fontanelles), then work down the side of his cheeks. Massage his forehead working from the centre out, moving across his eyebrows and ears.

Neck, shoulders, and arms
Using a downward motion, stroke his neck then move onto his shoulders, working from the neck out. Massage his arms by gently squeezing them as you move along. Massage his wrists, hands, and fingers, stroking each finger with your fingertips and thumbs.

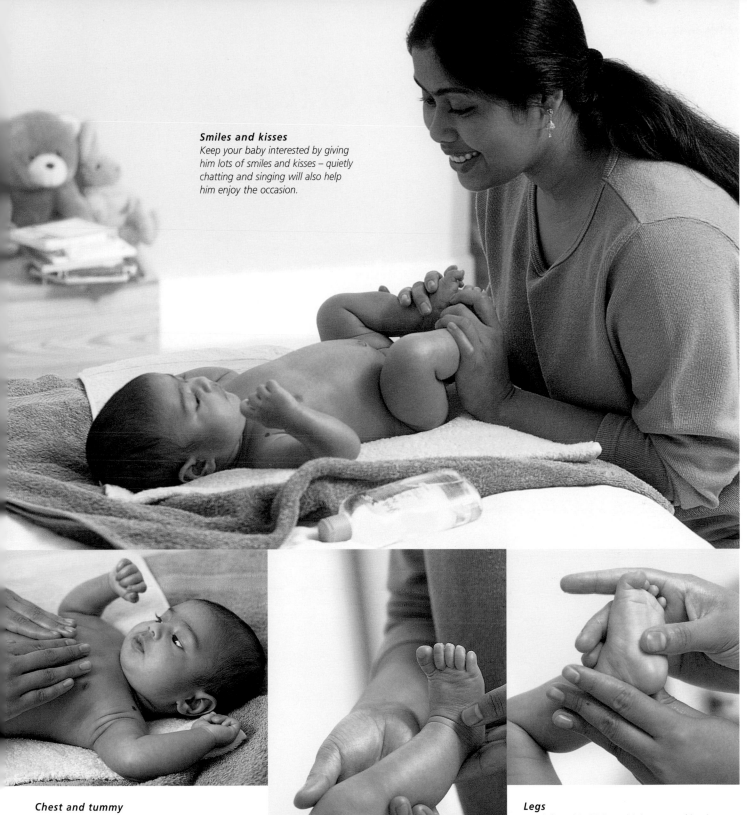

Smiles and kisses
Keep your baby interested by giving him lots of smiles and kisses – quietly chatting and singing will also help him enjoy the occasion.

Chest and tummy
Gently stroke your baby's chest using a downward motion. Rub his tummy using a circular motion, working clockwise and outwards from his tummy button with your fingertips.

Legs
Work from his thighs to his knees, stroking in a downward motion around the shins, gently squeezing them as you go.

Feet and toes
Rub ankles and feet, stroking from heel to toe and then gently massage each toe.

when your baby cries

Crying is normal for your baby. It is, after all, the only way she has of letting you know what her needs and feelings are. By learning what her different cries mean, you can respond and comfort her promptly, helping her feel safe and secure.

Happy interaction
Your baby will cry if she is left on her own for too long. Picking her up and playing with her will help keep her cheerful and smiling.

why babies cry

Although initially your baby's cries may all sound the same, you will soon discover that she has a crying "language" and that different cries mean different things.

Learning how to interpret her cries will help you respond effectively. Go to her promptly whenever she cries during her first few infant months. You cannot spoil a young baby by giving her attention; and if you answer her call for help, she will cry less overall.

Hunger
A cry that starts slowly and builds to a loud rhythm usually indicates that your baby is hungry. As this is the most likely reason your baby is crying, offer her a feed first, unless you are certain that she has had enough.

Pain
A baby in pain – because of an ear infection, for example – will cry in a very distinct way, beginning as a shrill scream, followed by silence and short gasps. The cycle is then repeated. If you think your baby is unwell take her to your GP.

Upset
Babies often cry in a fussy way when they are upset. The cry will increase in volume if you don't respond, and is distinct from a hunger cry. Your baby may need:
♦ **A cuddle** Newborns often just want physical comfort and being held in your arms may be enough to calm her down.
♦ **Sleep** Babies sometimes have trouble falling asleep and cry to express their frustration. Laying her down somewhere

Safe and secure
Sometimes babies cry simply because they need a cuddle. Holding your baby close, talking to her, and comforting her will often quickly soothe away her tears.

warm and quiet may help her settle herself down to sleep.

♦ **Stimulation** Even newborns get bored lying in their cots for long periods wide awake. Pick her up and talk to her.

♦ **Peace and quiet** Loud noises, bright lights, unexpected faces, a sneeze – all of these everyday occurrences can upset a newborn baby. Comfort her and keep her close.

♦ **A nappy change** Lots of babies hate being left in a dirty or wet nappy, especially if they have nappy rash, and a nappy change will not only relieve her discomfort but also distract her.

♦ **Cooling down or warming up** Your baby may be too hot or too cold. Newborns can't fully regulate their own temperature so you need to monitor and adjust the temperature of her environment. Ideally, the room should be about 16–20°C (61–68°F) for a baby dressed in a vest and sleep suit. You can check your baby's body temperature by feeling her tummy or the back of her neck – if her skin feels clammy she's probably too warm.

♦ **A chance to cry!** Some babies have crying spells, often at the same time every day. Try to comfort her using one of the following soothing techniques.

Soothing your baby

If your baby is crying for no obvious reason, try these ways to soothe her:

♦ carry her in a sling; keep her close to you

♦ rock her in your arms, in her pram, or sit and rock in a rocking chair

♦ swaddle her – some babies feel more secure when wrapped firmly (see page 100)

♦ sing to her or play soothing music; rhythmic noise or vibration can also help

♦ take her out for a walk either in the pram or sling, or for a ride in the car

♦ burp her to relieve any trapped gas bubbles

♦ give her a warm bath.

Coping with crying

On average, babies cry for one to four hours a day and you'll quickly get used to coping when she's unsettled. Sometimes, however, crying can be draining on your energy and emotions. When you need a break, put your baby in a safe place, such as her cot or pushchair, and take some time out to calm yourself; or let your partner, a friend, or relative take over for a while. Babies are alert to their mothers' moods and if you are tense or irritable your baby will feel it and cry more. No matter how tired or angry you feel, never shake your baby as this can cause blindness, brain damage or even death.

Twins and more...

Crying newborn twins rarely set each other off – although they often have similar needs at similar times. Mums of multiples discover clever ways of coping – putting the crying baby in a pram or bouncing cradle and rocking with a foot while feeding the other baby, for example. Dummies are also useful.

If you find you are struggling, don't forget that every new mum needs help – and you need it twice as much. Ideally, get help with chores as well as, or instead of, baby care.

---

intense **crying**

Intense, inconsolable crying is quite common in young babies. The crying often starts at the same time every day, usually in the early evening, and your baby may also pull up her legs and scrunch her face. These symptoms may be referred to as colic (see page 219). Ways to cope include:

♦ planning ahead – if the crying starts at the same time each night, try to have someone with you to take over when fatigue sets in

♦ experimenting with different carrying positions – try laying your baby across your forearm as a different position can help shift stomach or bowel contents (or gas)

♦ taking her out for some fresh air – this can work wonders.

Most babies learn to self-regulate and self-soothe by about four months.

sleep and your newborn

New babies spend most of their time feeding and sleeping – and at first they don't distinguish between day and night. It's natural to worry about your baby while he's asleep, but if you follow guidelines, such as putting him to sleep on his back, he will be safer.

helping your baby sleep

Your newborn will seek the amount of sleep his body needs: he will fall asleep when his body needs rest and wake up when he's recharged.

Newborns sleep an average of 16 hours a day – usually whenever they are not feeding. How long your baby sleeps will depend to a large extent on his weight and feeding requirements: the less your baby weighs, for example, the more often he will need feeding and the less he will sleep. However, all babies are individuals and tend to break the rules. Some new babies find it hard to settle down and may need extra special comfort.

baby **monitors**

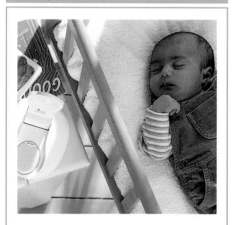

A baby monitor is useful if you live in a large flat or house and cannot hear your baby when she wakes in another room. The most common type is a sound monitor. This works through radio waves and has two units – one to transmit your baby's sounds and the other to receive the sounds. Systems may be mains or battery operated. Check for good reception.

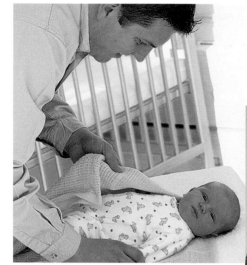

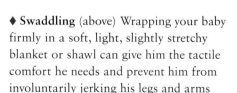

♦ **Swaddling** (above) Wrapping your baby firmly in a soft, light, slightly stretchy blanket or shawl can give him the tactile comfort he needs and prevent him from involuntarily jerking his legs and arms which may be keeping him awake.
♦ **Comfort sucking** A fretful baby will almost always be soothed if he has something to suck on – such as his finger or a dummy (sterilized before every use). The gentle rhythm of sucking can soothe him to sleep.

1 Lay your baby on a light, folded blanket, with his head placed on one of the corners and his arms by his side. Gently pull one side of the blanket across your baby's body.

2 Pull the other side of the blanket across and tuck it in so that your baby is swaddled. Place him on his back in his cot to sleep.

sleeping with your baby

During the first few weeks and months, you will want to have your baby close to you at night, not least because he will need feeding often. Some parents decide to put their baby in a crib or carrycot next to their bed. Parents in many cultures prefer to have their new baby in their own bed. Close contact not only feels wonderful, it may also decrease any anxiety you have about your baby's well-being. And night feeds – especially if you are breastfeeding – are less disruptive.

If you choose to sleep with your baby make sure you follow recognized safety guidelines (see *sleeping safely*, opposite). Don't share a bed if the bed is cramped, as your baby could get squashed or fall out.

sleeping **safely**

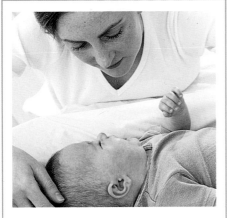

Sudden Infant Death Syndrome (SIDS)
Cot death (SIDS) is the most common cause of death in babies under one year of age (see page 225). It is therefore wise to take precautions known to reduce the risk.

Do....
♦ put your baby to sleep on his back with his feet at the foot of the cot to prevent him wriggling under the covers

♦ use cotton sheets and blankets

♦ tuck covers in securely

♦ make sure the mattress is firm, in good condition, easy to clean, dry, and well aired

♦ put your baby's cot in your room for the first six months

♦ keep the room temperature constant (about 16–20°C/61–68°F)

♦ learn infant CPR (see page 268).

Don't...
♦ use pillows, duvets, quilts, sheep skins, baby nests, bedding rolls, or cot bumpers

♦ ever put a hot water bottle or electric blanket in your baby's cot

♦ allow anyone to smoke in the same house as your baby. Not smoking in the same room does very little to reduce exposure to cigarette smoke toxins.

If you are sleeping with your baby...
♦ use light weight blankets not adult bedcovers for your baby

♦ make sure your duvet and pillows can't cover his head

♦ after cuddling or feeding your baby, put him back in his own cot if you or your partner smoke, have recently drunk alcohol, taken medication, or are especially tired.

Sweet dreams
The newest member of your family will spend most of his time sleeping.

how you'll feel

The first few weeks after birth are a unique time. You'll be coping with many emotional and physical changes and experiencing a huge range of feelings. However, as you and your baby slowly get to know and understand each other, life will start to settle down.

now that you're a parent

If this is your first baby, every baby-related task, from the first breastfeed or bath to the first outing, will be a new experience.

Sometimes the challenges and the responsibilities can seem daunting, especially in the early days when you feel tired and uncertain. You may find yourself asking your midwife and health visitor lots of questions. You may also feel you are given too much advice, as friends and family try to help you, too. With each passing day, however, your confidence will grow as you learn what works for you and your baby.

Your body after birth

You may feel some pain and discomfort in the early days as your body starts to recover from birth.

♦ You may have after-pains as your uterus contracts and decreases in size – and you will bleed for two to three weeks as the uterus sheds its lining. Slight loss may continue for up to six weeks.

♦ If you have had stitches, are bruised, or have piles, going to the toilet will feel uncomfortable for several days.

♦ When your milk comes in, around day three (see pages 86–89), your breasts will become very full and heavy, but the discomfort usually lasts only a day or so.

dealing with **tiredness**

The biggest adjustment you are likely to have to make is coping with broken nights. Try to make life easy for yourself:

♦ follow your baby's rhythms, and try to rest whenever your baby is napping

♦ don't be too concerned about sleeping, just unwinding – soaking in a warm bath, listening to music – will conserve your energy

♦ prioritize chores and do only those that are really essential; let others do the cleaning and preparation of meals

♦ look after yourself by eating regular nutritious meals

♦ accept all the help you can get, especially for household chores

♦ agree with your partner to take it in turns at the weekend to have a lie in – knowing you can catch up on sleep at least once a week will help you get through the other six days!

Bonding with your baby

During the first few weeks you need time and space to bond with your baby. Sometimes bonding begins as soon as you see your new baby; sometimes it takes longer to establish. Bonding has no time limit.

Many mothers feel overwhelmed by a flood of emotion as soon as they first see their baby. This is enhanced if they can hold their baby straight away and let her suckle.

Some mothers, however, feel dazed after childbirth – especially if they have had a difficult labour or their baby needs special care. Others feel anxious about their baby. Or maybe their baby looks different to how they imagined, or isn't the sex they longed for. In some cases, mothers who have difficulty bonding are experiencing postnatal depression (see page 78). If you think you aren't bonding, or you feel depressed, talk to your GP or health visitor. They can give you advice and support.

Whatever your experience, be reassured that if bonding doesn't happen straight away, it can happen just as happily weeks or months later. Try to help by spending special time with your baby: make eye contact, talk to her, and enjoy close physical contact as much as you can.

"The first few days at home after giving birth to Maddy were stressful – looking back I think I was trying to do too much. My midwife emphasized how important it was to rest. Now I take myself off for a sleep whenever Maddy naps."

KATRIN HAMBLE, MUM TO MADELEINE AGED 5 WEEKS

take a break

Getting time to yourself when you have a new baby can be a challenge. There will be days when finding even half an hour for making phone calls, let alone soaking in the bath, seems impossible. But it's important to remember that your baby doesn't need to be with you every minute of the day – and if you are lucky enough to have a friend or relative nearby who'll care for her every now and then, you should jump at the chance! At this age your baby will happily be cuddled, carried, or pushed round the park by someone else – and as long as she is handed over warm and well fed there should be no reason to worry.

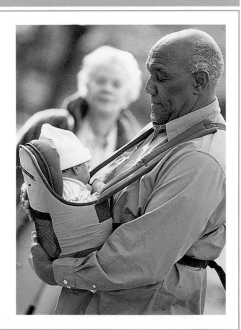

Grandparents are great
Grandparents are usually delighted to be given the opportunity to take their grandchild out for a walk by themselves – make the most of their help.

caring for your baby
6 weeks to 12 months

As your baby grows and develops, the skills you need to care for him will change: whether it's weaning him onto solids, coping with his increasing mobility, or simply getting him into a good routine.

Rapid change

Almost every day with your new baby brings change. The first few months will be spent keeping him warm, clean, and well-fed. Then as he grows and develops and starts to gain more control over his body – entrancing you with smiles and playing with anything he can lay his hands on, from his toes to your nose – you'll need new ways of nurturing and caring for him.

New challenges

Between four and six months he will have doubled his birth weight and be ready for real food to fuel his growing energy needs.

"I have to look at photos to remind myself that Ben was once a tiny newborn. He's such a solid boy now, and such a character – always on the go. We have a great routine – after breakfast we go shopping or to our local mother and toddler group. After lunch we might meet up with friends for a play or go to the park. Then it's teatime, bath, and bed."

KATIE JARRETT, MUM TO BEN AGED *12* MONTHS

He'll spend more of his day awake, playing, being with you as you go about your daily activities, and slowly you will start to develop a routine.

In his second six months, as he masters new and exciting skills – such as sitting up and crawling – he'll be off exploring his environment and taking his place as a vibrant member of the family.

Practical care – such as bath time and dressing – will become a new challenge, as will helping him learn how to pace himself and how to rest, sleep, and settle when he's tired or unhappy.

Back to work

Many mums return to work at some point during their baby's first year. This can be a particularly busy time for lots of families, but once you've found someone your baby feels loved by and secure with, you will discover that you can happily balance work and family life.

Outdoor activities
As your baby gets older the practicalities of caring for her change and outings, such as a trip to the park, can present a whole new set of challenges.

feeding and weaning

Feeding your baby real food for the first time is an exciting event. Between four
and six months she'll be ready for her first taste, and some time in the second
half of the first year she'll be sitting in a highchair joining in with family meals.

starting on solids

If your baby can hold her head up well, seems hungrier than normal, wakes more often during the night, or is interested in food you eat, she's probably ready for solids.

If you are unsure about when to start your baby on solids, talk to your health visitor. You don't want to start too early – your baby won't be able to digest foods properly before four months – but by six months breastmilk and/or formula alone will no longer provide all the nutrients and calories she needs.

Four to seven months

Begin by once a day offering her a teaspoon or two of runny fruit or vegetable purée and/or baby rice cereal mixed with boiled, cooled water, formula, or breast milk. Talk your baby through the process – "Mmmm . . . isn't this delicious". Once she is happy taking food from a spoon, build up from there. Most babies seem to prefer bland tastes initially. You could try:
♦ baby breakfast cereals
♦ purées of cooked apple or pear
♦ mashed banana
♦ purées of cooked vegetables such as sweet potato, carrot, parsnip, cauliflower, broccoli.

Offer one taste at a time so if your baby has an allergic reaction you'll know which food is the culprit. Stick to baby breakfast cereals and fruit and vegetable purées until she's seven months old, building up until you are offering her three solid meals a day. Never add baby rice or other solid food to your baby's bottle.

Eight to 12 months

At this age your baby needs between 750 and 900 Calories each day, about 400 to 500 of which should come from breast milk or formula (approximately 500–600ml/18–21fl oz a day).

Your baby will be ready for a whole range of tastes and can share many family meals – provided there's no added salt or sugar. To help get her used to textures, start mashing or chopping her food. If she spits the lumps out at first don't rush her. Instead, once she can hold them, help her discover new textures and give her lots of chewing practice with finger foods such as chunks of soft fruit, well-cooked pasta, toast, and small pieces of cooked vegetable. Always watch for choking in case she bites off a piece too big to swallow.

Ready for food
Starting your baby on solids is an exciting new stage. Take it slowly and as she starts to get the hang of it, you will find it an enjoyable and satisfying development.

Over the next few months you can introduce the following:
♦ bread, breadsticks, pasta, breakfast cereal, rice, potatoes, couscous
♦ meat, poultry, fish (check for bones), eggs (feed her only the yolks since their nutritional value is higher and they're less likely to cause allergies than the whites), lentils, beans (try to include at least one portion a day as these are good sources of protein and iron)
♦ more fruit and vegetables – try mango, melon, green beans, peas
♦ cheese, full-fat yogurt, fromage frais, cow's milk with cereal or in a cheese sauce.

Foods to avoid

Certain foods can pose health hazards and should be avoided in the early stages of your child's life. Others should be avoided to minimize the risk of allergies.
♦ **Up to six months** Milk products such as cheese, yogurt, and fromage frais; fish; citrus fruits (including orange juice); egg whites; wheat-, rye-, or barley-based foods such as bread, pasta, wheat flour, rusks; and some cereals, as they contain a substance called gluten which babies are sensitive to.
♦ **Up to 12 months** Avoid cow's milk as a drink – although from six months you can start to add it in small quantities to breakfast cereals or a cheese sauce; honey in liquid or solid form as it can contain spores that cause infant botulism – under one year old, babies' digestive systems are immature and spores can germinate and cause disease. (This doesn't apply to honey as an ingredient in commercially made baby foods as a different process is used.)

♦ **Up to four years** Don't give your child hard, smooth foods which need to be chewed because youngsters can't manage to chew with a grinding motion until the age of four. Whole peanuts shouldn't be given until age seven or older because they present an inhalation hazard. Peanut and other nut products (however smooth) shouldn't be given until your child is two years old because of the risk of allergies.

From bottle to cup

As your baby progresses to three meals a day, you can start to introduce a two-handled cup so she can take sips of water or diluted fruit juice during meal times. Those with soft spouts are easiest for first-timers. You'll need to hold and tip it for her to show her how it works to begin with.

Initially she may use it as a plaything, so it's worth choosing a non-drip system as chances are the cup will often be waved and

Homemade purées
Use a blender to purée steamed or lightly boiled fruit and vegetables, then freeze teaspoons of the purées in ice cube trays and defrost as required.

being **vegetarian**

If you are bringing your baby up as a non-meat-eater you will need to look at other sources to make sure she's getting enough protein and iron. After six months, she can eat egg yolk (excluding the egg white), beans, lentils, and fish. Try to give at least one portion per day. Iron supplements may also be a good idea. If you are excluding eggs and dairy products from her diet she may need supplements of vitamins B12 and D as well as riboflavin and calcium. Ask your GP or the Vegetarian Society for further advice.

thrown. Try to persevere, however, as it's important that your baby is weaned off the bottle earlier rather than later: drinks from a cup are better for her speech development and her teeth (the liquid spends less time in contact with the enamel coating), and if she stays on a bottle too long it may become a security object.

Common problems

♦ **Loss of appetite** Your older baby may go off her food and demand more milk instead if she's teething. Once the new tooth is through her appetite will pick up again.
♦ **Grabbing the spoon** Lots of babies prefer to feed themselves and from an early age will try to grab the spoon. Satisfy her need for independence by giving her a spoon of her own but use one yourself as well – slipping in mouthfuls when you can.
♦ **Refusal to eat** If your baby rejects food you give her, don't turn it into a big issue. Simply try again later.

bathing your baby

Bath time can be an enjoyable experience for you and your baby, although it's natural for babies and parents to be nervous initially. However, there are lots of ways to help build confidence and make bath time a success.

starting a routine

You don't need to give your baby a bath every day: at first two or three times a week is fine.

As he gets older you may want to increase this. Lots of mums find that once they feel confident, bath time is a relaxing and soothing experience and they like to make it a part of their everyday routine.

Between full baths and topping and tailing you can give him a sponge bath – simply hold him on your lap with a bowl of warm water nearby and, removing the minimum amount of clothes at a time, gently sponge him clean.

Bathing your older baby

Soon your baby will be ready for the big bath. Most babies make the transition easily, especially if they love playing in water and have some sponges, plastic mugs, and bath toys to keep them amused. To keep your baby safe see page 264 and follow these guidelines:

♦ keep the water shallow (up to 13cm/5in)
♦ always check the temperature of the bath water to make sure it's comfortable for your baby, regardless of his age
♦ wrap the taps with a flannel or small towel
♦ baby bath seats can help you support your baby, and help save your back
♦ don't allow your baby to pull himself up to standing unsupported in the bath
♦ never leave your baby alone in the bath, even for a second.

YOU WILL NEED   BABY BATH OR NON-SLIP MAT IF USING ADULT BATH • COTTON WOOL • COOLED, BOILED WATER • TWO THICK, FLUFFY TOWELS • BABY BATH, LOTION, AND/OR BABY SHAMPOO • CLEAN NAPPY

1   Keep the water shallow – up to 13cm (5in). Check the temperature with your elbow before putting your baby in – the water should be just warm. If you use a thermometer, it should register about 29°C (85°F).

2   Undress your baby, remove his nappy, then wrap him up in one of the towels. First, clean his face using cotton wool and cooled, boiled water (see topping and tailing, page 93).

3   Wash his hair by holding him firmly over the bath and cupping your hand to apply the water. Use a little baby bath or baby shampoo. Rinse well.

five steps to a
happy bath time

Step one
Your child is more likely to enjoy his bath if he's not tired, and is neither hungry nor has just eaten (straight after a feed he may be sick).

Step two
Babies become cold very quickly so bathe him in a warm room and keep a towel handy to wrap him in when you have finished.

Step three
Add some baby bath to the water – this will make cleaning your baby easy, and is less drying than soap.

Step four
Smile and chat soothingly to him – playing water games will help him associate water with having fun.

Step five
Dry him and dress him quickly to keep him as warm as possible.

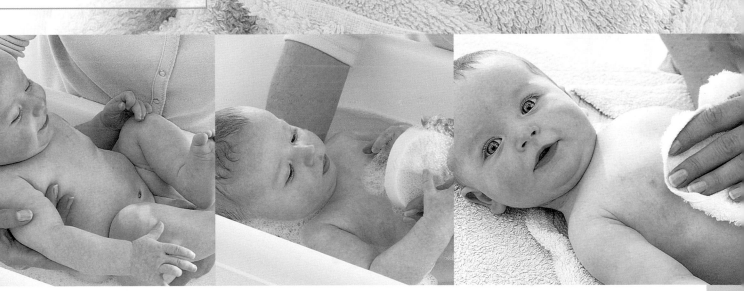

4 *Remove the towel and gently put your baby into the bath. Support his head and shoulders with one arm and his legs and bottom with the other.*

5 *Using the hand which was under his bottom, gently splash water over your baby's body. Give him time to kick his arms and legs if he wants to. A young baby needs constant support in water so never take your hand off him or leave him alone in the bath.*

6 *Lift your baby out of the bath, wrap him in a warm towel, and dry him thoroughly. Put on a clean nappy and dress him.*

taking care of your older baby

During the coming year your baby will learn how to sit up and crawl. As she becomes more mobile simple tasks, such as dressing her and keeping her clean and warm, may become more challenging.

dressing your baby

Dressing a wriggly baby can be difficult, but if you are patient and gentle it will become easier with practice.

Choose easy-to-fit clothes and distract your baby with smiles and chatter to keep her happy and relaxed. Lots of babies don't enjoy being dressed or undressed so try to make the procedure as quick and easy as possible by choosing clothes that are easy to put on and take off.

Remember to stretch neck openings wide before easing over your baby's head, and pull sleeves back over your baby's arms rather then tugging her arms through them. Wrap up your baby against the cold – hats are especially important as lots of body heat is lost through the head. Be sure to take off extra layers when you bring your baby inside again so she doesn't overheat.

Until your baby is walking well, all she needs on her feet are socks or similar items to keep them warm. Make sure they are soft and roomy – the bones in a baby's feet are very pliable and even tight socks may misshape the toes if they are worn a lot.

Lots of mums really enjoy choosing clothes for their baby. Check:
♦ style – look for snug clothes that will keep your baby warm and cosy. Popper fastenings and wide envelope necks are best as these make dressing and undressing your baby easier. All-in-one suits are ideal.
♦ fabric – look for soft, stretchy fabrics that are machine-washable and colour fast. Leaking nappies, dribbling, and possetting all mean your baby's clothes will need to withstand frequent washing. Your crawling baby will need sturdy fabrics that protect her knees but will not restrict her movement.

safety in **the sun**

If your baby is less than six months old she should be kept out of the sun.

♦ Keep her cool with lightweight clothing – in hot weather she needn't be dressed any more warmly than yourself.

♦ Older babies should be allowed in the sun only for a limited time and only if they are well protected. Dress them in light-coloured clothes made from lightweight, tightly woven fabric and cover any exposed parts of their faces and bodies with a suitable sunscreen (minimum sun protection factor 15 – consult the instructions on the bottle). Keep your child out of the sun when the peak ultraviolet rays occur.

♦ Use a sunshade or parasol to keep your baby in the shade. Make sure she wears a wide-brimmed hat to protect her face and eyes.

♦ See page 267 for more sun safety tips.

Let's get you dressed
Encourage your little one to let you get him dressed by making it fun – sing songs or play peekaboo, for example – and let him do the simple bits himself.

Ready to go?
It's important to make sure your baby is well wrapped up in cold weather. Hats and coats are essential – no matter what your baby's opinion!

Hat's on, hat's off
If the minute you put a hat or coat on your mischievous baby he whips it off, wait until you're out and he's distracted – then slip it back on again.

looking after your baby's nails

Your baby may already have long fingernails when she is born – and they will continue to grow rapidly.

It's natural to feel nervous about trimming them but knowing how and when it's best to trim will help you keep her free from scratches as she waves her arms around.

Fingernails

Scratch mittens are one way of preventing your baby scratching herself – but she needs to discover her hands so they are best avoided. Instead, check her nails every couple of days and trim when necessary.
♦ **What to use** Use a soft emery board, baby nail clippers, or blunt-nosed toenail scissors.

♦ **When to do it** You will find that your baby's nails are softer after a bath. If you can't get your baby to hold still while you cut her nails, have a go while she is asleep.
♦ **How to do it** Hold one finger at a time between your forefinger and thumb, safely

enclosing the rest of her hand with your remaining fingers. Try to press down on the finger pad, pulling it back out of the way while you cut.

Toenails

Your baby's toenails will grow much more slowly then her fingernails. Check them every couple of weeks. Toenails also need to be trimmed, with a similar technique to that used for fingernails (see above). You will notice that they often curl round at the end. Unless the skin around the nail looks red and inflamed there's no reason to worry. As your baby gets older the nail will harden and become better defined.

sleep and your older baby

Sleep is essential for your baby – it helps him grow and develop properly. Understanding your baby's sleep patterns and following some simple guidelines will help establish sound sleep habits – and give you all a good night's rest!

establishing a sleep routine

Not getting enough sleep will make your baby irritable and difficult. Encouraging good sleep habits now will him help avoid sleep problems later.

♦ **Distinguish between night and day** Help your baby learn that night-time is sleep time and daytime is play time with different rooms for night and day sleeps. During daytime naps keep the light on and sound at a normal level. At night, turn off the light and keep the room quiet.

♦ **Start a bedtime routine** As your baby's memory skills improve, he'll begin to look forward to this ritual and understand that it's a time to sleep, not play. Follow the same pattern every night – a warm bath, a cuddle/play/story, final feed, and then into the cot, drowsy but awake.

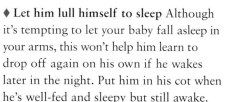

♦ **Let him lull himself to sleep** Although it's tempting to let your baby fall asleep in your arms, this won't help him learn to drop off again on his own if he wakes later in the night. Put him in his cot when he's well-fed and sleepy but still awake.

Teething troubles

Teething can keep babies awake at night. First teeth usually appear between six and nine months. Common signs of teething include one or all of the following: swollen, reddened gums; excessive drooling; an inflamed cheek; desire to bite down on anything he can get in his mouth. You could:

♦ give him a chilled teething ring to chew on, but it should be made of firm rubber
♦ gently rub a teething gel along his gums
♦ massage his gums with your fingertips.

"I give my baby something cold to chew on – teething rings are great but a chunk of frozen bagel works just as well."

Sophie Dewar, mum to Rory aged 8 months

wakeful babies

At night

Your older baby is likely to sleep as much as 12 hours a night without needing a middle-of-the-night feed. Beware of the possible problems ahead: as his separation anxieties intensify in the next few months (see page 171), he may start to resist going to bed. He may also wake up more often in the night looking for you. However, if your baby is used to settling himself down, he should quickly fall back into a deep sleep. If he cries until you comfort him, try the strategies on page 113 to help him sleep through.

During the day

Daytime naps are good for your baby – he probably still takes two: one in the morning and one in the afternoon. The more rested he is, the happier he'll be during the day and the easier to settle at night. However, as he gets older and becomes more interested in the world around him he may find it harder to nap. If your baby resists a daytime sleep yet obviously needs one, try to put him down before he gets overtired. If he still resists take him out for a walk or a drive. Many babies nap easily in the buggy or car and even 20 minutes will refresh him.

night-time **waking**

During the first six months or so, respond quickly to your baby – he may need changing or feeding. After six months your baby will be secure enough in your love to accept being left for a while. If his crying becomes desperate, check on him (see box below). If he seems fine, kiss him, tell him he's OK, and leave again.

You may have to do this repeatedly over several hours before he finally drops off. Persevere now and for the next few nights. At this age most babies learn by the sixth or seventh night that they are OK without you and discover they can get themselves back to sleep.

Why older babies cry

Your older baby may cry in the night because he's been disturbed. If he's still sleeping in your room after six months, he's more likely to wake up when you come to bed or cough or turn over in the night. Now may be a good time to move him into his own room.

He may also cry in the night if he is frightened of being separated from you. For the first time he is beginning to realize that you and he are different people – and when you vanish he has no idea when, or if, you will return. If your baby has become very clingy give him lots of reassurance. When you leave him during the day always give him a kiss and a hug as you say goodbye; looking happy and calm will help him feel reassured. The more secure he feels, the faster – and more smoothly – this phase will pass.

checklist: **is he OK?**

If your baby wakes during the night and can't settle himself down, he may:

♦ be too hot or too cold

♦ need his nappy changing

♦ be in pain because of teething, nappy rash, or illness

♦ be anxious about something, such as a new caregiver or a change in his routine.

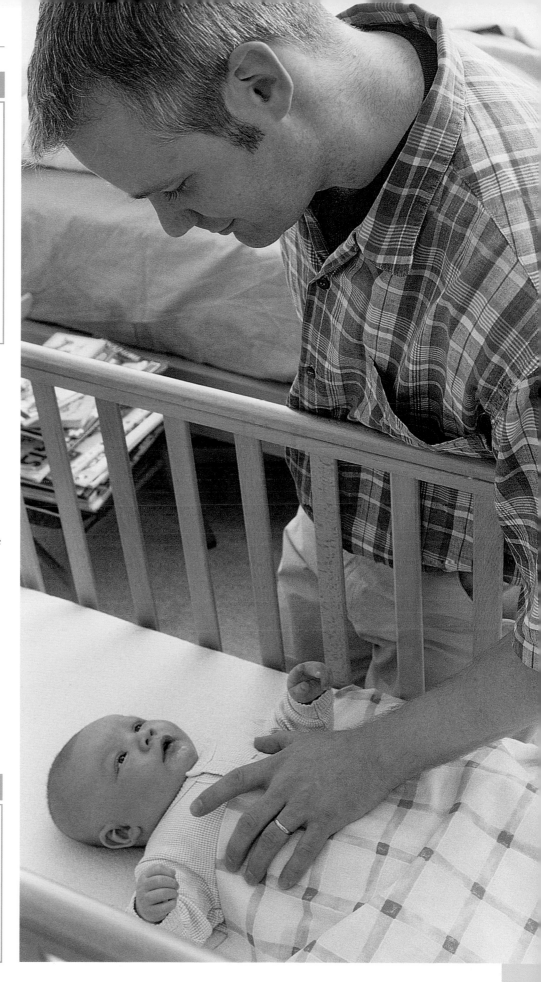

going back to work

Returning to work after you've had a baby can be an emotional time. Your main concern will be that your baby adjusts well and continues to feel loved and secure. The more time and preparation you give yourself, the easier the transition will be.

making it work for you

Finding the right person to care for your child when you return to work may take time, but it's important that you feel confident with your choice.

Introduce your baby to her caregiver early on and build up the time they spend together so she has the chance to adjust. Asking your caregiver to keep to your baby's routine will help your baby become used to being cared for by somebody else.

Childcare checklist

With the right person, your child will thrive. Whatever age your child, a good caregiver should:
♦ be warm and friendly – babies and toddlers need lots of physical affection and attention
♦ listen and watch carefully
♦ enjoy chatting to your child about what she is doing
♦ be fun and imaginative – older children especially need planned activities and creative play time
♦ be patient and prepared to go at your child's pace
♦ join in with her play without taking over
♦ be one step ahead – looking out for difficult situations before they happen
♦ be consistent about what your child can and can't do.
You will also need someone who:
♦ you feel you could get on well with
♦ agrees with your ideas on how to look after children
♦ knows how to keep your child safe, especially when learning to crawl and walk
♦ understands basic first aid.

You and your child's caregiver

Your child will benefit from seeing you getting on well with her caregiver, and good communication will help maintain good relations and a good standard of care. Treat her as a partner, not a rival.
♦ Help get your child settled before you leave, join in with chores at the end of the

Going to a childminder
Childminders, who look after children in their own homes, are often mums themselves and therefore sympathetic to the needs of your child.

day, help plan special events or activities.
♦ Find time each day to chat about what's happened – you need to know if your child is trying out a new skill or looks like she's coming down with a cold and always thank your childminder for her day's work.
♦ Have regular get-togethers to discuss any problems or changes. There's rarely a right or wrong way of doing something so be prepared to be open-minded.

Nursery care
A good day-care nursery will have plenty of toys and activities specially tailored to your baby's age – and she'll benefit from socializing with other babies.

Coping with tears

It's natural for babies to become more clingy as they grow older, and separation anxiety is an important emotional milestone. When you leave your baby she has no idea when, or if, you will return, so help her cope by:
♦ giving advance warning – 10 or 15 minutes before you leave tell her what's happening
♦ acting calmly – kiss your baby goodbye, give her a hug, and go without a fuss.

You may worry that by returning to work you are neglecting your baby or that she will become more attached to her new carer. Try not to worry – you will always be the most important person in your baby's life. And developing another warm and loving relationship will be good for her.

Stay-at-home dads

A growing number of dads are staying at home to care for their children. If you are planning to be a home dad, go along to mother-and-baby groups – they can share lots of information and advice. Ask your health visitor about other stay-at-home dads – building up a network of friends will help overcome isolation and provide playmates for your baby as she gets older.

Some mums have a close relative who is willing to care for their child. Otherwise, there are various childcare options to look into. Whether you decide to have your child cared for in your own home or you choose to take her to someone else's home or a childcare centre will depend on your finances and your own personal preferences.

Nannies and au pairs

For your child, being looked after by a nanny or au pair means staying in familiar surroundings and getting individual care and attention. Life will also be easier for you as you won't need to transport your child each morning and evening. However, nannies need not be registered – so you must carefully check references and suitability. They can also be expensive. And if the nanny is alone with your child, it will be difficult to check how well she is doing the job. Au pairs, although cheaper, are live-in and are not qualified in child care; they should not take on sole charge of a baby.

Childminders

Usually mums working in their own homes, childminders can be the most affordable type of child care. By law they must be registered with their local authority and there will be a fixed adult/child ratio. Your child will be in a friendly family environment, and will be able to join in lots of familiar household activities. She may also have other children to play with. As with nannies and au pairs, it's difficult to check what happens when you are not there, so it's important to get feedback from other parents who have used the same childminder.

Day nurseries

Often privately run, these also need to be registered with the local authority. Toddlers and pre-schoolers will find the structured programmes usually on offer stimulating and fun. There will be a number of staff, which means you won't be affected if one of them is unwell. Sometimes, however, staff turnover can be high, which may be unsettling for your child. Good nurseries get booked up quickly so make enquiries sooner rather than later.

your new family

Becoming a family is exhilarating and challenging. Shared love for your new baby will bring a new dimension to your relationship. Making time for yourselves as a couple is also important for everyone.

the joys of parenthood

As your baby grows so does the reality of family life, and you will find there are fewer and fewer times when you and your partner are alone together.

If your baby is not with one of you, he is with the other. Life revolves around his needs – which can't be put aside until later. As a result, time that was once spent with each other as a couple is now spent on your baby.

Shared parenting

Adjusting to this new way of life can be challenging. Few couples sail through the first year as parents without conflict of some sort. There's less time to talk, to feel close, to spend time caring for each other. Issues such as who's doing the most chores and getting the least sleep can be potential sources of conflict. Often, neither partner feels they are getting the love and attention they need; and as resentment builds there's a danger the relationship can begin to deteriorate.

Shared parenting can hugely reduce the stress on a relationship – taking on equal responsibility for childcare and household chores can benefit both parents, and be good for your baby, too. Even if one of you is working full-time, finding a way of sharing the domestic workload at weekends and in the evening can help create a happy household.

Family outing
Going out and spending time together as a family is as important for you as parents as it is for your new baby and his siblings.

Finding time for yourselves

Spending time together as a couple is vital. Make it a priority – when you and your partner are feeling close and supportive, any stress and strains will be easier to handle. Here are some suggestions:

♦ organize a weekly babysitter, or join a babysitting circle, so you can go out regularly together as a couple

♦ ask grandparents to help out, perhaps for the occasional weekend away

♦ one night a week agree to switch off the television, order a takeaway, and have a quiet evening together at home

♦ when possible get help with chores such as ironing and cleaning – and use your free time for each other

♦ book holidays with travel companies that offer on-site childcare so you can spend a couple of hours a day doing things together, such as sight-seeing or relaxing on the beach.

Additional children

If this is your second – or third – baby, you will probably find yourself feeling even more tired, and pulled in more directions emotionally and physically than you ever have before. From the moment baby number two comes on the scene it's all change – every moment of the day is spoken for and when they finally sink into their cot and bed, you'll probably collapse too!

Caring for more than one child can be extra difficult if your older child is feeling put out by the new baby's arrival. In step-families an older child can feel particularly excluded if you and your new partner have a baby together.

Keep family life as happy and relaxed as possible by being extra sensitive to your older child's needs.

♦ Make sure he still sees his friends, and keeps up with any activities or playgroups he was already going to – keep life as normal as possible.

♦ Encourage him to help – recognize that he will probably enjoy bringing you a clean nappy and playing with the baby at bathtime, as long as his help is encouraged and freely given.

♦ Give him special time on his own so that he still feels precious and important.

♦ Be positive – if he's acting boisterously

Time to talk
Making time just for you and your partner to be together may take some organization, but it is essential for maintaining a happy relationship. A meal out provides an ideal opportunity to enjoy each other's company uninterrupted.

around the baby or playing too loudly, suggest a different way of playing rather than simply telling him not to do something, so he doesn't become resentful of the new baby.

♦ Help nurture a good relationship – tell your older child how much the baby likes him by saying things like "Look, he's smiling at you" or "You make him laugh when you do that".

Single parents

Being a single parent isn't easy – in addition to the financial strain, caring for a baby on your own can be relentless, exhausting, and lonely. Trying to stay in control of your life is important for you both – the more confident and happy you feel, the more love and attention you will be able to give your baby.

♦ Take good care of yourself – eat well, exercise, and get plenty of rest.

♦ Try to ensure you have regular time away from your child so you can, for example, relax with friends, go to the gym, or see a film.

♦ Develop a good support network – friends, relatives, community services, and health professionals can give you practical and emotional help.

"I love my son and have no regrets about being a single mum. Occasionally I think it would be nice to have someone to share Jacob's achievements with – I wonder if my mum gets fed up with me telling her how wonderful he is! But otherwise I enjoy being able to do things my way – and my family are always there to help when I'm tired or just need a break."

CATHY WILCOX, MUM TO JACOB AGED 9 MONTHS

caring for your toddler
12 to 24 months

As your baby becomes a toddler, caring for her also means teaching her how to do lots of new things for herself. Whether it's washing her own face or starting to use a potty, she'll love learning how to be independent.

Stepping forward

Over the next few months your little one will become increasingly independent. She'll take her first steps, say her first words – and whether it's finding her favourite cup, sliding backwards down the stairs, or learning how to put on her hat, you'll be thrilled by her achievements.

As the year progresses, there will be lots of new and exciting experiences for both of you. She'll soon be ready, for example, to be fitted for her first pair of proper shoes, to make the move from her cot into a "big bed", have her first haircut, and take her first steps towards potty training.

Exploring the world

As your toddler becomes more physically adventurous, exploring her environment will be part of everyday life. Toddlers are into anything and everything. They love to feel, taste, touch, and empty things – it's how they learn about the world. Being prepared for mess – dressing your toddler in suitable clothing, using mess mats under the highchair, designating a particular corner of the room for activities such as painting and play dough – will help a lot.

Similarly, as she becomes more active you'll need to become increasingly careful about her safety. She needs space and a sense of freedom to explore her environment

"Emily is really steady on her feet now – and she's so excited about being able to walk. She seems much happier now that she can do more for herself."

JACKIE FRENCH, MUM TO EMILY AGED 16 MONTHS

– so wrapping her in cotton wool isn't the answer. But you can make sure she has a safe environment to explore. Check your house for hidden dangers, such as unstable furniture and unlocked windows, and install any necessary toddler safety devices, such as stair gates (these should be used as soon as your baby can roll over), safety covers for electrical outlets, locks for cupboards with household cleaners, door slam protectors, and corner guards on sharp cupboard and table corners (see pages 262–265).

Emotional outbursts

At some point during this year, your toddler may also have her first tantrums. Despite all her new physical skills, your child will often find she can't manage – or simply isn't allowed – to do what she wants. Tears, temper, and frustration are natural, but you'll quickly learn how to handle tricky behaviour such as this. And it's reassuring to know that at this age, upsets are quickly forgotten. Your toddler may be sobbing now, but she'll soon be smiling again.

feeding your toddler

Your toddler can now feed himself and enjoy most foods – but that doesn't necessarily mean he'll eat everything you put in front of him! Fussy eating is common at this age, but with the right approach you can avoid mealtime battles.

what he's eating

By now your toddler is eating mainly family meals, although they should be prepared with less salt and sugar than for an adult.

You will be offering him food that he can chew, although – apart from softer food such as banana – you will need to chop it up into bite-sized pieces. Be aware of food he might choke on, such as raw carrots, grapes, uncooked peas, celery, hard sweets, or other hard, round foods. Choking can also happen with meat products, such as burgers, sausages, and frankfurters, so these should be cut lengthwise and into smaller pieces. Always supervise your child while he is eating. Using a five-point highchair harness will prevent him falling and choking on food.

Use as many fresh ingredients as possible – processed foods are high in salt, sugars, and artificial flavourings. Choose foods from the four basic food groups:
♦ meat, fish, eggs, and other protein
♦ milk, cheese, yogurt, and other dairy products
♦ rice, cereals, potatoes, yams, bread, pasta, sweet potatoes, and other carbohydrates
♦ fruit and vegetables.

Remember that a low-fat, high-fibre diet isn't suitable for a child. Your toddler should have whole rather than skimmed milk, and full-fat dairy products.

Finger foods
Starting to feed herself will give your toddler a great sense of independence – but remember never to leave her alone with food because of the risk of choking.

Feeding himself

Your toddler will be able to feed himself but he may be slow and tempted to play with his food. You may want to spoon in the occasional mouthful yourself. Giving him finger food he can easily manage himself – such as small sandwiches and pieces of fruit – may help.

For the sake of his teeth, your toddler should also be drinking from a cup. Keep an eye on how much fluid he has. At this age a total of 330–420ml (12–15fl oz) of whole milk per day is more than enough. If he drinks more, he may not feel hungry at meal times.

Large quantities of fruit juice can have a similar effect, especially as the sugar content is usually high. It may also cause diarrhoea and increase the risk of tooth decay. Limit the amount of juice to 120ml (4fl oz) a day. Offer water as an alternative to juice and milk – at this age tap water is perfectly safe.

Fun with food
Make healthy food look inviting by letting loose your imagination: funny faces and food cut into interesting shapes will have great appeal for your child.

"It's not often we can all sit down for a meal together – Mark works long hours during the week. But we do try to have a family meal at the weekends. It means planning ahead and eating a bit earlier for Hannah's sake – she still has a nap in the afternoon and if she's tired then she's not interested in food. I always cook something I know she enjoys too, such as pasta, so there are no tantrums."

SHARON HILL, MUM TO HANNAH AGED 21 MONTHS

food **fads**

Lots of toddlers become fussy eaters. From around 18 months they have a surge of independence and want their own way whenever possible. Food inevitably becomes a battle ground – and lots of mums find their fuss-free babies become picky toddlers. You should never force-feed your child. Instead, stay as calm and neutral as possible and remember that it's just a phase. As long as your toddler is gaining weight and growing then his health won't be at risk. Meanwhile, encourage healthy eating by:

♦ giving your toddler a choice of two of his favourite foods. Children of this age are overwhelmed by an open-ended choice. They do respond well to: "Do you want to have X or Y?", for example, jam (X) or cheese (Y) sandwiches

♦ keeping meal times fun – sit down with your toddler and eat together. If he sees daddy eating sweetcorn he might try it too

♦ making the food look good – small piles of chopped food attractively arranged look tempting and not too overwhelming

♦ praising your toddler when he eats well or tries something new; and persevering – children's likes and dislikes change all the time.

healthy **snacks**

Toddlers are often on the move and using up lots of energy. Their small tummies digest meals quickly and they soon become hungry again. When this happens their blood sugar levels dip, making them irritable and tired. A healthy snack between meals is ideal for boosting their energy and lifting their spirits. When choosing what to give your toddler, think in terms of a nutritious mini-meal. Offer:

♦ thin vegetable sticks such as raw carrot and cucumber

♦ carrot or banana cake

♦ fresh, chopped fruit (dried fruit can stick to teeth)

♦ crackers, rice cakes, oat cakes with cream cheese

♦ mashed banana or Marmite on toast

♦ natural yogurt

♦ cubes of cheese and sliced baby tomatoes.

Always stay close to your child when he's eating in case he chokes.

sleep and your one year old

Your toddler is growing up fast and she'll soon be ready to make the move from her cot into a big bed. For healthy development she still needs plenty of sleep – at night and during the day – so continue to encourage good sleeping habits.

getting enough sleep

At a year old, your toddler will be sleeping for about 14 hours within a 24-hour period, although this may drop to about 12 hours by her second birthday.

Part of this will be taken as daytime naps. These are vital if your toddler is to get through the day without becoming cranky and also to prevent her getting overtired which can make night-time sleep a problem. Even if your toddler wakes early or is wakeful at night, don't be tempted to drop daytime naps. If your toddler needs waking from a nap, make sure she has plenty of time to adjust – rushing her to eat lunch or get dressed will only make her unhappy.

Good sleep habits

By now your toddler should be able to settle herself to sleep – and sleep through the night – without any help from you, the breast, or a bottle. Illness or going on holiday may temporarily disrupt your toddler, but once she has recovered or is back in familiar surroundings, she should settle back into her previously good sleep pattern.

If, however, you are still coping with bedtime battles or broken nights, it's not too late to help your child learn how to sleep well. Start with a regular bedtime routine (see page 112). With practice your child will learn she can happily settle down on her own, in her own bed. If she's still waking in the night, see *Night-time waking* below on how to help her sleep through.

from cot **to bed**

When your toddler tries to climb out of her cot or she is too big to sleep in it comfortably, it's time to move her into a grown-up bed. To help your child feel secure about the change:

◆ choose a time when her life is settled – if there's a new baby or new caregiver to get used to, or she is getting over an illness, for example, put the move off for now

◆ let her help you make up the bed and choose some favourite toys to be in it too

◆ entice her in by getting in yourself – children love imitating grown-ups!

◆ put some cushions on the floor next to the bed so if she falls out in the night she won't hurt herself

◆ if she is hesitant, let her start off with daytime naps in the big bed before taking down the cot for good.

sleep **solutions**

Bedtime battles
Calm your toddler down with a relaxing bedtime routine (see page 112). Reading a story in bed can help get her ready for sleep. Offer her a special teddy or blanket to cuddle, give her a kiss, say goodnight, lower the light and leave. Be calm but consistent. If she cries, wait a few minutes then go back and say "Goodnight sweetheart. I love you. You need to go to sleep. I am not going to pick you up. Goodnight." Then leave the room. You may have to do this every 15–20 minutes, and for the next few nights, too, but your toddler will eventually get the message.

Night-time waking
Check your toddler is OK, calm her down, then say goodnight and leave. If she cries again wait a few minutes to

see if she settles before repeating the procedure. You may have to do this through the night and for the next few nights too, but eventually your toddler will realize that she can go back to sleep without you being with her.

Early waking
Postpone bedtime by 10 minutes each night for a few nights until your toddler is going to bed an hour later and hopefully waking later too. Put heavy curtains or black-out blinds on the windows to keep the morning light out and leave some toys out to distract her when she wakes. If it's very early leave her to cry for a while – she may settle herself again. Or follow the procedure above – check on her, say goodnight and leave. Repeat until she gets the message.

staying in **her own bed**

If your toddler comes into your bed in the night and you want to discourage the habit, you need to be firm and put her straight back into her own bed every time she leaves it. This can be exhausting but your toddler will eventually get the message.

♦ Choose a couple of days when you can catch up with sleep during the day or decide to take it in turns – mum first night, dad second night.

♦ As soon as your toddler appears at your bedside, take her back to her room. Tuck her in and leave saying "Mummy's going back to her own bed now. See you in the morning".

♦ Give her something to take comfort from – maybe one of your T-shirts to cuddle.

♦ Stay calm and patient so your toddler feels secure about settling down on her own.

♦ Be prepared to get up numerous times on the first night and maybe the second too – however tempting it might be to give in one night, this will only confuse your toddler.

♦ Don't feel guilty – a good night's sleep is just as important for you as it is for your toddler.

Your toddler will still need a daytime nap to help her get through the day. Whether she appears ready to go back to bed late morning, before lunch, or early afternoon, setting up a routine will help her know what to expect. Try to put her down before she's overtired.

Sleep tight tips

A well-rested toddler means a well-rested parent – who'll have more energy for the day ahead. Keep these points in mind when dealing with sleep problems, and you should both get a good night's sleep:

♦ keep bedtime the same every night
♦ keep the bedtime routine relatively short, gently winding down
♦ stick to the same order of events each night to help your toddler know what to expect
♦ leave a night light on for reassurance
♦ don't use bedtime as a threat or a punishment.

Getting help

If your toddler continues to have sleep problems that are making life difficult for you, speak to your health visitor. Often support from an expert can give you the extra confidence needed to form good sleep habits. She may also refer you to a local sleep clinic, run by health visitors, where you'll be asked to keep a diary of your toddler's sleep patterns before being helped to devise an action-plan.

Early risers
If your child wakes up early then leave a few toys out for her to play with – these may distract her for long enough to allow you to get the extra sleep you need.

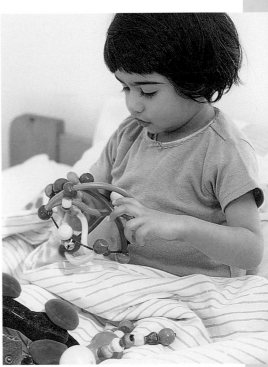

practical care of your toddler

Your curious toddler will need lots of care and attention when it comes to keeping clean. Some tasks – such as dressing and hair washing – may be more of a challenge than before. A few simple strategies will help you get the job done.

keeping your child clean

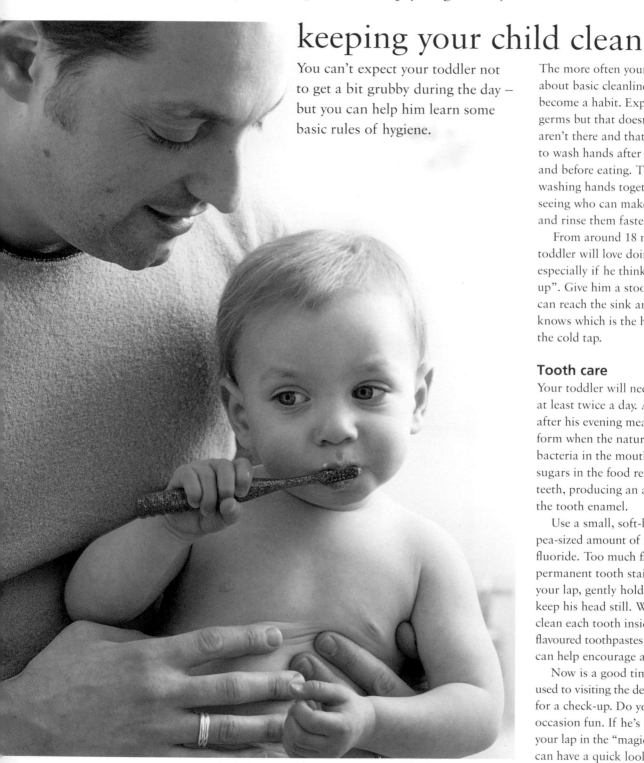

You can't expect your toddler not to get a bit grubby during the day – but you can help him learn some basic rules of hygiene.

The more often your toddler is reminded about basic cleanliness, the quicker it will become a habit. Explain that we can't see germs but that doesn't mean that they aren't there and that's why it's important to wash hands after going to the toilet and before eating. Then make it fun: washing hands together, for example, and seeing who can make them the soapiest and rinse them fastest is a good game.

From around 18 months onwards your toddler will love doing things for himself, especially if he thinks they are "grown-up". Give him a stool to stand on so he can reach the sink and check that he knows which is the hot and which is the cold tap.

Tooth care

Your toddler will need his teeth cleaned at least twice a day. After breakfast and after his evening meal is ideal as cavities form when the naturally occurring bacteria in the mouth combine with sugars in the food residues left on the teeth, producing an acid which attacks the tooth enamel.

Use a small, soft-bristled brush and a pea-sized amount of toothpaste containing fluoride. Too much fluoride could cause permanent tooth stains. Sit your child on your lap, gently holding his forehead to keep his head still. What's important is to clean each tooth inside and out. Different flavoured toothpastes and fun toothbrushes can help encourage a reluctant child.

Now is a good time to get your toddler used to visiting the dentist every six months for a check-up. Do your best to make the occasion fun. If he's nervous, sit him on your lap in the "magic" chair so the dentist can have a quick look inside his mouth.

Like a grown-up
Keep a stool handy for your toddler to stand on in front of the wash basin and she will be delighted to be able to start washing herself.

The magic of soap
Teaching your child good cleaning habits at this age will help ensure that she maintains them for the rest of her life.

Nail care

Keeping your toddler's fingernails and toenails trimmed will help him avoid scratching himself or others, and prevent the spread of infection as nails can harbour dirt and germs. Use specially designed blunt-ended scissors or nail clippers for safety and always trim toenails straight across (see page 111). If your toddler is frightened, try:
♦ trimming in the bath underwater – water is soothing and makes the nails softer
♦ doing your own nails first – show him what fun it is
♦ distracting him with a song such as "This Little Piggy".

Bath-time fun

Your toddler will probably spend many happy hours playing in the bath – especially if you provide him with lots of bath toys, such as empty and clean shampoo bottles, plastic boats, funnels, and cups. If your toddler refuses to get in the bath, try:
♦ focusing on his chance to have fun – "look at these lovely bubbles" – rather than just getting clean
♦ giving him a bath at an unexpected time – when it's not part of the everyday routine it may have more appeal
♦ jumping in with him – bathing together may be more fun than doing it alone.

Hair care

By now your toddler will probably have lots of hair and, though reluctant, will need to have it washed and cut more frequently.
♦ **Hair wash** Prevent tears by using a specially formulated baby shampoo. Ask your toddler if he wants to tip his head backwards or forwards – he may also like to hold a flannel over his eyes or even wear a pair of swimming goggles. Encourage him to help lather up the shampoo before rinsing quickly but thoroughly. The promise of a special game or story afterwards may help your toddler cooperate.
♦ **Haircut** Prepare your toddler for his first haircut with a game of "hairdressers" so he has an idea of what's going to happen. He may prefer to sit on your lap rather than in the hairdresser's chair to begin with. And it may be worth taking along some favourite snacks to distract him when necessary. Give him lots of praise for sitting still.

getting **dressed**

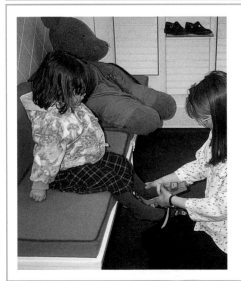

Your toddler's drive for independence may make dressing trickier than it used to be. She may no longer lie still and let you do all the work! The key to success is to make her feel involved in the process – give her a choice of what to wear, hold armholes and legs open for her to put her arms and legs in herself, and let her do the simple bits, such as pulling up her skirt, herself. Singing songs and playing games such as peekaboo can help.

Once your child has been walking well for a few weeks she can have her first pair of proper shoes. Go to a reputable shoe shop that will measure her feet – width and length – to find the correct fitting. Then check the fit of her shoes as often as once a month during this period (see page 185).

independence and tantrums

Your growing toddler is desperate to do things for herself. And although you'll need to stay calm and have lots of patience, encouraging her will build her confidence and help avoid frustration.

asserting her independence

As your toddler realizes that she is a separate person from you, she'll want to start doing things on her own.

Although letting her have a go may slow you down sometimes, in the long run, the more your toddler can do for herself the happier she'll be. She may, for example, soon be going to nursery or you may be expecting another baby – and you won't always be on hand to do things for her.

Independence is also vital for her emotional development; gaining a strong sense of herself by being able to do things on her own will do wonders for her sense of self-esteem.

Giving your support

Despite her desire for independence, your toddler still needs you. In fact, your support is more important than ever – she may want to manage on her own, but she is still trying to master lots of new skills and will often need your assistance. Give her lots of encouragement and praise to motivate her. She will love sharing how clever she is with you, so expect to spend a lot of time watching and applauding her!

Ways to help

♦ Allowing your toddler to have a go at something you know she can't manage then stepping in and taking over will probably leave her furious and tearful. Instead, be helpful but let her feel as if she's done it on her own.

What a clever girl!
Your enthusiasm and praise is the best reward when your toddler tries something new – even if she finds it difficult to master at first.

"I can dress myself!"
Your toddler loves being able to do things himself.

♦ Rather than prevent your toddler trying something because it will slow you down – such as getting herself dressed in the morning – build in extra time to let her be successful.

♦ Make sure your expectations are realistic. All children develop at different rates, so resist comparing your toddler with others. Instead, watch for when she wants to try something new, and help her step by step.

♦ Provide a safe environment – playgrounds can give your toddler the chance to be adventurous and help develop her sense of independence without putting her in danger.

Being consistent will help your toddler learn to accept certain limits – if the house rule is no biscuits before teatime stick with it, however hard she yells. At the same time, avoid too many limits. Setting as few as possible will help your child stay within the boundaries.

Gaining confidence
Providing a safe place to play and explore – sandpits are ideal – will help build your toddler's self-esteem and his confidence.

why your **toddler cries**

Your toddler may desperately want to be grown up, but she still needs lots of cuddles and comfort. Chances are she'll easily burst into tears during the day – and tears can sometimes turn to tantrums if not dealt with quickly. Common causes of tears at this age include:

♦ **Frustration** Either your toddler's desire to do something is ahead of her capabilities or else she is prevented by you from doing what she wants. Try to help her when you can and find as few reasons as possible to say no to her. Use redirection instead.

♦ **Tiredness** This is especially true at bedtime – try not to let your toddler become overtired as she'll be even harder to settle. A happy bedtime routine (see page 112) will help her relax and feel calm and secure.

♦ **Insecurity** Fear of being separated from you can last for many months (see page 171). Having a comfort object such as a special toy or blanket can provide the extra security she needs when you are not around.

♦ **Boredom** As your toddler is spending more time awake, there's more chance that she will get bored. And although she will love her toys, her attention span is

still quite short so they won't keep her amused for long. Although getting tasks done with a toddler in tow can slow you down, remember that being with you is her favourite activity.

♦ **Injury** Your toddler is more mobile than ever before and consequently will be much more prone to knocks and falls. Even a little scratch or bump can bring on serious sobbing. Always be sympathetic – your child will forget about the injury much faster if you tell her you know how much it hurts.

♦ **Teething** Between 10 and 14 months your toddler is likely to start cutting her first molars. These are harder to cut than incisors and could make your toddler feel miserable. Try the same remedies you used when she was younger (see page 112).

♦ **Hunger or thirst** If your toddler's blood sugar level drops because she's hungry or she's dehydrated from going short of fluids, she's more likely to be fretful and difficult. Make sure she has regular healthy snacks throughout the day – once in the morning, once in the afternoon, and even, if necessary, before brushing her teeth at bedtime. And encourage her to drink plenty of fluid – ideally plain water.

Temper, temper
When you first see your toddler throwing a tantrum it can be quite a shock, as she screams, kicks, and even hurls herself to the ground, oblivious to everyone and everything around her.

coping with tantrums

Not all toddlers have lots of tantrums – but around 18 months, when they experience a surge of independence, difficult behaviour is more common.

Your toddler has lots of new physical skills, can understand a lot and is determined to explore his capabilities. But he often finds he can't manage, or isn't allowed, to do what he wants. Tantrums – kicking and screaming if he can't get his own way, hitting out at other children, or refusing to cooperate over the simplest task – are an expression of the overwhelming frustration he feels when this happens.

Understanding your child

Tantrums often happen when your child is feeling less secure than usual or your attention is less closely focused on him. You might, for example, be with friends when your toddler wants something from

you. It's hard enough for him to make himself understood when he can't yet talk properly, and harder still if his parent is distracted and he is away from home and feels less secure than normal.

Thinking about the world from your toddler's point of view can sometimes help you see why he behaves the way he does. Knowing which situations your toddler finds hard to deal with can help avoid the frustrations that lead to tantrums.

Encouraging good behaviour

At this age it's important to help your child understand what good behaviour is. You can do this a number of ways:
♦ Give your toddler lots of praise and encouragement when he behaves well. Make your praise as specific as possible. Notice when he does something good, and tell him how pleased you are. He'll enjoy knowing that he's made you happy and this will encourage him to behave well again.

Don't expect too much – his learning will be slow as he has a very short attention span but over time he'll understand how he can get positive attention from you.
♦ Ignore some of the bad behaviour. If you get cross with him when he does something he shouldn't, he'll learn that one way to get your attention is to behave badly. Instead, if for example he throws a book which may hit another child, simply remove the book without saying a word.
♦ Redirect him when you can. If you see a potentially explosive situation arising – he refuses to put on his coat when it's time to go out, for example – sing him a funny song, and quickly slip his coat on while he's enjoying your antics.
♦ When you do help him get dressed or put on his shoes or finish a jigsaw, be subtle and diplomatic so he thinks he did it himself.
♦ Give him choices whenever you can. Letting him feel as if he has some control

over a situation can make all the difference. If, for example, he always refuses to wear the clothes you select, pull out a couple of suitable choices and let him decide which he'd like to wear.

♦ Recognize your toddler's flashpoints – and pre-empt them when you can.

♦ Avoid shouting or aggression – with him and with others, such as your partner. Children learn by example.

♦ Reward systems are great. The best rewards aren't treats or sweets, but attention from you.

♦ Don't take a firm stand if it's not important. Does it matter if he wears the red socks today, for instance? There is no point in inducing a tantrum by forcing him to wear the yellow ones that you chose.

♦ Use positive phrases to get him to do things. Toddlers are continually testing you and the boundaries you set, and if you listen to yourself you may realize you spend a large part of each day saying "No".

♦ Structure the day to avoid boredom and try to go out at least once a day. Think ahead for rainy days, and have a list of activities ready to amuse him.

Thinking ahead about which situations your child finds difficult – the supermarket shop when he's tired, or leaving a friend's house – can help you avoid them, or be ready with ways of dealing with them.

"Joe has already learned to scream to get his own way. I used to give in to him but when it kept happening I realized I had to be firm. Now, when he throws himself on the floor, I just walk away. Then he usually gets up and runs after me. I've also learned to be a bit crafty. He was banging on the TV the other day and the more I said 'no' the more he did it. So I got a biscuit tin and said: 'Come and bang on this, it sounds better.' He quickly forgot about the TV and really enjoyed banging on the tin!"

ANNE MARSHALL, MUM TO JOE
AGED **24** MONTHS

tantrums: **what you can do**

Even though it's natural for your toddler to want to assert himself, dealing with a tantrum – especially if it's in public – may test even the most calm parent. A full-blown tantrum is especially upsetting, for you and your toddler. Your child may fling himself on the floor, kick, scream, make himself retch and – most terrifying of all – hold his breath and turn blue in the face. Be reassured, however, that he won't harm himself – before he is in danger his own reflexes will force him to breathe again.

When your child has a tantrum:

♦ If possible, sit it out, as long as your child is not in danger. The sooner your child discovers that you are not responding the sooner he'll stop.

♦ Stay calm – remind yourself that you are the adult, he is the child. Show him by example what is acceptable behaviour.

♦ Improve your capacity to cope by not being embarrassed by your toddler's behaviour – every toddler has tantrums and any mother who might witness the tantrum is probably just relieved it's not her child.

♦ Remain kind but firm – if you change your mind, or give in, your toddler will simply learn that tantrums work. If he knows you won't change your mind, he will eventually realize that it's not worth the battle.

♦ Remember that tantrums are a normal part of a toddler's development and it's important not to take them personally; they are not aimed at you.

starting toilet training

You know your toddler is growing up when she makes the big step out of nappies into pants. This will not happen until your toddler's brain is developed enough to control her bowel and bladder, which can be any time between 18 and 36 months.

is she ready to start?

Social pressure to toilet train your toddler can be intense – but until she is physically and emotionally ready there's nothing you can do to help speed up the process.

First your child's nerve pathways from her bladder to her brain need to be fully mature. This usually happens around 18 months and means she will begin to realize when she's doing a wee or a poo. But she still won't be able to predict when she needs to empty her bowels or bladder – it will be some time before she's familiar with the feelings of needing to go and has the physical control to hang on. This usually happens by two and half, although it can be a lot earlier or a lot later.

Signs to watch out for

The more ready your child is for toilet training, the faster and easier it will be. Signs that she is ready include:
♦ knowing when she is doing a wee or a poo – she may stop playing, stand still, look at you, go red in the face, and even try and tell you what's happening
♦ if she is naked, looking at the puddle she has made and clutching herself
♦ understanding what you are talking about when you show her a potty and explain what it is for
♦ willingness to try sitting on the toilet or the potty – even if she isn't actually using it
♦ wanting to copy you, and use the toilet or wear proper pants.

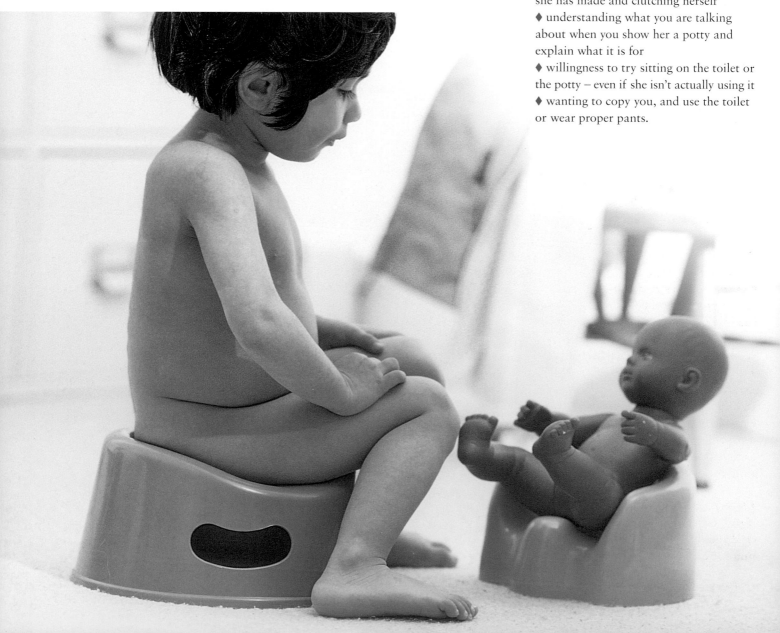

introducing **the potty**

Even though at 18 months your toddler probably isn't ready to start using the potty successfully, you may like to have a potty around the house to give her the chance to get used to it.

♦ Choose a potty that won't tip up when it's sat on or when your child stands up. It should be curved inside for easy cleaning with a moulded back support, have a splash guard at the front and a slot for carrying. Your toddler may like to help choose one.

♦ Put the potty in the bathroom next to the toilet and encourage her to sit on it before a bath when you take off her nappy. If she does anything praise her, if she doesn't don't worry. If she resists sitting on it, don't make a fuss – just try again a week or so later.

♦ Let your toddler see you using the toilet – most toddlers enjoy copying their parents.

♦ Remember this is just about introducing the idea of the potty – not getting your child out of nappies. The more prepared your toddler is the easier toilet training will be (see pages 138–139).

Make it fun

You should never force your child to sit on a potty or insist she stays on it when she's obviously had enough. There's no harm, however, in a little extra encouragement. Sometimes this is all that's needed to spark an interest in potty training. You could, for example, try:

♦ getting a child's picture book about using a potty from a bookshop or library and reading it with your toddler

♦ surrounding her potty with things to look at – such as her favourite books and toys

♦ suggesting she can watch a video while she sits on the potty

♦ playing games together which involve her teddies and dolls using the potty

♦ giving her lots of praise even if she sits on the potty but then gets up without having done anything.

Take your time

If you start trying to potty train your child and she has repeated accidents, then stop and go back to nappies for a few weeks. Don't be cross with your toddler – it's not a reflection on her or on you. Making an issue out of it may delay progress even further. And after all, there's no hurry – your toddler will get there in her own time. Even if you are expecting another baby and would prefer not to have to deal with two lots of nappies, you won't want to deal with

Getting ready to give up nappies
In the early days, while your child is getting used to the idea of using a potty, trainer pants made of towelling and with a waterproof backing – can be useful.

puddles and potties at the same time as coping with a newborn. Also, your toddler will be more responsive if she's not having to cope with other changes in her life such as getting used to a new sibling.

"From quite early on we had a potty in the bathroom, although it wasn't until Daniel was about 22 months that he was happy to try sitting on it. Occasionally this coincided with a wee – and I'd praise him ecstatically! But I didn't push it – he obviously wasn't really interested. When he was about two years and two months he clearly knew if he was doing a poo. As this generally happened around the same time each day – shortly after breakfast – I'd suggest he sat on the potty while I read him a book."

JOANNA HILL, MUM TO DANIEL AGED TWO AND A HALF

family life

One minute he's testing your patience, the next melting your heart – one thing is certain, with your toddler you will never be bored! Living with an emotional whirlwind can be tiring, so take a break occasionally and find time for yourself.

Part of the family
Your toddler will love joining in activities, although she may get frustrated if she can't keep up. Find a task she can manage and give her lots of praise.

riding a roller coaster

Life with a toddler is full of extremes. One minute he's clinging to you refusing to let go, the next he's wriggling out of your arms and refusing to be cuddled.

He's bursting with energy, and moves fast but usually in the opposite direction to you! He wants to be with you, copy you, and join in with everything you do, yet he also rages against you and it seems as if nothing you do is right. He's like an emotional whirlwind, and living with him can be tiring. Providing him with a safe environment – in the home, or out and about – will give him the chance to explore without putting himself in danger or forcing you to rein him in all the time (see pages 262–266).

Going at his pace – allowing yourself extra time to get to the post office, being there for cuddles when he wants them and not minding when he doesn't – will also help you both avoid feeling frustrated.

Handling your feelings
There will be times when your toddler pushes you to your limit with his irrational behaviour and your patience snaps. Losing your temper occasionally is understandable – talk to other mums of toddlers and you'll discover that you are not alone. Feeling guilty won't help – forgiving yourself will. Apologize to your toddler, explain that it was what he did –

having **another baby?**

You may find that you are starting to think about having another baby and wondering what the best age gap is between children. Some parents think that the closer in age children are the more likely they are to be friends, while others feel that the bigger the age gap the more time and energy there is for each child. There are no hard and fast rules – each family is different, and what works well for one may not work so well for another.

If you do decide to go ahead and expand your family, there will come a point in your pregnancy when you need to prepare your toddler for the arrival of his new sibling.

♦ Wait until the last few months of pregnancy before talking to your toddler about it – when he can see your bump he'll find it easier to understand what's happening.

♦ Explain to your toddler why your tummy is growing; let him touch and stroke your bump and say "hello" to the baby inside.

♦ Find a picture book in the library to help him identify with another little boy expecting a new baby in the family.

♦ Talk about friends and family who have younger brothers and sisters.

♦ Include him as much as possible in the preparations so he doesn't feel left out.

♦ Look at photos together of when your toddler was a baby; and give him lots of care and attention to help reassure him of your love.

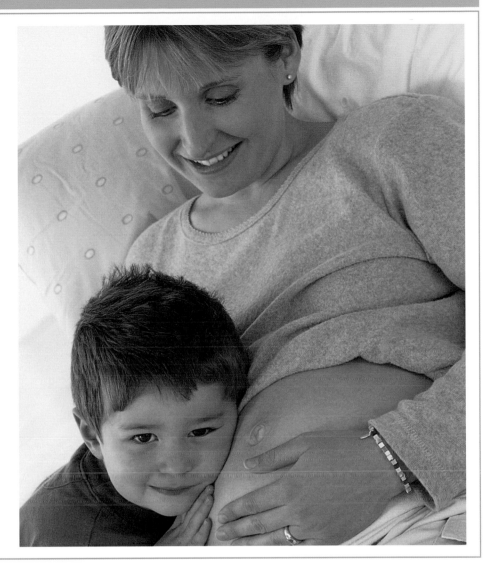

and not him – that you didn't like. Then give him a hug. He'll forget about it quickly, and it will help if you can, too.

Time for yourself

Spending quality time with your toddler, doing something you both enjoy, such as baking cakes or having a bath together, will help you feel close to him.

It's important also to spend some time on your own. Your toddler demands your constant attention and sometimes the daily routine can feel pretty relentless. You can give him your best only when you are feeling happy and refreshed. Have a break whenever you can – whether it's a weekend away with your partner or an afternoon spent shopping on your own.

"When he's not tired, hungry, or coming down with a cold Louis is angelic. He smothers me with affection, makes me laugh, and is a great companion. And as long as I'm one step ahead of him – ready with a snack when he needs one, avoiding tricky situations – the day goes smoothly. I try and make sure I get some adult contact during the day. Getting out of the house is really important – especially on days when Louis is a bit grizzly or clingy."

PHILIPPA DESMOND, MUM TO LOUIS AGED 20 MONTHS

caring for your toddler
24 to 36 months

Your toddler is growing up fast – she can run and jump, put on her own coat, and will soon be out of nappies and starting at nursery or playgroup. She's full of life – and desperate to be grown up – but she still needs lots of hugs and cuddles, too!

Growing up

This is an exciting year for you and your toddler. She is now a real companion – and you will have lots of fun together, whether it's walking in the park, looking at books, or making cakes. Family outings can be more ambitious – lunch out at your local pizza restaurant, for example, can be an enjoyable occasion for everyone, even if you have to take a few distractions with you.

Your toddler will enjoy playing with other children, too – and you may decide later in the year that she's ready for nursery school or playgroup. This is a big step for her, and you too. Knowing what to expect – and how to handle her feelings as well as your own – will help this be a happy experience.

Sometime during this stage you will probably say goodbye to nappies – at least during the day time. Recognizing when the time is right and giving your toddler lots of praise and encouragement will help make toilet training a success.

Facing fears

Although she's desperate to feel independent, your toddler will still sometimes feel anxious and come running back into your arms. She has a better understanding of the world around her, but she's not always sophisticated enough to make sense of it. It's common for children of this age to develop fears – whether it's being scared of the dark or frightened of dogs. Lots of support will help these fears pass.

Your time

As your toddler becomes increasingly independent, she may be less demanding at home as she discovers ways to occupy herself. And once she starts at nursery or playgroup, you may find yourself on your own for a few hours during the week.

Both you and your toddler will face a period of adjustment as you settle into your new routines. She may be extra tired when she comes home and test the boundaries more than usual. Meanwhile, unless there's a second baby to care for, you will be looking for ways to spend your newfound free time.

"Our favourite day is Tuesdays. We go to the park to feed the ducks together and then have a hot chocolate and croissant in the cafe. It's a treat for both of us!"

LIZZIE WOODS,
MUM TO JACK AGED NEARLY THREE

food and your child

Your toddler is eating a wide range of food and will love taking part in family meals – at home or in a restaurant. She's also mixing more with other toddlers and you may find sweets and sugary drinks become harder to avoid.

a healthy, balanced diet

Your child still needs protein for growth, carbohydrates and fats for energy, and fruit and vegetables for vitamins and fibre.

So continue to offer your toddler foods from the four main food groups (see page 106). Try to serve four small portions of fruit and vegetables a day – for example, a tangerine as a snack, carrots with lunch, diluted orange juice as a drink, and banana and custard as a pudding. If you can't buy fresh, offer frozen, canned, or dried varieties.

Your toddler can have semi-skimmed milk, although if she is very active she may benefit from the additional energy provided by full-fat milk. Limit milk intake. Too much milk may reduce her appetite for other important foods. She should have about quarter of a litre (half a pint) a day. If she won't drink milk, supplement her intake with full-fat cheese, fromage frais, and yogurt. Avoid low-fat foods as toddlers need fat as a source of energy, and don't give too many wholemeal products as the extra fibre can prevent minerals being absorbed properly.

Remember to include oily fish, such as salmon, mackerel, sardines, and pilchards, as well as white fish. Lentils and beans are a great meat alternative, but your toddler's digestive system won't be able to cope with large daily portions.

five tips for
healthy eating

♦ Avoid foods that are high in saturated fats and additional salt and sugar.

♦ Steam, bake, grill, or boil foods rather than frying or roasting.

♦ Use as many fresh ingredients as possible.

♦ Give her water or diluted fruit juice when she is thirsty.

♦ Offer raw vegetables (carrot, celery, or cucumber sticks), fruit, or bread as snacks.

Family meals
Getting together as a family at meal times is an important aspect of family life – but don't expect too much from your toddler.

Eating with the family

Life is so busy for lots of families that sitting down together for a family meal sometimes doesn't happen as much as we'd like. Eating together, however, is one of the best ways of encouraging your toddler to enjoy her food. She loves imitating, and is more likely to try something new if she sees mummy or daddy enjoying it.

Chatting around the table will also give her a chance to develop her social skills, and watching how you behave will help lay the foundations for good table manners. Try:

♦ eating together as often as possible – if you can't get everyone around the table at the same time, sit with your toddler so she's not eating alone

♦ getting your toddler involved – encouraging her to help you lay the table,

or take a dish out to the kitchen will help her enjoy the sense of occasion

♦ avoiding arguments – meal times should be a chance to relax and enjoy each other's company; try not to get drawn into battles over food likes and dislikes

♦ not to expect too much – your toddler won't have the patience to sit unoccupied at the table for too long. Once she's finished let her leave.

Dining out

Going out to eat can be fun for the whole family. Explain to your toddler beforehand what to expect and chances are she'll rise to the occasion.

♦ Time your outing – if your toddler is tired, or too hungry to endure a wait, she is unlikely to cope well.

♦ Choose a child-friendly place – lots of

restaurants provide highchairs, crayons and paper, plus a special children's menu.

♦ Take your own distractions – a favourite book or selection of small toys will help keep your child amused while she's waiting for her food or when she's finished.

♦ Go for speed – select a restaurant that serves food without much of a wait and choose what you want as quickly as possible. When your toddler has obviously had enough, you and your partner may need to take it in turns to take her outside for a change of scenery.

♦ Avoid the danger of spills by taking her own cup with a lid, even if she can usually manage a normal cup.

♦ Order her favourites – she will enjoy her meal more if she's served things she likes.

♦ Give her lots of praise – telling her how grown-up she has been will encourage her to behave well next time, too.

Eating on the go
Children often get hungry when you're out and about, so take with you lots of healthy snacks such as bread sticks or fruit.

protecting **her teeth**

♦ Avoid using sweets or desserts as a reward.

♦ Introduce a "sweety day" when your toddler has her weekly ration of sweets. Encourage her to choose chocolate rather than chewy sweets.

♦ Tell relatives and caregivers about your sweet policy so they can stick to it, too.

♦ Avoid sweetened or fizzy drinks.

♦ Remember that dried fruit contains lots of sugar, and can also cause tooth decay. Keep it for meal times or outings.

♦ Check food labels: sugar can appear in many forms, including dextrose, glucose, honey, maltose syrup, invert syrup, and concentrated fruit juice.

♦ Brush teeth after breakfast, at bedtime, and after sweets if possible.

toilet training

Your toddler is ready to come out of nappies and you've bought his first pair of pants. Choose a quiet day to try toilet training: be prepared for the occasional accident, and remember to give reminders and plenty of praise.

ready, steady, go

Some time this year your toddler will probably make the big step out of nappies and into pants, if it hasn't happened already.

Between the ages of 18 and 36 months his bowel and bladder muscles will mature, helping him to predict when he needs to go to the toilet. If you've already introduced the idea of the potty (see page 130) and he's watched you both using the toilet, your toddler will have a firm idea of what's expected. But how do you know when to take the plunge and start leaving his nappy off?

tips for **easy training**

♦ If you can, start toilet training in the summer when your toddler can run around in the garden without a nappy on.

♦ Dress your toddler in clothes he can easily manage himself – zips on trousers and clasps on dungarees are hard for small fingers. Pull-up trousers with elastic waistbands, skirts, and dresses are best.

♦ Suggest your toddler uses the potty after a meal – a story or video may provide an incentive.

♦ If you have just a few successes, persevere – switching back to nappies occasionally because it's more convenient may confuse your toddler.

♦ When he has an accident don't react negatively – just remind your toddler what the potty is for and change him without a fuss.

♦ Encourage your toddler with lots of praise and remind him how grown-up he is now.

Ask yourself:
♦ is he interested in using a potty?
♦ can he indicate when he has the urge to go? Watch out for the look on his face – is he clutching himself, aware that something is about to happen?
♦ can he pull his trousers and pants down without your help?

Leaving his nappy off

Buying some pants together will help focus your toddler's attention. Make it a special occasion – tell him he's a big boy now and let him choose which design he'd like. Choose a morning or afternoon when you are both at home together then take off his nappy and explain that without it on he will have to use the potty when he needs a wee or a poo. After the first couple of mornings or afternoons, start to leave the nappy off for longer and more frequent periods. Meanwhile, give him lots of reminders.

Staying calm

Expect accidents and don't be angry or make a fuss. For your toddler, using a potty instead of a nappy is all about learning a new skill. Put any pressure on him and he'll quickly decide it's not worth it!
♦ Never force your child to sit on the potty, even if you are sure he needs to use it – your toddler likes to think he's in charge and may prefer to assert himself by refusing to do what you want.
♦ Avoid words such as "good" or "bad" – if your toddler has an accident one day just remind him that tomorrow he may not.
♦ If your toddler does have an accident try to hide any feelings of disgust you may have – it may not be pleasant, but your toddler may be upset or worried about doing a poo if he sees you reacting badly.
♦ If there are lots of accidents it may be a sign that he's not quite ready yet. Leave it a week or more before trying again.

Out and about

Minimize the chance of accidents by always putting your toddler on the potty before you go out. You could also take the potty with you. Just in case, take a spare set of clothes out with you, too. Lots of

I'm so grown up
Teach your toddler how to flush the loo and wash her hands each time she uses it so good hygiene quickly becomes a habit.

mums use trainer pants for outings as they absorb accidents yet can be pulled up and down just like ordinary pants.

Using a toilet

Once your toddler is happy using a potty he may like to try the toilet. He'll need a sturdy stool to step up on and a toilet trainer seat so he feels safe. Your toddler may like you to hold him while he's on the toilet. Even if he can get up and down easily and pull up his own pants and trousers, he will still need help wiping himself for a while yet. For a girl, that means teaching her to wipe from front to back, particularly after bowel movements, because contact between the faeces and urethra or vagina can lead to urinary tract or vaginal infections.

Night-time training

Even when your toddler is dry during the day, he may still need nappies for daytime naps and at bedtime. Encourage him to use the potty before going to sleep. Once you've noticed that he is regularly waking up early in the morning with a dry nappy, you can leave it off at night. As there may still be the occasional accident, put a waterproof cover on his mattress.

why is he having accidents again?

Sometimes a toddler who has been happily out of nappies for a while will suddenly start refusing to use the potty and having accidents. If there's no medical cause (such as a urinary tract infection) it might be that your toddler is feeling anxious about something – such as a new baby in the family – or is reacting to the pressure to perform. Or maybe your toddler isn't getting to the potty or toilet in time because he wants you with him – it can be many months before children of this age are able to manage in the bathroom entirely on their own.

Show your toddler that accidents are not a problem – simply change him, while reminding him gently about the potty. A bit of variety might help – a different coloured potty, new toilet seat, some more grown-up pants, or fancy loo paper. Encourage your toddler to feel grown-up in other areas of his life, and he may feel less of a need to assert himself when it comes to using the potty.

crying and sleep

Your toddler's ability to cope with his active life will depend a lot on how much sleep he has. Many seemingly trivial things will make him cry as he struggles to understand the world around him.

a need for sleep

Your toddler needs between 10 and 12 hours sleep within each 24-hour period, although during a growth spurt you may find he needs more.

Depending on how early he goes to bed, when he wakes up, and how much stimulation he has during the day, your toddler may or may not still need an afternoon nap. Some manage a couple of days without a nap, then each third day or so make up for it with a long afternoon sleep.

Crying and comforting

Toddlers at this age can cry a lot. Being overtired is a common cause for tears. Low-grade whining is usual, too, especially

"Our neighbour's dog always barked when we went to visit. Violet was terrified of the noise and became frightened of all dogs. When we went to the park, she'd run crying into my arms if one came anywhere near her. Then we went on holiday with friends, and they brought their dog Rosie, too. Violet saw the other children playing with Rosie, and my husband and I made a point of stroking and talking to the dog as well. During the week Violet became calmer when Rosie was around and even tentatively tried to stroke her. She's now much less scared of all animals – and more confident in herself."

EMMA COLE, MUM TO VIOLET
AGED 36 MONTHS

when your toddler wants something he can't have. Your child is also experiencing lots of new emotions – such as guilt, jealousy, and dislike – and sometimes these feelings will cause him to cry. Until he learns to manage these feelings they may simply overwhelm him. One way to help is to tune into your toddler – and then change your own mood. If you are irritated when he gets cross, for example, try being gentle instead. Meeting his anger with yours will only make him more upset, whereas sympathy and understanding can make all the difference.

It's also common for children of this age to become easily frightened. Although you might not be able to banish fear from your child's life, you can make a huge difference to the way he handles it. Telling your child, for example, that he's silly will only make him more scared as he has to face his fear without your support. Instead, take his fears seriously and encourage him to talk to you about them. Your child trusts you and if he sees you are not worried his own fear will start to be manageable.

Bedwetting

It's not unusual for a toddler who is otherwise dry at night to occasionally wet the bed. Night-time accidents often

Night-time comfort
Lots of toddlers like to take a special dolly, teddy, or blanket to bed to help them feel calm and relaxed as they fall asleep.

continue up to five or six years, especially in boys. Check your toddler always uses the toilet before bedtime and use a waterproof cover to protect the mattress. Stay calm when accidents happen so your child doesn't become anxious. If accidents continue, you may want to go back into night-time nappies for a while. If bedwetting persists, however, check with your GP.

coping with **nightmares**

Nightmares
Occasionally children have bad dreams. If your child seems happy during the day there's no reason to worry – although you might want to find out if he saw something scary or unsuitable on television or in a book. If your child wakes in the night go to him straight away, and reassure him that it was just a dream and dreams can't hurt him. Tell him that everyone has dreams – and when he goes back to sleep it will be gone. Show him that he's safe in his bedroom, then stay with him until he falls back to sleep.

Night terrors
If your child appears awake – eyes open – but very frightened and thrashing around the bed, he may be having a night terror. Seeing your child like this is very upsetting but you need to stay calm. Sit next to him to make sure he doesn't hurt himself, but don't try to wake him. Remember that he is not actually awake, even though he may look as if he is, and anything he can see or feel is only part of the night terror. After a while he will become calm and, without waking, settle back down. In the morning, he will remember nothing about it.

starting playgroup or nursery

Your older toddler will enjoy making new friends and playing with new toys at playgroup or nursery – but how will she cope with leaving you? Choosing the right pre-school, and knowing how to settle her in, will help her relish this new experience.

preparing **your child**

♦ The more secure your toddler feels, the more easily she'll be able to cope with new situations. Long before she starts at pre-school remember to keep heaping on the praise and boosting her confidence.

♦ Going together to a parent-and-toddler group will help your child be comfortable with other children – once she starts wandering away from you to play, you know she'll soon be ready for playgroup.

♦ Once you've chosen a playgroup or nursery go along for a visit so she knows where everything is and can meet the staff.

♦ Find out how each session is run and, a few days before she starts, talk to your toddler about what to expect.

♦ Help her learn a few skills such as how to put on and take off her coat, drink from a cup, go to the toilet on her own.

♦ Don't overwhelm her with the newness of it all – too big a build-up may make her feel anxious.

♦ Be positive – acknowledge any worries she has and talk about them, but don't let your child pick up on any anxieties you may have. She will gain confidence from you and your calmness will be reassuring.

what to expect

Pre-school is good for your toddler – she'll learn how to play with other children, experience new ideas, and get used to being away from home.

But starting nursery or playgroup can still be unsettling. Although your toddler is desperate to be independent, she also needs lots of reassurance. She has little concept of time, and although you tell her you'll be back in half an hour, she will learn only through experience what this actually means.

Settling her in

The first day will probably be difficult for both of you. If you've prepared your toddler beforehand (see opposite) settling her in may be a little easier.

Most playgroups and nurseries will encourage you to stay at least for the first session. Sitting quietly watching will allow your child to get involved without worrying that you're going to disappear suddenly. Once you can see your child happily involved in an activity, tell her you're going to pop to the shops and will be back shortly (and do come back when you said you would).

Say goodbye and leave calmly and without hesitation: if your toddler sees you hovering around the door she'll think you don't want to leave her there. But never slip away without telling your child you are going – tears may be upsetting for you but if your child is feeling unsettled, disappearing without warning will only make matters worse.

If your child is clingy and cries, you may want to build up gradually the time you are away over the next few days until she is happy to see you go. If the crying continues every time you leave it could be just for your benefit – staff will probably tell you that once you have left she is fine, and you can always peep through the window to check for yourself!

Choosing the right place

At this age, you have two choices when considering pre-school for your child.
♦ **Playgroups** These are less formal than nursery schools and often take children from as early as two and a half.
♦ **Nursery school** These usually offer a more structured session. State-run nurseries may not offer your child a place until she is in her fourth year, although some may take younger children.

Both playgroups and nurseries offer similar activities, including sand and water play, fantasy play, outdoor games, story time, cooking, and creative play – and your child will have lots of opportunity to play with other children, essential for helping her develop her social skills.

Before you make any decisions about which pre-school is best for your child, try

to visit several. Points to look for include:
♦ are staff welcoming and friendly, and do they look as if they enjoy their work?
♦ how many children are there? Do they seem happy? How are they disciplined?
♦ what is the standard of the facilities? Is it a stimulating environment?

Ask if you can sit in for a session so you can get a feel for the school. And think about the needs of your own child. If your child is energetic and outgoing, she may thrive best somewhere with lots of outdoor space. If your child is shy and cautious, you may want to look for a small and intimate pre-school.

dressing **herself**

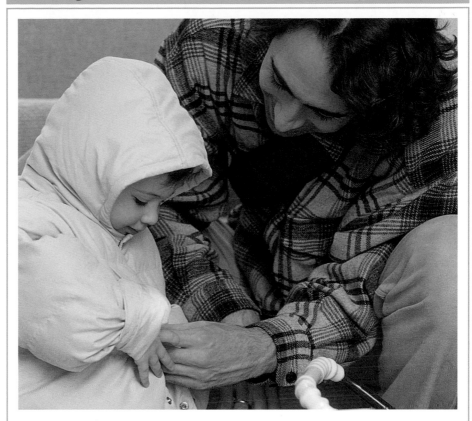

Teaching your child a few practical skills such as dressing herself can make settling into nursery school a little easier. Choose clothes with fastenings that are not too fiddly to manage.

♦ Help her practise taking her coat on and off by herself – if it has a zip fastening attach a ring to the zip tab to make it easier for her to pull up and down.

♦ Most toddlers can manage shoes that are done up with Velcro better than buckles and laces, although they won't necessarily get them on the right feet!

♦ Trousers that are elasticated at the waist are much easier to pull up and down than those with zip fastenings. Show her how to sit down to put her feet into the trouser legs before standing up to pull them up.

♦ Dresses with fastenings at the front rather than the back will be easier for your daughter to do up on her own.

"In our village all the children start off at the local playgroup. Katrina loves going but she's mature for her age and we're hoping she'll be offered a place at the local primary school's nursery when she's four. A more structured environment would suit her better now."

SALLY HUGHES, MUM TO KATRINA AGED NEARLY THREE

the next step

Starting your toddler at nursery school or playgroup will be a big step for you as well as him. You may be thrilled by your new-found freedom, or experience a sense of loss as he starts to develop a life of his own. Being prepared can help.

a new routine

When your toddler starts nursery or playgroup you may have conflicting feelings.

On the one hand you are proud of his step towards independence – and probably excited too about the freedom it gives you. On the other, you are anxious about his safety and wellbeing – suddenly he is out of your sight for part of the day and you have no control over what he's doing. You want him to be happy and feel special, but you may also feel jealous about the close relationship he has with his teacher.

It's natural to feel protective of your child – but it's important not to hold him back because of your own fears. Feeling confident about your choice of pre-school will help calm a lot of worries. Talking to the staff about any concerns you may have and getting to know other parents and their children will also help. Try not to let your toddler sense your worries: appearing relaxed and confident about this big step will help him take it in his stride.

Time for yourself

Once your toddler starts playgroup or nursery you will have a couple of free hours to yourself. Unless you have a new baby to care for, it may feel odd being without your toddler. You may miss his company and wonder what to do with yourself. Or you might feel overwhelmed by all the things you can do now your hands are free.

Bear in mind that a few hours each day passes very quickly. Trying to cram a hundred and one tasks into that short amount of time will leave you feeling exhausted. Doing nothing, however, may leave you feeling lonely. Managing your time so there's a balance between doing something for yourself and keeping up with the chores will be more satisfying. If you can't think what to do, here are some ideas you might like to build into your new weekly routine.

♦ **Exercising** You could join a gym, go swimming, or meet up with friends for a jog round the park. Exercise is great for boosting your energy and lifting your spirits, and if you are planning another baby now's a good time to get fit for pregnancy.

Shaping up
Enjoy your new-found free time once your toddler starts nursery or playschool. Exercise at home or out and about can give a great boost to your spirits.

♦ **Relaxing** On the sofa with a good book, soaking in a hot bath, sunbathing in the garden – giving yourself a chance to recharge your batteries helps family life go more smoothly.

♦ **Meeting friends for a coffee** Meet up with ex-work colleagues or friends who don't have children. Taking a mental break from parenthood is as important as physically taking a break.

♦ **Taking a class** Whether it's to continue your education or explore a new interest, this can be stimulating and sociable.

At home

In the early days your toddler is bound to be more tired after his sessions at nursery school or playgroup and you may find him grumpy and difficult to deal with. This is an age when toddlers are typically testing the limits set down by their parents – and tiredness can make children dig their heels in even more if they don't like what they are being told.

Tears and tantrums can be especially upsetting if you've missed your toddler while he was away. Try to remember, however, that it's because he feels secure and happy with you that he can behave the way he does.

♦ Don't expect too much from him when he's back at home – sitting down quietly reading stories together or watching a video might be more relaxing than a trip round the supermarket or tea with friends.

♦ Avoid confrontations as much as possible. Although it's important to continue to set secure limits, try not to say "no" too often – instead use humour or a gentle challenge (can you finish your peas before I finish mine?) to get him to do what you want.

♦ Give him lots of support and reassurance – knowing that you can cope with his feelings, even if he can't, will eventually teach him how to manage them himself.

Sibling rivalry

Life at home with your toddler may be extra hard if you have a new baby. Toddlers often display either overwhelming love or extreme dislike for a new arrival – sometimes both feelings almost simultaneously. Feeling threatened by a new brother or sister is

Brothers and sisters
With time and patience your toddler will learn to love his baby brother or sister – and one day soon they will be great playmates.

entirely natural – although you can do lots to help smooth the way by preparing your toddler in advance (see page 133). Once the baby has arrived and her novelty has worn off, try to minimize sibling rivalry by making sure your toddler has his own space and toys to play with well out of the baby's inquisitive reach.

Spending time together playing games both your baby and toddler will enjoy – such as hide and seek or singing songs and doing the actions – will encourage your toddler to see the baby as a potential playmate. And don't forget to put aside some special time every day when you can be alone with your toddler so he knows he is still important.

"When the girls were just over two they dropped their afternoon sleep. By teatime they were often very tired and emotional – and early evenings were a nightmare! I also felt very frustrated – I no longer had a couple of free hours when they were asleep to get things done. Now they are at playgroup and we are all happier. Martha and Josie love it – and having time for myself is wonderful."

CAROLINE WATTON, MUM TO TWINS MARTHA AND JOSIE AGED THREE YEARS

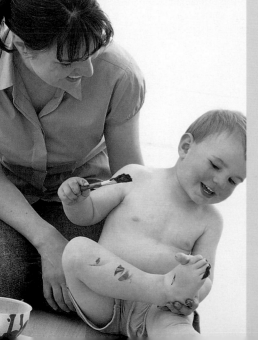

development

Watching your child grow and learn is one of the most satisfying aspects of being a parent. From reaching out to grasp your finger, to crawling or learning to draw, her physical growth and social, emotional, and intellectual development are inextricably linked. The following pages explain a young child's development at every stage, and guide you on choosing the right playthings and activities so that your child can make the most of learning through play. You will discover how to bring out the best in your child, and, equally importantly, how to let her enjoy just being a child.

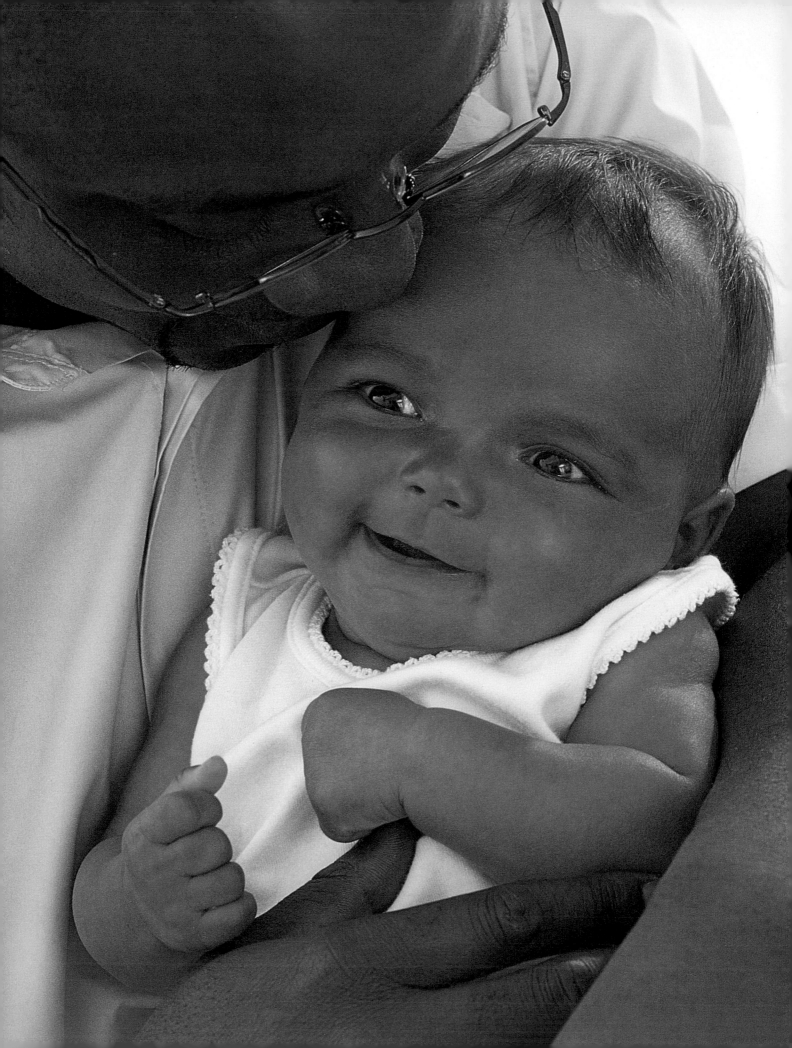

your developing baby
birth to 6 months

From the moment she is born, your baby will develop at an amazing pace. At the same time, every achievement that she makes, every new milestone that she passes, is a result of all that you do to make sure she is happy, secure, and loved.

Your baby is unique

The most important point to remember as your newborn grows is that babies develop at different rates. Like all babies, yours will eventually smile, lift her head, babble, and grab things, all at her own pace. She won't do something just because a book says she will or because you want her to. The "right time" will be when she is ready.

Charts and books such as this one can offer only general guides to how babies develop. You cannot speed up the development timetable, but if you are giving your baby lots of love and attention, you are giving her exactly what she needs: the wherewithal to develop at her own pace.

Your baby's development doesn't happen in isolation from the rest of the world; she can learn and progress only by being part of it. Having you, your partner, siblings, friends, and family members there is fundamental to her learning and developing.

Not only does she learn by example, she needs acknowledgement, love, and encouragement from the people around her in order to reach her full potential. So by doing what comes naturally – cuddling her, talking to her, going to her when she cries – you are giving her a sense of security and confidence that allows her to learn.

You are developing, too

As your baby learns to do more and more, your skills as a parent will adapt to meet her new needs. By your baby's four-month birthday, you will probably have established a daily routine for her, revolving around feeding, napping, going for a walk, bathing, and going to sleep at night. A routine will help you both feel secure and confident, and will provide the foundations of your life together as a family.

The development process

Development is rarely a linear process: occasionally your baby's development may seem to take a step backwards. For example, she may have slept through the night for several weeks and then suddenly start waking up every three hours again for no obvious reason. Such seemingly backward steps are perfectly normal – in fact, they are often a sign that she is about to take a developmental leap forward. You may find that a week or two down the line, she is considerably more alert and responsive to people and events around her, or she is sleeping less during the day than before.

By playing games such as "This Little Piggy" on your two month old's toes, you are introducing her to the delights of anticipation (in this particular case, the tickle at the end) as well as the nature of counting rhythms. A game of "Hide the Teddy" with your five month old will help her understand that objects exist even when she cannot see them.

playing is learning

Playing with your baby provides the fabric of her learning experiences. Every time you play or interact with her, you are not just entertaining her – you're teaching her valuable lessons about herself, about you, and about the world.

For example, by shaking a rattle for your new baby, you are helping her learn to focus, as well as introducing her to the concept of cause and effect – after a while she will begin to understand that shaking the rattle is what makes the noise.

While playing simple games, you'll find your baby is developing her own sense of humour, and she will soon start to let you know just how funny she finds your jokes!

the first 6 months

Each time you pick him up, play with him, talk or sing to him, smile at him, or soothe him, you are giving your baby information about his world and what it means to be a human being. Above all, you are teaching him that he is loved.

how your baby learns

The security you give your baby gives him the confidence to explore his environment. As the weeks and months pass, he will delight and impress you with a dazzling array of new skills.

He will start to control his own body, and learn that he can influence his environment (by kicking at his toys hanging from his baby gym to make them move, for example). He will respond to you with real excitement, communicate his needs and desires, and

know just how to make you laugh. He will also respond to the sounds, rhythms, and tones of language and will love to practise his own. He will be fascinated by his environment, and is an active participant in everything going on around him.

Best of all, your baby will become adept at expressing real pleasure in life – smiling, gurgling, cooing – and he will know just how to make you feel this pleasure, too.

Being your baby's "teacher" doesn't mean you have to give him constant stimulation or surround him with bits of coloured plastic. "Playing" with your

baby during these early months is about providing for his basic needs: food, warmth, comfort, touch, and love.

Helping his development

Research shows that parents tend to do this naturally, but here are some pointers on how to help him get the best out of his developing sense of awareness.

♦ **Stimulate his senses** Before he can move about independently, your baby explores the world with his five senses – sight, touch, taste, hearing, and smell.

♦ **Face him** Make eye contact with your baby. This will help him learn to communicate and to feel secure.

♦ **Get him involved** Point out things, describe them, and talk to him all the time. By doing this, you are helping him pick up language as well as stimulating his curiosity.

♦ **Repeat yourself** Babies learn by repetition, and you'll help him by repeating words to promote recognition.

♦ **Take his lead** Don't push your baby to play if he's not in the mood; learn to read his cues.

♦ **Act it out** Describe and demonstrate whatever you are saying or doing. Babies really respond to exaggerated expressions.

♦ **Entertain him** Play new games, think of new songs, and give him new experiences

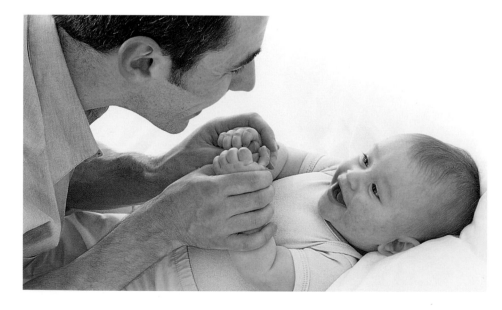

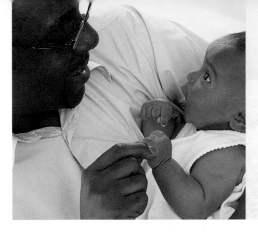

when you can, so he doesn't get bored.

♦ **Respond to him** If he cries, cuddle him. If he laughs, laugh with him. Acknowledge how he's feeling.

♦ **Tell him he's fantastic** Just like adults, babies love to be encouraged and told how clever they are.

Your baby's temperament

Many factors contribute to your baby's temperament. Genetics, gender, social environment, and number of siblings all play a large part. Of course, most of these factors are not within your control, and you will become well aware that you cannot choose your baby's personality.

But by far the most important of all influences on your baby during the first months – and years – of his life is his relationship with you. You may not be able to choose what "type" of baby you have, but the way you interact with him and respond to him now can have an incredible influence on his developing character.

Evolving personality

Whatever personality he has, he will benefit from your love and attention. By following his cues, and being as nurturing as possible, tending to his needs and responding to his cries when he is tiny, you can help him establish a strong sense of confidence and self-worth. Feeling confident and secure is not only a major asset in life, it is also fundamental to development.

Remember that your baby's personality is constantly evolving. Try not to stick any labels on him, such as "shy" or "cranky", as this can affect the way you respond to him. Nobody can predict what sort of person he will be. You will undoubtedly delight in discovering all aspects of your baby's emerging personality.

birth to 6 months: **your baby's milestones**

The following is a general guide to baby development. Remember, there is a wide range of what's "normal" for each month. If you have questions, ask your baby's doctor.

The first month
♦ recognizes your voice and smell
♦ may try to lift his head when on his tummy
♦ sticks out his tongue in response to you doing it
♦ starts to uncurl from fetal position

The second month
♦ lifts his head for a few seconds
♦ smiles for the first time
♦ coos in response to you
♦ loses some newborn reflexes
♦ makes smoother movements
♦ shows excitement when he knows you are near
♦ can see things further away
♦ opens and closes his mouth in imitation of you when you talk to him

The third month
♦ becomes more interested in people around him
♦ starts to notice his hands
♦ can open and close his hands and play with his fingers
♦ may hold his head without support for a few seconds
♦ may briefly push himself up on his arms when lying on his tummy
♦ clasps a toy in his hand
♦ swipes at toys
♦ reaches out and grabs at things
♦ experiments with vowel sounds
♦ may gurgle

The fourth month
♦ head control becomes steady
♦ uses hands to explore his own face and objects of interest
♦ may make recognizable sounds
♦ can remember some things – for example, that a rattle makes a noise
♦ can recognize people closest to him as individuals, and will have a distinct reaction to different voices
♦ is naturally outgoing and not at all shy or self-conscious

The fifth month
♦ grabs his toes and puts them in his mouth
♦ may try to take his weight on his legs when held upright
♦ starts rolling over from front to back
♦ turns his head away when he doesn't want any more food
♦ reaches for toys he wants
♦ concentrates for short periods
♦ puts everything in his mouth
♦ raises his arms to be picked up
♦ wants to be included in everything
♦ becomes excited at the prospect of food

The sixth month
♦ holds his head steady
♦ keeps his head in line with his body when pulled to sitting position
♦ grasps objects
♦ enjoys sitting up with support
♦ starts to chuckle
♦ blows bubbles and raspberries
♦ changes tone of voice to express himself
♦ initiates interaction: knows he can get your attention by making sounds and banging objects

birth to 2 months

It may seem that all your newborn does is eat, sleep, and cry – but from the moment she is born, she is developing new skills with incredible speed. By the end of her second month, her personality will really begin to shine through.

physical development

During the early weeks, your baby will still be curled up, with her legs drawn in and her hands clenched.

Even before she was born, your baby was exercising her muscles – and now she has a lot more space to do it in. When she is awake and alert, she will punch the air and kick her legs vigorously, especially in response to stimulation or when she is agitated or crying. These movements are jerky, random, and uncontrolled at the moment, but they strengthen her muscles and stimulate her nervous system, paving the way for more controlled attempts later on.

During her second month your baby will spend more time awake. You could try putting her under a baby gym on the floor, so that she has something to swipe at. She will miss most of the time to begin with, because, even though her arm movements are becoming more purposeful, her coordination and her ability to judge the distance between objects are still developing.

Remember that babies want and need to be with their parents when they are awake, so try to keep to a minimum the time your baby spends entertaining herself. She would much rather be interacting with you.

A nose for security
A newborn baby will recognize her mother's unique smell just hours after birth and quickly associates it with the comfort of being held in her arms.

Head control

Before your baby can control her body, she needs to master the art of holding her head unsupported. Until she has full head control – which may not come until she is four months old – you must always make sure you support her head when you are holding her.

Over the next few weeks her neck muscles and the muscles at the top of her spine will gradually strengthen, allowing her to support her head herself. By eight weeks she may be able to raise her head to a 45-degree angle for a second or two when lying on her tummy.

Uncurling and stretching

During her first few weeks your baby will begin to stretch out and uncurl from her fetal position. Her knees and hips will be stronger, and they won't be as flexed as before. And the tightly clenched fingers of your newborn will unfold one by one into an open hand, ready for clasping objects.

By the end of this stage, if you put a rattle into the palm of your baby's hand she will probably try to grasp it automatically and hold on to it for a little while.

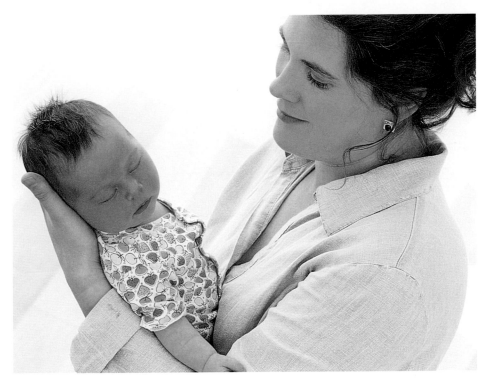

learning skills

Your baby is learning and developing all the time – and the main way she does this is through her relationship with you.

She is incredibly receptive to any kind of contact you have with her: notice how she calms and concentrates when she hears your voice, or how she watches your moving lips with fascination as you talk to her. Watch her carefully and you may see her move her body in excitement when she knows you are near. She gets enormous pleasure from this relationship, and her brain is being stimulated too, making it easier and more pleasurable for her to respond to loved ones in the future.

Vision

Your baby's senses are exquisitely attuned to help her take in all the information she needs for survival and development.

Her vision will go through many changes during the first month. At first, she'll see only the edges of things because the centre of her visual field is still blurred. She'll like to look at objects held about 20–35cm (8–15in) in front of her – just the right distance for watching your face as you feed or hold her. Focusing on your face and the faces of other family members is important to your baby. By one month she'll be able to focus on things as far away as 90cm (3ft).

first **smile**

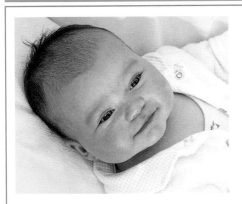

Your baby's first real or responsive smile will appear at about six weeks. You'll know it's a real smile because her eyes light up at the same time, and, as you respond by smiling back, it becomes stronger.

Although she may have made previous practice runs during the early weeks of her life, you'll recognize the real thing because she'll use her whole face, especially her eyes.

This is a real breakthrough in her development. The more she smiles at you, the more you will smile back and talk to her. Her happy face cannot help but engage you in interaction with her, and this is exactly what she needs to develop into a social human being.

Happy days

Once she has learned to smile, there will be no stopping her. She will smile at anyone she sees to begin with, especially if someone is looking at and talking to her. But within just a few weeks, you will notice that she is more choosy about who she smiles at; she will quickly learn to tell the difference between familiar and strange faces.

More than anything else, this is a very enjoyable stage in your baby's development. Her smile is telling you that she is happy to be with you. So smile back at her and let her know you're happy, too!

toy box

Mobiles

Newborns prefer a mobile with bold colours and contrasting patterns. Musical mobiles that go round will also fascinate her and help her develop her "tracking" skills. Be sure to attach the mobile securely to the side rails of her cot. Hang it high enough so your baby cannot reach it to pull it down, and remove it when she is able to get up on her hands and knees or when she reaches five months, whichever comes first.

Mirrors

Buy an unbreakable mirror that's specially made to attach to the inside of your baby's cot or playpen, so she can entertain herself when you're not nearby.

Books

It's never too early to introduce your baby to books. Choose board books designed for young babies, which have clear, bold pictures of faces, babies, animals, or patterns. They will help your baby familiarize herself with everyday faces and objects. Sit her on your lap and talk about the pictures, pointing out things as you look at the different pages. To begin with, she won't want long sessions with a book, but as her vision and mind develop, she will get more and more out of them.

Rattles

Your baby will love to hold a rattle and enjoy the sound it makes when you shake it for her, even if she can't do much with it herself at the moment.

Baby gym

A baby gym or cradle gym (one that you hang over a pram or cot) has an array of interesting objects hanging from it to interest your baby. Choose a gym with toys that make a noise as well as those that are colourful. She'll love things that squeak, rustle, or rattle. Move her position from time to time so that she can look at all the different toys.

Share what you've learned with others. Show siblings and other family members how to hold her so that she can respond most fully.

Talk to your baby

Even at this stage, your baby is tuning in to the tones and rhythms of language all the time. Talk to her as much as you can, and try to use exaggerated modulation in your speech. It's OK to use "baby talk" at this stage of her development. You are beginning to teach her the building blocks of conversation. It won't be long before her understanding of language becomes more sophisticated and she may start to respond to you by making little noises or moving her mouth when you talk to her.

Memory for detail

Although your baby's memory is very short-term in the early weeks, her ability to remember is improving and becoming more sophisticated all the time. To help stimulate her memory, let her experience things with more than one sense. For example, she is far more likely to remember a toy if she has been allowed to touch it as well as look at it, because her memory will include details such as shape and texture as well as outline and colour.

emotional development

Your newborn is a little bundle of emotions. From the first few moments of life, she is very sensitive to the moods and feelings of the people she is close to.

You may notice, for example, that your baby becomes agitated if you are feeling upset or worried, and that she seems more calm and content when you are feeling relaxed. This emotional sensitivity is an important newborn characteristic.

In later stages of development, it will help her adjust her behaviour and enable her to respond appropriately to the people around her. In other words, her awareness of the moods and feelings of others is fundamental to her development into a social human being.

You will probably find, particularly in the early days, that it is hard to work out exactly how your baby is feeling or what it is that she needs or wants. But over time, as your relationship develops, she will soon become easier to read, and both you and your baby will find the time you spend together increasingly emotionally rewarding.

By her second month, your baby is learning to recognize and respond to you. The most rewarding response at this stage is undoubtedly the appearance of her first social smile at about six weeks old (see page 153).

Calm contentment

You will be able to tell when your baby is feeling happy or content because she will lie peacefully, looking intently into your eyes or at her surroundings. These moments may be short-lived to begin with, because most of her time will be spent feeding or sleeping, but they will be very pleasurable for you both when they do occur.

Quiet, content times are very important for your baby for many reasons. They give her brain the chance to take over. This means she can exercise her curiosity, practise focusing on things, and, most important of all, give you some undivided attention. And just being with you will make her feel secure and happy. These periods when your baby is quiet yet alert are some of the special moments when you and your baby can really get to know one another.

Knowing that your baby is content can be incredibly emotionally fulfilling – it is a sign that you are meeting her needs. This will increase your confidence as a parent, and, at the same time, strengthen your bond with your baby.

A time to cry

For now, your baby's physical requirements take priority over everything else, and she will express herself accordingly. She will cry to let you know she is hungry, tired, or uncomfortable, or feeling vulnerable and in need of a cuddle (see page 98).

Respond to your baby's cries and make sure you give her all the reassurance she needs. Lots of attention and love now will teach her how to respond positively to you, and will help her develop into a secure and confident baby.

After a few weeks, although she will still cry as all babies do, she will also begin to discover other ways to get your attention and communicate with you. You will notice she starts to use her whole face and body to get the response she wants.

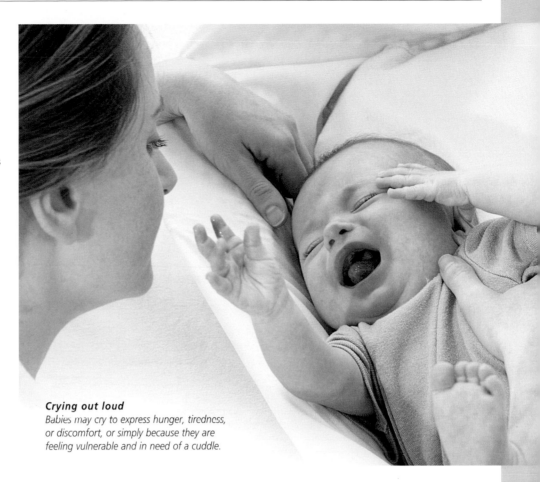

Crying out loud
Babies may cry to express hunger, tiredness, or discomfort, or simply because they are feeling vulnerable and in need of a cuddle.

---

learning through play

You are your baby's number one favourite plaything. Talk to her, rock her, sing to her, or put on some music and dance around the room with her – all these activities will bring her pleasure and stimulate her, with positive results.

Copy cat!

Try sticking out your tongue at your baby every 20 seconds when she is looking into your eyes, and you may soon see a tiny tongue sticking back at you. Be patient – it may take her a minute or two to respond.

Light and shade

Your baby's attention will be caught by objects with bold patterns of light and shade: your face, a Venetian blind, or a black-and-white picture, for example. This is because strong contrasts are easily picked out even with poor vision.

♦ Draw black-and-white patterns and faces and stick them onto the wall by her cot.

♦ Place her cot near a window where there is a play of light and shade.

Playful interaction
Supporting her head with his body, this father plays "This Little Piggy" with his baby's toes.

Sensory stimulation

♦ Splash water in the bath with her feet while you hold her carefully supported in your arms. This will stimulate her sense of touch without making her feel insecure.

♦ Prop your baby up in a car seat or a bouncy chair so she gets a good view of what's going on around her. Talk to her from different places in the room and watch how she tries to locate the sound. Games like this help her to coordinate sight and sound.

♦ Play "Round and Round the Garden" or "This Little Piggy" to encourage her fingers and toes to relax. Open out her fingers and toes as you say the rhymes. This also reinforces your baby's ideas about enjoyment and interaction.

♦ Repeat the same song a few times, and see how long it takes before she learns to anticipate the tickle at the end.

♦ Your baby may also like it if you stroke the palm of her hand and her fingertips with anything soft or furry in texture. Try it and see how she responds.

2 to 4 months

Your baby is now more in control of his movements, and will become more communicative towards you, using gurgles and smiles. He will be able to hold his head steady, and he has discovered a source of great pleasure: his hands.

physical development

As your baby gains control over his body, he will begin to understand how he can use it to learn more about his world.

His neck muscles will now be so strong that, when he lies on his back, he can lift his head and hold it up for several seconds. When you grasp his hands and pull him to a sitting position, his head may no longer flop back, but will lift up as his body is pulled upwards. Sit him in a bouncy chair or a baby play nest, and he may be able to hold his head steady. Lie him on his stomach and he'll begin doing mini push-ups, lifting himself with his hands and arms, and turning his head.

He may not be able to hold these positions for long at first, but every time he does it his muscles are strengthening. This gives him much more opportunity to take in his surroundings, and he will become increasingly curious about them.

Get ready to roll

His developing neck control marks the beginning of a whole new adventure for your baby. His increased strength, confidence, and ability to manoeuvre himself up on to his hands means that sometime over the next few months, much to his surprise, and yours, he will suddenly find himself rolling over. Active rolling can start any time from about three months onwards, but it can occasionally take place earlier and unexpectedly.

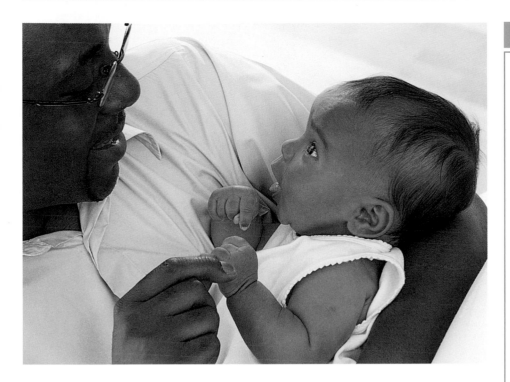

Your baby's hand control will become far more refined, and by his fourth month he may be able to grab hold of a rattle or toy if you give it to him, although he may not be able to let go of it as yet.

♦ He will be fascinated by what his hands can do. They, along with his mouth, are his tools for the exploration of his world. He will use them for searching out and exploring parts of his own face, such as his nose and his mouth. He will also use one hand simply to play with the other.

♦ He will still enjoy swiping at toys within reach and will occasionally manage to grab hold of one. When this happens he won't quite know what to do with the toy – except, of course, to put it in his mouth to explore it with his tongue and mouth.

♦ He will be intrigued by the sensation of holding different textured objects, such as a soft, squashy toy and a cool, smooth plastic one.

Do not leave your child unattended on a bed, changing table, or any surface raised above floor level, as he might choose this moment to roll over for the first time, and fall off.

Fascinating fingers

They may have been there all along, but your baby has only just noticed his hands. These will now become an ever-present source of fascination to him, and he will spend a lot of time lying still and intently examining his new-found fingers, watching as they interact with one another.

He will quickly learn to bring his hands together and play with his fingers, jamming them in his mouth, where he will enjoy sucking them. He will love to watch his hands as they clasp and unclasp, and will press his palms together in a clapping motion.

toy **box**

Textured toys

Now that he is grabbing hold of things, it's worth giving your baby lots of different textures to experience.

♦ Let him have a range of toys to explore: smooth plastic toys; toys that are squashy; beanie toys that change shape as you hold them; toys with bumpy surfaces. Make sure they are safe for a baby to play with before you buy them.

♦ Allow him to touch different materials, such as fur, silk, velvet, water, warm skin.

♦ His cradle gym and play mat may also become more fascinating now. Let him lie on a play mat

that has lots of different textures carefully sewn on it or velcroed to it.

Noisy toys

Toys that make a noise, such as a squeaky duck, will now be very entertaining. You'll need to help him squeak these for a while, as they may still be too hard for him to manipulate, but he will love the surprise sound they make.

Once he has learned how to make a toy squeak, he'll get even more pleasure from it – and, what is more, he'll be continuing to learn about cause and effect.

Ball play

Your baby will be fascinated by objects that move – especially if he can control them. Try lying him on his tummy and rolling a brightly coloured ball in front of him across his line of vision, about 60cm (2ft) away from his body. At first he will watch the ball intently as it moves from one side to the other, but he will soon come to anticipate this action and try to reach out to grab it on subsequent rolls.

Rattles and baby gym

He will like to hold a rattle, and he will pull at toys hanging from his baby gym with more confidence.

learning through play

Now that your baby is responding to you and conversing with you more, you will have even more fun playing and interacting with him. He still needs all the cuddles, words of encouragement, and reassurance, but you can expand your repertoire with more adventurous activities, such as bouncing games and singalongs.

Singing games
♦ Gently bounce your baby on your knee to the beat of many babies' favourite song: "Horsey, Horsey".
♦ Sing splashing songs in the bath, counting songs when you play with his fingers, lullabies when it's time to go to sleep – he'll love them all!
♦ Try patting out the rhythm of the songs on his tummy or hands as you sing to him. This will give your baby even more enjoyment.

Playing with finger puppets
Your baby will be fascinated by the distinctive and friendly faces of finger puppets. Bring them to life by moving your fingers, perhaps integrating the movement with a song or story.

Make a noise
♦ Now that he has found his hands, your baby might enjoy having a wrist toy or bell bracelet Velcroed around his wrist. He'll learn that by shaking it he's making the noise.
♦ Your baby will like to hold a rattle and will enjoy the noise he makes when he shakes it.

learning skills

Your baby is already a keen thinker. He is now fascinated by his own body and is beginning to understand that he can make it move by himself when he wants to.

This is an important first step in your baby's understanding of the concept of cause and effect. He is also beginning to connect seeing with doing, which is the first step in developing hand-eye coordination.

Memory advance
Your baby's memory will now have developed sufficiently for him to remember certain people and events. One study of babies of this age found that they quickly learn how to kick a mobile attached to their cot to make it move. When the mobile was taken away for a week and then put back in place, the babies could still remember what to do.

Clarity of vision
His eyesight will have greatly improved since those first hazy newborn days, and your baby can now use both eyes together to focus on something, whether it's close up or right on the other side of the room. This means that he is more able to judge the distance between himself and the things he is looking at, so his hand-eye coordination will be much better now.

This clarity of vision also means he can clearly focus even on something as small as a button, and follow a moving object if held a few centimetres away. When the object disappears, you may notice him continuing to stare at the space where he last saw it.

Sound combinations
Your baby will begin to experiment more with vowel sounds, and his vocabulary will range from brief, one-syllable squeaks and squeals to long "eh" and "oh" vowel sounds. He is beginning to discover which sounds are made by which combinations of throat, tongue, and mouth actions.

At first, these cooing, throaty gurgles will seem completely random, but you will gradually notice that the sounds your baby is making are directed at you when you talk to him. He is enjoying socializing with you, as well as the sound of his own voice.

emotional development

Your baby is learning that being friendly is rewarding because of the way you respond to him with cuddles, love, and soothing sounds.

Now that he understands this, he will smile even more, knowing that you will smile back. He will also welcome you with definite waves and wriggles when he knows you are coming to him.

Response and recognition

One of the most significant developments that your baby's sharpened memory brings is that he now has a very detailed memory of the people closest to him, so he can recognize them as individuals. This starts to influence the way he interacts with you, your partner, his siblings, and anyone else he has a lot of contact with.

For example, now that he knows you, he may have very distinct responses to your voice, which are quite different to his responses to your partner's voice: seeing or hearing you may calm him down, while hearing his father's voice may make him excited, for instance.

Skilled expression

Your baby's different little noises are beginning to be recognizable now. He is becoming more skilled at expressing himself. For example, he may show his feelings of pleasure by making attempts to "coo" to you. He may even shriek with pleasure, and giggle to express his delight. He will also be learning that loud screeching will bring you running to his side – another lesson in cause and effect!

Although your baby cannot repeat any words, he is listening to you and storing them all for the future, so the more you talk to your baby, the better.

Feeling secure

At this stage, your baby will probably be naturally outgoing and not at all shy or self conscious. He will charm everyone with his smile, and although he'll prefer

Love and laughter
Your baby will not only smile when you smile now, he may even laugh out loud in delight when you do something he enjoys.

you to anyone, he will love to "talk" to people – other babies, complete strangers, even his own reflection. He is learning to take the lead, which is important for his self-confidence, and, as you follow his lead, you learn even more about his emerging character and sense of fun.

By his fourth month, you may have decided to start a routine of regular naptimes, walks outside, feeding, bath, and bedtime. This helps him learn to

anticipate the events of the day, and teaches him that his life has a pattern to it. It helps him feel emotionally secure and increases his confidence. Establishing a routine also helps him to trust that you are near, even if he cannot see you.

Having a structure to your day and getting out and about will increase your pleasure, too. You may find that it boosts your confidence, and helps you feel in control of your new job as a parent.

4 to 6 months

Your baby will now be making controlled movements and may be starting to use her limbs to manoeuvre herself by rolling from front to back. She's becoming more aware of new situations, and can detect changes in her surroundings.

physical development

Improved muscle control and understanding of what her body can do means that your baby's movements are now quite deliberate.

You will notice that she is much more effective in reaching and grabbing hold of what she wants or positioning herself on the floor to play, for example.

Keeping steady

Your baby will now be able to hold her head steady when held upright, and will keep her head in line with her body without letting it lag behind when pulled from sitting – a major developmental milestone.

Although she may not be able to support herself sitting up yet, she will definitely feel happiest propped up in a sitting position, so that she can keep an eye on what's going on around her and join in with everything. You may find she takes great delight in kicking the sides of her bath when she's in the water, or kicking out at any surface within reach of her toes.

Mighty muscles

Your baby will enjoy any activity that gives her a chance to push with her legs and feet – and doing this will help strengthen her muscles ready for crawling. If you hold on to her hands she may try to bounce up and down, although she won't be able to hold a standing position for very long. Don't let go of her, as she does not yet have the muscle strength or physical coordination skills to take her own weight on her feet.

Baby love
At six months your baby will really demonstrate her love for you: she will want to touch your face, grab your hair, and will hold out her arms to be picked up.

When she is lying down the improved control she has over her limbs means she can now begin to roll over on to her back from her front. This is an important milestone, as she is gaining control over her whole body, and paving the way for learning to crawl.

Staying focused

Your baby's eyesight and her hand-eye coordination have improved so much that it is almost as good as yours. She can now deliberately reach for an object and bring it straight to her mouth. Faces are still her favourite thing to look at, and she is able to distinguish facial expressions now. She can tell a happy face from a sad face.

coordination **skills**

Your baby's visual skills now mean that she is able to judge how far away a toy is and manoeuvre herself to reach out for it and grab it with one or both hands.

♦ She will be able to hold a toy firmly in her grasp, with her fingers securely curled around it. If she holds a rattle, she may now know what to do with it (thanks to her improved memory).

♦ Her own body still holds great fascination for her, and she will love to grab hold of her foot and suck her toes when the mood takes her.

learning skills

Your baby is increasing her non-verbal forms of communication, using her body to make her point.

She will push you away if she wants to do something else; reach for something she wants to play with; or turn her head away to let you know she doesn't want something.

Learning to speak

Your baby is keen to communicate with you, and will try to make different sounds with her mouth.

She will practise using her tongue, poking it out and blowing raspberries with her lips to make different sounds. Listen to her carefully. As she realizes that people use different noises to communicate, your baby may become more adept at changing her tone of voice in the hope that you will turn and look at her.

She is probably more vocal in letting you know what she wants by making particular babbling sounds, which mean "Pick me up" or "I want to play with that".

Listening to you

Although she doesn't understand the meaning of many of your words yet, she will understand their tone. She will be very sensitive to changes in the tone of your voice. A firm tone will stop her, but is also likely to make her cry. If overused, it will discourage her natural curiosity and learning later on. Reserve using "No!" for situations of danger.

Through watching your facial expressions she will begin to learn what you are saying. By allowing her to watch you as you speak, you are continuing to lay important foundations that will later help her to form words through imitation.

By her sixth month your baby is beginning to understand a little more of what you say. She may start to turn her head towards you when she hears you use her name in conversation and will understand often-repeated words such as her own name, "mummy", or "bedtime".

Concentration skills

Your baby will really be able to concentrate now, and some toys, games, and activities will hold her interest for longer periods.

Face to face
Faces are still your baby's favourite thing to look at, and she can now distinguish different expressions.

toy **box**

Surprise
Your baby will love games with an element of surprise. A jack-in-the-box, a pop-up clown, or a toy that makes a noise if you press it in a certain place will be great fun now. Encourage her to interact and use her hand and visual skills by helping her to push down on toys to make them pop up.

Music and movement
Your baby will enjoy toys that she can play with easily. A baby tambourine or a clear rattle with colourful beans inside will be great fun, and will teach her about the power she has over things. Let her be the conductor of her own little orchestra.

Squeak?
Put a different toy into each of your baby's hands. Make sure they are pliable enough to make a noise with just one hand. Watch as she tries to work out which hand the squeak is coming from when she presses.

Mat exploration
Her play mat will now be more useful. Although she is not crawling yet, your baby will be able to move herself around a little by rolling or using her arms. A brightly coloured activity mat with attached toys will keep her amused as she explores the different areas on it.

Cuddly toys
Your baby will love soft toys with faces now. Encourage her to be gentle with them – role-play by cuddling a favourite teddy and saying "Aah" (to teach your baby about sociability, gentleness and kindness). It won't be long before she will start "looking after" her toys, too.

Make sure that all your child's toys meet the required safety standards (see page 262).

Not only will she hold a toy, she will examine it, manipulate it, and feel and taste it by putting it in her mouth. This is her most sensitive area, so it's a natural place for her to put things to find out more about them. Always make sure that small objects are not within your baby's reach, as she could easily choke on them.

Broader understanding
Your baby's greater comprehension of what is going on around her means that she will now concentrate on subjects for longer, whether it's looking at a toy in her hands or watching you.

She can now focus intently on one thing at a time – listening to music, watching you, examining a picture in a book, or scooping up a building brick with her hands – before becoming distracted and moving on to a new activity. You can help increase her attention span by gradually minimizing distractions and gently redirecting her to a shared activity when her attention starts to wander.

emotional development

By now you will have a good idea of your baby's personality and her growing individual characteristics.

Although she may be happy to be held by strangers, she is now able to distinguish between people she knows and those she doesn't, and will show a definite preference for familiar faces – yours most of all.

She will get a lot of enjoyment from social situations, such as watching other children play, sitting in her highchair at family meal times, and being taken to the park. These events also help her to interact with other people, and to feel comfortable in new situations when they occur.

Interactive family

Let her be a part of everything that is going on. Encourage her as she tries new things, and acknowledge her when she makes her own contributions – whether it's a gurgle or a hand lifted up with a toy in it to show you. Encourage everyone around her to respond to her in this way, too. Siblings, friends, your partner – they will all be sources of endless fascination for your baby, and the more attention she gets from them, the better.

This interaction also makes her feel part of the family, contributing to her emotional security and helping her develop social skills. These extremely important skills fall into two categories: learning how others think and feel, and learning how to care about them.

Getting emotional

As your baby becomes more mature emotionally, she will show a wider range of emotions in different situations. She can show you by bouncing up and down that she is excited, by gurgling with pleasure that she has seen something that gives her joy, by remaining quiet and watching warily that she is unsure of a situation, or by crying that her needs are not being met.

learning through play

Your baby will still love singalongs, bouncing, and clapping games, and you will be able to be a little more physically playful with her now that she's stronger.

Hide and seek
To help your baby learn the concept of permanence, try hiding her teddy bear under a blanket. Pull away the blanket and watch your baby's face when the teddy suddenly reappears. Or, hide behind a curtain then peep out. Your baby will slowly begin to realize you were there all along (see object permanence, page 182).

Physical fun
Because your baby's upper body is so strong and her head control is complete, she will probably now know how to roll over from front to back. Try playing floor games with her that allow her to show off her new skill and allow you to help her perfect it. She'll also enjoy being tickled – blow raspberries on her tummy and see her delight.

Cause and effect
Your baby will be delighted at her own skill at pressing buttons on simple toys to make sounds or a face pop up. She will also love knocking down a tower of plastic blocks, or swiping at a roly-poly doll that rights itself after it has been pushed over.

Change and growth

Although genes play a part in determining your baby's personality, she will already have developed many of her own characteristics, likes, and dislikes.

Many of the traits you see in your baby now will not necessarily stay with her for the rest of her life. For example, she may be impatient for solids at every meal or frustrated by not yet being able to move around freely and reach the things she wants, but this does not mean that she will grow into an impatient or frustrated child.

Remember that your baby has a long way to go before she can understand, reason, or use language to communicate effectively what she is thinking or wants. Your baby also still needs quiet time and may even sometimes want to be left alone. If a fun game suddenly ends in tears, try to recognize her need for a break, and give her time to calm down and refocus.

your developing baby
6 to 12 months

During his second six months, your baby will develop new skills to help him explore his environment, assert his own will, and discover his independence. By encouraging him along the way, you will give him the confidence and self-esteem he needs.

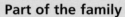

The wider world

Reaching his natural milestones – such as discovering how to sit, crawl, and communicate – enables your baby to start really interacting with the wider world. He can see a favourite toy and move forwards to grab it. His older brother may pull a funny face to make him laugh and he can pull one back. If he meets another baby he can reach out with interest towards him.

Watching your baby acquiring new skills is exciting, and will give you a sense of his developing independence. The fact that he can sit on his own, crawl happily around the floor, amuse himself with a new toy, and feed himself at the table gives you a little taste of freedom – every now and then you may even have time to sit down with a cup of coffee! A daily outing in the buggy is another step in introducing your baby to the wider world, and gives you both important "out and about" time together.

New relationships

Your baby will also become more involved and responsive with other people, especially close family members. With their instinctive sociability, babies at six months and older can start to develop a close bond with people other than their parents, such as grandparents and caregivers. This is a good time to help your baby establish separate relationships with people who will become important in his life – especially as, in a few months' time, "stranger anxiety" may make new friendships a lot harder.

Part of the family

During these next six months your baby will also really begin to enjoy his siblings, or love to watch an older toddler or child bouncing around. And as he begins to move about himself and becomes capable of doing more things, many activities can be shared, such as singing songs together, playing clapping games, or having a game of chase (on all fours!) around the room.

Older children can also play the role of teacher for your baby. He'll love to imitate them and may try hard to look at a book or blow raspberries like his big brother or sister.

Shared reading
Your baby will start to take a greater interest in books as his concentration skills develop. Your baby will love looking at books with you and he will benefit from the closeness.

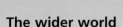

making **friends**

If this is your first baby, his encounters with other babies will probably be a result of the friendships you have made during pregnancy and after birth. Over the next six months, your baby and your friends' babies may start to interact: gurgling, touching, imitating each other. However, don't worry if your baby doesn't pay attention to others – some do, some don't.

the second 6 months

Your baby's mastery of physical and mental skills is staggering, especially when you think how she started life – as a tiny bundle with little sense of herself and the world around her. So how do these incredible changes take place?

how your baby learns

Genetics play a part in your baby's continuing development, but much of her progress depends on the kind of stimulation and attention she receives from you.

From the moment of her birth your baby is absorbing information, especially from the people closest to her. You are her first teacher.

This isn't as overwhelming as it sounds, since your baby's natural way of learning is through play: if she shakes a rattle and discovers that it makes a fantastic noise, she's learning about cause and effect; when she tries to crawl over a mountain of cushions you've built for her, she's finding out how to balance and coordinate her limbs; and when she listens to you sing a nursery rhyme, she's starting to understand emotions and language.

Encouraging your baby

How is your baby motivated? Again, partly through a built-in drive to discover and learn. But your encouragement and support are also incredibly important. When, for example, she eventually manages to wave goodbye as a friend leaves, it's your delight and praise that boost her sense of achievement, and convince her that learning is fun.

Taking your lead from your baby is key to motivating her. When she's ready to try a new challenge, you'll see the signs. Understanding how and when your baby develops can help you prepare for each stage and be ready with the right kind of games and activities to stretch her and fulfil her needs. In fact, making sure the family environment is fun and stimulating is one of the most valuable things you can do for her.

Playing with your baby brings you closer together and helps develop her self-esteem and sense of security, proving that you love her unconditionally for who she is, not just what she can do.

A question of gender

Even though your baby may be showing clear character traits at a young age, her personality is still emerging. And in the same way that her character traits affect the way you respond to her, so your responses will have an impact on her personality.

Getting upright
During the next six months your baby will learn to pull himself upright and stand on his own, albeit probably only with the aid of furniture or you for support.

Although you may not consciously realize what you are doing, chances are that the way you care for and respond to your baby will also be affected by gender.

If you dressed a group of one-year old boys and girls in the same outfits and put them in a room together, you would find it difficult to tell the boys from the girls. At this age, the differences in skill development are tiny. But, based on traditions, some parents treat boys and girls differently, encouraging different toys and games for each sex. If left to their own devices, both are attracted to all of the toys, and they will benefit from being allowed to play with both "boy" and "girl" toys. What matters most is the love and respect the parent gives the child as a person, regardless of their sex. This helps build self-esteem.

While boys and girls are naturally different – for example, girls do tend to be more sociable and less adventurous, and boys are usually more physical and inquisitive – the way we adults respond to them also tends to reinforce these gender differences. Tempering your behaviour towards them – encouraging your boy's gentler side, or stimulating your girl's sense of independence – will begin to help eliminate sexual stereotyping and allow your baby's own individuality to emerge.

6 to 12 months: your baby's milestones

Your baby will master a lot of new skills and reach many important milestones over the next few months. It's important to remember, however, that while each baby will reach all of the following milestones, the time it takes to reach them will vary from baby to baby. After all, every baby develops differently.

If you ever become concerned about your baby's development, speak to your doctor or health visitor.

Movement milestones
By 12 months she will probably:
- sit unsupported
- begin to crawl
- pull herself up to a standing position
- "cruise", holding onto furniture
- stand momentarily without any support
- be able to walk two or three steps on her own.

Hand and finger milestones
By 12 months she will probably:
- bang two blocks together
- use her hands rather than her mouth to investigate new objects
- feed herself finger foods

- try to hold more than one object in her hand at a time
- put objects in a container and take them out again
- let go of objects in her hand when she wants to
- point with her finger
- use the pincer grip (hold a tiny object with her forefinger and thumb).

Social and emotional milestones
By 12 months she will probably:
- cry when you leave her
- become anxious and cling to you if strangers directly approach her
- enjoy imitating people.

Language milestones
By 12 months she will probably:
- babble; may even be able to say two or three recognizable words
- understand many words and start to imitate sounds
- listen carefully to you when you talk to her
- respond to simple commands
- recognize her name and other familiar words, such as "bye-bye"

- use gestures, such as shaking her head for "no"
- try to imitate words.

Intellectual milestones
By 12 months she will probably:
- understand the meaning of "no"
- follow simple questions, such as "where are your shoes?", and reply by pointing
- have an abundant curiosity
- find hidden objects easily
- explore objects in different ways (e.g. banging, throwing, dropping)
- understand cause and effect (when she shakes her rattle, it makes a noise)
- start to understand how objects are used (drink from a cup, brush her hair, listen into a telephone)
- know that something still exists even when she can no longer see it.

Some babies may also be able to stack blocks, for example, or say "mama" or "dada" with meaning. These milestones aren't just about achievements. They are also indicators of your baby's healthy emotional and social development.

6 to 8 months

Now more than half way through his first year of life, your baby is beginning to take a greater interest in the world around him. Being able to sit upright gives him a whole new perspective on his environment.

physical development

Constantly exercising his body over the last few months has helped your baby develop his muscles, balance, and control.

He may now be able to roll from side to side with ease, flipping himself onto his back and over again. He may also sit for long periods and lean forward without falling over. However, he still can't twist sideways or swivel at the waist, and may topple over when trying to reach for a toy.

On his own two feet

Your baby is growing stronger by the day and will be keen to flex his muscles and show off his skills. Pretty soon just sitting won't be exciting enough for him. Always looking for a new challenge, he will be keen to try standing, and may make his first attempt by hauling himself up in his cot while hanging on to the rails. To begin with he'll collapse in a heap or remain stranded and yell for help – he hasn't yet developed the balance or coordination to lower himself down gently.

Reach for the toys
Once your baby can sit upright without using his arms for support, he will start stretching forward to grab anything nearby that looks interesting.

When you come to his rescue, support his weight and allow him to relax so that he can gently slide into a sitting position. All of this is great practice for the next important milestones: crawling, standing, walking.

On the move

By his eighth month, your baby may be attempting to crawl. To crawl properly, your baby needs to be strong enough to push himself up on all fours and then discover that by pushing down with his knees he can move forwards. First crawls are often backwards, and it may be a week or so before he learns how to move forwards.

Many babies don't learn how to crawl until they are between eight and 10 months; some don't begin to move until they are a few weeks older; and some never crawl at all, but go straight from shuffling on their bottom to walking.

Playing with toys

Once he learns how to sit upright and no longer needs his arms to keep himself supported, your baby will be working hard to grab anything nearby that excites him. Make sure there are always some toys, safe household objects, or baby books nearby to keep him interested – but don't expect too much. His concentration skills are still developing and even something he has never seen before will hold his attention for only a few minutes.

Hand-eye coordination

As his grip develops, your baby will be able to hold objects more firmly and steadily, turn them over to have a good look at them and put them in his mouth, pass them from one hand to the other, and even bang two objects together.

As his hand-eye coordination improves, he'll be grabbing a spoon as soon as it's in sight, and probably overturning it before it reaches his mouth. You may like to offer him a two-handled cup to drink from. Before long, he may be drinking from it without your help. You may also want to start offering him finger foods, such as a piece of bread or rice cake. Never leave him alone with finger food in case he chokes.

learning **to sit**

Thanks to all the wriggling, twisting, kicking, and stretching he has been practising in his first six months, your baby can now sit up on his own – at least for a few minutes, and probably longer. Sitting up enables him to look around more easily, watch family members coming and going, and reach out for toys to keep himself entertained – if only for a little while.

learning skills

Your baby's everyday routines are now very familiar to him. He can remember things that have happened before, and begins to recognize sounds and objects.

Your baby is starting to learn about object permanence. Up until now, when something disappears, your baby thinks it no longer exists. During this stage, he will begin to realize that just because he can't see something it doesn't mean it isn't there. You can see this in action by partially hiding a toy under a towel. Chances are he'll try to lift the towel to find the toy – and by the end of his eighth month he'll look for it even when it's fully hidden.

Gestures and expressions

You'll notice your baby's understanding of language is developing faster than his ability to talk. He recognizes his own name and will turn his head when he hears you calling. He is also starting to

respond to the names of familiar objects and people, glancing over at a favourite toy you've just mentioned, for example, or looking at his sister when you call her name.

First conversations

Real speech is still some way off, but your baby has lots of ways of letting you know what he's thinking. Gestures, for example, are now a regular part of his vocabulary – see him open and shut his hand if he wants something, shake his head or push you away if you're doing something he doesn't like, or try to wave when you say "bye-bye". Watch his face, too – his facial expressions will convey a variety of emotions.

At this stage your baby practises his babbling. You may start to notice that his sing-song "conversations" sound increasingly like proper words, such as "dada" or "mama". He will love to repeat strings of familiar sounds so give him lots of encouragement and he will soon learn how to say the words correctly.

Comparing sounds

The covering of a nerve that connects the ear to the brain – allowing your baby to pinpoint where a sound is coming from – is complete by about his eighth month. Now he can compare his sounds with yours, and over the next few months he will increasingly attempt to imitate your sounds.

Discovery zone

Once he can propel himself in a chosen direction, your baby will be into everything: cupboards, drawers, and wastepaper baskets. He has an overwhelming sense of curiosity to discover more about each object's shape, size, and texture. Does it taste good? Does it do anything exciting? Although he can use his hands to great effect, your baby will still put things in his mouth so take steps to child-proof your home (see pages 262–265).

Your baby's understanding of objects is growing every day. He may now be beginning to see how things relate to each other – how a small box fits inside a big box, for example. More importantly, he is learning that something still exists even if he can no longer see it.

toy box

Cars and trucks
As your baby becomes more adept at sitting unaided, he'll begin to enjoy pushing cars and other wheeled toys along the ground. Get him a few in bright colours that are easy to handle and safe to put in his mouth.

Hand puppets
Use soft hand puppets with simply drawn faces that meet current safety standards. As your baby won't be able to hold them himself yet, they should also fit adult hands.

Nursery rhymes cassette player
If your baby enjoys listening to you sing familiar tunes to him, record a few songs on tape, or play a cassette of nursery rhymes while he has a quiet time. Encourage other family members to record stories and songs as well.

Bath-time toys
Toys to amuse your baby while he's in the bath can really come into their own now. Some stick to the side of the bath or to the tiles, others float or need filling with water. Even a simple floating ball or duck will give your baby lots of fun. Bath books are also a good idea. Do wipe them dry after use to prevent growth of mould.

Squeaky, noisy, and musical toys
Babies love the sounds of squeaky toys. They will also enjoy the repetition of hearing a particular little tune over and over again. Buy toys that they can grasp easily and operate themselves.

Plastic stacking cups
Try to buy different-sized cups in bright, contrasting colours that fit together well.

emotional development

Your baby is very loving – he'll kiss you when encouraged, hold his arms out to be lifted up, and pet his toys.

You'll notice that your baby is becoming more sociable, turning to listen to voices around him. He'll also want to join in conversations, responding to you, not just with baby babble but also with a range of gestures and facial expressions. Watch him look at himself in a mirror, too. He doesn't realize that he is looking at himself but he is interested in the baby he sees, and will gurgle away in the hope of a response.

Loving you

You are still your child's favourite plaything. Has he dropped that toy again – and is he looking for you to come and help? Maybe it's not the toy he's after, but a chance to smile and laugh with you.

The pleasure your baby takes in your company is a sign that he is forming a deep and genuine bond with you, his main carer. You may find towards the end of this stage that if you vanish from sight for a moment, his bottom lip begins to wobble as he fears you've gone forever. Return before the tears are in full flow, and he'll beam and bounce with happiness.

A separate person

Part of this deepening attachment comes from his realization that he is a separate person to you. This is a huge and important milestone. Over the next few months, he may become much more clingy and increasingly anxious when separated from you, even for a moment. Separation anxiety can be upsetting, but it is perfectly normal and often continues through toddlerhood. Reassure him with lots of love and attention and in time he'll realize that parents always come back.

Meanwhile, he will also start to develop attachments to other important people in his life – his siblings, granny,

learning through play

Your baby is fast demonstrating that he has a growing curiosity he needs to satisfy, and an urge to explore everything. Give him a selection of activities to keep him busy for a short while, or help him discover how to crawl towards the toys he is showing interest in.

◆ By now your baby will love to play with pop-up toys that burst out when a button is pushed or a dial turned. Show him how to push them back down himself, and he'll develop strength and coordination in his hands and arms.

◆ Satisfy your baby's desire to discover new things by giving him a box that you have filled with harmless but interesting household objects for him to play with. This will give him a chance to explore them in his own time, and will teach him more about the shape, size, and texture of different things. If he begins to tire of them, make a few small changes, such as putting a ball in the bowl to rekindle his curiosity in it.

◆ Help your baby learn more about the relationship between objects by giving him some plastic stacking cups in different colours, shapes, and sizes. It will be many months before he can fit them into each other the right way – or even stack them himself – but he'll enjoy trying. And when he needs a change you can build a tower and encourage him to try knocking it down – a game he'll love.

◆ There are lots of ways you can encourage your baby to crawl: make sure he has plenty of opportunities by putting him down on the floor whenever you can and placing a toy or something interesting just out of his reach to encourage him to try moving forwards to grasp it. Keep his knees well covered so that crawling isn't painful or uncomfortable.

◆ It's never too early to start reading to your baby. Choose a few soft books that your baby can dribble and chew on. You can also have more special books which you get out to read, then put away safely.

or caregiver, for example. Encouraging these relationships helps him adapt to being without you when he needs to be cared for by someone else.

Fear of strangers

Your baby may be sociable and confident one minute, then fearful and shy the next. When he meets people he doesn't know well, he may bury his face in your shoulder, cling to you, and cry. Becoming anxious when unfamiliar people directly

approach him is one of his first emotional milestones. Stranger anxiety is normal and can last for up to two years or so.

Try not to force your baby to be friendly and don't tell him he's being silly if he is shy as this will undermine his confidence – instead, praise him when he has the confidence to smile back at someone new. It's also worth encouraging newcomers to be gentle when they interact with your baby.

8 to 10 months

Your baby's personality is really beginning to shine through, and as her physical skills continue to develop, and she becomes more confident, she'll start to show you that she really has a mind of her own when she wants something.

physical development

Your baby may now be able to sit by herself for quite a while, as well as lean forwards for a toy without toppling over.

Don't expect her to play like this for too long though: the physical effort of maintaining her balance is tiring, so after 10 minutes or so she'll be ready for a change.

Once your baby discovers how to move herself around – whether she's crawling or shuffling – she'll move faster very quickly. It'll be a question of now you see her, now you don't, so you'll need to keep a constant eye on her and be sure she's safe.

If your baby is now crawling, she may attempt more challenging manoeuvres such as crawling upstairs. Although stair-climbing may help her learn how to judge height and depth and develop her sense of

balance, it's important to install stair gates so she can't attempt to climb them without you on hand to help (see page 262). Going up is easier than coming down, and it will be a while before she's ready to learn the skills needed to make a safe descent.

Cruising around

Very mobile babies may now be attempting to take a few steps while holding on to a piece of furniture. If your baby is becoming

more confident, she'll soon discover how to move across a room using pieces of furniture as balancing aids (see *safety*, page 262). Learning how to "cruise" like this is the last physical skill your baby needs to master before she begins walking without assistance.

Hand control

As she now begins to spend less time putting things in her mouth and more time exploring them with her hands, her hand movements are becoming agile and controlled. You may notice, for example, that she turns the pages of her books herself, even though it's usually several at a time. And she can accurately guide small pieces of food into her mouth with her fingers, making meal times slightly less messy than before. She can also bang two objects together by holding one in each hand.

Learning to point

If your baby is starting to point, this is an important milestone. Controlling the index finger is the first step to mastering a pincer grip – being able to close the thumb and forefinger together to pick up tiny objects. It also helps her

attention **span**

Your baby's sense of her environment is growing rapidly. She now notices and is interested in people and things up to three metres (10 feet) away. At the same time, her attention span is increasing: she is becoming more absorbed in activities she enjoys, and you'll find it harder to distract her when, for example, you need to take something away from her.

communicate with you by pointing out things she wants. Encourage her by looking at books together and pointing at things as you name them. And let her practise picking up tiny things such as raisins or cooked kernels of sweetcorn.

Roll play

Since her birth, your baby has been refining her visual skills and now she can judge the size of an object up to one metre (three feet) away. She'll know, for example, that a ball rolled from this distance will get larger as it comes towards her. Watch how she holds out her arms to catch it. Ask her to roll it back, and initially she may swing at it with no effect, but eventually she'll be able to return it in your direction.

learning skills

By now your baby is beginning to communicate more, letting you know that she is an important family member with something to say.

By the end of her ninth month, your baby may be able to recognize up to 20 familiar words such as "cup" or "teddy". She'll also laugh in the right places when you sing her favourite songs, look for her cup if you ask her where it is, and associate actions with certain words, such as saying "bye-bye" and waving her hand.

Making conversation

Your baby loves interacting with people, and will enjoy social get-togethers such as meal times. She will try to join in conversations. Her babbling is developing

toy **box**

Touch-and-feel books
A selection of different activity books will give your baby a new perspective on the world. Choose strong, brightly illustrated books with clear images and pictures and shapes made out of different textures.

Toy piano
If your baby has a toy with buttons to push, encourage her to practise pushing down and releasing the buttons. A toy piano or xylophone are toys your baby can grow into. For now, she will enjoy the random sounds she can make while also developing her listening skills.

Household objects
The simplest objects provide fun for a baby. When you are busy in the kitchen, your baby may love to play with some simple, safe kitchen utensils. Let her have fun with a few unused items such as a saucepan, plastic bowl, or wooden spoon.
She may also like to pick up an orange from a small cardboard box and pop it back in again, or take dry clothes out of a plastic laundry basket and put her toys or dolls in it.

all the time, and she may add new sounds to her vocabulary, such as "t" and "w". Her strings of babble will start to follow clearly the rise and fall of an adult conversation. And although on the whole it may still sound like nonsense, it is important for you to listen and respond, since this encourages her to keep trying.

Real words

Having discovered your delight when she says "dada" or "mama", your baby will probably now understand their meanings and use them to attract your attention.

If you make the sounds of specific words, such as "cat" or "bath", in time your baby may start to imitate you and repeat these sounds. Complete words won't emerge for another few months, but keep repeating the sounds and she may soon learn how to say the words back to you.

Understanding language

Your baby's understanding of language continues to increase faster than her ability to use it. She may also use gestures as well as sound to get your attention – perhaps waving at you or pulling your clothes – and will even repeat herself if you don't understand what she is trying to say.

learning through play

Around this age your baby can start to show off her problem-solving skills – as long as you can resist helping her when she faces a difficulty. Facing everyday challenges will help her learn to work things out for herself.

♦ Satisfy your baby's urge to explore, and her growing ability to problem-solve, with an activity board. Choose a board with cylinders that can whirl, dials that spin, and buttons that squeak. Show her how it works to begin with, and then let her have a go and investigate it in her own time. At first she may only be able to do the simple activities, such as sticking her finger in a dial, but during the following months she'll soon figure out how to work the other activities.

♦ Playing peekaboo and hide-and-seek with your baby at this age helps teach her

about object permanence, and there are lots of variations: cover your head with a towel and let her pull it off, then let her try; hide behind the door with just a hand or toe showing, before popping out and gently surprising her.

♦ Fill a basin with water and, using different spoons, cups, and containers, show your baby how she can fill and pour. Emptying and filling games are a good way to help your baby practise her hand movements and develop dexterity and hand-eye coordination. Water games are great for bath-time play, too.

♦ If your baby loves moving objects from one container to another, why not make a surprise box full of interesting and harmless objects for her to handle, explore, put back in and take out again. To make the game more interesting you could wrap some of the

emotional development

Your baby is unique, with her own likes and dislikes. She may object if you take a toy away or want to play the same game again.

As her self-awareness develops, your baby will become more assertive and turn any everyday activity into a battle of wills. You may find she is beginning to arch her back when she doesn't want to be put in her car seat, or shake her head if you try to feed her something she doesn't like.

As frustrating as this behaviour can be, don't forget how easily your little bundle of energy can be distracted! Her memory is short, and some fast thinking can refocus her attention: if she hates being dressed, sing her a funny song to help her forget why she made a fuss – or try redirecting your child's thoughts to what she can, rather than can't, do.

Her sense of humour

Your baby's first laughs were probably prompted by physical games such as being bounced on your knee or lifted high up in the air, and later by visual jokes such as you shaking your hair about or putting her bib on your head like a hat. Now that she is more mobile, she'll enjoy teasing you by doing things you don't like – heading out through a forbidden door and then looking back to see if you're watching, for example, or pushing the off button on the TV.

Developing fears

At the other extreme, this is the time when your baby may develop fears about things that haven't upset her before – the noise of the vacuum cleaner, perhaps. If she seems frightened of something, stay relaxed, comfort her, and reassure her that she won't come to any harm. This will help deepen her trust in herself and others.

Slowly familiarizing your baby with the object of her fear can help conquer this tendency. For example, let her examine the vacuum cleaner once it has been switched off and unplugged. Take things one step at a time and in time she will manage her fears.

Laughing together
As your baby's sense of humour develops she will love to tease you – and you will still get a lot of laughs from her when you bounce her on your knees or lift her high into the air.

items in paper – she'll love ripping them open to see what's hidden inside. Never leave your baby alone with paper to play with as she may put it in her mouth and choke on it.

♦ Listening to different sounds will help develop your baby's emerging language skills. If you play a familiar tune that she'll recognize on a xylophone or a toy piano, it will spark her interest and may encourage her to try creating some wonderful sounds herself.

♦ Your baby may become more aware of the noises animals make, so now is the time to introduce some animal songs. Look at animal books together and let her hear you mimic all the different sounds they make. Once your baby learns to imitate lots of animal noises, her success will encourage her to copy other sounds, too.

♦ Babies at this age are intrigued by space – they love crawling behind sofas or around the backs of chairs. Your baby will probably also love to crawl through a play tunnel. Roll a ball towards her inside the tunnel so that she can see how it works. As she becomes confident, she'll love crawling through the tunnel or hiding from you inside.

♦ A daily trip out to the park or local playground provides a good chance to spend time together. It also means you can encourage your baby's sense of spatial awareness, and improve her visual skills as you point things out to her.

♦ Satisfy your baby's need to explore with her hands – and encourage her sense of touch – with a "touch-and-feel" activity book that contains pictures and shapes made out of different textures.

10 to 12 months

As your precious baby approaches his first birthday, you will look back in amazement at the incredible changes that have taken place. He now has a unique personality, a wide range of emotions, and a strong sense of his place in the family.

physical development

At this age babies vary enormously in their physical achievement. Some have been crawling for a few weeks, while others are just getting started.

Your baby's balance has improved tremendously. He can lean sideways while sitting without toppling over, and twist round to reach something behind him, enabling him to reach for things himself.

First steps

Towards the end of this stage your baby may take his first steps – a really exciting development. If he has perfected his balance while cruising around your furniture, he may start to let go occasionally, grabbing hold of something only if he totters. See page 262 to make sure you have taken adequate steps to ensure his safety if he should fall.

Initially, he may manage only one or two steps before falling; encourage him to try again, and before long he'll manage more and more steps on his own. Moving the furniture slightly further apart will also help him gain confidence. But be prepared for your baby to go at his own pace – lots of babies don't walk until they are 13 or 14 months old, and some not before 18 months. Don't worry if your baby is taking things slowly, as long as his developmental patterns seem to be normal. If you have concerns, discuss them with his doctor.

Feeding himself

Now your baby has much more control over his hand movements, he is more accurate in everything he does with them, including feeding himself with finger

foods with no difficulty. Using a spoon isn't as easy to master, since it involves difficult hand-eye coordination in addition to good muscle control. But now that he can rotate his hand he is much better at getting food into his mouth, although it will still be a messy business.

It is worth encouraging your baby to feed himself, since sometimes he may refuse someone else feeding him, and he shouldn't rely on you entirely for all his food. On the other hand, it's still too early to leave it all up to him. Although he may start each meal enthusiastically, he'll quickly get tired and you may have to intervene to make sure that he is eating enough.

Throwing

Exploring different objects is still one of your baby's favourite activities, but now he will probably have stopped putting everything that he picks up into his mouth. How an object feels in his hands is more important to him, and he will experiment more and more with his hands.

For example, he will try to hold more than one item – such as two building blocks – in his hand at a time. This may be difficult at first as he drops one or both. Having discovered how to let go of something, he can now have great fun throwing things on purpose.

learning skills

You and your baby may be able to communicate together well, and his understanding of what makes the world go round is developing fast.

Your baby may still not be saying very much, but his understanding of language and communication is coming on in leaps and bounds. He can now follow simple questions such as "Where is your cup?" and will probably reply by pointing or looking in the direction of the cup. If you ask a simple question such as "Do you want a drink?", he may respond with a smile and move towards the cup.

If your baby has older brothers or sisters, they will find this a rewarding time, since they, too, can begin to interpret what he is trying to express.

Some babies may be able to say two or three words by their first birthday, although often only you and the rest of the family can understand them. It may be weeks before your baby uses more words, which is quite normal.

Understanding concepts

As your baby's intellectual skills develop you'll be able to watch him making more sense of his immediate world. Now, when he sees a picture of a dog in his book, he'll perhaps relate it to his grandfather's

dog or the dog he saw in the park, and begin to realize that even though every dog he sees looks different, they are all in fact dogs.

He can now also grasp the idea of opposites. With the help of your explanations, he will understand the difference between wet and dry, hot and cold, big and little, and in and out.

Linking objects to events

Your baby's understanding of cause and effect is now well developed – he knows exactly what will happen when he bangs his drum (it makes a noise) or drops his block (you will probably pick it up!).

He's also beginning to match objects to their intended purpose. For example, he'll put a toy telephone to his ear just as you do with a real telephone, or pick up the flannel in the bathroom and wash his face with it. This is an important step forward, since he will use this understanding to help him when he starts to match what he says to the objects he wants to talk about.

Concentration and memory

You may notice your baby can listen to very short stories right through. This is partly because he can now understand you, and because he can give you his attention for longer. His developing memory and past experiences affect his

Becoming a book lover
As your child's concentration improves, he will start to listen to stories all the way through. Learning to enjoy books now will help him enjoy them throughout his life.

actions and behaviour. You may notice this in the way he loves to cause chaos to his routine – crawling away when you want to get him ready for a bath or put his coat on, for example. Knowing what's going to happen next gives him a great opportunity to play a joke – at your expense.

emotional development

Your baby is keen to get involved in household chores, loves being with other babies, and may now become more attached to a comfort object.

By now, your baby will enjoy seeing other babies his own age – and may get excited when you invite friends around who have babies of their own. He can learn a lot by watching other children – and feeling at ease in company will help him take his first steps towards learning how to make friends.

Now is a good time to join a parent-and-toddler group, particularly if your baby doesn't have brothers and sisters at home. He'll still want to stay close to you, but he will be fascinated to watch and imitate the other babies and toddlers around him.

At this age, however, don't expect him to actively mix, join in, or share with the others. Your baby still thinks the world revolves around him and while he'll be very happy playing alongside other children, he'll naturally assume that every toy is there just for him. He won't be able to understand the reasons for sharing for another year or more.

your growing **relationship**

Your baby is very loving towards you and will shower you with hugs and respond to kisses when he chooses to. He can also become very self-focused, believing that he should come first when it comes to getting attention from you. At the same time, his sense of independence is increasing and his desire to explore means he won't sit contentedly in your arms for long.

Hugs and kisses
Your baby will enjoy the attention you shower on him – but he could be off to his next activity any minute now!

Copying and helping
Your baby is understanding the world around him more clearly than ever before, and he wants to be involved in whatever is going on. If he sees you busy wiping his highchair after a meal or sweeping the floor, he'll want to join in and he may try to copy you brushing your hair or washing your face, too.

He may also try to help speed your progress when you dress him by slipping his arm into his sleeve, or getting his padders for you to put on his feet. Make sure you always tell him what you're doing and why. Give him a chance to have a go, too, although don't expect him always to

do exactly what you anticipate: many a baby has tried to brush their hair with their toothbrush, for example.

Comforting objects
Around this time, lots of babies become attached to a special object such as a blanket or soft toy, which they insist on taking everywhere with them. Known as a "transitional object", this item will have a special place in your baby's life, helping him sleep when he's tired, and reassuring him if he's unhappy, especially if you are not around to comfort him. This is especially true for babies still dealing with separation anxiety.

Your baby will probably rely on his comforter for some time to come. Only when he finds other ways to deal with upsets will he gradually give it up. Meanwhile, if you are concerned about cleanliness, try and have two identical comforters to hand in case one needs to be washed. This will also come in handy if one is lost.

Social skills
Although at this age your baby doesn't understand how, or why, he needs to have good manners, he loves imitating you and his siblings. Learning the way you behave will help him get on with other people as he gets older. Even before he can talk, your baby can learn social rituals such as how to wave bye-bye. And if he hears you using polite words, he is more likely to use those words himself once he can talk.

toy **box**

Posting box
Posting boxes should be durable and incorporate a selection of simple, recognizable shapes. Make sure the shapes are not so small that they fit easily into your baby's mouth.

Nursery rhymes
Nursery rhyme books and songs will give your baby huge pleasure as he becomes more familiar with the words and tunes.

Pull-along toy
If your baby is becoming actively mobile, he might enjoy playing

with a pull-along toy on wheels that he can trail behind him. These are often available in the form of animals or trains. For safety reasons, make sure the string on this type of toy is no longer than 20cm (8in).

Soft toys
Soft toys can become treasured possessions. Choose dolls that have expressive or appealing faces to attract your baby's attention.

Toy telephone
Your baby will enjoy pretend toys such as telephones – especially those that make noises. Buy a safe, well-made version – the chances are it could be in use for a very long time.

learning through play

Help your baby expand his understanding, and particularly his knowledge of the names of objects, with familiar songs and books. Try also to encourage him to share well-loved toys, and develop his coordination and rhythm by playing clapping games with him.

♦ As your baby learns to turn the pages of a book, make sure he has plenty of them to look at, especially board books. Try and establish some regular quiet time together so that books become part of his everyday life.

♦ Your baby may now be able to hold his hands flat when he claps them together; if not, let him hold your hands as you clap them together. Let him sit on your lap, or on the floor facing you, so he can watch and join in clapping games and songs. Putting words, gestures, and music together will help with first words as well as giving him the chance to play with and imitate you.

♦ Play "give and take" with your baby by offering him something new to look at. When he's finished exploring it, hold your hand out for him to return it. Most likely he will. If so, encourage his sharing by saying "Thank you!" If not, try again another time.

♦ Soft toys such as teddy bears and clowns and dolls will give him lots of play opportunities for many years to come. Use them now to help him learn social rituals – encourage him to kiss his favourites goodnight, or say goodbye when he goes out for the day.

♦ Your baby will love listening to song tapes and looking at books again and again. This repetition will help encourage his first words and improve his memory.

♦ If your baby is beginning to walk, he may be ready for his first push-along trolley. At first you may need to help him along, but he'll soon enjoy pushing the trolley himself.

your developing toddler
12 to 24 months

Having spent the first year learning about your baby's physical and emotional needs, the focus now changes. This second year is more about helping your toddler become a self-sufficient individual, branching out into the world, with you as a guide.

A whole new world

Your toddler continues to need your active encouragement to explore her capabilities and her surroundings. She will also need you to return to as a safe emotional base because, for all her apparent independence, she needs your love and reassurance.

Developmentally, the physical change is enormous. Once your child learns to walk, her horizons expand. And learning to talk opens up her world to you, and the whole world to her, in a new and exciting way. Your toddler will constantly attempt to move ahead of her immediate capabilities, which may lead to enormous frustration for her. Learning about limits, her own and those set by you, is new for both of you. With patient teaching and encouragement, she can learn to follow basic safety rules and to cooperate with your expectations.

Recognizing limits

Toddlers cannot self-limit their activity. They tend to move straight from one activity to another without pause and to put every ounce of their energy into each. Your toddler will rely on you to help set the pace, so that she can manage to enjoy activities without overdoing them to the point of exhaustion, which is sometimes where the flashpoint of frustration ignites into a tantrum.

establishing a safe environment

Your toddler continues to explore things with her hands, but now this isn't limited to those toys given to her. She can move around her home, and everything is worth investigating, whether it's the dog's bowl or the CD player. How can she tell the difference between those buttons she can press and those she can't? It's not possible without your help, so remove items that can hurt her or be damaged (see *safety*, page 262), and direct her attention to activities that take advantage of her natural curiosity and pleasure in exploration.

Varying the pace

Toddlers still need lots of rest, and most will probably continue to need at least one daytime nap during this year. Well-rested toddlers will manage life better than those who are tired. And if your toddler is a poor sleeper at night, don't be tempted to keep her going all day in the hope that she will sleep continuously through the night. The more tired she is, the less easy she will find it to relax into a good sleep pattern.

Ultimately, this is a wonderfully exciting time for you and your toddler, full of new experiences. Understanding just what makes your toddler tick, and what her needs are, will help you create those opportunities that bring out the best in her.

the second year

By the beginning of the second year your baby will have developed a wealth of skills on which to build new ones. He has progressed from an infant, dependent on you to meet all his needs, to a very definite personality in his own right.

how your toddler learns

Where initially your baby's skills were geared to basic survival, now they are enabling him to explore and expand his world with your help.

During your baby's second year he is using all of his senses to gain experience and understanding of his world. Physical skills are greatly increased through mobility, and mobility is increased through the development and practice of physical skills. As a result, your toddler's cognitive, or learning, skills are influenced by his new view of the world. And emotional development moves ahead as your child utilizes these new skills to interact with others, and learns to become more social.

By the age of 24 months, your toddler will have more in common with an adult than with his newborn self in terms of abilities.

Increased mobility

This period is one of increased mobility for your baby. It is about exploring further afield through a newly developed ability to move from A to B. Initially this may be through crawling, but it also occurs through learning to walk upright, which enables greater movement and also frees up the hands. Once a skill such as walking

has been learned, progress comes through getting better at it. Learning comes from doing something over and over.

As your child becomes more proficient at moving around, he is able to see things in context and develop his spatial skills further. For example, it's hard to imagine a chair in context unless you can move around it. Also, if your toy rolls behind a chair, and you can get to it, you learn that when things disappear from view they don't actually disappear altogether. This is part of a learning process that the psychologists call "object permanence", meaning that something continues to exist, even after you can no longer see it.

Communication skills

Long before first words appear, comprehension and a developing understanding of the meaning of what you are saying emerges. It is not until

the meaning of a word is understood that the spoken word follows, which is why repetition is so important. As you do something, constantly talk to your toddler, telling him what you are doing.

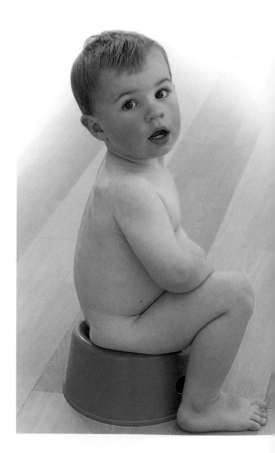

Potty at the ready
A major developmental milestone is reached when your child is ready to start using a potty, which can happen any time after about 18 months.

Eventually it becomes clear that your child understands simple words through his response to what you say. Long before he can say the word "shoes", he will help you look for his shoes when you ask him, for example.

Individuality

The rate of your baby's development depends partly on opportunities provided to develop different skills, but it also depends on the inclination and individuality of your child.

Some babies love to sit and focus on one thing for a time, absorbed in something quite stationary, while others are always on the go and keen to get up and about. Some will manage to get to where they want through crawling, and show no inclination to walk, while others may spend a short time bottom shuffling before moving swiftly to walking, never having actually crawled at all.

Boisterous children

Some children need more activity than others. Boys tend to become more restless more often and concentrate for shorter periods on quieter activities (such as playing with blocks or toy animals) than girls.

If your toddler, girl or boy, becomes restless or frustrated, instigate a short period of physical activity, such as a walk round the block with his push-along trolley or a game of being chased by you in the garden or park. Once he has let off steam, he will be happy to sit down with his crayons or toy cars again.

Calming activities, such as sitting together reading a book or listening to soft gentle music while being cuddled, can help your child enjoy some peaceful relaxing time.

1 to 2 years: your toddler's milestones

Your baby's milestones during the next 12 months are an important indicator of his developmental progress. Although all children develop at their own pace, there are a number of achievements that you can expect of your child during this year.

Movement milestones
- learns to walk unsupported
- walks, stops, and turns
- may be able to run, although may have difficulty slowing down to go round corners
- can squat to pick up something and return to standing position
- carries something in his hand while walking; may carry two items, one in each hand
- climbs safely onto a chair

Hand and finger milestones
- self-feeds with a spoon
- graduates from a feeder cup to a normal cup
- learns to let go of objects
- throws an object, even if not in a straight line
- can use his finger to point at something he wants
- tends to use both hands equally
- may try to carry two items, one in each hand
- rotates wrist to unscrew an item

Social and emotional milestones
- learns to be happily apart from you for longer periods
- plays alongside another child
- likes to watch what other children are doing and imitate them, especially if the children are older
- shows loving behaviour to a toy, pet, or another child
- picks up on your happiness or sadness, even if he is unable to understand it
- forms close attachments to parents, caregivers, and other close family members
- begins to think about how he feels and how others feel
- understands what annoys and what pleases you
- may help you with simple tasks

Language milestones
- talks about what he is seeing and learning
- progresses from single words to two-word utterances
- vocabulary extends to include up to 200 words
- responds verbally to questions you ask
- enjoys naming everyday objects when he sees them

Intellectual milestones
- remembers simple events that occur regularly
- makes connections between live objects and pictures
- learns the difference between what is real and what is not: can distinguish between the family car and a toy car, for example
- his imagination becomes more developed and he will love pretend play
- will enjoy looking at books both with you and on his own
- begins to understand the concept of possession
- may start to demonstrate an interest in potty training towards the end of his second year

12 to 16 months

Your baby's increasing ability to interact with her world is becoming more and more evident now. She will take every opportunity to explore as she enjoys her new-found mobility and as she develops her cognitive skills.

physical development

Almost half of all babies learn to walk during this time, although many will still topple if they lose momentum.

Your baby may already have taken her first steps, either cruising from one object or person to another, or setting off by herself. But if she has been walking since 10 months, or doesn't bother until 18 months, that is normal too.

Provide lots of opportunities to use and strengthen the leg muscles in preparation for walking. Start by holding her hands as she practises putting her body weight on her feet while taking a few tentative steps. Babies' heads are big in comparison to their bodies, and heavy. Until their legs strengthen, balance is a little unsteady as a result.

When your baby begins to walk, she'll walk with her feet wide apart, toes pointing out, to give herself as broad a base as possible to improve her balance. And as she walks alone, her arms are held away from her body to help her balance. With time, instead of toppling over, she will probably sit down quite deliberately if she feels she is losing her balance.

Fine motor skills

Your baby's fine motor skills – smaller movements of the hands – are also improving through practice, along with hand-eye coordination. Learning to let go of something provides a quite dramatic shift in ability, and brings together a number of skills.

As a baby, if you gave her an object, she would tend to clasp it and hold on to it until she dropped it accidentally, or had it taken from her. This was because of the reflex to hold on that she was born with. Initially so strong, this ability to cling so tightly diminishes over the first three months. Now she is reaching out, placing her hand over the object, deliberately picking it up, moving it to another place, and letting it go.

Hand movements are becoming more sophisticated. Your baby is beginning to turn her wrist in order to place an object more specifically into the place where she wants it to go. This movement is a bit haphazard at first, as the physical development of the bones, which allows for greater manipulation, occurs over the first few years, just as the child is growing in maturity and dexterity. All this picking up and dropping of things – maddening though it can be at times – is part of the activity needed to practise these movements.

Point and pick

Your baby now begins to stretch out her fingers into the right position to pick something up – she is anticipating what she intends to do. She will also stretch out her arm towards something that she wants, to convey to you what it is.

At first, toddlers tend to point with their finger, hand, and whole arm when they want something, but over time they learn to use just the finger to communicate their wishes to you.

Left or right?

At this age your toddler will probably use both hands equally. Some toddlers may begin to show a preference for using either the right or left hand when playing, feeding, or drinking from a cup, but most children do not consistently use one hand rather than the other until they reach about three years old.

The hand a child shows preference for is genetically determined. If both parents are right-handed, there is a 98 per cent chance of their child being so, too. When one parent is left-handed, there is a 17 per cent chance of a child being left-handed, and where both parents are left-handed, the probability increases to 50 per cent. Don't try to deliberately influence which hand your toddler uses: she will use the one that feels most natural to her.

learning **to walk**

When babies are learning to walk, it is much more useful for them to learn with bare feet. A baby can tell a lot about the surface on which she is walking through what she can feel through the soles of her feet – whether the surface is smooth and soft, or hard and lumpy. Don't be tempted to encase your toddler's feet in anything but the softest-soled shoes and allow lots of opportunity for safe barefoot exploration. It is essential that you get your toddler's feet measured for length and width to ensure that the shoes you choose fit correctly. She will need properly soled shoes only when walking outside. You will probably notice that walking with feet encased in shoes demands a slight adjustment at first (see page 125).

learning skills

With the right balance of stimulation and time to assimilate new experiences, your baby's cognitive development is expanding in leaps and bounds now.

Your child's attention span is beginning to lengthen and, if she isn't distracted by feeling tired, thirsty, or hungry, she can focus on an activity for a little longer. This is because she is beginning to develop memory, through repeated activity, so she is beginning to anticipate the pleasure of a book when you suggest it, for example, or going for a walk, or having a bath. And during an activity, if she is distracted for a moment and discontinues it, she will return to what she was doing after a break.

Through the daily routine, your child develops an understanding of what might happen next. This understanding can then begin to be transferred to other events.

A sense of touch

We are all born with a need to be touched, but its development is dependent on having the experience of touching and feeling things as well.

Manual dexterity
This baby is enjoying her new-found ability to pick up toys and put them exactly where she wants them to be.

Our ability to distinguish between different textures comes from our experience of feeling them. Touching an object to see what it feels like also provides a baby or toddler with the opportunity to use her hands in a different way, that is not to manipulate an object but to use her sense of touch to find out something about it. She can learn to explore and experiment by touching different substances and textures, such as water or fabrics.

Verbal skills

Your baby's first words are evidence of her cognitive development, and the beginning of an amazing new stage where communication extends into verbal language. Toddlers learn language by hearing the spoken word, so talk to your toddler.

At this stage your child will probably be saying, or attempting to say, a few words. Children vary enormously: some will say nothing at all for months then suddenly come out with a three-word sentence, while others will continually attempt to say individual words, however inaccurately, until they make themselves understood. Often a child will begin by saying one word, such as "dog" or "daddy", but apply it to all animals or to all men.

toy box

Stacking toys
These toys provide an opportunity to learn about sizes, and how things fit together. Playing with stacking toys such as blocks also involves using the hand to pick up and put down. Show her how to stack two blocks, one on top of the other, and she will try to copy you. At first she will probably manage to stack only two blocks, but with playful practice she will soon progress to stacking three and four blocks at a time without any difficulty at all.

Push-down/pop-up toys
Although these toys rely on hand-eye coordination, they also help your child learn about cause and effect. When I do this – push down – then this happens – it pops up. It engages her attention because she is learning that one event leads to another, but doesn't yet know for sure that it will happen every time. Show her how it works, then let her make her own efforts. Is it easier to push down with the whole hand, or just one finger?

Push-along toys
Pushing something along can be done for its own sake, or it can be incorporated into early, imaginative play – for example, putting a favourite soft toy into a miniature buggy or pushchair, and taking it "for a walk".

♦ A toy wheelbarrow in which things can be carried elsewhere is also fun, as is a toy vacuum cleaner that can be used alongside an adult using the real thing.

♦ Some push-along toys are designed to make a musical noise when used, while others may include a dog on wheels (which incorporates the pleasure of a soft toy into imaginative play).

♦ Some push-along trolleys come complete with a set of building bricks, which provide extra fun in being loaded and unloaded.

Textured toys
Use a variety of textured items – egg boxes, joining bricks, shiny paper, crinkly fabric, soft toys – and allow your child to explore their properties, while you supervise.

learning through play

Water play really begins from birth when your baby enjoys her first bath. Water is great fun to play with, and has lots of interesting properties that make it useful for exploration. Just pouring water from one plastic cup into another helps your child develop hand-eye coordination.

Bath and basin games
Provide a variety of different-sized plastic containers. Great fun can be had with a plastic tea set with a small teapot, which challenges coordination further when trying to pour from the spout. Playing somewhere where spills don't matter or helping to clear up when they do encourages your toddler to gain confidence.

♦ Lots of bath toys provide opportunities for pouring, while some also include other possibilities, such as turning a tap to allow water through or not.

♦ Supervised water play introduces the idea of different weights – a cup of water feels heavier than an empty one – and provides opportunities to learn about other properties of water. For example, it always flows down, not up – and here are the beginnings of understanding why rain falls down and rivers

don't run uphill. Your toddler can also learn about things that float, such as a leaf or a lolly stick made of wood, and those that sink, such as a pebble – but remember never to leave your child alone with items that could be a choking hazard.

Paddling pool play
Water play can be extended from baths to baby pools, where your toddler will learn to feel comfortable sharing space with other children, getting splashed, and participating in the rough and tumble of communal play. The confidence in water that this develops paves the way eventually towards the confidence to learn to swim.

♦ Never leave your toddler, even for a few seconds, in or near a body of water without supervision. This includes a bucket of water, bath, paddling pool, swimming pool, fish pond, lake, or the sea.

emotional development

Every baby is individual with a unique personality. Ensuring that all the physical needs of your baby are met really helps her emotional development at this stage.

It's hard to concentrate on learning to walk, or to deal with new people in your life, if you are tired, cranky, or hungry. Whenever possible, plan new activities or experiences for your baby when she is well rested, to ensure that an enjoyable time is had by both of you.

By now, close attachments have been formed to a parent, a caregiver, and other close family members. Often there is an especially close attachment to one or two people if there is a parent and childminder sharing the daily care. It is within this secure emotional environment that babies continue their development and learning.

Babies who are cherished, cuddled, and kissed learn, by example, how to pass on similar expressions of positive emotion to others, and you may also see this extended to their toys. Young children are often very

responsive to the emotional environment in which they live. They may not understand it but they often pick up on your happiness or sadness – laughing with you, or stroking your face if you are sad.

The role of soft toys
A favourite toy, to which a child can form an attachment, can help some children make the transition from your company to being happily alone. It can become a "transitional object". Many young

children find the presence of a familiar toy reassuring at bedtime.

Soft toys can also help develop a child's imagination as they give their toy characteristics, or act out happy or sad times with it. They can also use their soft toys to act out feelings. Talking to your toddler about feelings through a favourite soft toy can help her learn how to empathize. Does she look sad? Why does she look sad? How can we make her feel happy?

16 to 20 months

Toddlers are naturally curious, and will learn to make important discoveries by themselves. Make sure you allow your child the time and space to develop his own ability to find out things for himself.

physical development

With his walking skills getting better and better, and with his arms free, it now becomes possible for your toddler to pick up and carry an object while walking.

This usually requires two hands, so balance has to have improved enough not to need the arms. Being able to walk, and stand securely, also opens up the possibility of reaching for objects that were previously out of reach. Don't underestimate how far a toddler can reach: make sure objects are placed far enough away to be out of danger. It's all too easy for a toddler to grab a cup of hot coffee left too close to the edge of a table.

Smaller movements

Because your child's fine motor skills are improving, he is more able to grasp a small object using his thumb and forefinger. This makes much smaller movements possible, such as zipping and unzipping a coat, although it may take some concentration and effort at first, and some children of this age will not quite be able to do it on their own.

Activities that encourage fine motor skills, such as pressing and turning knobs and twisting handles, now make your child more successful when playing games that involve pushing a shape through a matching hole. Accuracy improves through play. Being able to achieve tasks independently – such as drinking from a cup – demonstrates his mastery of these skills.

Playing outdoors

Using their bodies in an energetic and expressive way helps children develop balance, coordination, and strength, and much of this sort of play needs to be done outdoors. Make sure that your child wears

188

suitable clothing when playing outdoors – clothes that you won't mind getting muddy, and that won't catch when your child is trying to negotiate a slide with your help.

Learning to be adventurous on swings and slides doesn't come naturally to every child, and yours might need some encouragement. But when he sees other children having fun, this will encourage him, too. Playing with other children also helps him to learn about taking turns.

Outdoor play can include first games with balls. Choose a medium-size ball – a bit smaller than a football and much lighter, so it won't knock your toddler over if thrown too hard, and so he can hold it in both hands. At first there will be very little hand-eye coordination, which is what makes actually catching a ball possible. This takes a lot of practice, but for now it is worth introducing the idea.

Learning to run

Your toddler may now be able to walk faster, and even run a little without stumbling, although children at this age vary considerably in what they can and want to achieve. If he is gently chased or excited when playing, your toddler can speed up quite considerably. The large muscle groups in the legs have become much stronger through use, and give your child more control over stopping and starting when he is walking or running.

His movements are generally much more controlled now, and may include taking backwards and sideways steps. What also becomes possible, with better balance and greater strength in the legs, is a kicking movement. At first, standing on one leg momentarily can be destabilizing and it takes practice to become proficient at doing so and then kicking out. Accuracy will be poor at first and, instead of actually kicking the ball, your child may effectively stand on it, which won't achieve his objective – yet!

Throwing a ball

Once your toddler has learned how to let go, the next challenge is throwing. Although first attempts demonstrate that toddlers cannot throw with any degree of accuracy, this will improve with practice. Give your toddler scrunched-up paper balls or soft foam balls to throw. Make a game of throwing, rolling, and catching balls. Keep heavy objects out of reach.

learning skills

By this stage your toddler's understanding has increased to the point where he can easily carry out simple requests, such as "Give me the cup". But he may struggle with more complex requests.

If you ask him to put down his book, fetch his shoes, and close the door, this could be beyond his ability because it requires him to remember a sequence of events in order. He would probably be able to do all three things if you asked him to do them one at a time.

Language development

Your toddler's developing language may still be limited to one word at a time, but voiced in a different tone to convey different meaning. "Dadda!" might mean "Come here!", while "Dadda?", as he holds out a toy, might suggest "Help me". And "Dadda" said while pointing at a cup might mean "I want a drink".

Soon two-word sentences begin, so you might hear "Dadda, here!" or "Dadda, please?" or "Dadda, drink". Reinforce what you hear by asking, "Would you like a drink?" This way, you let him know you've understood his request, and help him to understand how to say things correctly.

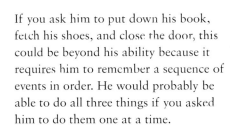

handy **work**

Little fingers and busy minds enjoy building bricks such as those that fit together and come apart without too much effort. To begin with, your child may simply admire the shapes and spend time working out how one piece can lock with another – he may also chew the pieces when teething. But soon he will use the different pieces in more complex ways to turn them into a variety of increasingly sophisticated constructions. This kind of toy is a good buy as it lasts well – and children of both sexes often have fun playing and learning with these bricks well beyond their second birthday.

toy box

Building blocks

Blocks that fit together take the possibilities of building blocks a little further. They require a bit more in the way of deliberate coordination as the fit needs to be a little more accurate, and it takes more strength to push them together. But the rewards are greater, as the blocks stay together.

Playing with building blocks that fit together is great for boys and girls. With a little prompting from you, they will soon learn to use their imaginations to build a house, or a garage, or just put the colours together in particular patterns.

Modelling clay

Making shapes out of soft, pliable, coloured, non-toxic dough can give your toddler hours of creative play. Clear a space on the kitchen table and show him how to roll the dough with his fingers to make sausage shapes. He could also have fun making flat shapes, using a child's rolling pin and some plastic pastry cutters or shape moulds.

Sand play

Sand has all sorts of interesting properties that can be explored. It trickles through the fingers or a toy. It feels gritty, and sticks to your hands. If you put a lot of sand into a large container, it gets heavy. If you make sand wet, it sticks together and will keep the shape of another object. If you have a garden, it's worth having a sandpit. Sand must be fine and clean. You will need a selection of plastic containers, spades, and other plastic toys to play with.

Improving vocabulary

Towards the end of this period your toddler will probably have a vocabulary of between 50 and 200 words. The development of memory and language are closely linked, so you may be aware of a big leap in his general understanding of the way the world works as his speech improves.

What he says is now becoming more sophisticated, too. Whereas before it was more a question of naming objects – dog, car, shoe – or linking an adjective with an object – a red bus – now he may be using abstract concepts. He may also show that he is beginning to understand that objects belong to people: "my car", for example.

Learning responsibility

At the end of a play session encourage your toddler to put the toys away. At this age, doing this is just as much of a game as anything else, and if it is presented as such it starts to pave the way towards caring for things and putting them away after using them.

We call it tidying up, and presume our child will find it boring – don't make that assumption and they won't either! Don't refer to it as "helping me"; it's a game and one he wants to play if you make it interesting, talking all the time – "Here's the red one. Can you find the green one for me?", "And... put it in the box! Now it's my turn." This will help him learn to value and take care of his possessions.

learning through play

Making a permanent mark, even if it's just a streak of purple on a white page, is quite a thrill when done for the first time. It is very clear evidence that you can make something happen! And if this is joined by other colours, and eventually celebrated and pinned on the wall, it is a very rewarding process for a toddler.

Paper and crayons

First scribbles are very important – they are early expressions of creativity. Provide lots of paper – it doesn't have to be new, the back of junk mail is good – and half a dozen colourful, thick wax crayons that are easy to grip, in an easily accessible container for your child. You will need to make it clear that only paper should be drawn on, but if yours is a particularly expressive and experimental child then other surfaces may be considered fair game at first. You can quite see why a nice white wall might be thought suitable, so you will need to be very clear about what's OK and what's not.

♦ Don't concern yourself with which hand he chooses to use for drawing at this stage, as he may use both equally before he opts more and more for one than the other when he is about three years old.

♦ Your child's first experiences of drawing on paper give him an idea of what he can achieve, and, over time, using crayons in this way helps him learn to control the movements of his hand. Using the thicker wax crayons, allow your toddler to experiment with his own ways of holding the crayon when scribbling.

♦ Movements are large at first, covering wide areas of the paper, and become smaller later as his fine motor control – the small movements he needs to make in order to manage writing later on – improves.

♦ Scribbling with crayons (these should be non-toxic) allows your toddler to practice twisting and turning movements of his hand. His hand-eye coordination as well as fine motor control need to come together to do this. Encourage your toddler to have fun, and enjoy the patterns he makes, so that he wants to continue to make more scribbles.

A time to read

By now your toddler will probably have quite a good selection of books, and visiting the local library to choose and borrow books is another activity that can be routinely enjoyed. Have a special shelf or book box where you keep your child's books and where he can get them for himself. And always keep a favourite book in your bag when you are out and about as it will give your toddler something to look at and talk about if you are waiting somewhere.

Find time at least once a day to sit and read stories to your toddler. This quiet, absorbing activity will give you some peaceful, restorative time together. If you have more than one child, ask them each to choose a story, and read each story in turn. This will also help them to learn about taking turns and patience. Children need individual storytelling and reading as often as possible.

Hearing stories read aloud encourages imagination and helps your toddler learn to focus on your voice while having fun. Talk about the stories you read, asking questions about the pictures, as well as reading the words.

emotional development

You may notice that your child now knows what pleases you and may try out different behaviours to see what your reaction is.

This is an extension of his learning about how he can influence his world, and is a way that he learns to engage your attention. It is best simply to ignore any behaviours that displease you, so that he does not get attention for doing them. At this stage, he will want to please you, so it's worth giving specific feedback for desirable behaviour: "Thank you for letting your friend play with your tractor" or "Well done – you've put all your toys back in their box", for example.

Becoming independent

You may also find that your toddler is quite happy to be independent of you in a group, just occasionally checking to see that you are available to him if he needs you. Sometimes, however, in new situations, the need for reassurance is temporarily increased. You may find a period of clinginess arises as a new adaptation is needed. This is normal behaviour while getting used to a new situation. Give your toddler the reassurance he needs but don't become overprotective: it will pass.

Playing with other children

Although your toddler might begin to understand about an object belonging to him, at this stage of his development he is unlikely to get too upset if it is taken away. Unless he has an emotional dependency on a favourite toy, he is more likely simply to reach for another toy to play with and continue his game. His interactions with other children are limited, and although he will enjoy being around other children of similar age, any playing he does is in parallel rather than interacting with them.

By this stage he may smile at other children of all ages, and may like to watch what they are doing and imitate them, especially if they are slightly older.

20 to 24 months

Your toddler has become increasingly independent, but she still needs your unconditional love and understanding. She always will! Meeting her emotional needs means being aware of her fluctuating moods and adapting to support them.

physical development

The difference between the baby who couldn't walk just over a year ago, and the toddler who can now walk, run, and kick, demonstrates the amazing range of physical skills acquired over the second year.

Climbing on and off low furniture and low climbing frames is probably routinely attempted and achieved. If you watch your toddler you can see that she is usually quite cautious, looking round to judge distances and stretching one leg to find the ground and then the other. If you have stairs, teach your child to come down them backwards, on her hands and knees, which is much safer than trying to come down facing forwards. If you are coming downstairs with her, she can walk down slowly, holding on to your hand.

Some toddlers try to jump up and down, but their feet may not leave the ground. All the time muscles are being strengthened and coordinated, and activities such as kicking a ball become possible through practice.

Your toddler's ability to squat down and pick up something, then return easily to a standing position, is now quite proficient because of the increased strength and flexibility in her hip and knee joints. But her running may still be a little stiff, and she may have insufficient strength and coordination to manage running around corners without slowing down.

Using her hands

Carrying something in her hands as she walks is probably routine now if the object is not too large, and she may try to carry two objects, one in each hand. Her fine motor skills are now more developed, meaning that not only can your child use her hands to greater effect, she can also use tools more efficiently. This can range from digging in a sandpit with a plastic spade, to scribbling on paper, to banging a drum.

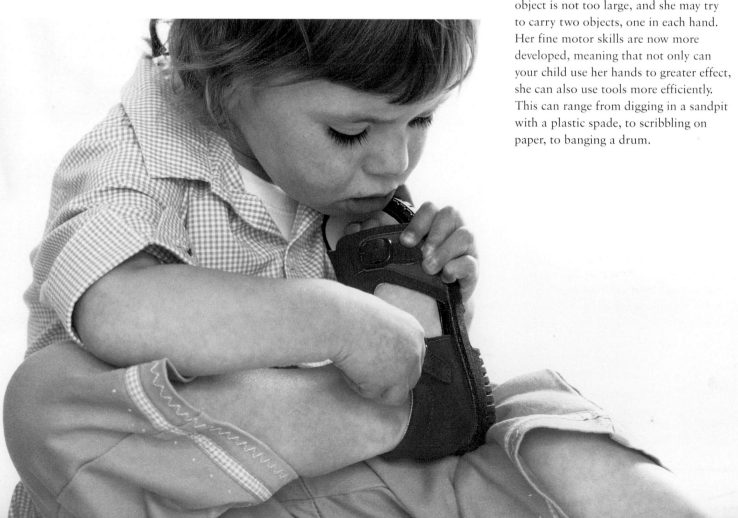

Fun with sand
This child is enjoying playing in his sandpit with his mum, who shares the fun while also being on hand to supervise.

responses. This exchange causes a massive shift in understanding as language and memory develop.

Language and memory

Memory and language are closely linked. It is much easier to remember something when it has a name than when it is just an abstract object. Talk to your toddler, as this will help her cognitive development enormously. If you reinforce her efforts to communicate, it encourages her to go on trying. In addition, if you repeat what she says and build on it, this helps, too. For example, when she points and says, "Car", you say "Yes, that's your car. That's your blue car. Would you like to put your teddy in your blue car?" Not only are you responding to and reinforcing what she is saying, you are giving her a lot more relevant information.

You are also helping her develop the ability to think about what to do next, which helps develop her imagination. On another occasion when she is playing with her car and teddy, she will put the teddy in the car and move her language along, saying "Teddy in", for example. Then, over time, "Teddy in car" or "Teddy in blue car".

learning skills

By constantly building on what she already knows, your toddler continues to extend her understanding of the world.

Physical experiences help develop your toddler's cognitive skills. For example:

♦ She knows that toy cars go "brrrmmmm, brrrmmmm" but a plastic cow goes "moooo".

♦ Your child knows that a toy hammer is for banging with and should use it correctly now, instead of another toy.

♦ She can make connections between a toy car and the family car; a plastic cow and one in a book or in a field. She knows that each car has similar properties but that they are different: one is real, the other is not.

And all the time your child is talking about what she is seeing and learning, which means that you are reinforcing her knowledge with your questions and

toy **box**

Tray puzzles
Matching shapes in tray puzzles is a development of shape sorting, and a precursor to simple jigsaw puzzles. It is all about identifying and matching shapes. You may have to show your child what is expected of her before encouraging her to have a go.

♦ Tip out the pieces and choose one. Show her how you look at it.

♦ Together, find the matching shape on the board.

♦ Place the shape alongside its home so she can see how they match up before putting the piece in place.

♦ Take your cue from your child – some children welcome help while others want to work things out for themselves.

Crayons and paper
Having been introduced to the idea of crayons and paper at an earlier stage, your child will want to scribble and draw regularly by now.

♦ Her hand movements are crude at first, but through experimentation with colours and shapes she will learn that she can exert greater control.

♦ Allow her to experiment with a variety of non-toxic crayons and felt pens. Talk to her about the colours and what she is trying to express through her scribbles.

♦ Don't assume that you can interpret what your child is trying to draw – let her tell you about it.

fun with **finger paint**

Your child can use paints in a variety of ways without using a brush – she simply needs hands and feet. You need thick, non-toxic, water-based paint in the three primary colours – red, yellow, and blue.

You can experiment with one colour at a time, or mix two to make a third, or mix them all together to make a dirty brown, which begins the exploration of the different properties of colour.

Finger painting
Finger painting is fun because it's messy and very tactile, and gives your child a real hands-on experience of making her mark. You will probably need several sheets of paper to experiment with different effects.

Hand prints
Hand prints require a slightly different technique, and possibly some adult help to paint one hand at a time, all over, and then to press down carefully. First attempts may be a little smudged, but this activity provides a good opportunity to talk about fingerprints and individuality.

Footprints
Footprints require adult help if you are to avoid paint being trodden elsewhere, especially as balancing alone on one foot isn't possible yet. Footprints make a unique record of your child's growth, and you can compare children's hand and foot sizes, talking about whose is bigger or smaller.

Hands-on experience
This toddler's mother helps him paint thick, dark blue paint onto the palm of his left hand. Once his hand is covered in paint, he spreads his fingers and presses his hand on the paper to make a print. She is helping him develop his own hand print, and he loves doing it.

Pretend play
The development of imagination is helped enormously by encouraging pretend play. Pretend play usually begins through imitation, so, for example, when you played peekaboo, you pretended you had gone away by hiding your face and reappearing, and your baby copied you. This extends into other activities.

She will pretend to pour tea from a toy teapot into a cup, and milk from a toy milk jug. Then she will put in sugar and stir. She remembers a sequence of events and pretends to do it as part of her game. All the time your toddler is playing these games she is beginning to understand the distinction between what's real and what's not.

Learning about nature
Playing outdoors gives a child the opportunity to experience the natural world. It's difficult to be aware of the weather, for example, when indoors – but you can feel the wind and see its effect on

learning through **play**

Toys, such as first cars, trains, teddies, dolls, and toy figures, provide great opportunities for imaginative play, whether your child is a boy or a girl. These toys also help your child develop her own stories and events, which she can play out with them.

Playing with dolls and toy figures
You will probably find that your child concentrates quite hard while playing imaginatively with her toy figure or doll, and she may talk about what is happening in her game, chattering away to herself.

♦ Boys tend to talk less when they play with dolls or toy figures, as their games tend to be more active.

♦ Both boys and girls copy what they've seen in real life, and at this age will probably copy various parenting activities they have experienced.

♦ Your toddler may pretend to feed a doll, put it to bed, or give it a bath.

♦ Looking after a sick doll – giving it pretend medicine, putting bandages on its knees, or bandaging its arm is a great game.

the trees when you are outdoors. Walking in the countryside or a park provides an opportunity to look at leaves, and other growing things, as well as older children riding bikes, scooters, or skateboards.

Talk about the leaves on the trees, the seasons of the year, how the temperature influences the way things grow. Keep it simple, but point things out and name them. All of this will help her observation skills and vocabulary. You can also point out things such as reflections in puddles and the shapes made by clouds in the sky.

Reading

By now, reading to your child is part of your regular routine. Although books are something that you can share with your child, also encourage her to use books on her own, perhaps suggesting that she looks at a book in bed while waiting for you to come and settle her into bed at night, or when she is having a quiet time during the day.

emotional development

Learning to think about others takes a long time, but as your toddler becomes more self-aware, physically and then emotionally, she will begin to extend her feelings about herself to others.

Empathy starts with those who are closest to her, which is why you may see some evidence of this in her relationship with you – on whom she is still so dependent – but not necessarily with others.

Loving family members create the emotional security that allows your toddler to consider the feelings of other people. For example, if you point out that an older child is upset, your toddler may express sympathy by giving the child a kiss and a hug.

As your child experiences more of the world, and develops the language to talk about her experiences, she begins to think more about both how she feels and how others feel. This may become apparent first of all through expressions of her own feelings – happiness, anger, sadness – which can sometimes feel overwhelming and may be expressed in a tantrum.

Managing feelings

Feelings can now be expressed in a variety of ways and learning how to manage them, especially in a group, is the beginning of your child's social development. Your child's inability to manage overwhelming feelings may result in unacceptable behaviour towards other children. You will want to help your child deal with this, but she has to have experience with a social group in order to practise managing her feelings. Remember that a hungry, tired, or bored toddler is much more likely to exhibit unwanted behaviours.

♦ Toys don't need to be sophisticated: an old shoebox and a tea towel makes a very good bed and blanket for a teddy to sleep in.

♦ Toddlers sometimes act out their own experiences with their dolls, helping to make sense of events in their daily lives.

Playing with cars
Both girls and boys enjoy playing with cars and trains.

♦ At this age toddlers still tend to play alongside each other, although elements of social play are beginning to emerge. Sharing a group of cars may not work, but if each child has his or her own car they may happily play together.

♦ Look for opportunities to acknowledge and praise sharing, and head off any potential conflicts before they occur. Children need coaches not judges.

Car in the making
This toddler makes a car with his building blocks. He can then play with it, moving it around an imaginary world.

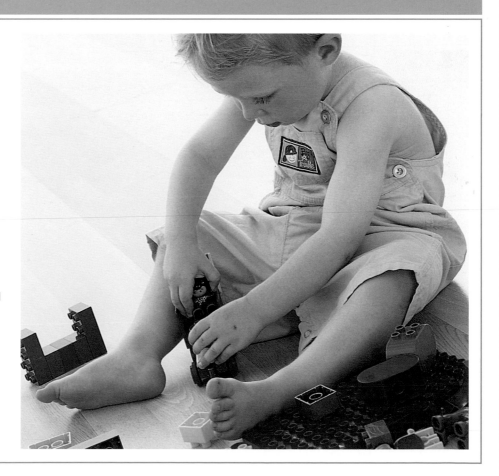

your developing toddler
24 to 36 months

During the third year of life your child will continue to develop into a physically dexterous, verbally competent, and emotionally expressive individual. He will also begin to experience just what a magical, if sometimes frustrating, place the wider world can be.

Emerging independence
This is a time when your child progresses from being almost completely self-centred and limited in his outlook to becoming more aware of other people and events around him. It is also a time spent juggling your child's growing desire for greater independence with the limits of his abilities, which can often be out of line with each other, and he will frequently require your help.

Growing closer
This can also be the best of times for you as a growing family. Spending time together provides all sorts of learning opportunities as well as being fun – whether you are visiting the park, reading a book, or even walking to the shops. Your child may also delight you with spontaneous outbursts of affection, disarming you with his endearing hugs, irresistible smiles, or infectious laughter; while you in turn can respond in an equally spontaneous way.

Accentuating the positive
Although it may sometimes seem at this stage as if your child's favourite pastime is saying "no", it may be because this is one of the words he hears most from the grown-ups around him.

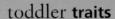

toddler **traits**

It is important not to confuse family characteristics or potential personality traits with challenging toddler attributes. A stubborn or argumentative streak in a two year old is a typical form of behaviour for a child of this age, and is not necessarily setting up key character traits for later life. Even so, it can sometimes be challenging to live with a two-year-old child who just doesn't want you to put on his shoes or who seems to say "no" to every request you make! Be patient – the likelihood is that this is a developmental stage and it will pass.

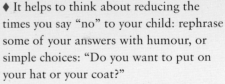

♦ It helps to think about reducing the times you say "no" to your child: rephrase some of your answers with humour, or simple choices: "Do you want to put on your hat or your coat?"
♦ Reinforce positive behaviour with plenty of praise.
♦ Remember, too, that when your child says "no" it is a reflection of his growing sense of self, which is positive and important – this is his way of learning what it means to be an independent person.

Your child needs your guidance, reassurance, and unconditional love. It's not easy, and can sometimes bring out the two year old in the best of us! So remember which one of you is the adult and retain your sense of balance as you make this journey from toddler to pre-schooler together.

the third year

The biggest change you will probably notice in your child's abilities as he enters his third year is his increased understanding of his own world and his relationship to it, including the people around him.

how your toddler learns

During this year, your child's language skills will develop tremendously, opening up a whole new world of communication.

You may also find that your child is becoming more interested in what you are doing. By letting him join in as much as possible with your everyday activities, he will learn new skills as well as enjoy just being with you.

Talk to your child as you do things together. Describing objects, colours, and shapes, for example, will help to increase his vocabulary and language development. Acquiring the ability to communicate verbally is the start of a whole new aspect of your child's life.

Taming tantrums

At this age, it can be hard for small children to know how to wind down if they are tired or accept that something has to finish. You may find your child resists

Puzzle power
Advancing fine motor skills is a key factor in your child's development as his increased abilities allow him the independence to enjoy more activities on his own.

or rebels against ending a game he is enjoying because you have to go out, for example. It takes improving memory skills to understand that finishing something enjoyable doesn't mean that it can't be done again another day. Explain this to your child and allow him time to digest the idea.

Acquiring social skills

Most of what children learn about respecting other people's feeling is acquired through example and by observing others. If your child is treated with fairness and consideration, and then sees this repeated in the extended family and wider community, he will, in time, begin to understand what it means to be considerate of others.

Likewise, despite his typical toddler attributes of self-focus and possessiveness, it is important to encourage your child to mix with other children to help his social development. For instance, if an older child, who has already learned to share, plays with your child, he can in turn learn from the example of the older child.

Fine motor development

Your child's hand movements are becoming more precise. Turning the pages of a book one at a time, holding a pencil correctly, and using a cup with one hand, are all examples of the greater dexterity he is now developing.

Your child is learning to focus on a single activity for longer periods of time. This in turn gives him the ability and concentration he needs to develop more creative tendencies, such as beginning to draw or play with puzzles using his improved imagination and observation skills.

2 to 3 years: **your toddler's milestones**

In terms of overall physical growth, which slows down between the second and third birthday, the most noticeable change during this third year is your child's body proportions. As his limbs lengthen and his muscles strengthen from being used, his posture becomes more upright, with a flatter tummy.

Movement milestones
Your child's expanding physical abilities in turn give him increased coordination and balance. Now he can walk quickly, for example, and carry toys in his hand as he walks.

By the end of this year you can expect your child to be able to:

♦ walk upstairs using alternate feet

♦ bend down to retrieve a toy without falling over

♦ hop and skip

♦ pedal a tricycle.

Hand and finger milestones
By the end of this year you can expect your child to be able to:

♦ use a crayon to copy a circle on a piece of paper

♦ turn the pages of a book one at a time

♦ rotate his wrist and unscrew jar tops.

Social and emotional milestones
With the development of the idea of the self, and of possessions, comes difficulty in sharing – sharing you, or his possessions.

As your child becomes more social, he'll start to anticipate events and express pleasure at certain activities, or begin to recognize particular children and grown-ups. His emotional range is broad, including anything from sheer pleasure and delight to frustrated rage.

By the end of this year you can expect your child to be able to:

♦ happily spend time away from you

♦ express affection to you and to other close family members

♦ show interest in other children.

Intellectual and language milestones
Until this point, your child's physical development, and what he learned from it, gave him the impression that what happens in his world is the result of something he has done.

This self-orientated view of the world means that a child of this age often takes things literally. He finds it difficult to differentiate between fantasy and reality: if you say, for example, "If you eat any more, you'll burst!", it is just possible, from his point of view, that this could happen.

Imaginative play also becomes important as your child tries to make sense of and seek explanations for events by acting them out, and learns to distinguish fact from fantasy.

By the end of this year you can expect your child to be able to:

♦ follow a two-part instruction

♦ speak in sentences of four or five words

♦ be understood by non-family members

♦ play imaginative games

♦ match an object to a picture in a book

♦ sort objects into groups by colour

♦ understand the concept of "two".

Making sense of it all
The journey that you take with your child over this year happens in fits and starts, and the challenge for you is to help your child make sense of it all through opportunity and activity, with you as his guide.

24 to 28 months

Your two year old's growing independence and the pleasure she derives from her discoveries makes this an exciting time. You can still expect her to let you know just how she is feeling – she will express herself openly with tears and smiles.

key milestones

♦ can hop, skip, and jump, as balance and coordination improve

♦ understands concepts such as up and down, in and out

♦ becomes more sociable; starts to learn to consider others

physical development

Your two year old's physical ability has progressed in leaps and bounds over the last 12 months and now she can walk, run, and climb.

What she needs over this next period are lots of opportunities to use her body and explore her capabilities, building greater strength in her limbs and increasing her coordination.

Although your child may be unable to continually jump and hop at this stage, for example, it won't be long before she incorporates an occasional hop, skip, or jump as she runs or walks. These skills have their own momentum and will become easier with practice.

Fine motor control

While your child's gross motor skills – such as walking and running – are improving, so, too, are her fine motor skills, which enable her to use her hands in specific ways to accomplish tasks.

At birth, your child's wrist and palm consisted of only three bones, in comparison to the 28 bones in an adult's hand. It isn't until the relevant bones grow and can be manipulated that the brain's ability to influence the supporting muscles can be more fully exerted. Once this happens, using tools (in your child's case, these are usually toys) becomes easier, whether it is a stick to beat a drum, a crayon for drawing, or a spoon to feed herself.

Practice makes perfect

As a baby, your child began by swiping at an object, then she was able to grasp it with her whole fist, and now she can delicately pick up something quite small between her thumb and forefinger. Not only that, her ability to pick up something, twist her wrist, and place it carefully down again is a considerable physical achievement.

Initially, every effort was put into trying to place and balance just one block on top of another, for example. Practice has made this easy, and now she may try to balance as many blocks as possible before they topple over – or are deliberately knocked down! Thus her ability to pick up an object in her hand has matured immeasurably: she can now do this with greater accuracy and judge far more easily where to place the brick so that it will balance.

At play in the park

Playing in the park can also help improve your child's fine motor skills, although she still needs careful supervision since her high energy levels and expectations of her abilities can sometimes get her into unexpected difficulties.

love of **repetition**

You may find your child requests the same story book over and over again. Children of this age love repetition, and sometimes object if you deviate from exactly what is written. They feel comfortable hearing the same stories over and over, and this repetition helps them to learn. They may also remember or recognize the odd word, and then notice it again if they later see the word printed somewhere else. You will probably find they like playing the same action songs, rhymes, and clapping games over again, too.

learning skills

Your child will make great progress throughout this year as her language skills develop and she begins to gather and express information in ways other than physical exploration alone.

Physical advances continue, too, of course, but it is the bringing together of her language and physical skills – for example, "When I do this, this happens" – that really helps her cognitive development.

The continued development of her memory, together with improving language skills, means that your child is beginning to form mental images of how things happen, which leads to an understanding of concepts.

Concepts such as in and out, over and under, are abstract ideas to a toddler. Showing your child the meaning – up the stairs, down the stairs; in the door, out the door – will further her understanding. Talk to your child about going inside your house, or show her how you put one stacking cup inside another, for example.

You will be able to see your child's understanding evolve as you watch her play and as you talk and explain things to her. For example, if she sees you put her teddy bear inside a box and you then ask, "Where is the teddy bear?", she will soon comprehend what it means for something to be inside the box. Keep demonstrating and then explaining things to her, and she will gradually begin to understand more about how the world around her works.

Improving concentration

You can also see the effectiveness of your child's memory at this age if you interrupt her activity to ask her a question. She can focus on you and then return to whatever it was she was doing. This is because she can now not only remember what she was doing, but what stage she had reached doing it. Part of being able to develop this technique involves what psychologists call "selective (or focal) attention" – the ability to switch off from outside stimuli and concentrate on one thing at a time.

toy box

Picture lotto
Choose a chunky picture lotto game that your child can grasp easily, and with simple images. Use only a few pieces to begin with; as she gets older she can memorize more pictures.

Cassette player
Some children's cassette players enable children to record their own voice talking and singing, or are even equipped with headphones for listening quietly to a favourite tape.

Books
Although your child will love reading the same stories over and over again, make sure you keep her stimulated by occasionally borrowing other books from your local library to vary the complexity of pictures and introduce new types of stories.

Scrapbook materials
Choose round-ended scissors that are easy for your child to open and shut with one hand, and a water-based glue that actually sticks but which can be easily washed off hands and clothes.

Painting equipment
Choose paint specially designed for young children and that will wash out of clothing. Thick finger paints in bright colours are the best choice. If you buy brushes, choose large brushes that are easy to hold.

Tricycle
Tricycles are good for outdoor play. Let your child get used to pushing herself along with her legs and learn how to steer before showing her how to use the pedals.

The benefits of books

If you say you are going to read a story to your child, her memory of what this involves and the pleasure she knows she will derive from it make her more willing to focus on the book for the time it takes to read a story.

She can then use this knowledge about what books involve and how to enjoy them to look at books by herself. This helps with developing her concentration and lengthening her attention span, while also gradually extending the range of her vocabulary.

Over the past two years you have probably collected numerous children's stories, from treasured first board books and favourite picture books to more sophisticated stories. All of these provide unique access to an imaginative world that helps your child learn about new ideas, cause and effect, feelings, and facts.

This is the start of your child learning to read, so it is important to help her develop a natural curiosity about books and stories.

emotional development

Emotionally, your two year old will still appear quite selfish. This is our adult interpretation of her behaviour. Her inclination is to put her needs first. Help her to think of the needs of others, too.

Encouraging your child to share teaches her to consider other people. It will also help increase her socialization skills, which are learned primarily through imitation. If she is treated with respect and affection, she will learn to treat others in the same way. However, if you are overly concerned with the feelings of others at the expense of those of your own child, you will diminish her self-esteem. Other people are just as important as she is, but not more so.

At this age you may also have the advantage of your child wanting to please you, so through your relationship with her she can learn to extend her consideration to others around her. Focusing on this aspect will help her develop the idea that if something is nice for her, then it would be nice for someone else, too.

Expressing emotion

You can expect spontaneous and genuine shows of affection from your child by this stage, especially if similar attention has been lavished on her. It makes it much easier for her to accept and value other people's feelings if she feels accepted and valued, too.

Try to watch the language you use when managing your child's emotional behaviour. She is not being naughty if she doesn't want to wait her turn to play with a toy, she merely needs a gentle reminder or explanation of how the process works or what her part in playing with other children is. If she can't grasp what you mean at first, wait with her, or suggest that she play alongside you until she learns that taking turns is a positive thing to do.

The emotional range of a two year old is broad, extending from sheer delight to frustrated rage. While the ability to express emotions freely is considered healthy, what your child needs to learn is to manage her emotions and know which feelings are appropriate. This takes practice and needs your help.

Managing emotion

Children may feel overwhelmed by the force of their emotions sometimes, hence the full-blown tantrum. These situations need specific management skills, but it also helps to keep in mind what might trigger such extremes of emotion. Some children cannot manage emotionally as well as others when they are tired or hungry, for example.

In the middle of an emotional maelstrom it is worth remembering that your child is also capable of expressing positive emotions. So finding an activity to share, which she enjoys and allows her to express her happier side, will help her self-esteem, and increase your own pleasure.

learning through play

Giving your child lots of opportunities to explore what her body is capable of doing can help her physical development and her self-esteem. Help her develop her memory skills, too, by playing tapes and matching picture games.

♦ Outdoor playgrounds with swings and slides to enjoy are good as there are usually other children to share the experience, which also helps your child learn about taking turns.

♦ Soft modelling clay is a delight in itself, and your child may enjoy just squeezing it through her fingers before getting involved in more imaginative play. Creating flat shapes and making impressions in the

dough with pastry cutters or even just making hand prints allows her to explore all sorts of interesting possibilities with modelling clay.

♦ Matching shapes or pictures is an important observational and pre-maths skill. You may have given your child a shape-sorter, and then moved on to a puzzle where she has to select and place a flat shape into a matching place on the board. Now this skill can be developed into a simple game of similarities and dissimilarities. This in turn helps extend language skills to communicate ideas, observations, and feelings.

♦ A cassette player designed to be used by little fingers will give your child access to music and favourite stories on tape. You may also like to record yourself reading a favourite story for your child, and if there are stories with which she is familiar, she can look at the book while listening to the tape. This will increase the access your child has to the spoken word. Learning to listen attentively will be of great benefit to her, especially when she joins nursery school or playgroup. Make sure the volume can't be raised beyond a certain level, to avoid damaging your child's ears.

28 to 32 months

During these early years, you are your child's first teacher, and time spent together is invaluable. Even when life is very busy, find time to be together. Giving your child your undivided attention will give you both pleasure.

physical development

Your child needs plenty of physical activity to help expend some of the enormous amount of energy she exhibits at this age.

All forms of exercise help your child's spatial understanding, and, by extension, her balance and coordination skills. Getting plenty of exercise not only burns off excess energy, it establishes a positive body image and a sense of self-esteem in your child's mind.

In addition, the connections built up between neurones in the brain, known as neural pathways, are formulated by regular physical, as well as cognitive, activity. This is why, once we have learned how to ride a bicycle we never forget, unless something interferes with those specific neural patterns imprinted in our brains. Therefore, a child needs practice in the larger physical skills – running, kicking, climbing, or pedalling a tricycle – to become competent, as well as build strength and use up energy.

With growing concerns about today's rising rates of childhood obesity, our

Getting physical
Outdoor play gives young children the opportunity to develop important physical skills such as coordination and balance, as well as improve stamina and strength.

sedentary lifestyles, and children's lack of exercise, it is as well to foster an enjoyment of exercise. Let your child walk rather than take the car, allowing her to sit in her buggy if she gets tired, or park further away from the shops than usual and walk there.

Hand proficiency

Given the opportunity, it's amazing what a difference practice can make to your child's ability to use her hands proficiently.

By this stage, you can expect your child to use her hands to do a variety of different things, from carefully turning the pages of a book to holding a pencil or unscrewing a jar. Practising undoing buttons on clothes, for instance, can help her fine motor skills and develop her independence.

This maturing of fine motor skills helps in all sorts of ways, including encouraging your child to develop the self-confidence to try other things that were once quite difficult. Seeing her own progress, and enjoying the pleasure and satisfaction that it brings, encourages her to try other new activities.

awareness of self

Your child probably now knows that she is a girl – or he is a boy – and can distinguish between the sexes, although she may not always know why. She will also be able to refer to herself as "I" and may be able to describe herself in simple sentences: "I am hungry", for example. This growing awareness of self began months before, but its expression is now becoming clearer, and as your child's language skills improve she may be able to convey her thoughts more easily.

toy box

Jigsaw puzzles
Choose colourful puzzles that are not too difficult for your child. Some children will still be on six- or seven-piece puzzles while others may have graduated to enjoying more complex ones. Well-made wooden jigsaw puzzles with clear, simple pictures are most suitable for small fingers and will hold a child's attention.

Ball play
Buy a medium-sized, lightweight ball that your child can easily wrap her arms around to hold securely. Soft tennis balls are another option.

Toy tea set
A brightly coloured, well-made plastic tea set will give hours of pleasure. Make sure the pieces are sturdy enough for little hands and not so flimsy that they keep toppling over.

Dolls and dolls' clothes
You can buy dolls with appropriate clothes that are specially made to help young children learn about the process of dressing and undressing. Dolls stimulate imagination and also encourage role-playing games.

Picture dominoes
Make sure that the dominoes are large enough for young children to pick up and put down easily.

Plastic blocks
The chunkier the plastic pieces are, the more chance your two year old will have of being able to use her coordination skills and the strength in her hands to fit blocks together without becoming frustrated.

learning skills

Since memory is such an important part of what helps children develop intellectually, it is worth helping your child try to improve her memory skills.

At this stage it is still easier for children to remember language that is reinforced by physical activity, such as action songs. In the same way, when you tell your child how to do something, show her at the same time – turn the page of a book carefully, or close a door gently, for example. This is especially important when your child struggles with abstract concepts.

Creating an impact
For all of us, remembering routines that happen every day is harder than remembering single events. You may notice that if you ask your child

she had for breakfast – even if it was only an hour ago – she may look at you blankly since the food she eats every day is not of much consequence to her. But if you ask her what she had for tea on her last visit to her grandma's house, she may easily remember.

Children are very much "of the moment", and remembering the mundane holds little interest for them. Something that may have been planned, discussed, and involved a change in the normal routine becomes an exciting event, and thus has a greater impact on a child.

Language skills

By now your child's vocabulary may include as many as 200–300 words. She may also be using connecting words between phrases, such as "and", while also adding details to her descriptions. Bilingual children may initially tend to mix words from each language when they speak, but overall they should speak as fluently as their peers.

Asking questions

With this acquired vocabulary comes the question, "Why?" The process of questioning is valuable to your child as it helps her to understand, and it is likely to continue for many months. Answer the question simply, allowing for development of thought, rather than overwhelming your child with a complicated explanation.

Answering a two year old's incessant questioning is rather an art, and there can't be many parents who haven't resorted occasionally to saying, "Because I say so!" However, be prepared for the comeback "Why?" You may even want to respond with your own question in a friendly tone, "What do you think?"

Speaking clearly

Children of this age may still speak unclearly or mispronounce words. This may be connected to the development of facial muscles. If your child still mispronounces most words, it is important to check with your doctor to make sure she hasn't suffered any hearing loss and then pursue a speech/language evaluation.

Time for tea
A toy tea set will provide lots of fun as your child practises pretend play.

emotional development

You may find that as your child becomes more social she starts to anticipate events and express pleasure at one activity over another.

She may also begin to express her excitement when she sees a friend she enjoys playing with. Forming attachments outside the immediate family circle is evidence of your child's widening emotional development. She is making relationships based on her own positive feelings about being a person, independent of you.

It is important to try and validate your child's emotions, even if doing so sometimes seems at odds with your own feelings. With her improving language skills, articulating how she feels about someone, or something, becomes a greater possibility. She may not know what she feels at first, but you can help her explore her emotions. Don't disregard her feelings or tell her not to be silly if she appears hesitant about playing with another child, for example. Gently determine what it is that she doesn't feel comfortable about.

Expressing pleasure

In the same way, when a person or an event generates particular pleasure, ask your child what it is that feels good about the experience. Use this opportunity to

learning through play

Simple jigsaw puzzles are an excellent way of training your child's eye to recognize matching shapes and to look at how things fit together. You can also help her manage a small task and improve her fine motor skills by giving her a doll to undress. Try playing singing games to improve her ability to listen to different sounds and follow rhythms.

◆ Introduce the idea of rhythm to your child by beating time. Pick out the rhythm of different words, or combinations of words, for example, the rhythm in your child's name: Martin becomes Mar-tin, Samantha becomes Sa-man-tha, and so you introduce the idea of syllables with a game. Maybe an older sibling could play an instrument while you and your two year old beat time, clapping your hands or tapping glasses filled with different volumes of water.

◆ Getting dressed and undressed is a part of your child's routine, and something she may be happy to attempt on her own. It can provide the chance to learn to undo various clothes fastenings, such as buttons and zips, which require small, precise movements of the fingers. But these are skills of great value, and something your child needs to be competent at doing in due course. It also allows her to develop the sort

of confidence needed to manage small tasks alone, which will stand her in good stead when she has to manage away from one-to-one support, perhaps when she starts nursery school.

◆ You may also like to play picture dominoes with your child. This makes demands on her observation and memory skills and improves her ability to spot similarities. Although she is still too young to play this game on her own, she may enjoy playing with you.

◆ Simple jigsaw puzzles take the process of matching up shapes to a higher level, since they require good observation skills. Children find great satisfaction in trying to find the right piece and putting it in the right place. Learning to look at something in this very specific way is also good training for the identification of letter shapes later on.

---

talk to her about feelings, but keep it simple. By being attuned to your child's feelings and acknowledging them, and encouraging her to articulate them when she's ready, you are paving the way for her to learn how to explore and express her own feelings.

Other people's feelings

If your child learns at this early age that her feelings are valued, it will eventually enable her to consider other people's feelings in the same way. Respecting your child's feelings in turn teaches her that respecting another individual's emotions is equally important.

A child's viewpoint

Your child has probably developed a clear idea of what possessions are, but she still needs reminding that she can share what she has. Understanding what's "mine" at this age can result in a certain amount of possessiveness in children. However, all this is really just part of how they view the world around them from their own, very singular, point of view. Act as a guide to your child, by helping her open up her focus and incorporate a wider viewpoint.

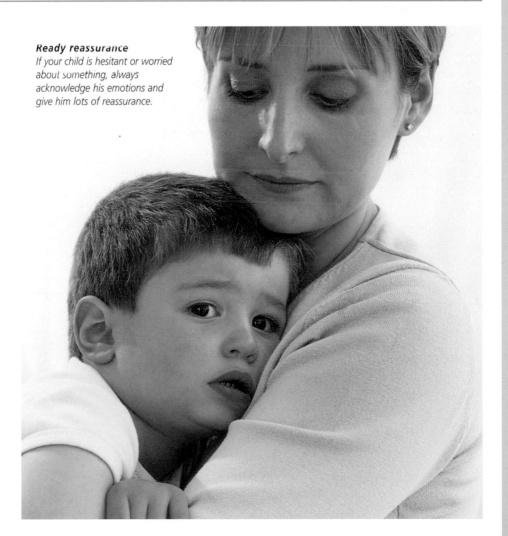

Ready reassurance
If your child is hesitant or worried about something, always acknowledge his emotions and give him lots of reassurance.

32 to 36 months

Your almost three year old is much more independent now, with his own developing interests and opinions. His personality is also becoming more clearly established, and he is learning to experiment and express his own ideas.

physical development

Your child now builds on the strength he has developed so far in his limbs to climb up and down stairs, walk on tiptoe, and control his hand movements more accurately.

If you live in a house with a flight of stairs, your two year old may now be confident going up and down them safely on his own using alternate feet rather than taking just one step at a time. If you do not have stairs in your home, your child will inevitably have had less practice at this skill. However, he is probably beginning to climb stairs he encounters using alternate feet. Regardless of his ability, you should never leave your child completely unattended near stairs.

Improving motor skills

Jumping with two feet may now be possible for your child, although he may still be rather flat-footed. You might like to suggest games that encourage him to walk on tiptoe in bare feet. This activity strengthens his feet and gives flexibility and balance.

Imagination and inventiveness
Allow your child to spend some time playing with his toys by himself. Inventing his own games starts when he is given opportunities to develop his imagination.

the concept **of time**

Your child may be advanced enough in his understanding now to grasp the abstract concept of time – for instance, before and after. He may understand if you say he can get down and play, "after you've finished your lunch". This understanding is possible because of his developing experience and memory, and repeated activities such as meal times help define the course of his day.

Your child may also be getting better at washing and drying his hands. Some fine motor skills, such as eating with a spoon or fork, are also improving, but may still be difficult.

Individual development

Some children may seem physically less able than others because they are so impatient to get from one place to another, or achieve a specific task; they may manage better if they slow down and take things more gently. Other children can be very impulsive and don't allow themselves time to assess physical risk, so again, they may need some encouragement to slow down a little. If they show little natural fear or reservation, they may need help understanding that what they are doing could put themselves at risk.

Structured activities

You may feel naturally inclined to reduce the level of physical activity undertaken by your child if he appears to be less physically able. However, guard against this tendency as it won't help him. In fact, increasing the amount of structured activities to help your child learn to manage physical skills more easily will be to his advantage.

As long as it helps him in an uncompetitive and fun way, think about whether he may benefit from joining a gymnastics or dance class for young children at your local sports centre. Remember to keep giving him lots of encouragement to raise his self-esteem.

toy **box**

Simple board games
Focus on simple games with your child, such as board games that are age appropriate. Go slowly and patiently as you play with him, and you may find he soon begins to pick up the rules of the game.

Dressing-up box
It is worth keeping a large box full of old grown-ups' cast-offs and dressing-up clothes for children to play with. Encourage them to think imaginatively about how they can adapt the clothes to suit who they want to pretend to be.

Picture lotto
If you have already begun playing a simple version of picture lotto with your child, you may want to buy a slightly more sophisticated version of the game if he is becoming proficient at it. Or you can make your own version of picture lotto using pictures cut from old magazines and glued on to square pieces of card.

Pens and paper
Buy large, non-toxic crayons, felt-tips, and bright-coloured paper to give your child many hours of fun.

Foam letters
Many toy shops sell containers of foam letters and numbers that will stick to the side of the bath when wet. Choose large pieces that help your child begin to recognize letters and numbers.

learning skills

Your child is now beginning to grasp the concept of simple number sequences and different categories.

Your child's knowledge of numbers began when you first sang number rhymes to him, although it wouldn't have been clear then what these words represented. Through your frequent repetition, your child may have learned to "count" to five, or even 10, although in reality he has just been repeating a sequence of sounds.

Now, he will begin to use these familiar words to represent the more tangible concept of counting. The development of this understanding begins with forming groups, or sequences, of objects. Just counting three cars or two spoons is a start. Your child may also grasp the idea of different categories soon: 10 plastic animals in total, but three cows, five pigs, and two horses. You may even find him repeating numbers and number sequences in his games.

Nursery rhymes

Have you ever wondered why parents pass down favourite nursery rhymes through the generations? Perhaps it's from an intuitive knowledge that talking to your child helps him develop speech, but the repetition of nursery rhymes is also a useful preparation for reading. The constant repetition of the rhymes in early life means that your child becomes familiar with different word sounds. They also engage his attention, helping him pick up information about language and how it works.

Personal references

Your child should now be able to converse with you in short sentences rather than just in phrases, and he may now be able to continue talking about a topic for a short period.

Your child will probably now refer to himself as "I" rather than by his name, say "you" rather than use the third person, and refer to friends and family by name. This demonstrates how his cognitive skills have advanced over the year in identifying himself as an individual within his family, and referring to himself as such.

Visual memories

As his language skills improve, you will notice how good your child's memory and observation skills are becoming. Children have very visual memories, so if your child has a broad range of vocabulary you may be surprised by how much detail he can give you about something. Encourage this skill by asking him to describe events or experiences in more detail.

emotional development

Attention-seeking behaviour in two-year-old children can take different forms and having a tantrum is often one of them.

At this age, tantrums in children can be due to changes or events, or a learned response. If they surface in a previously peaceable child, consider why his behaviour may have changed. Once the tantrum is over, calmly communicate that his behaviour is not appropriate.

Emotional frustration

It's important to try and understand why a child responds to situations in an anti-social way. This can be difficult if a tantrum gets him what he wants in the short term. Tantrums are usually linked to a child's frustration and inability to communicate effectively. A two year old does not fully understand that there are things he cannot have (see pages 126–129).

Children need quiet time to imagine and be creative. This helps develop self-reliance, stimulates new ideas, and builds self-esteem. Children also have an emotional need for lots of attention, and while positive attention is better than negative, they tend not to

make that distinction – any attention will do if a child feels he isn't getting enough.

The challenge of parenting is being attuned to your child so that you can accommodate his needs as they change. The basic principle is to ignore negative behaviour and to be generous in your reward and praise of good behaviour.

Managing separation

By this age, your child should be reasonably happy when separated from you with a familiar caregiver for an extended period of time, although some children manage

this progression with less anxiety than others. In order to feel comfortable about spending time away from you, your child needs to be able to hold on to the thought of you and know that you will return to him, which is learned partly through experience.

How you handle separation will also convey to your child what is expected of him. If you appear confident, you will convey to him your confidence in his ability to manage. If you are anxious or hesitant, he may pick up on this emotion, which might make it more difficult for him to feel confident without you.

learning through play

Imaginative play is very important for young children. Through it they learn to work out certain abstract concepts, act out story lines, "try on" different ideas, explore feelings, and ways of behaving – all within their own imaginations.

♦ Playing with other children is a learned skill, and is all about socializing, taking turns, and thinking about others. Help your child learn these skills by playing simple board games that are appropriate to his age group and encourage him to take turns. In addition, playing a counting game enables you to help him learn about numbers, plus their names and sequences. Focus on the pleasure and excitement of playing the game, irrespective of who wins, so that winning is not your child's only goal when playing. By playing a game repeatedly over time,

the experience of winning or losing will become a less important aspect of playing the game. It is more important at this age to have fun than to focus on winning.

♦ All young children should be encouraged to play games that rely on their own internal resources, and dressing-up games help to stimulate this ability. They also make a game of developing those skills your child needs to learn in order to dress himself. A big square of material can be a princess's cloak, a magician's cape, a magic carpet, a baby blanket, or Red Riding Hood's granny's shawl. Adults' clothes and accessories such as old hats or high-heeled shoes are another great attraction. Shop-bought outfits, perhaps based on popular fictional characters, are also an option, as are doctors' and nurses' outfits and other costumes.

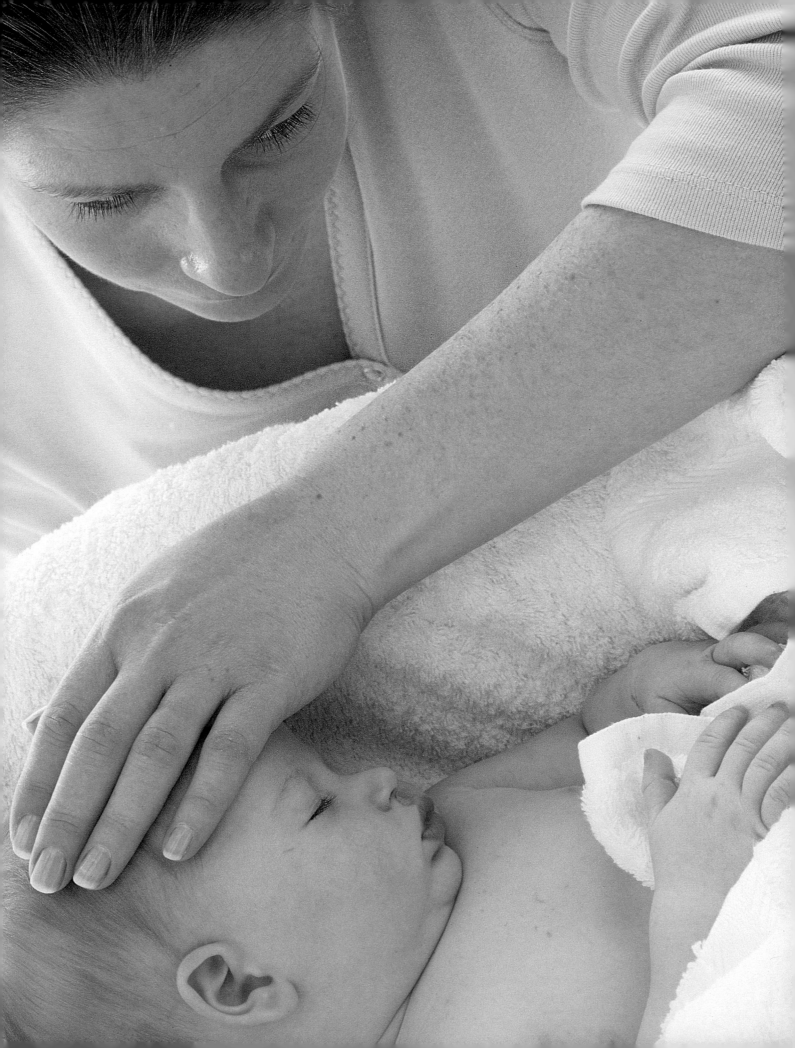

health

All parents want their children to be healthy, to enjoy life to the full, and to develop normally. As the immune system matures, minor illnesses are common in young children. It's always distressing for parents when their baby or child is ill, and it can be hard to know what to do. Always check with your doctor or health visitor if you have questions about your child's health. In this section, you'll find information to help you keep your child healthy and on what to do when your child is not feeling well. There is also advice on injury prevention and first aid to help you deal with emergencies should they arise.

keeping healthy

Babies and young children can develop minor illnesses, and babies, in particular, can become ill very quickly. Many common childhood illnesses are due to viruses and will resolve on their own. Happily, there is much you can do to help keep your child in the best of health.

home life

At first, even minor illnesses can be a challenge for you and your child, but as a parent you soon become adept at interpreting symptoms and knowing how to make him feel better – and get better – as quickly as possible.

Good health is partly a matter of luck. However, there is a lot you can do to keep your child well. A warm, loving bond with you provides the right environment for children to thrive. There has even been evidence that this can help your child fight minor illnesses.

People in a household tend to harbour the same germs, so you don't normally have to worry about kissing your baby. However, if you have cold sores or shingles, ask your doctor for advice.

Parents often know instinctively when their child is ill. The more in tune you are with your baby when he is well, the more quickly you will know if there is something amiss.

Infections are especially likely to spread in winter when there is more indoor play, but unless your child has an immune disorder, it's better for him to socialize and catch a few colds and other minor illnesses.

Exercise

A daily outing is a good idea from a young age, even if you just push your baby around in his pram. Toddlers appreciate the space to wander about, so a trip to the park is a good idea. Take a pushchair with you even if your toddler is a good walker because he might appreciate a ride home. In bad weather, dress your child warmly before taking him outside.

Out and about
Regular exercise, even just a short trip to the park, will help to keep your child healthy, and is great fun for the whole family.

key **points**

♦ Good habits can prevent a lot of childhood illnesses, but not all.

♦ As a parent you play the most important role in keeping your child healthy.

♦ Think ahead about safety as your baby grows.

♦ Learn the basics about common illnesses before they occur.

hygiene

Cleanliness in the home, especially around your baby, is vital. Babies, their bottles, and playthings all need to be kept clean to minimize the risk of infection, particularly when they start putting everything into their mouths. Good hygiene practices, such as always washing your hands after nappy changes, are vital.

Always try to stay a step ahead of your child. Before long, a baby grows into a toddler, who needs to learn how to wash his hands, handle food properly, and acquire good toilet habits.

Hygiene in the kitchen

The whole family should be scrupulous about kitchen hygiene.

♦ Take extra care when preparing your baby's meals or bottles.

♦ Don't keep food that's already been served in his bowl; there are always bacteria on hands and cutlery, and these thrive on leftovers.

♦ Change your dishcloth often and keep towels clean.

♦ Use different implements for handling raw and cooked foods, and for raw meat and vegetables.

♦ Bacteria thrive in warmth, so check the temperature of your fridge (0–5°C/ 32–41°F) for optimum efficiency.

♦ Keep cooked food near the top of the fridge, and raw food below. Germs from raw foods can contaminate cooked meals.

♦ Abide by food use-by dates.

♦ For more kitchen safety advice see pages 262–263.

Household pets

Animals are part of many homes and they often give a family a lot of pleasure. Young children who grow up with a pet get a chance to learn about being gentle and responsible, and may even get a lesson in reproductive biology. Walking the pet can promote a healthier lifestyle.

However, pets do harbour germs, so it's important for your child to wash his

Safe meal times
Your baby relies on you, as a parent, to keep her surroundings as clean and germ-free as possible, both at home and out and about.

hands after playing with an animal, especially before a meal. If you have a dog, make sure that he is regularly wormed. Keep pets off the beds and preferably out of your child's bedroom. If you have a cat, keep the litter tray clean and teach your child not to touch it. If you have a sandpit in your garden, make sure that there's a cover for it and that it goes on when the sandpit's not in use; even if you don't have a cat, other pets in your neighbourhood may use it as a litter tray.

Research suggests that having mild infections in early life can protect against some illnesses later, but experts believe that animals may trigger asthma and other symptoms in families who have lots of allergies. So if allergies are common in your family, you may need to think twice about getting a furry pet for your child.

the effects of **smoking**

The air that your child breathes has a profound effect on his health. Smoking reduces the ability of the air passages to fight off infection, and also reduces the amount of oxygen carried in the blood. Ideally, you and your partner should not smoke at all. If you do smoke, don't do so anywhere near babies and children, or in the house.

♦ Passive smoking is thought to be linked to a quarter of all sudden infant deaths (see page 225).

♦ Young children of smokers are more likely to suffer allergies, asthma, chest infections, and ear infections.

♦ Children whose parents smoke are often shorter than children from non-smoking families.

♦ Cigarette smoke contains carbon monoxide, ammonia, cyanide, and chemicals that are known to cause cancer.

♦ Many fatal house fires are started by cigarettes and matches.

immunizations

Immunization is an important means of protecting your child from certain life-threatening illnesses. Thanks to immunization programmes, many serious illnesses have been more or less eradicated.

understanding immunization

All of the diseases your child is immunized against are serious and unpleasant infections. The more children are vaccinated, the better the protection for the population.

A vaccine stimulates the immune system into making antibodies (proteins that can fight infection). A vaccine is a virus or bacterium, altered so that it can't cause illness but can trigger antibodies which protect your child if she comes into contact with the disease.

When to delay immunization

♦ If you have any concerns about immunization, consult your health visitor or doctor for advice.

♦ A mild cold needn't deter you from immunizing your baby.

♦ If your baby has a feverish illness, delay the immunization until she is better.

♦ Speak to your GP or health visitor if your baby has had a serious reaction to any previous injection, has an allergy to eggs or anything else, has had a convulsion, is having treatment for cancer, or has any disease that weakens the immune system. It may still be safe for her to have the vaccine, but it might be necessary to take additional precautions.

immunization **timetable**

This is a schedule for the UK. Your doctor or health visitor will give your baby these immunizations, and you will be notified when each is due. In babies, injections are usually given into the front of a thigh, while for a child the upper arm is usual.

2 months	Polio (by mouth); Hib, diphtheria, tetanus, whooping cough (one injection); meningitis C (one injection)
3 months	Polio (by mouth); Hib, diphtheria, tetanus, whooping cough (one injection); meningitis C (one injection)
4 months	Polio (by mouth); Hib, diphtheria, tetanus, whooping cough (one injection); meningitis C (one injection)
12–15 months	Measles, mumps, rubella (MMR) (one injection)
3–5 years	Polio (by mouth); diphtheria, tetanus, whooping cough (one injection); measles, mumps, rubella (MMR) (one injection)

Routine immunizations

Your baby or child usually needs immunization against the following infections and viruses:

♦ **Polio** (*poliomyelitis*) A virus that causes damage to the nervous system and can result in permanent paralysis or even death.

♦ **Diphtheria** A bacterial disease that starts in the throat and can spread to the heart and the nervous system.

♦ **Tetanus** This is a potentially fatal bacterial infection that can cause paralysis of the muscles.

♦ **Whooping cough** (*pertussis*) A bacterial illness sometimes with mild fever and often with violent coughing spasms. These spasms can result in vomiting, seizures, and lung damage.

♦ **Hib** (*haemophilus influenzae B*) A bacterial infection that can cause a range of illnesses, including meningitis and pneumonia.

♦ **Meningitis C** This is one of the most serious causes of the potentially fatal bacterial meningitis.

measles, mumps, and rubella (MMR)

There has been a lot of debate – and often parental anxiety – about the MMR vaccine, which was first introduced in Britain in 1988. Concerns centre around whether MMR can be linked with Crohn's disease (an inflammatory disease of the bowel) and/or autism (a disorder of development that affects a child's social skills). Both these have become more common over the years. However, after a lot of laboratory research and following up children who had MMR jabs, the evidence is that MMR almost certainly doesn't cause any long-term problems. Like all vaccines, MMR can have some short-term side-effects: mainly fever (which can be very high) and a mild measles-like rash about 10 days after the injection is given.

It's worth remembering that measles, mumps, and rubella can all be very unpleasant and occasionally fatal. That's why most doctors believe the benefits of MMR greatly outweigh any risks. The effectiveness of the immunization programme relies on as many children as possible being immunized.

♦ **Measles** A virus that can cause chest infections, seizures, meningitis, and permanent brain damage.

♦ **Mumps** A virus that causes painful swelling of the salivary glands. It can also cause meningitis and deafness.

♦ **Rubella** This is a virus that can cause serious birth defects in unborn babies. Although for the majority of children rubella is not serious, it can also result in joint pains and encephalitis (inflammation of the brain).

♦ **Tuberculosis** (TB) This is a bacterial infection that mainly affects the lungs. If you live in an area where tuberculosis is relatively common, your baby may be offered this immunization at birth or a little later.

questions & answers

q What side-effects do vaccines have?

a The needle itself causes transient pain, so it's usual for a young baby to cry. Often this is several seconds after the injection. You can breastfeed your baby or use a dummy to comfort her. Soreness and slight redness are common at the injection site. A small lump can form, but this is harmless and usually painless, and resolves on its own. It's normal for a baby to be a bit unhappy for a few hours or even a day or so after her jab, and she may have a slight fever. Tender loving care will make a big difference to how your baby feels afterwards. You can give a small dose of paracetamol syrup for pain or fever. Follow your doctor's instructions for dosing.

q My baby missed an immunization. Should she start all over again?

a No. It's best to stick to the timetable if possible, but if your baby misses a dose, then she should have it late. She doesn't need to start the whole course of vaccines all over again.

Protecting your child
Although taking your baby for her immunizations can be upsetting for you as a parent, there is a lot you can do to comfort her afterwards, and you should be reassured that you are doing your best to protect her health for years to come.

q When do I need to call the doctor about side-effects?

a It's unusual to need the doctor after an immunization. However, you should call your doctor if your baby or child has a fit (convulsion) after her immunization, or if she develops a fever over 39°C (102.2°F). You should tell your doctor if your baby has a lot of pain or redness at the site of the jab or has a more widespread rash. If your baby or child has any other symptoms that you don't understand, or you have any concerns, ask your health visitor or doctor.

q What side-effects does the polio vaccine have?

a Usually none at all. However, polio vaccine is a live virus and it appears in the baby's stools for several weeks after immunization. There is therefore a tiny risk of an adult catching polio from a baby who's recently had the vaccine. So, while you should always wash your hands after changing your baby's nappy, it's even more important after she's been immunized.

your baby's health

It's natural to worry about your baby's health. If you're a new parent, you may also be uncertain as to what's normal. Looking after a sick child can be a challenge. You'll want to do all you can to make him better, and to reassure yourself that you're doing the right thing.

illness in newborn babies

Infants under one year of age can have some of the same ailments as older children, but they can't express themselves in the same way.

Their immune system is also less developed, so illnesses that an older baby might shrug off can occasionally develop into something more serious. On the other hand, for about the first six months of his life a young baby has the benefit of antibodies he has acquired from his mother. This is why babies under one year old tend not to get common childhood infections such as chicken pox and measles.

Often parents just know when their baby isn't feeling well. This instinct develops over time, and as you get to know your baby, you will understand what is normal for him.

Common ailments

There are a number of ailments that are particularly prevalent in very young babies.

- **Dry skin** This is very common in babies, especially those born past their due date. Dry, flaky skin is usually found over the ankles and feet, or in the nappy area. This is nothing to do with eczema. Apply baby lotion or oil after a bath (see pages 94–95) to soothe and relieve dry skin.

- **Nappy rash** Ammonia and other chemicals in urine can irritate a baby's sensitive skin. It is more likely to happen if a nappy is left on too long – that's why it is important to change your baby regularly, especially if he has loose stools. Fabric nappies are not better than disposables for avoiding nappy rash. Modern disposables probably keep a baby's bottom far drier.

If your baby develops a rash, when you've cleaned him, dry him thoroughly and let him lie on a mat or towel without a nappy for 10–20 minutes and stay with him. You may need to do this three or more times a day until the rash clears. Smooth on a thin layer of barrier cream before putting on a clean nappy.

Nappy rash can also be due to thrush, an infection caused by a yeast called candida or monilia. If the rash doesn't improve, see your health visitor or doctor.

Learning about your baby
As you and your baby get to know one another you will learn to recognize common symptoms. With a young baby you should consult your doctor or health visitor if you are concerned.

spots and **rashes**

Babies can have many spots and rashes (see page 94). Most are quite harmless, but it is a good idea to familiarize yourself with some common conditions and to check with your health visitor or doctor.

Harlequin colour change
Some areas of your baby's skin may be

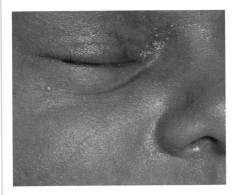

Milia
These are small white dots, usually over the nose. They need no treatment, but see your health visitor or doctor if any become very red.

paler than others. If you change his position, the pale part becomes brighter pink while the pinker part fades. This is a harmless sign of immature blood vessel control.

Small facial spots
These may develop in the first few days and weeks. They come and go quickly. If they look red and infected, ask your health visitor.

Stork marks (flat angiomata)
These are red or purplish V-shaped marks on the back of the neck or eyelids. They are usually harmless, and most will fade over the first few months of life.

Mongolian blue spots
Fairly large greyish-blue patches on your baby's buttocks or limbs; these are harmless.

Strawberry marks (haemangiomas)
Your baby may develop marks with a surface that resembles a strawberry. These stop growing at about six months, and then slowly recede. Ask your doctor for advice.

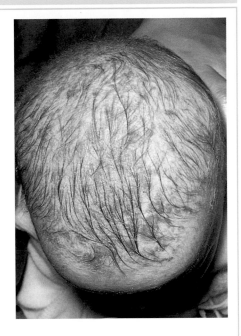

Cradle cap
These greasy scales on the scalp are caused by dead skin. It is not infected, nor does your baby have dandruff or eczema.

♦ **Colic** Long bouts of loud, inconsolable crying, usually starting at about two weeks of age, are often referred to as colic. These bouts of intense crying are common in the first three months, particularly in the evening, and may last for two to three hours. A baby may pull up his knees, go red in the face, and clench his fists during a colic attack. The cause is unknown, but recent research suggests that in the majority of cases colic is simply a more extreme form of normal crying.

For a small number of babies, physical problems (particularly digestive disorders) may be the cause of unexplained crying. Consult your doctor to rule out any possibility that your baby is ill and for advice on coping with colic. Try different ways of soothing your baby (see page 99), but avoid overstimulating him.

Take comfort from the fact that colic usually passes by three to four months of age. In the meantime, call on your family and friends for help during this period.
♦ **Trapped wind** Most babies suffer from trapped wind after feeding at one time or another, although some are more

susceptible than others. Frequent winding during and after feeds is important. If your baby seems prone to trapped wind, talk to your health visitor or doctor who may recommend drops that are available over the counter and contain simethicone, which has an anti-foaming and gas-absorbing action. Use only products that are formulated for babies and seek advice first.
♦ **Reflux** Caused by stomach acid and food flowing up the oesophagus (food tube) during and after feeds, reflux can lead to abdominal pain. The "valve" at the lower end of the oesophagus is immature and may not close properly. Symptoms are similar to colic but tend to occur with, or after, every feed. Keeping your baby in a more upright position, especially while feeding, can help. If symptoms persist, speak to your doctor.
♦ **Dehydration** Babies can lose fluid very easily when they have vomiting or diarrhoea; even more so when they have both at the same time, as in gastroenteritis. This is why babies with diarrhoea and vomiting need to see the doctor. It's important to

recognize the warning signs of dehydration. You may find that your baby's nappies are drier than usual. As dehydration progresses, his skin will become less elastic than normal. Over his tummy, for instance, it can look dry and wrinkled. His fontanelle may be sunken, his eyes may seem more deeply set, and he may become floppy and lethargic. These are signs of serious dehydration. Contact your doctor without delay if your baby shows any of them.
♦ **Navel bulge** If your baby's umbilical cord seems to push outwards when he cries, he may have an umbilical hernia. Your doctor or health visitor will confirm the diagnosis. These hernias, unlike those in the groin, usually resolve on their own, although they can take months or sometimes even years to do so.
♦ **Sticky eye** Wipe each eye with a fresh piece of cotton wool and cooled, boiled water – wipe gently outwards away from the nose, and avoid touching the eyeball. Consult your doctor if symptoms persist. Babies under a year old are prone to conjunctivitis (see page 249). If the eyeball looks red or the eyelid swells, see the doctor.

six-week check

Six weeks after the birth, your doctor will give your baby a development check. The aim is to assess your baby's physical growth, behavioural development, and overall state of health.

what your doctor looks for

Your doctor will check your baby's body control and social responses, paying special attention to vision and hearing.

Not all babies cooperate, so your own observations are very important, too. This is a good time to mention any concerns you may have.

♦ **Hearing** The doctor will check that a sudden noise startles her.
♦ **Muscle tone** The doctor will move your baby's arms and legs to assess muscle tone.
♦ **Reflexes** Certain reflexes that were present at birth will be disappearing by now (see page 83). Your doctor may look for the grasp reflex: when a newborn baby's palm is stroked, her hand closes on the finger, but this reflex may have gone by six weeks. The stepping reflex is a walking-like action most new babies make when the sole of a foot is pressed on the couch. This too disappears by six weeks of age.

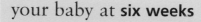

your baby at **six weeks**

At six weeks, your baby will start to:
♦ watch faces intently
♦ follow a light or a dangling toy
♦ lie still to concentrate on your voice
♦ smile, especially on hearing your voice
♦ control her head more
♦ make some noises back at you
– when she's in the right mood.

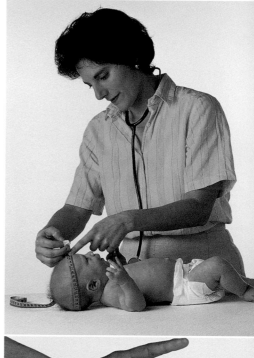

Head circumference (right)
This provides vital information about how your baby is growing and developing.

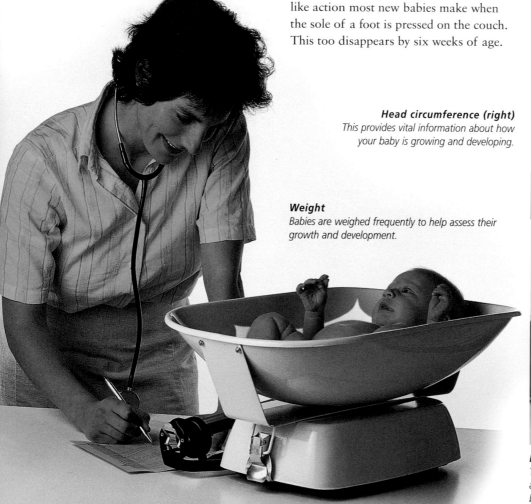

Weight
Babies are weighed frequently to help assess their growth and development.

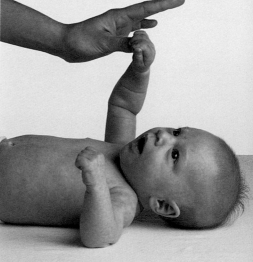

Reflexes
The birth reflexes will begin disappearing soon. At birth, a newborn can tightly grasp a finger placed in her palm, but by six to eight weeks this reflex normally goes. The stepping reflex also disappears by six weeks of age.

premature **babies**

Your bond with your baby is as important as all the technology in the special care baby unit (SCBU), so try to be as close to her as circumstances allow. Many parents feel intimidated by the equipment and the level of staffing, but you can still help care for your baby. She already knows your voice, so talk to her and touch her through the port-holes of the incubator. This gentle stimulation is good for her. Skin-to-skin hugging may be impossible for now, but even nappy changes will help to form a bond. And there's evidence that a parent's loving touch can help premature or vulnerable babies thrive.

Sometimes it is hard for parents to feel confident in handling such a small baby. If you don't feel quite ready to hold your premature baby, ask the staff to show you what to do and how to do it. With a little practice, your baby will reap the rewards of your tender care.

It can be a challenge to be optimistic, but try to stay positive. Your baby can feel this. Remember that every baby is different, so don't compare your baby's progress to that of other babies in SCBU.

It's reassuring to know that premature babies usually develop at the same rate as any other babies, but because they were born earlier they will take longer to reach the same level of development. So, at six months, a baby born three months premature can be expected to have the social skills of a three-month-old baby. In time, any discrepancies become less obvious, and by the time your child is two years old there will be little or no difference between your baby and one who was born at term.

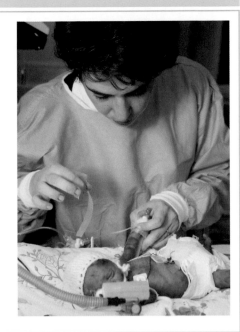

The doctor will also check for:
♦ eye abnormalities
♦ congenital dislocation of the hip
♦ signs of congenital heart disease
♦ undescended testes in a boy
♦ small abnormalities such as birthmarks.

Measuring weight, length, and head circumference enables your baby's growth to be plotted on a chart. This will give a good indication of development. Don't worry too much about her exact length. This measurement tends to be approximate because babies still hold themselves curled up at this age.

Remember to take a spare nappy, and a feed if you're bottle-feeding. A dummy can also be a good idea if she uses one. The best time to schedule a check-up is when your baby is awake but not hungry: an hour after a feed, for instance. This isn't always possible. Moreover, young babies are unpredictable and don't necessarily stick to a routine. There's no need to worry if your doctor asks you to come back at a later date to complete the behavioural parts of the examination.

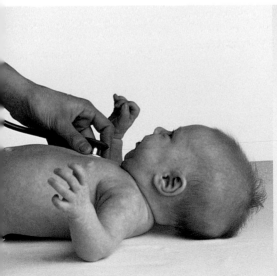

Checking the heartbeat
Until your baby is about one year old, her heartbeat will be about 120 beats per minute; much faster than a child or adult heart. The doctor will use a stethoscope to listen to your baby's heart.

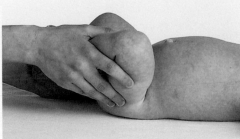

Checking the hips
Your baby will have been checked for hip dislocation after birth, but it is still a possibility, so the doctor will manipulate her legs again at the six-week check.

Head control
The doctor will hold up your baby on her front in the air. She may also pull her up to a sitting position to see how strong her back is.

caring for a sick baby

If you think your baby may be ill, call your doctor. Together you can decide what's best – whether your baby needs to be seen by the doctor or can be cared for at home.

what to expect

As you and your baby get to know each other, you will become more adept at diagnosing minor symptoms. Your health visitor will also advise you on managing minor illnesses.

When your baby is feeling ill, he is likely to be clingy and unwilling to be put down. He may also be less playful than usual, less smiling or even miserable.

He's likely to need more time with his feeds, especially if he has a cough or cold. Give him all the cuddles he needs and keep him close. Tender loving care is very important to a sick baby's recovery.

Understanding symptoms

Babies under a year old have trouble communicating their symptoms. All you may notice is that your baby is not feeding well, cries more than usual, or is just not quite himself. Many babies vomit or have diarrhoea when the real cause of the trouble isn't in the stomach or gut at all; it can, for instance, be the result of an ear infection. The chart opposite lists some of the most common ailments and their symptoms. See pages 238–256 for more information on diagnosis.

If you are concerned

If you are ever in any doubt about what is wrong with your child, see the doctor, especially when the baby is very young. Parents often worry about troubling the doctor unnecessarily, but it is better to be cautious and go to see him or her, if only to put your mind at rest. Remember that parents do not magically acquire the ability to interpret every symptom correctly; learning to cope when your baby is ill is a gradual process.

Do think carefully before you request a home visit from your doctor. Your child will probably be seen more quickly if you can go to the surgery.

sleep

When he's ill, your baby may sleep more than usual. Sleep is restorative, so this is natural. However, you should be able to wake him when necessary. If you can't wake him, call the doctor immediately.

If he usually sleeps in his own room, move his cot or crib into your room temporarily, so that you can keep an eye on him at all times. Don't worry that this will deprive everyone of rest; sleeping in the same room will benefit all of you as you will actually sleep more easily knowing you can go to him if he cries or vomits, and he will be reassured by your presence.

How to help

Some babies sleep less when they're not feeling well, if for instance a cough or stuffy nose keeps them awake. This can make your baby tired and irritable, and he may be more clingy than usual. Try to comfort him and let him doze off in your arms if that's what he wants.

Chores and other household tasks will have to wait until he is feeling better. Right now, your baby is the highest priority, so ask for help around the house if you need it. When he does fall asleep, take the opportunity to put your feet up and have a rest yourself. You will need to conserve your energy to be able to look after him properly.

dealing with **illness**

ILLNESS	SYMPTOMS	WHAT YOU CAN DO
Common cold Caused by any one of many viruses. Very common in all ages.	Sneezing, stuffy or runny nose, trouble feeding, slight grumpiness, possibly mild fever.	Wipe baby's nose with cotton wool or soft tissue. Call doctor if baby doesn't improve or is wheezy.
Ear infection (*otitis media*) Can be due to viruses or bacteria. More common in babies and children because of the shape of the Eustachian tube linking throat and middle ear.	Screaming, feverish baby. May refuse feeds and be inconsolable. Irritability, especially at night. May vomit or have diarrhoea. An older baby may pull his ear, but most don't.	See doctor for diagnosis. A course of antibiotics may be prescribed.
Croup Usually caused by a viral infection in the upper airways. Most common from three months to three years. Can recur.	Harsh, barking cough, especially at night, with wheezing and hoarseness. In severe cases, blueness from lack of oxygen.	Call your doctor. Inhaling steam may help (see page 247), at the direction of your doctor.
Bronchiolitis An inflammation of the small breathing tubes (bronchioles). Occurs most often in infants. Possible link with asthma later in life. (Bronchiolitis is not to be confused with bronchitis.)	Runny nose, cough, and sometimes fever, followed by wheezing and rapid, laboured breathing. Baby may fight for breath and chest may look sucked in between the ribs. In severe cases, baby is blue.	See doctor without delay. Bronchiolitis is usually due to a virus so antibiotics don't help. Home treatment includes use of a humidifier and nasal aspirator.
Chest infection Infection somewhere in the respiratory system (sometimes called pneumonia or bronchitis).	Breathless, rapid breathing and/or feverish baby. May have a cough. May wheeze, especially at night.	See doctor without delay. If pneumonia is caused by a virus, there is no specific treatment except rest and fever management.
Pyloric stenosis Over-development of the duodenum muscle that controls passage of food from stomach to bowels. Occurs more commonly in boys under three months old.	Frequent forceful vomiting – called "projectile". If untreated, results in severe dehydration.	See doctor for diagnosis. Surgery is usually required to open the narrowed area.
Gastroenteritis (infectious diarrhoea) May be caught from someone or from bacteria in food (see pages 255).	Frequent loose bowel motions. May vomit and refuse feeds. Baby may be feverish and unwell from dehydration.	If baby has more than a couple of runny stools, vomits more than once, or seems unwell, call doctor without delay.
Meningitis (See page 244) Serious, but rare.	High-pitched cry; lethargy; pale, blotchy skin.	Seek medical help urgently.

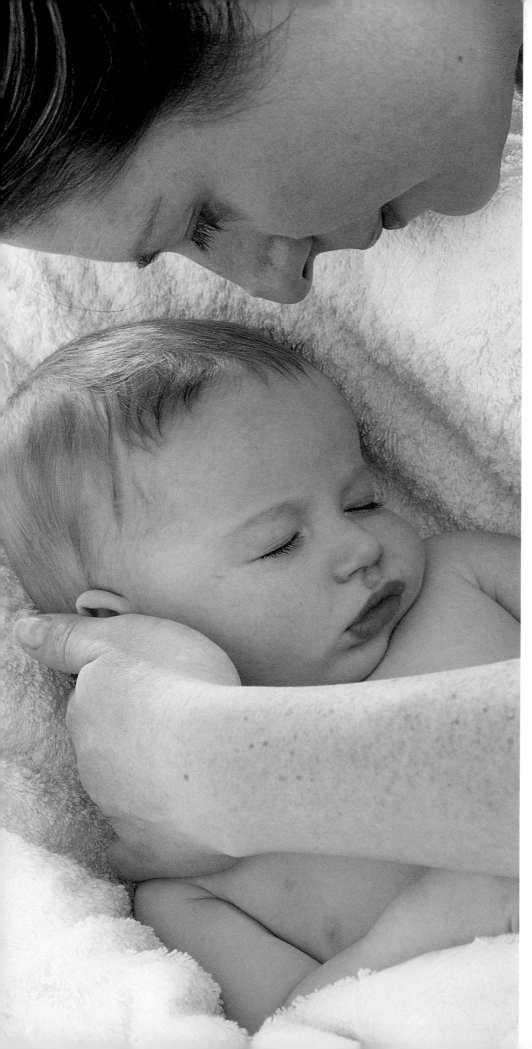

understanding temperature

Babies can't control their body temperature as accurately as children and adults, and they can't tell you they're hot or remove clothing.

Babies lose more heat from their heads, so they can easily get too cool, but they can also become unpredictably hot.

Fever may make your baby uncomfortable, can lead to dehydration, and may lead to seizures. It is important to check with your doctor to determine the cause of your baby's fever. Febrile seizures are especially common between the ages of five months and five years. They are distressing, and after one there may be a risk of another (see page 272).

Normal body temperature

For a baby this is about 36.5–37°C (97.7–98.6°F). Taken from the armpit, anything over 37°C (98.6°F) is a fever. You may suspect your baby has a fever if he is irritable. Or he may be flushed or sweaty, especially on the back of the neck. These are good guides to skin temperature, but you can only be sure he has a fever (a high inner temperature) by using a thermometer (see page 226). Consult your doctor if you are worried: the younger your baby, the sooner you need medical advice.

Reducing a fever

♦ Check your baby's temperature, consult your doctor, and give paracetamol syrup if your baby's temperature is over 38°C (100.4°F).
♦ Keep his room comfortably cool and dress him in lightweight clothing.
♦ Sponge his head and limbs gently with lukewarm water.
♦ Give him plenty of fluids to drink, and reassess his temperature in half an hour.
♦ Take his temperature every two to three hours until you're sure it is dropping without fever medications. If you're worried, call the doctor.
♦ NEVER GIVE YOUR CHILD ASPIRIN. Aspirin has been linked to Reye's syndrome, a serious liver disorder.

Sleeping safely
Make sure you follow the SIDS safety guidelines when putting your baby to sleep (see page 101).

Although rare, Sudden Infant Death Syndrome (SIDS) – also known as cot death – is still the biggest cause of death in babies under a year old. Campaigns to educate parents and carers have brought about huge falls in the number of incidences, however.

Nobody knows the exact cause, but it's probably due to a combination of factors, such as overheating and infection. Although SIDS can affect any baby, it's more common in babies who are small, underweight, or who were premature. Some babies had been unwell beforehand. Perhaps their immune system was too weak to cope with a minor illness.

Try not to spend a lot of time worrying about SIDS, but do take precautions (see page 101) and if your baby is ill, get medical advice promptly.

If you ever find your baby motionless or you cannot rouse him, call an ambulance and start resuscitation (see page 268).

giving medicine

As a parent, it is useful to develop a good technique for administering medicine. Choose whichever method suits you both best.

Your doctor may prescribe treatment, or you may need to give your baby over-the-counter medicine. Consult your doctor, health visitor, or pharmacist before giving your baby any medicine. This is also true of complementary therapies (see pages 236–237). Remedies formulated for adults and older children can be dangerous for babies. Follow dosages carefully and use only the dispenser supplied.

Giving medicine from a syringe
A sterilized medicine syringe is useful for very young babies, and for doses under 2.5ml. Fill the syringe from the bottle before picking up your baby. Place the mouthpiece on his lower lip and gently press the plunger so the medicine goes slowly into his mouth.

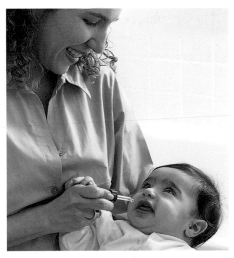

Giving medicine using a dropper
Fill the dropper from the measured dose in a spoon before you pick up your baby. Lean him back slightly to help the medicine down. Place the tip of the dropper inside his lower lip or the corner of his mouth. Squeeze to release the medicine, making sure it is all released.

Giving medicine using a spoon
Babies from about six weeks old can take medicine from a spoon. Use the correct, clean measuring spoon, sterilized for a very young baby. Measure the dose before you pick up your baby. Touch the spoon to his bottom lip, then gently tip the spoon.

your child's health

Now that your child is growing up and is no longer a baby, you'll be able to tell more easily when she is ill, as she may say that something hurts, point to a painful area such as her ear or her tummy, or tell you that she feels ill.

general symptoms

Even if she doesn't tell you how she feels, your child might be pale, or her cheeks may be flushed from fever.

She may not be feeding well, or may be drinking either less than usual, or perhaps more than usual because a fever is making her thirsty. Sometimes a sick child vomits dramatically and without warning.

Your child may be less playful or smiling than normal, she might cry more readily, or she may just be more demanding of your attention.

What you can do

If you do not know what the problem is, note your child's symptoms and call your doctor. If you think you know what's wrong with your child, turn to the section in this book that deals with her ailment for more information (see *childhood illnesses*, pages 238–261), then call the doctor if need be. In the case of urgent problems, you may need to summon emergency medical help. In these circumstances, it's natural for a parent to be worried, but try to act swiftly without panicking, as your reaction will affect your child.

checking temperature

Check if your child's cheeks are flushed (the area around the mouth may appear to be pale by comparison), or feel her forehead. A child's normal body temperature taken from the mouth is about 36.5–37°C (97.7–98.6°F). Armpit temperature is about 0.5°C (1°F) lower. Rectal temperature (which is rarely used now) is approximately 1°C (2°F) higher than armpit temperature. To be certain of your child's temperature, use a thermometer. Choose from:

♦ A digital thermometer (see right), which provides a clear digital read-out of your child's temperature. Settle her comfortably on your lap while taking the reading.

♦ An ear sensor (see far right), which is easier to use if your child is restless, but the measurements need to be taken three times to be sure of an accurate reading.

♦ A liquid-crystal strip, which is heat-sensitive and records the skin temperature when held to your child's forehead for 30 seconds. This method is popular because it's quick and easy, but it is not generally recommended by doctors.

Digital thermometer
This is battery operated, accurate, and almost unbreakable, so it's ideal for babies. For a baby, take the temperature from the armpit. A child's temperature can be taken from the mouth.

Ear sensor
This measures infra-red (heat) radiation in the ear canal and takes a second, so it disturbs your child very little. Pull gently up and back on the ear to take the temperature. The measurements vary, so use the same ear during an illness, and take three readings.

looking after a feverish child

When your child is ill, it's important to give plenty of fluids. Lower the fever if she is uncomfortable or if her temperature is over 38°C (100.4°F).

A fever is not an illness. It's a sign that the body is trying to fight off illness, so fever doesn't always need treatment. However, high fever can, occasionally, cause seizures, called febrile seizures (see page 272), especially before the age of five. Bringing your child's temperature under control can prevent this. Fever can contribute to dehydration and may cause a headache. Dehydration, in turn, may cause fever, so it is important to break this cycle by giving fluids.

How your child will feel

A feverish child is hot and may be in discomfort, especially if dehydrated. She may be listless and seem to be very unwell. Once the fever abates, she'll often begin to perk up. When your child has a fever, she may shiver. This is because the surrounding air feels relatively cool to her hot skin. Despite this, avoid over-dressing a feverish child or keeping the room too hot as this prevents heat loss. Her temperature may rise even higher and she will feel worse.

home **medicine cabinet**

Useful items to have at home are:

♦ calamine lotion for itches and stings

♦ antiseptic spray or cream

♦ a thermometer

♦ assorted plasters for minor injuries

♦ paracetamol or ibuprofen syrup, useful to reduce fever and ease pain. (Aspirin should not be used in children under 16 years old because of the small but important risk of Reye's syndrome, a serious liver disorder.)

Keep the medicine cabinet out of your child's reach, and preferably locked.

What you can do

Remove layers of clothing when your child is feverish. She may need only her underwear, pyjamas, or something else lightweight when she's indoors. Giving her plenty of fluids helps control her temperature and counteract dehydration, so make sure she has drinks on hand in a favourite cup. If she's reluctant to drink, try offering her drinks she doesn't usually have. Sweet drinks are not good for teeth, but they do provide energy and can tempt the taste-buds.

If her temperature is over 38°C (100.4°F), give a dose of paracetamol or ibuprofen syrup. If her temperature is over 39°C (102.2°F), sponge her with tepid water. Don't use cold water as this makes blood vessels constrict and slows down heat loss. Alternatively, give her a lukewarm bath. Check her temperature again in about 20 minutes. Continue to monitor her temperature while she is ill, and call the doctor if it reaches 39.5°C (103°F) or more, if it lasts more than 24 hours, or if her appearance worries you.

Avoiding dehydration
Encourage your child to drink by letting her choose her drinks and have them from a favourite cup.

caring for a sick child

Like a baby, a child who is ill tends to be more clingy and she may still want to be hugged a lot. Give her the reassurance of having you close by.

what to expect

You'll want to be with your child as much as possible. Let her climb onto your lap as often as she likes to get the comfort she needs. She may also want to use a favourite old toy, or a discarded blanket or comforter.

Even an older child can become clingy when she's unwell, so don't be surprised if your child becomes less independent. She may want to follow if you leave the room.

Feeding your child
Allow your child plenty of time to eat. A little of her favourite food may tempt her, but don't worry if she doesn't seem very hungry.

If she has recently become potty-trained, she may also be reluctant to use the toilet and lose bladder or bowel control temporarily. She could be as upset by this as you are, so don't be annoyed. Clean up the mess without making a fuss. Things will improve when she recovers, meanwhile use plastic sheeting on the bed, and wear old clothes yourself.

Many children vomit when they're unwell, some more readily than others, and they don't usually make it to the toilet or sink in time. A bucket by the sofa may not look attractive, but if your child has been sick it can be reassuring for both of you to have it at hand.

practical care

A sick child needn't usually be confined to her bedroom. Unless your doctor has said otherwise, let your child decide whether to get up.

If your child is very ill, she may prefer to be in her cot or bed so she can sleep, but most children are happy to be up and about, and this should do them no harm.

Clothing

To keep fever under control, it's important not to overdress your child (see page 227). Pyjamas or a nightdress are usually sufficient around the house. A dressing-gown, cardigan, sweatshirt, and/or slippers may be needed as well, depending on room temperature. If your child is hot and sweaty, or has been vomiting, a bath and change of clothes will help keep her feeling fresh. For practical reasons, you may want to dress her in old clothes. However, newer, nice-looking clothes often wash just as easily as less attractive ones, and it's worth letting her wear whatever makes her most comfortable if you can.

Drinking

Your child may not be hungry when she's ill, but she will need plenty to drink. Fluids speed up recovery and help replace

the body fluid lost through sweating. This is particularly important if your child has diarrhoea or has been vomiting. If very severe, dehydration can cause kidney damage and can even be fatal.

Some children are especially thirsty when they're ill or feverish, but not all. Thirst can be a poor indicator of fluid need, so you may have to remind your child to drink. To entice her, you can let her have more or less anything she likes, as long as it's not caffeinated or too salty. A straw can be fun and may make her drink more. Give her small amounts often; this is particularly important if she has vomited, as her stomach won't tolerate large quantities.

Eating

Don't worry about food unless your child is hungry. Unless your doctor has advised otherwise, your child doesn't need to eat while she's ill. For now, fluids are more important than food. Her appetite will come back as she gets better. Sometimes this happens gradually, other times it's very quick.

If she has a sore mouth, she may feel like food but be unable to eat it. Offering soft foods such as mashed potato and ice cream can help. Ice cream is especially soothing for sore throats, and is often a favourite with young children.

Reassuring your child

Your child may be feeling ill and missing her friends and the routine at playgroup or nursery. Try not to worry, as your anxiety can affect her, and try to be with her as much as you can.

Leave non-essential chores around the house for now, saving your time and energy for your child. You may not be very active physically, but looking after a sick child can be tiring, so you should accept any offers of help.

See whether you or your partner can negotiate for time off work, or take work home with you. If you can't get time off and have to leave your child with someone else while you are at work, give clear instructions for her care and leave a telephone number where you can be reached at all times.

Being together
Most people in a household harbour the same germs, so unless your doctor has said otherwise, you can still cuddle up as a family.

entertaining **your child**

A sick child may have less energy than usual, but she still needs to pass the time. Reading to her is a great comfort and will give you both added closeness. She may particularly appreciate an old favourite book, over and over again. To vary things, you could also let her listen to stories on audio tape. Undemanding puzzles and games will also please her.

If you need something new to do, you could cut up old magazines and catalogues together. You can make easy puzzles out of old greeting or birthday cards. To avoid boredom, you may also want to let her watch a special video but be sure to stay with her and watch it together.

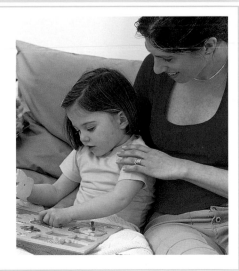

when to call the doctor

It's important to distinguish minor ailments from more serious illnesses, so call the doctor whenever you have concerns. The younger your child, the sooner you should seek medical help.

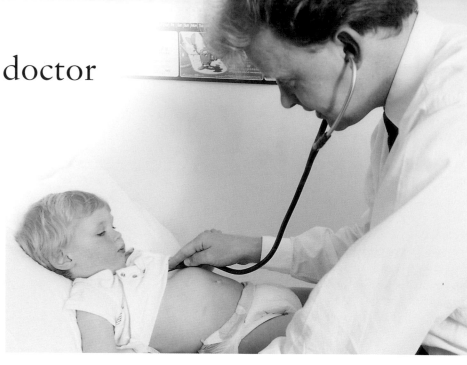

Young children can have fever and a headache together. Headache is rare in young children and can be an important symptom. Although it may be due to fever, headache may be a sign of serious illness so consult your doctor.

Coughs and colds don't always need medical advice. Contact the doctor if your child appears short of breath, wheezes, or his breathing seems laboured. If your child has abdominal pain, the abdomen may not be the cause of trouble – his symptoms need assessment by a doctor.

Sometimes you may need a house-call. However, your child will generally be seen quicker at the doctor's surgery. Feverish children don't get worse when you take them out for a short while, and most doctors will try to fit in a sick youngster. Ring before you set off. If your child might be infectious, the staff may arrange for you to sit away from the other patients. If you're not sure whether you need to see a doctor, telephone the surgery first or speak to your health visitor.

Call your doctor if your child:
- is breathing very noisily or rapidly
- has trouble swallowing
- is unusually drowsy or irritable
- has abdominal pain
- has severe or persistent pain anywhere
- has a swelling in the groin or testis
- has a rash, or a high or persistent fever.

understanding symptoms

SYMPTOM	WHAT IT MIGHT BE	WHAT YOU CAN DO
Fever	Common causes include upper respiratory infections, tonsillitis, ear infection, chest infection, urine infection.	See the doctor if the cause isn't obvious, and, following the doctor's advice, give one dose of paracetamol.
Sore throat	This can be tonsillitis or the start of a cold.	See if the throat looks red or there are white spots. If your child is unwell or symptoms persist, see the doctor.
Cough	A common symptom, often due to a cold, upper respiratory infection, chest infection, or asthma.	See the doctor if your child is unwell, short of breath, or has a persistent cough, especially without a cold.
Headache	A worrying symptom for parents, the most frequent cause is fever. Other causes include meningitis and head injury.	See the doctor if headache persists after fever is reduced. If your child is unwell, consult the doctor urgently.
Swelling in the neck	Usually caused by enlarged lymph nodes, in response to viral illness or tonsillitis. These can take a while to reduce.	Feel along the underside of your child's jaw and on the side of his neck for swellings or tenderness. If the swelling is large or he is unwell, see the doctor.
Abdominal pain	Can be due to tonsillitis. Other causes include urine infection, gastroenteritis, appendicitis, and anxiety.	Always see the doctor the same day.
Rash	Many causes, including eczema, allergies, and infectious illnesses such as measles, scarlet fever, roseola infantum, and bacterial diseases.	A mild itchy rash in a well child is unlikely to be serious – use calamine lotion and see how things develop. If the rash doesn't itch, check with the doctor. If your child is unwell at the same time, don't delay.

giving medicines

Many medicines have flavours and colours that appeal to young children, so they're less reluctant to take them. But this also means you need to take special care to keep them out of your child's reach.

When he's ill, your child may need to take over-the-counter medicines, medicines from your doctor, or sometimes both. Tastes differ dramatically. What one child loves, another may hate. It's not unknown for a child to spit out his medicine. If so, wait for him to be calm and try again.

It can help to use a favourite spoon, to mix the medicine with jam, or to reward him with a nice drink afterwards.

However, do not add your child's medicine to a drink as it may cling to the side of the glass or cup, and you won't know how much of the medicine he has actually swallowed.

Drops

It's useful to be able to give drops quickly and confidently, to minimize any upset. Some children do not mind drops and will cooperate happily, but others are quite resistant, so be prepared.

♦ **Eye drops** Sit or lie your child down comfortably on your lap, or on a bed or sofa. Hold his head steady with one arm. Gently pull down his lower eyelid and apply the drop or drops to the space between the eyeball and the lower lid. Wipe, or let him wipe, his cheek afterwards. If your child resists, hold him more firmly, or ask another adult to help.

♦ **Ear drops** Lay your child's head on your lap with his head to the side, so that he is comfortable. He will have to stay in this position for a minute or so. Hold his ear firmly but gently then let the drops fall into the ear canal. Keep your child still for a few seconds. If he gets up too soon, most of the drops will come out.

in an **emergency**!

Go to the nearest accident and emergency department, or call an ambulance, if your child:

♦ has difficulty breathing or is so short of breath he can't talk

♦ has a seizure (convulsion)

♦ loses consciousness

♦ has a serious burn (see page 271)

♦ has an accident and can't move a limb

♦ is bleeding severely

♦ has a headache, dislike of bright lights, or a rash that doesn't go away when pressed with the side of a glass (see page 244).

♦ **Nose drops** Lie your child on his back on your lap, and tilt his head back. Gently but firmly hold his head with one hand and drop the nose drops into the nostril. Repeat for the other nostril if required. Try to get your child to sniff afterwards; this will help the drops reach up the nose.

Eye drops
These often need to be given three or four times a day so it is important to develop a good technique.

Ear drops
Have your child lay his head on its side on your lap. To allow the drops to go in easily, gently pull his ear up and back.

check-ups and hospitals

Every child is different. Your child may feel perfectly at ease going to see the doctor, or she may feel inhibited, insecure, or even apprehensive. Fortunately, there is a lot you can do to help reassure your child.

visiting the doctor

Your child's doctor or nurse can make a big difference to how your child feels during an examination. A doctor who has an interest in children's health usually has an easy welcoming manner with youngsters and their parents.

It's also important to have a doctor whose professional judgement you trust. This will make the whole process easier for you, and your confidence will rub off on and comfort your child.

Examining your child
At first your doctor will merely observe your child as you describe the symptoms. This is an important part of the consultation, and allows the doctor to get an idea of how ill your child is and what's wrong. At the same time as the doctor is assessing your child, your child is sizing up the doctor, and assessing the working relationship you have with him!

The doctor will examine your child's neck for enlarged lymph glands and check her ears with an auriscope. This may be uncomfortable but is not usually painful. It helps if you hold your child on your lap or on the examination table, steadying her with your hands.

The doctor will listen to your child's chest with a stethoscope, and feel her abdomen with his hand. Again, this can

be ticklish, and many children laugh. If your youngster is still in nappies, the doctor might want to look at the nappy area. If your child is particularly ill with diarrhoea or has blood in her stools, the doctor may find it useful to look at a stool sample.

Your doctor may also need to look at your child's throat. Babies and younger children tend to resist this, so many

questions **to ask**

♦ Is my child sick? Is it serious?
♦ What does the treatment involve?
♦ What else can I do to help?
♦ For how long will my child feel unwell?
♦ Is it infectious?
♦ When should I bring her back? What should I do if she doesn't get better?
♦ When can my child return to playgroup or nursery?
♦ Are there usually after-effects?

doctors leave this bit of the examination until last. Don't worry if your child cries while her throat is being examined. You can rest assured that she will soon stop and, incidentally, a lusty cry generally gives the doctor a really good view.

Preparing your child
Treat visits to the doctor as fun and try not to let your child see if you are concerned. A good family doctor will be experienced at putting young children at ease.

having an **operation**

It's natural to be concerned about an operation, and to want to minimize any discomfort. Most operations are short and routine, and children recover particularly quickly. You may be able to take your child home the same day, although she will need extra care from you for a while.

It is important to prepare your child. She needs to know what to expect. An anaesthetist usually visits you and your child on the ward beforehand, and you can ask how your child will be put to sleep. This may be using a gas given by mask (which children don't usually mind), or by injection into an area made numb with anaesthetic cream (this is painless).

Tell your child that she'll wake up in a special recovery room, so that she's not alarmed at finding herself somewhere unfamiliar. Try to be as calm as you can, whatever your own emotions may be.

A reassuring smile and a cuddle from you will boost her spirits. While you're waiting to go to the operating theatre, you could read a book or play a quiet game. Depending on the operation, your child may have medicine by mouth about an hour and a half before to make her drowsy. Even if she's very sleepy, she'll know you're there if you hold her hand.

You can usually accompany your child as she is taken to the operating theatre (you can often carry a baby yourself). In general, you'll be able to stay with her in the anaesthetic room until she is asleep, and you can be in the recovery room as she wakes. Depending on the operation, your child may be in pain. If so, ask for pain relief.

Checklist for operations
♦ Be as calm as you can and stay with your child as much as possible.

♦ Get the details you need from the surgeon, anaesthetist, and nurses.

♦ Tell your child about the operation and give a simple explanation of why it will make her better.

♦ Explain that she can't eat or drink just beforehand.

♦ Reassure your child that you'll be there when she goes to sleep and wakes.

♦ Tell her she'll be in a special recovery room just afterwards.

♦ Read a favourite book out loud to entertain your child and help pass the time.

♦ Talk about the things you'll do when she leaves hospital, but avoid rash promises.

♦ Don't forget to smile.

a hospital stay

Tell your child well beforehand about her hospital stay.

You can help prepare your child by:
♦ answering any of her questions honestly and simply, without excess detail
♦ looking out for toys and books related to doctors and hospitals
♦ encouraging her to practise her stethoscope skills on her dolls or teddy bears.

What you can do

Most parents expect to stay in with their child if possible. You may be given a bed, or you may have to doze in an armchair. Your presence will help your child overcome any anxieties she has, and can really aid her recovery. On most children's wards, parents take over the routine non-medical care such as feeding and washing, which is good for your child and also saves nursing time. If you can't stay with your child, be there with her as much as possible and make sure that you're with her for any tests, operations, removal of stitches, or other procedures.

Packing a bag for hospital

Hospital stays for children are usually very short, but you'll still need a number of essential items if your child has to go into hospital for more than a day. Pack a small case containing:
♦ bib and your child's favourite eating implements
♦ pyjamas or nightdresses
♦ dressing gown
♦ slippers
♦ towel and face-cloth
♦ soap
♦ toothbrush and toothpaste
♦ hairbrush or comb
♦ favourite soft toy, books, and a small toy or game
♦ nappies and nappy-changing equipment if you need them.

In addition, don't forget to pack a bag of overnight things for yourself if you are going to be staying in the hospital with your child.

special needs

The term special needs applies to those children whose development, behaviour, or ability to communicate and learn are such that they need extra special care to realize their potential and lead happy lives.

where to **find help**

♦ Ask your health visitor, GP, or paediatrician about support groups.

♦ For rare conditions, talk to your paediatrician or get in touch with Contact-a-Family (see page 280).

♦ Try local and national voluntary bodies.

♦ Search the Internet, but bear in mind that many websites may not be authoritative or accurate.

what are special needs?

Some babies and children have a long-term health condition that can affect their development. It is really important to focus on what your child can achieve rather than on what he can't manage.

A child with special needs may have any one of a broad range of conditions, some of which arise before birth, while others develop later. Cystic fibrosis, for example, is inherited (see page 260). Down syndrome (see page 260) is not usually inherited, but it is congenital, meaning that a baby is born with it. Sometimes a child develops special needs because he is severely affected by a common condition such as asthma (see page 259), or because he has had a serious infection, such as bacterial meningitis (see page 244).

Getting help

In the UK, home care for a child with special needs normally starts with an assessment at the local child development centre and then the coordination of a team of professionals to support your child's development. Depending on the condition and how it affects the family, the team helping your child may include a speech therapist, physiotherapist, child psychiatrist, social workers, educational psychologists, teachers, and support groups or charity workers. If you need any extra help or want to discuss other avenues, you can access further medical, practical, and financial help for your family through your doctor, health visitor, or hospital or community paediatrician.

Other support

Although a team of professionals will support you and your child, parents of a child with special needs can sometimes feel isolated socially. Most families benefit greatly from contact with others who are in a similar situation. Talking to someone who has already faced and overcome the same challenges can inspire you to feel more positive and make it easier to handle day-to-day practicalities. This can be anything from getting more information about financial assistance to finding someone to care for your child while you enjoy an occasional evening out. You can usually contact such families through self-help and support groups. Many national organizations,

Encouraging your child
As a parent, there is often a lot you can do to help your child lead a fulfilling life.

which are usually charities, have a network of local groups or patient registers. A network such as this can lend invaluable practical and emotional support to you and your family. These organizations may also run helplines as well as publish useful information about the condition and the latest news on any ongoing research. See pages 280–281 for more information.

Playing and learning

Your child may be able to attend an ordinary toddler group, playgroup, or nursery. This will help you be a part of the community, and will enable your child to socialize. Very young children will accept and play with a child who may look or behave differently to them.

Sometimes a child with special needs is offered specialized play and learning facilities. Many children will gain more

advantages from this than from attending a regular group where they may feel out of their depth or miss out on the kind of therapy they need. It all depends on the child and her particular needs, and you will want to give her the best chance of growing up and leading a fulfilling life. A child's needs can change over time, so it's always worth keeping things under review and attending any follow-ups with paediatricians, therapists, and other members of the team.

Unusual conditions

Occasionally, a child with special needs has a condition so rare that there are very few other children with it, and little information available for parents. Sometimes, there may not even be a firm diagnosis. In these cases, parents can find the services of Contact-a-Family valuable (see page 280).

(see page 280)

coping with **your feelings**

You may feel you have missed out on the chance to have a healthy child and lead a "normal" family life. This is understandable and you may experience some of the emotions that often accompany bereavement.

♦ At first, you may feel shock and find the news difficult to believe. An element of denial is common in the early days.

♦ When things don't go to plan, it's natural to try to find a cause or apportion blame. You might be angry with health professionals, or you may feel resentment against your partner or even yourself.

♦ Feeling negative, low, or depressed may follow. Some parents worry about being able to care adequately for their child.

♦ As you become more adept at coping with the challenges, you can learn to enjoy family life.

parenting a special-needs child

Patience and understanding will help you get the best from your child. It takes special skills to be a parent to any small child, and usually even more so if your child has special needs.

There will be unique rewards for you and your family. You are likely to develop a particularly deep bond with your child. Children with special needs can be very happy and affectionate, making them especially loving and a delight to care for.

There may be times when you are feeling tired and are therefore feeling less upbeat. It's worth remembering that not every so-called "normal" child is easy all the time. Try not to be hard on yourself or your partner as you are probably already doing an excellent parenting job.

Keeping yourself in good health is a high priority, and making time for each other, and for any other children in the family, is also important. It is normal for parents of children with special needs to

ask themselves what might have happened had things been done differently. It's important to be able to talk these feelings through to help you to come to terms with your situation, and other parents in similar circumstances are often best qualified to help.

Joining in
Depending on your child's needs, he may be able to interact well with other children. This sort of relationship can be beneficial to all involved.

complementary therapies

Parents often turn to simple self-help remedies to treat minor childhood ailments, and complementary and alternative therapies, such as massage and homeopathy, are also becoming a popular choice today.

a different approach

Complementary and alternative therapies are growing in popularity. Practitioners aim to treat the whole person and can spend plenty of time in consultation, which many parents find comforting.

Complementary therapies are generally used *alongside* conventional medicine, while alternative therapies are used *in place of* conventional medicine. Many of the therapies claim to promote a feeling of wellbeing and represent an appealing opportunity for parents to have more involvement in their child's health care. However, it's important to bear in mind that there's little or no scientific proof that many complementary and alternative remedies work, although there are a few areas where there is some evidence of their efficacy – a good example is massage for helping babies to relax.

Talk to your doctor

If you're considering trying a complementary or alternative remedy on your child, you should always discuss it with your doctor first. If you don't, you may risk your doctor missing or delaying diagnosis

of your child's condition. She will talk to you about the safety and effectiveness of the therapy and will advise against it if there's a risk it will interfere with any medical treatment your child is receiving.

Finding a therapist

In the UK, there is a register of qualified osteopaths. There is no register for homeopaths, although there are some qualified homeopaths, including doctors using homeopathy.

Love and reassurance
The simplest and most pleasurable self-help remedy is to give your child plenty of love and reassurance when he's feeling ill.

types of treatment

There are many complementary and alternative treatments based on different theories, but they all differ from orthodox (allopathic) medicine as prescribed by conventional doctors.

A one-off remedy may be enough to help symptoms or, depending on your child's condition, you may be recommended an ongoing programme of treatment. Such treatment can be costly, so be realistic about how much you can afford.

Osteopathy

This is a system of manipulation. The method most suitable for babies and children is the cranio-sacral approach, which is very gentle. Cranial osteopathy focuses on the skull. Some parents find it relieves sleeping problems and colic.

Massage

Massage is a centuries-old art of nurturing and healing. It's widely used to relax babies, improve their sleep patterns, and calm them when they are irritable. It's also been shown to help the development of premature babies in special care units. See page 96 to learn how to massage your baby, and ask your health visitor for advice.

Homeopathy

Homeopathy is a treatment based on the theory that a substance that in large doses causes specific symptoms can, in minute doses, relieve the same symptoms. Always consult a qualified practitioner for advice as these remedies should be taken under supervision. Homeopathic treatments are available from pharmacies and health shops. Common remedies for children include arnica for cuts and bruises, and camomile for teething pain. Treatments often need only a single dose.

Aromatherapy

Aromatherapy is based on herbal oils (essential oils), which can be inhaled as a vapour using a special burner or mixed with a neutral oil, called a carrier, then used as a massage oil. Essential oils must never be used undiluted. Many are toxic, so your child shouldn't taste or swallow even diluted oils. Ensure any essential oil or carrier oil is suitable for young children – nut oils in particular are best avoided because of the risk of allergies.
♦ Tea-tree oil is mildly antiseptic. Used as a rinse when washing fabric nappies, it may help prevent or treat nappy rash.
♦ Lavender and tea-tree oils may help relieve the itch of chicken pox.
♦ A blend of tea-tree, rose, eucalyptus, lemon, lavender, and geranium oils is sometimes recommended for headlice.

Herbal medicine

Chinese herbal medicine may be useful for severe ezcema, while Western herbal treatments may be used for recurrent infections. Herbs can be very potent. In fact, some strong conventional medicines originate from plants. Herbal treatments can have serious side-effects and can also interact adversely with other medicines. Consult a medically qualified herbalist and always talk to your doctor first.

home remedies

Apart from complementary medicines, there are a number of home treatments and simple over-the-counter remedies that may ease your child's symptoms.

♦ **Rubs (ointments) and vapours** These may help decongest the nose and throat. Some can be rubbed onto clothing or bedding, while others can be applied directly to the chest of older children. Follow instructions carefully, and ask your pharmacist if in any doubt about the suitability of any remedy.
♦ **Linctus** This is a syrup-like medicine, available over the counter, that's usually considered by doctors to be of limited use. But it is soothing for the throat and can therefore help an irritating cough.
♦ **Fluids** These prevent dehydration and can also ease a sore throat. Lemon and honey drinks are especially good for throats. Only use honey for a child over one year old.
♦ **Soup** This is nourishing, and is a traditional home remedy for feverish illnesses in patients of most ages. It can also soothe the throat.

Steam inhalation
Sit with your child while hot water runs into the bath and let him inhale the steam. This can help alleviate catarrh and chesty coughs.

childhood illnesses

As she grows up, your child is likely to suffer acute (short-term) illnesses lasting a few days or a week. These are usually minor and often need no treatment other than loving care from you, and attention to fluid intake. Some conditions will need your doctor's help, and perhaps even admission to hospital.

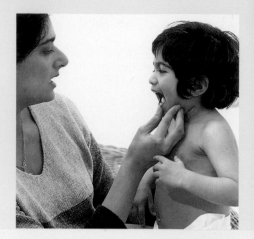

This section is a guide for parents on a variety of common and not-so-common childhood illnesses.

You will find an explanation of each condition, a description of the typical symptoms, and advice on what you can do to care for your child after she has been diagnosed by a doctor. This includes guidance on how to recognize complications and when to call your doctor.

The information in this section is designed to provide you with insight to better understand what might be affecting your child.

The early part of the section covers acute illnesses, divided into related topics, such as skin and hair, for easy reference.

The later part of the section covers chronic conditions, in other words long-term diseases and disorders. These chronic conditions can rarely be totally cured, although the symptoms may wax and wane and there are often long periods of time when your child is completely well and free of any symptoms.

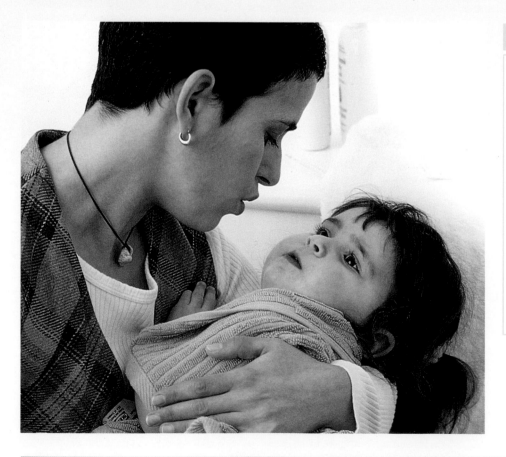

calling the **doctor**

It's natural to be concerned when your child's not at his best. Remember that your doctor is there for reassurance and advice, as well as for prescribing treatment.

Call the doctor if:

♦ you suspect that your child may be ill

♦ you're not sure that you're caring for her in the right way

♦ you know what's wrong but your child isn't improving as you would have expected

♦ your child's symptoms do not fit the description of the disease

♦ your child's symptoms change, or she develops a new one.

infectious illnesses

Thanks to immunization, the pattern of many infectious illnesses is changing. Some, such as measles, are less common than they were, while others, such as parvovirus (slapped cheek disease), seem more common. Growing awareness may be the reason for this, but it's also possible that young children having more contact with each other at playgroup, toddler group, or nursery could increase spread.

CONTENTS

viruses and bacteria

There are many differences between viruses and bacteria, but the main one is that antibiotics don't work against viruses, only bacteria. An antibiotic may combat a range of bacteria, which is useful when your doctor isn't sure which your child has. However, these broad-spectrum antibiotics interfere with harmless bacteria, too, which is why they should be taken only when needed.

Many bacteria and viruses spread in invisible water droplets in the air when someone coughs, sneezes, or speaks. Another method of spread is direct contact, especially from hands. Objects such as toys can also carry germs. Some infections spread from the gut of one person to the mouth of another, via dirty hands.

IN AN EMERGENCY!

Seek medical help urgently if:
♦ your child is unusually drowsy
♦ she has a headache or stiff neck
♦ she has a seizure (convulsion)
♦ she develops dark red or purplish spots that don't fade when pressed with the side of a glass (see *The tumbler test*, page 244).

roseola infantum

This is a surprisingly common infection that affects babies over six months and children under two years old. Occasionally, you may hear doctors mention it by its other names: *exanthem subitum*, sixth disease, and even baby measles, although it actually has nothing at all to do with measles.

Offer reassurance and plenty of fluids when your child has a fever.

SYMPTOMS

♦ a sudden onset of fever 38.9°C (102°F) to 40.5°C (105°F), lasting three to five days
♦ runny nose, slightly puffy eyes
♦ mild diarrhoea
♦ tiredness or irritability, and reduced appetite
♦ after the fever subsides, a rash of spots over the body and often the face and limbs

Making the diagnosis

Before the rash appears, the diagnosis is difficult to make. Consult your doctor.

What to do for your child

There's a risk of febrile seizures (see page 272) so bring down her temperature with fluids and paracetamol.

CALL THE DOCTOR if your child's fever persists once the rash has appeared.

IN AN EMERGENCY!

Seek medical help urgently if your child has a seizure.

chicken pox

Chicken pox is common in children over a year old, and is caused by the herpes varicella-zoster virus. Highly catching, it spreads from another person with the disease, or with shingles, which is caused by the same virus.

SYMPTOMS

♦ a feeling of being unwell before the rash appears
♦ spots that start as small red dots and turn into itchy, oval blisters that crust over
♦ sometimes, sores in the mouth that make it hard to eat

Making the diagnosis

This is usually easy as the rash is distinctive. It's most infectious in the early stages, a day before the rash appears, and it's catching until every spot has turned into a firm, dry crust. The incubation period is 14 to 21 days. One attack usually gives life-long immunity.

What to do for your child

Keep your child cool and lightly clothed to make him more comfortable. Soothe itching with calamine lotion. He may also appreciate a lukewarm bath to

which you've added a tablespoon of sodium bicarbonate (baking soda). Keep his fingernails short to minimize damage from scratching – scratched blisters tend to become infected and are more likely to scar, too. If itching is severe, try an antihistamine syrup, especially at night.

If your child's mouth is sore, give soft foods, soothing drinks, and plenty of fluids. As chicken pox is so catching, keep him away from other children, and from any adults who haven't had the disease – chicken pox can be worse for grown-ups.

CALL THE DOCTOR if:

♦ your child is unwell in himself
♦ he has a high fever you can't control
♦ he refuses to drink anything
♦ he has a very large number of blisters, particularly near his eyes
♦ you or your partner have never had chicken pox.

Gently dab on calamine lotion to soothe itching.

parvovirus (slapped cheek disease)

Parvovirus is a mild illness in children that's also known as slapped cheek disease, fifth disease, and *erythema infectiosum*. It's caused by a virus called parvovirus B19, which you can catch only from another person, by direct contact and through infected droplets in the air.

SYMPTOMS

♦ a facial rash with a well-defined edge
♦ a fine, lacy red rash on the arms or trunk
♦ sometimes, a mild fever or cold symptoms before the rash appears

Making the diagnosis

This is often obvious, but blood tests can be carried out if needed.

Children with sickle-cell disease (see page 259) tend to become more seriously ill with parvovirus and can develop severe

anaemia. The disease is also more serious in adults, who may miss out on the rash and instead develop joint pains, with or without swelling. These symptoms can last a week or two but occasionally the disease persists for months.

About half of all pregnant women are immune to parvovirus. However, those who aren't can sometimes miscarry as a result of infection in the early stages of pregnancy. There is probably less than a one in 20 chance of this happening, but it is wise to tell your doctor or midwife if

you're pregnant and suspect you may have come into contact with parvovirus. The incubation period is from five to 20 days.

What to do for your child

There is no special treatment other than keeping your child comfortable and well hydrated. As the disease is no longer catching once the rash appears, your child can usually carry on going to playgroup or nursery.

CALL THE DOCTOR if:

♦ your child is unwell in himself or is particularly feverish
♦ your child is known to have sickle-cell disease
♦ you are in the first half of pregnancy
♦ the diagnosis is in doubt.

hand, foot, and mouth disease

Hand, foot, and mouth disease is caused by a virus of the coxsackie group, and has no connection with the serious condition that afflicts farm animals called foot and mouth. The disease is spread in moisture droplets through the air but is not very catching, so not everyone who comes into contact with it develops symptoms.

SYMPTOMS

♦ spots and blisters on the hands and feet (mostly the palms and soles)
♦ spots in the mouth that make it hard to eat
♦ spots that don't appear all at the same time
♦ a mild fever a day or two before the rash

Making the diagnosis

It is usually easy for your doctor to recognize hand, foot, and mouth, especially if there have been cases of it at your child's nursery or toddler group.

Unlike chicken pox, the spots aren't itchy, and don't usually occur much on the trunk. The incubation period is about 10 days.

Because several different strains of coxsackie virus can cause the illness, it's possible to get it more than once.

What to do for your child

Most children with hand, foot, and mouth disease are well. If your child has a fever, treat it in the usual way with fluids and paracetamol (see pages 226–227). Monitor his temperature to keep it under control.

You needn't put anything on the spots. However, if your child's mouth is sore, he'll appreciate soft or sloppy foods so that he doesn't have to chew. Ice cream is a perennial favourite. You can also try him with yogurt, milk shakes, mashed potato, puréed vegetables or fruit (but avoid citrus fruits and drinks because they can make the mouth feel worse). A straw will make it easier for him to drink.

Most youngsters with hand, foot, and mouth disease don't need to stay off nursery or playgroup, unless they're feverish or feeling unwell.

CALL THE DOCTOR if:
♦ your child has a high temperature that you can't bring down
♦ you're unsure of the diagnosis
♦ he refuses to eat or drink.

measles

Measles is an uncommon infection but it is unpleasant and can be very serious, occasionally fatal. It's caused by a virus of the paramyxovirus group and spreads by infected moisture droplets in the air. Measles is very catching. More than nine out of 10 children who are exposed to it can expect to get it. Measles vaccine (the "M" in MMR) prevents most cases.

SYMPTOMS

♦ feeling ill, a high fever for up to four days, a cough, and a runny nose; during this stage, small spots inside the mouth
♦ a rash appearing on about the fifth day on the face and neck, then the trunk
♦ puffy, red eyes

Making the diagnosis

You should always consult your doctor if you think your child has measles. The incubation period is 10 to 14 days.

Measles vaccine, as MMR, offers good protection, especially if two doses of MMR are used (see page 217). One attack of the disease usually gives permanent immunity.

What to do for your child

Treat any fever (see pages 226–227), give your child plenty to drink, and soft foods

if his mouth is sore. He will probably feel miserable and won't be well enough to go out. Keep him away from other children.

CALL THE DOCTOR if:
♦ you suspect measles
♦ call him a second time if your child seems to be getting worse, especially if he won't drink, is drowsy, short of breath, or has earache.

Regularly check his temperature.

mumps

Mumps is caused by a virus of the myxovirus group and spreads by moisture droplets in the air and direct contact. Thanks to the MMR vaccine, outbreaks are rare, but it is fairly common in those who haven't had the vaccine.

SYMPTOMS

♦ feeling unwell with a mild fever lasting no more than four days; headache; appetite loss
♦ pain and swelling of one or both parotid glands (saliva glands on each side of the face)

Making the diagnosis

When both sides of the jaw swell up and your child has pain when she eats, it's usually easy to diagnose. The incubation period is 17 to 19 days. Mumps is catching from a few days before the glands enlarge until they are back to normal. One attack gives permanent protection.

Children can occasionally develop pancreatitis, or mumps meningitis (which can cause permanent deafness). Older boys may get inflammation of the testes.

What to do for your child

Treat a fever and keep an eye on her temperature to ensure it stays under control (see pages 226–227). Chewing makes pain worse, so give your child soothing drinks and soft, sloppy foods. Drinks are easier to swallow with a straw. Avoid citrus fruit, which tend to make the saliva flow and can increase discomfort.

If possible, keep your child away from other children until the swelling has gone.

CALL THE DOCTOR if:

♦ you think your child has mumps
♦ she has a persistent high fever
♦ she won't take any fluids
♦ she becomes unusually drowsy.

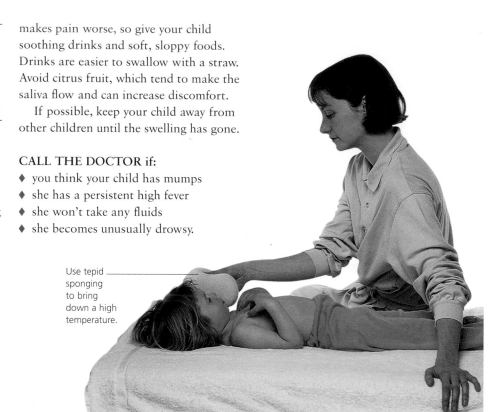

Use tepid sponging to bring down a high temperature.

rubella

Rubella (German measles) is a mild infectious disease, but it's important because it can cause serious birth defects if a pregnant woman catches it. The cause is a virus of the togavirus group. It's very catching and can be spread by those who have symptoms and by those without them, which is why it's important to eradicate rubella by immunization (see pages 216–217).

SYMPTOMS

♦ a rash, often starting as small pink patches, on the neck, face, trunk, and limbs
♦ enlarged glands high in the back of the neck
♦ feeling slightly ill

Making the diagnosis

Rubella is difficult to diagnose because the rash can look like many other conditions, including other viral infections. If it's vital to have a precise diagnosis, your doctor can arrange a blood test, but children rarely need one.

Rubella spreads by moisture droplets in the air and is catching for about two to three weeks, starting from one week before symptoms start. The incubation period is 14 to 21 days.

What to do for your child

Keep your child comfortable. Because of the risk of birth defects, warn any women your child has been in recent contact with, and keep her away from anyone who may be in early stages of pregnancy.

CALL THE DOCTOR if:

♦ you think your child has rubella, because you're unlikely to be able to diagnose it yourself, and also it's a notifiable disease (which means it must be reported to the local health authorities)
♦ your child isn't better in four days
♦ you are pregnant.

whooping cough

Whooping cough (pertussis) is a serious and distressing infection that inflames the whole respiratory system from nose to lungs. Although it can occur at any age, it tends to be worse in the under-twos and very severe in premature babies. It can be prevented by the pertussis vaccine (DTP).

SYMPTOMS

- runny nose, cough, fever, and sore eyes
- worsening cough with uncontrollable bouts, sometimes followed by the typical "whoop"
- during a coughing bout, vomiting or even turning blue through lack of oxygen
- occasionally, seizures can occur

Making the diagnosis

A typical case of whooping cough is easy to spot once bouts of coughing and whooping begin. However, it's harder to diagnose in the early stages, when symptoms resemble a bad cold.

The cause is a bacterium called *Bordetella pertussis*. It spreads from one infected person to another in droplets in the air when coughing or sneezing. The incubation period is one to three weeks. There is a vaccine for whooping cough (see *Immunizations*, page 216).

What to do for your child

Give her plenty of fluids in between coughing bouts. She also needs small meals to reduce the risk of vomiting.

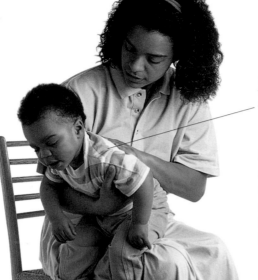

Lean your child forward during a coughing bout.

Keep a bowl nearby in case she is sick. Avoid smoky atmospheres and over-excitement as these can trigger coughing. Antibiotics may shorten the illness, but have to be started early, which is rarely possible.

A child with whooping cough can be scared as well as distressed, so it's wise to sleep in the same room while she's ill. This may not give you much sleep, but you'll both gain reassurance from being close.

CALL THE DOCTOR if you think your child has whooping cough, as she may need hospital treatment.

kawasaki disease

This is a fairly common illness in children under two that was almost unheard of 40 years ago and now seems to be getting more common. Its exact cause is unknown, but it's probably an infection. It affects many parts of the body and, although full recovery is usual, it can have long-term effects on the heart.

SYMPTOMS

- high fever that persists for five days or more
- red rash on the trunk, similar to measles
- enlarged lymph glands in the neck
- sore, red eyes
- sore, cracked mouth
- swollen or peeling hands and feet

Making the diagnosis

Kawasaki disease is not difficult to diagnose when the symptoms are typical. Your child is likely to have it if she has five of any of the six symptoms listed, left.

What to do for your child

Keep your child comfortable and contact the doctor. Aspirin is sometimes used for Kawasaki disease but it also has risks (see page 227), so don't ever give it to your child except under specialist supervision.

CALL THE DOCTOR if you have any reason to suspect your child has Kawasaki disease.

meningitis

Meningitis means inflammation of the meninges, the membranes that protect the brain. It can be caused by many viruses and bacteria. A lot of the germs that cause meningitis live in the throat or nose of healthy people and cause no harm at all. It's not clear what triggers disease in some people, but it's more common where there's overcrowding and in households where people smoke.

SYMPTOMS

Baby
- a high-pitched or moaning cry
- refusing feeds and irritability when picked up
- drowsiness with limp limbs, or else limbs that are stiffer than usual
- pale, blotchy, sometimes clammy skin
- a tense, bulging fontanelle (soft spot)

Child
- severe headache and a dislike of bright lights
- stiff neck
- fever
- drowsiness and confusion, with flu-like aches and pains

At any age
- a rash of red or brown pin-point spots, or large bruises and purplish marks that don't fade when pressed with the side of a glass

Making the diagnosis

In the advanced stages, meningitis is easy to diagnose. However, the ideal is to spot it early, when complete cure is most likely. The disease can develop very quickly. A child may seem well one moment, then within a few hours be extremely ill. In other cases, it may take one or two days to develop. Another problem is that the symptoms can be difficult to distinguish from other, less serious infections. If you suspect meningitis, always tell your doctor what you're thinking of.

Symptoms vary according to the age of the child. A baby or child with meningitis may not have all the symptoms listed, but he will be ill in himself and may get rapidly worse.

The incubation period for bacterial meningitis is between two and 10 days, and for viral meningitis it can be up to three weeks.

What to do for your child

Call your doctor urgently or go straight to hospital (the accident and emergency department) if you think your child has meningitis. Tell the hospital you suspect meningitis as soon as you arrive. Never wait for a rash to develop as this is a late symptom and it's better to diagnose the disease earlier.

Tests must be done to confirm the diagnosis. If your child has meningitis, antibiotics are the usual treatment, often given in intensive care together with any other help he may need.

types of **meningitis**

Viral meningitis is milder and complete recovery is usual. Bacterial meningitis is more serious and always needs urgent treatment in hospital.

Meningococcal meningitis One of the most serious forms of bacterial meningitis, this can also cause septicaemia (blood poisoning). Although treatment can still cure the disease, a child who reaches this stage is very ill and every second counts. There are several different types of meningococcal meningitis. Type B infection is more common in the UK and other Western countries, while type C occurs in outbreaks. Type A is more common in parts of Africa and Asia. The vaccine against meningococcal C infection gives very good protection (see pages 216–217), while a vaccine against meningococcal B infection is still being developed.

Pneumococcal meningitis Another very serious bacterial form of meningitis. It especially affects children under two years old and is linked with septicaemia and other infections such as chest and ear infections. Long-term complications are common with pneumococcal meningitis. There are several different strains of pneumococcal bacteria, so one attack doesn't protect against any future infection. A vaccine to prevent pneumococcal infections in babies and children is due to be introduced soon.

Haemophilus influenzae B (Hib) Once a common cause of bacterial meningitis in children, but thankfully it has become much rarer now that babies are given the Hib vaccine (see pages 216–217).

respiratory infections

Respiratory infections are common in babies and children because there are many different viruses and bacteria, and babies' immune systems have yet to mature. It's sometimes hard to tell which part is infected. Doctors often use the terms upper respiratory tract infection (URTI) for infections of the nose, throat, and larynx, and lower respiratory tract infection (LRTI) for infections in the trachea, bronchi, or lungs.

colds

The common cold is exactly that – very common. It's caused by a virus, but this can be any one of several hundred viruses, mostly of the rhinovirus group. Because babies and young children need to build up immunity to each virus one at a time, they get a huge number of colds as they grow up – more than six a year is not at all unusual while they are young, especially once they start nursery or playgroup.

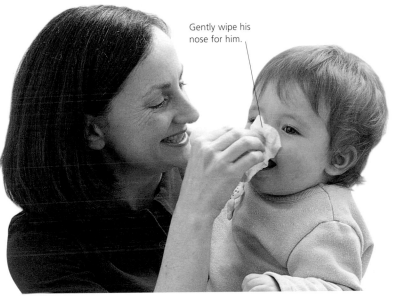

Gently wipe his nose for him.

SYMPTOMS

♦ sneezing, and a stuffy or runny nose
♦ a sore throat and watery, sticky eyes
♦ a mild cough, especially at night when secretions run down the back of the throat
♦ a mild fever

Making the diagnosis

It's usually easy to tell if your child has a cold from the typical symptoms. Colds spread on moisture droplets in the air when coughing, sneezing, or talking. Your child will usually suffer more colds in winter as more time is spent indoors with other people. The incubation period is about two days and a cold can last up to three weeks. Complications include middle ear infection (see page 248) and chest infection (see page 247).

What to do for your child

There's no cure as such, but there's a lot you can do as a parent when your child has a cold. Children can't blow their noses, so wipe your child's nose gently for him. Use cotton wool rather than tissues because it's softer on a baby's tender skin.

Give your child lots of fluids to drink. Babies with a cold are often slow to feed because they find it hard to breathe and suck at the same time. So be patient with feeds, giving your baby plenty of time to suck.

Over-the-counter preparations can be useful to decongest your child's nose. Check with your pharmacist, doctor, or health visitor that the preparation you buy is appropriate for your child's age. Saline nose drops can help unblock a baby's nose, but medical opinion is divided as to whether they're a good idea.

CALL THE DOCTOR if:

♦ your infant's temperature is higher than 38°C (100.4°F) for more than 24 hours
♦ your child seems to be ill
♦ you notice any new symptoms developing, such as wheezing, shortness of breath, or earache.

flu

Flu, or influenza, is always caused by a virus. There are many different strains of flu virus, the two main groups being influenza A and influenza B. Influenza A changes over time, and can therefore cause major outbreaks or pandemics (worldwide epidemics). Incidentally, flu is not caused by the bacterium *Haemophilus influenzae* B (see *Hib*, pages 216–217).

Soothe your child with a loving cuddle.

SYMPTOMS

- a fever, often very high
- aches and pains
- a slightly runny nose or sore throat
- vomiting, diarrhoea, or abdominal pain
- listlessness and generally feeling unwell

Making the diagnosis

Flu spreads in moisture droplets in the air. Adults are more likely to get flu, but young children can develop it, especially between December and March. The incubation period is one to three days.

Because flu is uncommon in the very young, it's important not to assume that it is flu – he may be ill with something else, such as an infection of the ear, throat, chest, or urine, or even early meningitis. Even your doctor may be unable to tell at first, and may need to see your child again.

What to do for your child

Keep your child comfortable and treat his fever if necessary (see pages 226–227) – he'll feel much better when his temperature is under control. Give your child plenty to drink, and tender loving care.

CALL THE DOCTOR if:

- you're not sure if it's flu
- his fever lasts for more than 24 hours
- he's increasingly listless
- he develops new symptoms, such as earache or breathlessness.

bronchiolitis

Bronchiolitis is an infection of the bronchioles, which are tiny air passages in the lungs. It usually affects babies under 12 months, but toddlers can get it, too. Bronchiolitis differs from bronchitis, which involves large air passages.

SYMPTOMS

- cold and fever, progressing quickly to coughing, rapid breathing, and wheezing
- crackly or bubbling breathing sounds
- in severe cases, an indrawing of the chest between and below the ribs, shortness of breath, and turning blue from lack of oxygen

Making the diagnosis

Consult your doctor if your child has any of the above symptoms. Diagnosis is easy for your doctor to make, especially during outbreaks, but symptoms can resemble asthma (see page 259) and chest infection (see opposite). Bronchiolitis tends to occur in early winter and is caused by a virus, usually respiratory syncytial virus (RSV). It has an incubation period of just a few days and spreads by droplets in the air. Some cases are milder than others but, on the whole, the younger your baby, the more serious it tends to be. Some children need to be hospitalized. Bronchiolitis can recur.

What to do for your child

Follow your doctor's instructions. If your child is mildly ill, give plenty of fluids and treat fever, if necessary. You can also sit your child in a steamy room, such as in the

IN AN EMERGENCY!

Bronchiolitis can be an emergency, so don't delay. If in doubt, call an ambulance.

bathroom with the hot water running, to decongest her air passages and ease her breathing. Doing this several times a day for 10 minutes seems to help. You may want to sleep in the same room as your child, to keep watch over her and to comfort her.

CALL THE DOCTOR if:

- your child is distressed
- she is unable to take even fluids
- her chest is sucked in with each breath
- her breathing becomes more rapid
- she turns blue.

croup

Croup is a form of laryngitis that occurs from three months to three years. It's usually due to a virus, often RSV, the same virus that causes bronchiolitis. However, croup can be caused by other viruses, too. The larynx (voice-box) of a young child is different from an adult's, which is why children get croup. The symptoms occur because the airways are narrowed, making breathing difficult.

IN AN EMERGENCY!

In severe cases, croup can be an emergency. Don't delay – call for an ambulance.

SYMPTOMS

- a harsh, barking cough and noisy breathing, especially on breathing in
- hoarseness – may be worse in the morning
- in severe cases, rapid breathing and turning blue from lack of oxygen

Making the diagnosis

Although the cough can sound typical, croup isn't always easy to diagnose because it can be similar to two other conditions, epiglottitis and inhaled foreign body. Epiglottitis is inflammation of the epiglottis, the flap of tissue just above the voice-box that covers the airways during swallowing. Epiglottitis is rare, but often due to infection with *Haemophilus influenzae* B (Hib). As it's bacterial, it responds to antibiotics. With epiglottitis, the child often sits forwards to relieve the blockage, and he may drool because he can't swallow saliva. NEVER put anything into your child's throat, or look down it, when he is hoarse or wheezing. If it's epiglottitis, this can cause the epiglottis to block the airway, with possibly fatal results.

Inhaled foreign bodies, like beads or nuts, can also block the airway if they lodge in the windpipe (see page 270).

The incubation period of croup is a matter of days. Because of the different viruses, it's possible to have it several times, and some children are prone to it.

What to do for your child

A child with croup is often distressed. Keep calm yourself and reassure him. For a mild attack of croup, treat any fever, if necessary, and give plenty of fluids.

Help decongest your child's airways by sitting him in a steamy room (see bronchiolitis, page 246).

CALL THE DOCTOR if:

- you're not sure it's croup
- your child's breathing gets worse
- he turns blue.

chest infection

Chest infection means any infection in the chest, from bronchitis to pneumonia. Often the doctor can't tell exactly where the trouble is, so chest infection is a term that may be vague but is more honest. The term lower respiratory tract infection (LRTI) is the same as chest infection.

IN AN EMERGENCY!

Call for an ambulance if your child is distressed or turns blue.

SYMPTOMS

- cough, shortness of breath, and a fever
- harsh breathing sounds, or breathing that's faster than usual
- sometimes, vomiting

Making the diagnosis

You may suspect a chest infection from your child's symptoms, but your doctor needs to listen to his chest with a stethoscope to be sure.

Viruses and bacteria can both cause chest infections. Pneumococcus is one of the most serious bacteria, and it also causes meningitis and septicaemia (see page 244). Most chest infections spread via phlegm and saliva droplets. The incubation period is short for all of these germs.

What to do for your child

Reassure your child. Regularly check her temperature and give her plenty of fluids. Keep meals small and frequent if she's coughing a lot or short of breath. A baby needs plenty of time to feed.

Young children's chest infections can change rapidly, usually for the better, but not always so watch your child carefully. Few children bring up phlegm when they are ill, but if yours does, encourage her to spit it out on a tissue rather than swallow it. Give prescribed medicines as directed.

CALL THE DOCTOR if:

- your child becomes short of breath
- her breathing is laboured
- she fails to improve on treatment.

TUBERCULOSIS (TB)

TB is a chronic infection that's caused by a bacterium called *Mycobacterium tuberculosis*. It's common in many parts of the world, including inner cities in the UK. The vaccine gives good but far from perfect protection.

Infection often begins in the lungs, then spreads to the lymph glands inside the chest. From there, it can spread elsewhere. The incubation period is several weeks. There may be a cough, poor appetite, weight loss, fever, tiredness, and enlarged glands in the neck.

Doctors may suspect TB if you have any relatives with it or you have been in contact with anyone else who has it. The treatment is prescribed drugs from a specialist. Always see your doctor if you think your child has been exposed to TB.

eye, ear, nose, and throat

Eye, ear, nose, and throat infections are among the most common childhood ailments. A child's immune system has yet to mature, and he's exposed to new viruses and bacteria almost daily. Lymph tissue in the nose (adenoids) and the throat (tonsils) mops up infection and mounts an immune response.

ear infections

These can affect the outer ear, which channels sound towards the ear drum, or the middle ear, which transmits sound vibrations to the inner ear mechanism with the help of three tiny bones. The inner ear, which sends coded sound signals to the brain, does not usually become infected.

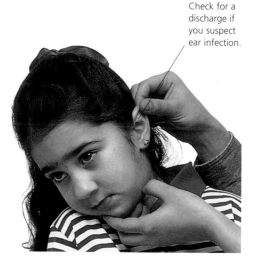

Check for a discharge if you suspect ear infection.

OUTER EAR INFECTION (otitis externa)

In an outer ear infection, the ear canal itself is inflamed, often due to bacteria. This can happen if your child has eczema, or if he goes swimming a lot. Children also poke their fingers in their ears, which is another possible source of infection. Although it's called an outer ear infection, you may not be able to see anything from the outside.

SYMPTOMS

♦ earache or itching
♦ discharge from the ear
♦ repeated pulling or rubbing the ear

Making the diagnosis

Your doctor will examine your child's ears with an auriscope (also known as an otoscope) to see into the canals.

What to do for your child

Give your child paracetamol or ibuprofen for pain relief, and use ear drops as directed. Avoid getting his ear wet.

Keep him away from other children for a day or so as the discharge is usually infected. Gently wipe away any discharge from the ear, but avoid putting cotton buds, or anything else, inside the canal.

MIDDLE EAR INFECTION (acute otitis media)

This means infection or inflammation in the space behind the ear drum. Sometimes only one ear is affected, but occasionally it's both. Viruses cause as many as half of all middle ear infections, but it's not always possible for your doctor to know whether viruses or bacteria are the cause.

Infection reaches the middle ear from the throat via the Eustachian tube, which is narrower and shorter than an adult's. Some children are prone to repeated ear infections while they are growing up.

SYMPTOMS

♦ earache and fever
♦ inconsolable crying
♦ discharge from the ear

Making the diagnosis

Your doctor should examine your child's ears with an auriscope to see the drums.

What to do for your child

Relieve your child's pain with a warm compress over the ear. Give him pain relief in the form of paracetamol or ibuprofen. If the cause is a mild virus, he may begin to improve on his own. Treat fever, if necessary, and offer plenty of fluids. Give antibiotics if prescribed.

CALL THE DOCTOR if:

♦ you suspect an ear infection
♦ you can't control his earache, he has a high fever, or he seems unusually ill.

GLUE EAR

Glue ear is a build-up of sticky fluid in the middle ear. Initially, your doctor may prescribe a decongestant, but a simple operation may be needed if the fluid persists and causes impaired hearing. Under anaesthetic, a tiny tube (known as a grommet) is inserted into the ear drum. The grommet equalizes the air pressure on either side of the ear drum and allows the ear to dry out. After several months, the grommet will fall out, the hole will heal, and hearing will be back to normal.

tonsillitis

Tonsillitis means inflammation or infection of the tonsils. Tonsils are usually large in children. They're also the doorway through which many germs pass, so are often infected with any of a wide range of airborne viruses and bacteria. Your child may recover from tonsillitis on his own, but antibiotics may be given if the cause is thought to be bacteria, such as streptococcus (strep).

SYMPTOMS

- fever, sore throat, and difficulty in swallowing
- tender, swollen lymph glands in the neck
- abdominal pain from enlarged lymph glands in the abdomen
- sometimes, a rash that starts with spots on the trunk, spreading to the rest of the body

Making the diagnosis

Tonsillitis is difficult to diagnose if your child is suffering from mainly abdominal pain. However, you will probably suspect it if he complains of a sore throat, has difficulty swallowing, and is running a fever.

You may also notice that he has bad breath and a raw-looking throat, possibly with creamy spots where the tonsils are. NEVER attempt to look down your child's throat if he is hoarse or wheezy, and never force open his mouth as it may do more harm than good.

What to do for your child

Give your child tender loving care. Offer him plenty of soothing drinks, preferably warm, unless he takes more readily to cold drinks and ice cream. Sweetened lemon drinks can be particularly helpful. Give pain and fever relief in the form of paracetamol or ibuprofen (see pages 226–227).

IN AN EMERGENCY!

Get medical help urgently if your child has trouble breathing.

CALL THE DOCTOR if:

- your child has a fever for more than 24 hours
- he has stomach pain, or can't swallow
- he doesn't improve within 48 hours.

conjunctivitis

This is an inflammation or infection of the lining of the eyeball or eyelids, and can be bacterial, viral, or allergic. It affects one or both eyes. The stickier the eyes are in the morning, the more likely it is to be bacterial. Babies get bacterial conjunctivitis because their tear ducts aren't properly formed until six months.

SYMPTOMS

- eyes that are sticky or crusty with pus first thing in the morning or after a nap
- a blob of pus in the corner of the eye
- rubbing the eyes in discomfort
- bloodshot eyes and/or swollen eyelids

Making the diagnosis

Conjunctivitis is usually obvious from the symptoms. However, your child may also have sticky eyes when he has a cold, and this often needs no special treatment.

Both viral and bacterial forms of conjunctivitis are catching, spreading in the air and by direct contact. The incubation period is usually short.

Allergic conjunctivitis is uncommon in the under-threes, but can be linked with hay fever and other allergies. It tends to make eyes itchy or watery as well as sore.

What to do for your child

If your child has only mild conjunctivitis, with slightly sticky eyes on waking, you may not need to see the doctor at all. Wash your hands, then gently wipe off the pus from his eyelids with cotton wool that has been dipped in cooled, boiled water. Always wipe from the nose towards the outside of the eye. Use a clean piece of cotton wool for each eye, and take care not to touch the eyeball itself. Wash your hands again.

If you have been prescribed eye drops by your doctor, use them as directed (see page 231) and make sure that you complete the course, which is usually five days. While your child's eyes are inflamed, keep him away from nursery or playgroup because conjunctivitis is catching until your child has had treatment for at least the first 24 hours.

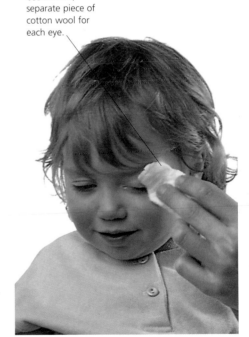

Use a clean, separate piece of cotton wool for each eye.

CALL THE DOCTOR if:

- your child's eyes need wiping more than twice a day
- his eye is bloodshot or very sore
- his eyelids look swollen.

styes

A stye is a localized infection at the base of one of the eyelashes. It forms a small boil on the upper or lower lid. This is sore and painful, and the whole lid looks red in the early stages. Bacteria usually cause styes. Toddlers and older children get them because they often rub their eyes with less-than-clean fingers.

SYMPTOMS
♦ a red swelling on one of the eyelids
♦ a pus-filled lump in the swelling a day or two later
♦ a discharge before the stye dries up

Making the diagnosis
The typical appearance will probably tell you that your child has a stye. However, in the early stages a stye can look like conjunctivitis or an eye injury, so it helps if your child is old enough to be able to tell what, if anything, happened.

What to do for your child
Although styes are painful, they aren't usually serious and you can treat most of them yourself. To relieve your child's symptoms and ease swelling, wash your hands and make a warm compress for the eye. Dip a wad or ball of cotton wool into hot water, squeeze it out, then press it gently onto your child's closed eye for a few minutes. A few drops of water may trickle down her face, so give her a tissue to wipe her cheek if she wants to. Using compresses several times a day will help bring the stye to a head. When it bursts or discharges, just wipe away the pus with cotton wool dipped in cooled, boiled water.

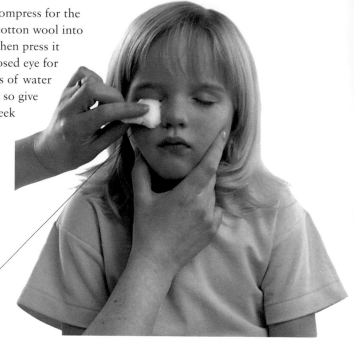

Press gently, taking care not to touch the eyeball.

CALL THE DOCTOR if:
♦ the stye doesn't improve within a week
♦ the redness spreads
♦ the whole eyelid is swollen and her eye looks bloodshot.

cold sores

Cold sores are a localized infection on the lip, or less often the nostril. They're caused by the herpes simplex virus and are very catching. They often appear during a cold, hence the name cold sore. Once your child has a cold sore, the virus then lies dormant. Your child may get further attacks triggered by minor illness, strong sunlight, or nose-picking. Babies or young children with herpes simplex can get a more widespread sore mouth with painful blisters.

SYMPTOMS
♦ tingling or pain on the lip or in the nostril
♦ a blister or a cluster of small blisters that appear a few hours later
♦ weepy blisters a day or two later that crust over and form a scab

Making the diagnosis
Cold sores can look typical, but sometimes may be hard to distinguish from impetigo (see page 252), which needs different treatment.

What to do for your child
If your child only has tingling, try wrapping an ice-cube in a clean cloth and applying it to the tingling area for five to 10 minutes. This may stop the cold sore developing.

If you notice cold sore symptoms early, they often respond to acyclovir cream. This is an antiviral cream that needs to be applied regularly, several times daily – ask your doctor or pharmacist.

Stop your child from touching her cold sore, and keep her away from other children until the sore is completely dry and scabbed. Also, prevent her sharing toys that she's likely to have put in her mouth because they may be carrying the virus.

CALL THE DOCTOR if:
♦ this is your child's first cold sore attack
♦ she has more than one area affected
♦ the cold sore is near the eye
♦ your child looks unwell
♦ she is not eating or drinking
♦ the cold sore looks infected.

skin and hair

Babies and children have beautiful healthy skin most of the time. However, it's easy for them to pick up infections and their delicate skin can look inflamed or irritated. Your child may scratch, causing more damage and scabbing. Once a scab forms, she may pick at it, which delays healing. You can't always stop her doing this, but it is important to teach your child good hygiene from an early age, to help avoid infections.

pimples and boils

A pimple is a small infected red swelling anywhere on the skin. A boil is bigger and more painful. It contains pus which eventually points in the middle and discharges creamy-yellow material. Both pimples and boils are caused by bacterial infection and can occur at any age. Most pimples are nothing to worry about, and nor is the occasional small boil. However, if your child gets frequent boils it may indicate that she has an underlying illness, such as diabetes (see page 258).

SYMPTOMS

Pimples

♦ a small, red, painless lump, usually with a white or yellow centre

Boils

♦ a painful, angry-looking, red lump, perhaps with a white or yellow head in the centre

♦ sometimes, tender enlarged lymph glands

Making the diagnosis

This is usually obvious from the appearance of your child's skin, but splinters, foreign bodies, and infected cuts or grazes can look similar. Sometimes lymph glands near the site of the boil can become swollen and tender, for example a boil on the arm will cause swollen glands in the armpit, while a boil on the scalp will make glands behind the ears enlarge.

What to do for your child

Pimples usually clear up in a few days without any treatment. Just keep your child's skin clean in the usual way. Don't be tempted to squeeze pimples or boils as you can spread infection, and may cause scarring. After a boil bursts, simply clean the discharged pus with cotton wool dipped in antiseptic, or in cooled, boiled water. If the area looks raw, cover it with a non-fluffy dressing. If your child has a boil in a painful place, such as her bottom, she may be more comfortable if you pad it with plenty of cotton wool or gauze, held on with sticky tape.

A large or deep boil may need lancing to let the pus out. Some boils are so inflamed and red that antibiotics are needed to help them clear up, but most of them are not. Your doctor will advise you on the best course of treatment.

CALL THE DOCTOR if:

♦ your child has a large or painful boil

♦ she has frequent boils

♦ she has many pimples.

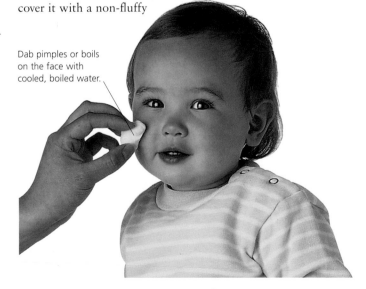

Dab pimples or boils on the face with cooled, boiled water.

urticaria

Urticaria literally means nettle rash, because that's what it looks like, but it's not caused by nettles. Also known as hives, urticaria is an allergic skin reaction to any of a number of triggers, ranging from foods and drugs to viral infections. It can also be caused by sunlight. Urticaria can occur at any age, but it's most common in young children.

SYMPTOMS

- raised areas of intensely itchy, red skin that spread and merge together
- rash lasting a few days or fading within hours

Making the diagnosis

Diagnosing urticaria isn't hard if your child has the typical rash, but working out what caused it is more of a challenge. In nearly nine out of 10 cases, the trigger remains a mystery.

What to do for your child

Keep your child comfortable by applying an even layer of calamine lotion onto the affected area. If the rash covers most of his body, a lukewarm bath, to which you've added about two tablespoons of bicarbonate of soda (baking soda), can be helpful first. You may also need to give your child an antihistamine syrup to ease severe itching – ask your pharmacist, health visitor, or doctor.

Try to work out what caused your child's urticaria. For instance, think about any unusual foods he has eaten in the last day or so, or any new garden plants he may have touched.

CALL THE DOCTOR if:
- your child is very distressed
- your child suffers from frequent attacks of urticaria.

IN AN EMERGENCY!

Call your doctor urgently, or phone for an ambulance, if your child's face, mouth, or tongue is swollen, or if he has trouble breathing. He could be suffering an anaphylactic shock (see page 272).

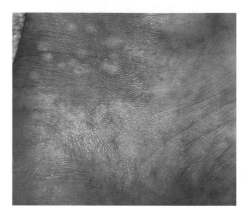

Urticaria
With urticaria, or hives, the typical red, raised, itchy patches spread and merge together. They may last a few hours or a few days.

impetigo

Impetigo is a skin infection most commonly caused by the streptococcus or the staphylococcus bacterium. It's common in children over one year old, and gets into the skin when it's cracked, irritated, or has been picked. Impetigo usually starts near the mouth or nose, but can be almost anywhere on the skin, and spreads rapidly from the area where it first began.

SYMPTOMS

- a small cluster of red spots and blisters, often near the corner of the mouth
- enlarging spots that become yellow, burst, and form honey-coloured crusts

Making the diagnosis

In the early stages, it's not always easy even for a doctor to tell impetigo apart from cold sores (see page 250). Both are contagious, but need different treatment.

Impetigo spreads by direct contact from person to person and is very catching. Serious complications are rare, though kidney damage is a remote possibility. In children, impetigo is not usually serious, but young babies who get it can become very ill.

What to do for your child

There's a lot you can do to keep your child comfortable and stop impetigo from spreading. Discourage him from touching or picking at the area as this can make the infection more widespread and scarring more likely. Keep his face-cloth and towels separate from the rest of the family's. Wash the affected area daily by dabbing it with cotton wool dipped in warm water, then pat dry with paper tissues or kitchen towel and throw this away immediately to reduce the risk of infecting others. Don't take the crusts off unless they're already sliding off as you clean your child's skin.

Your child will need antibiotic cream or ointment on prescription, and your doctor may also prescribe antibiotics by mouth. Make sure he takes the whole course of treatment. Meanwhile, keep him away from other children, especially babies.

CALL THE DOCTOR if:
- you think your child has impetigo
- it's widespread despite treatment
- your child becomes feverish or unwell.

warts

Warts are small lumps in the skin caused by infection with wart virus. The lump itself is made up of several layers of dead skin. A wart on the sole of the foot (often called a verruca) looks a bit different because constant pressure prevents it rising above the rest of the skin.

SYMPTOMS

♦ small, hard lumps of dry-looking skin that may occur singly or in clusters anywhere on the body, but especially the hands and feet
♦ tiny black spots in the centre of each lump

Making the diagnosis

In the early stages, you could think your child has a splinter or some minor injury, but soon the appearance becomes more typical of a wart. Check your child's body for warts elsewhere, too.

Warts are catching and spread by direct contact. They sometimes also spread from one part of the body to another. They are very common and no treatment is needed because the body's immune system makes warts go away within two to five years.

What to do for your child

Some children are bothered by their warts, but they're painless and harmless, so it's best not to make a fuss. They go away without treatment. Just cover them up if your child goes swimming, and keep his towels and face-cloths separate.

If your child wants to get rid of his warts, you can try over-the-counter wart preparations – ask your pharmacist. They work by dissolving the wart, and treatment can be uncomfortable. Don't use any wart preparations on your child's face or genitals as these areas are too delicate.

CALL THE DOCTOR if:

♦ you're not sure it's warts
♦ your child's warts multiply rapidly
♦ a wart appears on your child's face or genitals.

MOLLUSCUM

Molluscum contagiosum is a collection of warts with a characteristic pearly appearance and a pit in the centre. It occurs in clusters and is common in children. It starts as small fleshy bumps, then takes on a shell-like look. Although contagious, molluscum is nothing to worry about, and usually clears up on its own after a while.

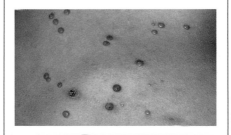

headlice

Headlice are a common infestation in children, especially at nursery or playschool. Lice are small wingless insects that crawl on human heads, cling to the hair shaft, and suck tiny amounts of blood from the scalp to survive. Since lice can't jump or fly, they spread by direct head-to-head contact. Each louse lives for up to three weeks. Lice are said to prefer clean hair, but in truth they're probably not fussy.

SYMPTOMS

♦ brownish lice moving in your child's hair
♦ pinhead-sized louse eggs, close to the scalp
♦ gritty brown powder on your child's bed, or empty white egg cases (nits) clinging to hair
♦ possibly itching, but this is a late symptom

Making the diagnosis

The best way to detect lice is to comb your child's damp hair with a special fine-toothed lice comb bought from the chemist. Do this over a white surface such as a paper towel or hand-basin to see what comes out. If you're not sure whether they are lice, you can put the bits onto sticky tape and take them to your health visitor.

What to do for your child

Relax. Headlice are not serious, nor are they a disgrace, and they're definitely not an emergency. The treatment is special insecticide lotion or shampoo, applied to the scalp. Ask your health visitor which one to buy from the chemist, as these change over time to combat resistance.

The comb-and-conditioner technique is a non-drug way of treating lice: saturate your child's hair with ordinary hair conditioner and comb it until the lice come out. Repeat the process every four days for at least two weeks. This is a popular method, but its effectiveness isn't entirely proved.

Check the rest of the family's hair for lice. There's no need to keep your child off nursery or playgroup, but do tell his teachers, childminder, or any other carers that treatment has begun.

CALL THE DOCTOR if you and your health visitor aren't sure it's headlice.

Use a fine-toothed comb to remove the lice.

bowels and bladder

Children often have trouble with their bowels or bladder, and probably can't tell you how they feel. However, there are several signs to look out for that may suggest your child has a problem, in particular frequent, runny stools, vomiting, or smelly or bloody urine.

stomach ache

Stomach ache can be a symptom of gastroenteritis (see right), when it occurs usually just before a bowel movement. Sometimes it's caused by over-eating. But stomach ache doesn't always mean trouble in the stomach. Lymph glands in the belly can be painful if your child has tonsillitis, or other infections.

Appendicitis is another possible cause. The pain is likely to start in the middle before settling on the right side. It's rare in young children but can be serious, so get help urgently. Children can also get stomach ache when they're worried about something. A stomach ache and headache at the same time could be a form of migraine.

IN AN EMERGENCY!

Seek medical help urgently if:
♦ your child is screaming with stomach ache
♦ she has stomach ache and a fever
♦ she passes blood in the stools
♦ she has stools like redcurrant jelly
♦ she shows signs of dehydration (see page 219).

urinary tract infection

Infection can affect any part of a child's urinary system, from the bladder right up to the kidneys. Most infections are bacterial. Bacteria get into the urinary system through the urethra, the channel that leads from the bladder to the outside.

SYMPTOMS

Baby or young child
♦ a fever, listlessness, or drowsiness
♦ refusing to feed or crying more than usual

Older child
♦ passing urine more often
♦ burning or stinging when passing urine
♦ stomach ache and fever
♦ cloudy, smelly urine, possibly with traces of blood in it

Making the diagnosis

Your doctor will test your child's urine. The ideal is to catch a sample in a sterile container to send to the lab – easiest with toilet-trained boys; with baby girls, stick-on bags may be used to collect urine.

Some young children have minor abnormalities in their urinary systems, which means that when bacteria enter the bladder they multiply and take hold.

What to do for your child

Make sure your child has plenty to drink, to help flush out bacteria. Keep an eye on her temperature and report this to your doctor, who will prescribe an antibiotic to clear up the infection. If your child has a proven urine infection, she will need tests to rule out any abnormalities.

During toilet training, encourage good habits in your child by teaching her to wipe from front to back to help prevent bacteria entering the urethra.

CALL THE DOCTOR if you suspect that your child has a urine infection.

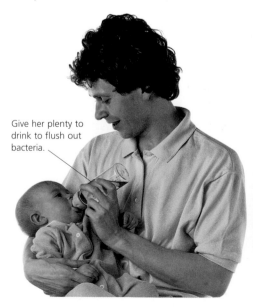

Give her plenty to drink to flush out bacteria.

diarrhoea and vomiting

Gastroenteritis (infectious diarrhoea) is the most common reason for diarrhoea and vomiting. It can be serious in babies because they quickly become dehydrated. Breastfeeding protects against gastroenteritis so breast-fed babies, when they get it at all, don't become as ill as bottle-fed babies.

SYMPTOMS

♦ diarrhoea and vomiting, and refusing food
♦ a stomach ache before a bowel movement
♦ a fever, particularly with dehydration

Making the diagnosis

It's usually enough to know that a child has gastroenteritis, and in most cases there's no need to identify the germ responsible. If your child fails to improve, your doctor may take a stool sample to test. A variety of bacteria and viruses cause gastroenteritis. They spread in contaminated food, or from the stools of someone else with the germs, which is why hand hygiene and thorough cooking are so important.

What to do for your child

To guard against dehydration, give her plenty to drink. Water is fine in most cases, or your health visitor may recommend a glucose drink. Alternatively, if your child is over two years old she can

Keep a bowl close in case she's sick.

have a cola drink, which you have stirred first to remove the fizz. Your doctor may recommend a rehydration powder, available by prescription or from pharmacies. Give it to your child small sips at a time, or it will soon find its way back up again.

Ensure there's a potty close by at all times, or if your child has recently grown out of nappies, consider putting her back in them while she's ill. A bowl nearby in case she's sick will also help. Frequent baths or topping and tailing will help your child feel fresh.

Control your child's fever if necessary (see pages 226–227). Wash your hands often, especially when handling food, changing nappies, or cleaning the potty.

CALL THE DOCTOR if:

♦ your baby is under a year old
♦ your baby or child is becoming dehydrated
♦ she is not improving
♦ she passes blood in her stools
♦ she has persistent stomach ache.

threadworms and worms

Threadworms (also known as pinworms) are thin worms that resemble a piece of white cotton or thread about 1cm (½in) long – hence their name. Although anyone can get threadworms, young children are most likely to have them.

SYMPTOMS

♦ an itchy bottom, particularly at night
♦ worms wriggling on the stool in the potty
♦ sometimes, no symptoms at all

Making the diagnosis

Threadworms live in the gut. Their eggs spread from the stools of an infected person via dirty hands, as well as on toys and other objects. If your child has threadworms, she can reinfect herself with her own hands.

If you see the worms, you can be confident of the diagnosis. Otherwise, see your doctor. Alternatively, position a small strip of double-sided sticky tape near your child's anus and leave it overnight. Take

anything that's collected to your health visitor or doctor for an opinion.

What to do for your child

Medicine is available on prescription or over the counter from pharmacies. The whole household needs treatment.

Bathe your child the morning after her threadworm treatment to get rid of any shed worms and eggs. To make sure that the worms are killed, wash all of her clothing, bedding, and towels in very hot water, ideally 60°C (140°F). Iron her sheets and nightwear.

Keep your child's fingernails short and ensure she washes her hands well after using the toilet, and before eating.

CALL THE DOCTOR if:

♦ your child is under two and has threadworms
♦ you're not sure if your child has threadworms
♦ you are or might be pregnant.

TOXOCARA CANIS

Toxocara canis is a worm found in the gut of dogs. It can cause serious illness in children, with stomach ache, fever, and even blindness. That's why it's important to worm puppies and dogs, and to keep your child away from dog faeces.

intussusception

This is a rare condition in which part of a child's small bowel telescopes into the bit ahead of it, as if it were swallowing itself. This makes the gut swell and creates a blockage. It is acutely painful and requires urgent hospital treatment. Intussusception most often affects babies under 12 months.

SYMPTOMS

- ◆ intense crying and pulling up legs with pain
- ◆ pallor, feverishness, and vomiting
- ◆ stools containing mucus and blood, resembling chicken fat and redcurrant jelly

Making the diagnosis

The cause isn't known for sure. It's not an infection, but it's thought that enlarged lymph tissue in the gut is linked with some of the cases. Intussusception usually needs a barium enema test in hospital to diagnose it. This means pumping in a small amount of liquid barium into your baby's rectum to show his bowels on an x-ray. Sometimes this test actually relieves the condition, but if it doesn't then your baby will need an operation. Although it's natural for a parent to be concerned when this happens, you can rest assured that the vast majority of babies recover very quickly – much faster than would most adults.

What to do for your child

Comfort your child and check his nappy, looking for any blood or mucus, and get medical advice without delay.

CALL THE DOCTOR if:

- ◆ you think your baby might have intussusception
- ◆ your baby has blood in the stools
- ◆ your baby has had intussusception before and now has tummy ache again.

balanitis

This means inflammation of the tip of the penis. It's usually caused by bacterial infection, although yeasts such as candida can also be responsible. It's fairly common in uncircumcised boys because it's normal not to be able to pull back the foreskin, but balanitis may also be part of a more general nappy rash.

CALL THE DOCTOR if:

- ◆ your child's penis looks sore
- ◆ he seems to be in pain
- ◆ he finds it difficult to urinate
- ◆ he doesn't seem to urinate properly after an attack of balanitis.

SYMPTOMS

- ◆ pain when urinating
- ◆ frequent rubbing or clutching of genitals
- ◆ pus in nappies or on underpants
- ◆ red, sore-looking penis tip, perhaps with swollen foreskin

Making the diagnosis

Balanitis is painful and often needs antibiotics. Your doctor will be able to diagnose it just by looking at your son, but may need to do a swab test to find out exactly which germs are causing it. This involves gently dabbing the tip of the penis with a sterile cotton bud then sending it to the lab to see if it grows any bacteria or yeasts (see *thrush*, page 218).

Usually, the infection affects only the penis and foreskin. However, your doctor may also want to test your little boy's urine to make sure it's not infected, too.

What to do for your child

Give your child frequent warm or lukewarm baths to ease the pain, and paracetamol syrup if he needs it. Don't try to pull back the foreskin as this can do more harm than good (it's best not to pull back a young boy's foreskin anyway).

Give him the antibiotics prescribed by your doctor, which may be in cream or medicine form, or sometimes both.

After an attack of balanitis, your son's penis should return to normal. Recurrent attacks can occasionally cause scarring, which could mean you'll be advised to have him circumcised for medical reasons. However, this is fairly rare. Even if you have to see a specialist, surgery isn't always necessary as things often settle down by the time a boy is four or five.

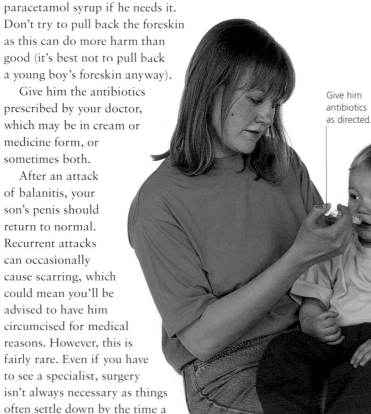

Give him antibiotics as directed.

chronic conditions

Most diseases are short term, from which a child recovers completely. However, some disorders can cause long-term effects. There is a range of these more chronic (long-term) conditions. Some, such as mild hearing difficulties, are noticeable only in certain situations, while others are more serious, posing greater challenges for the child and his family. Whatever your child's condition, there's a lot you can do to help him to get the most out of life, and to help others around him understand his condition.

how to help

It can be distressing for parents to learn that their child has a chronic condition, but children themselves often cope well with all kinds of restrictions and take the treatment in their stride.

Positive parenting
By making the most of each achievement and adopting an upbeat approach to her treatment and care, you'll help your child meet every challenge.

Adopting an upbeat approach yourself is one of the best ways to help your child. It will also encourage others, such as carers and grandparents, to be positive, too.

Some disorders, such as cerebral palsy or cystic fibrosis, may mean your child isn't able to do the things other children of his age take for granted. Sometimes, the condition fluctuates, so that your child may be well most of the time, but has limitations when the condition flares up. Asthma often falls into this category, so even children with severe asthma can have very good spells.

Try not to label your child or over-medicalize his condition. These days, health professionals prefer to talk about "a child who has epileptic seizures", for instance, rather than "an epileptic". The distinction is subtle, but not trivial.

Individual needs

Whatever your child's diagnosis, remember that he's an individual, and that each family is different, too. Therefore, not every generalization about a particular condition will apply to your child. There are many sources of information available (see *further information*, above), including self-help groups. These usually involve getting together with other parents who have children with a similar condition and can offer support and practical advice.

It's important to focus on what your child can do and make the most of this. As he grows up, encourage him and give him opportunities to do more of the activities he can manage. Try not to over-protect him. In time, he needs to grow up, meet others, and gain as much independence as he can.

further **information**

Always bear in mind that your child is an individual, so if you're not sure whether a particular treatment or course of action might benefit him, seek further advice.

Good sources of information include:
♦ your health visitor and your doctor
♦ your hospital or community paediatrician
♦ self-help and support groups
♦ libraries
♦ the Internet.

Remember that not all publications and Internet sites contain information you can trust, so be selective.

hearing loss

Hearing impairment in children is usually partial, but can be total. In some cases, the middle ear doesn't conduct sound well (conductive deafness), often during or after an infection. In others, nerves in the inner ear don't send accurate signals to the brain (sensori-neural or nerve deafness).

Symptoms

The signs depend on the degree of impairment, and which sounds are affected. Your baby may not respond to your voice, or may not hear you approaching and look surprised as you come into view. Your child may fail to do what you ask. This can be normal toddler behaviour, but hearing loss can genuinely make a child less biddable. Look out for slow or immature speech – your child may speak less than expected or may repeat words less accurately than children her age.

Sign language

If your child's hearing is severely impaired, sign language will help you communicate. This is good for her progress and doesn't stop speech from developing.

What to do for your child

Routine development checks can pick up hearing loss but if you're worried at any time, consult your doctor or health visitor. Look directly at your child when talking, speak clearly, and give her time to express herself. Minimize background noise. Your child may need specialist treatment, such as grommets for glue ear (see page 248).

squint

Although it's normal for a newborn to look cross-eyed, after about eight weeks of age this may mean there's an imbalance of the eye muscles, or poor vision. It's important to treat a squint promptly, otherwise vision will suffer.

Symptoms

Your child's eyes may face different ways, especially if she tries to follow your finger or a rattle. Her eyes may face away from each other or towards each other.

What to do for your child

Consult your doctor if you suspect a squint. Encourage your child if she needs to wear glasses, or a patch over the stronger eye. Most young children accept the wearing of glasses and eye patches if their parents and friends take it in their stride, too.

Occasionally, surgery, or injections into the muscles at or after the age of two is carried out to correct muscle imbalance. Older children may be given exercises to strengthen the eye muscles. Make sure your child does these as directed by incorporating them into her daily routine.

diabetes

Diabetes is due to lack of insulin, the hormone that gets glucose (sugar) into the body cells. The cause isn't known, but it might be a reaction to an infection. Children with diabetes often develop symptoms suddenly and almost always need long-term insulin treatment to control their disease.

IN AN EMERGENCY!

Give her a sweet drink if she has stomach pain, is dizzy, and/or confused.

Symptoms

Your child may be very thirsty, or pass large amounts of urine. She could lose weight, or have tummy ache, vomiting, and become dehydrated. You may smell ketones on her breath – like nail varnish remover. Some children suffer frequent chest and urine infections (see pages 247 and 254).

What to do for your child

Once the diagnosis has been made, your child will need hospital treatment, initially as an in-patient.

Although the treatment of childhood diabetes is very specialized, there's much you can do to help your child take it in her stride and keep the condition on an even keel. Give your child her insulin injections regularly. Reassure her and stay calm yourself. Learn all you can about diabetes, and make sure that relatives and any other carers are well informed, too. Your child will need a carefully regulated diet and her blood sugar levels will need regular monitoring.

asthma

With asthma, the airways in the lungs are inflamed and become narrow during attacks. This can be triggered by infection, exercise, cold air, air pollution, and allergies. It's more common in the over-twos. Severe asthma is easier to diagnose than mild cases. Your doctor may prescribe medicine to prevent constriction or to dilate the airways – if this helps, it's more likely to be asthma.

Symptoms

Your child may cough or wheeze, especially at night, and she may be short of breath following exertion. The symptoms often first start just after she's had a bad cold. Acute attacks can be frightening for a child and for those around her. She could start to turn blue from lack of oxygen.

Encourage her to use an inhaler regularly.

IN AN EMERGENCY!

Always get medical help urgently if your child has a severe attack – for instance, if she becomes too breathless to speak or starts turning blue from lack of oxygen.

What to do for your child

Keep calm and help your child breathe slowly, without panicking. Encourage her to use her inhalers regularly, and to accept this as normal. If she has a steroid inhaler, ensure she rinses her mouth afterwards. Avoid possible triggers, such as cigarette smoke, furry pets, and house dust.

sickle-cell anaemia

This is an inherited condition in which the red blood cells are sickle-shaped because they contain an unusual form of haemoglobin. A child can only have sickle-cell anaemia if both parents carry it. It's most common in those of African or Caribbean origin, and is diagnosed by a blood test.

IN AN EMERGENCY!

Get medical help urgently if she has pain in her legs or severe stomach ache.

Symptoms

Symptoms are wide ranging as sickle-cell disease can be mild or severe. Anaemia can set in after a baby is four to six months old, with tiredness the main symptom. Frequent infections also occur.

Attacks can be triggered by dehydration, infection, cold weather, or lack of oxygen.

What to do for your child

Make sure your child has all her immunizations. She may also be offered an injection against pneumonia. Guard against her becoming dehydrated, and protect her in cold weather. Learn all you can about the condition, and make sure that other carers are well informed about it, too.

eczema

Eczema is a skin condition that's common from four months. It may clear up as a child gets older, but not always. Eczema can run in families with asthma, hay fever, or other allergies. It often appears when a baby is weaned, but is less often due to food allergy than most parents think. In some cases, however, elimination tests under medical supervision can help diagnose allergy.

Symptoms

Eczema is itchy, so you may notice your child scratching, especially at night. There can be dry or raw-looking areas on the face, or in the creases of the knees or elbows. Because eczema makes skin dry and cracked, it can become infected with bacteria, particularly in the nappy area which can blister and weep.

What to do for your child

Clothe her in cotton fabrics that have been washed in a mild, non-biological detergent, and rinsed well. Keep your child's nails short to deter scratching. Avoid using soap on her skin – emollients in the bath and creams afterwards will help. Your doctor may prescribe a mild steroid ointment.

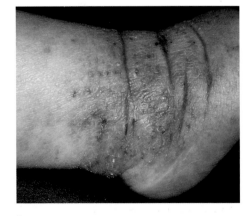

Eczema
Itchy, red, cracked, and raw-looking skin is a typical sign of eczema. If the area becomes infected with bacteria, it can start to blister and weep.

cystic fibrosis

Cystic fibrosis (CF) affects glands that make mucus and certain enzymes. Sticky mucus collects in the lungs, which become infected, while lack of enzymes in the gut makes it hard to absorb fats. Treatment helps, but there's no cure. CF is inherited – it can be passed on if both parents are carriers.

Symptoms

A baby may not pass meconium stools (see page 92) at birth. Later, he may have constipation, diarrhoea, or alternate between the two. His tummy may look swollen. Recurrent chest infections or a chronic, rattly cough are common. Children with CF have a higher than normal salt level in the sweat, and this is how the condition is diagnosed.

What to do for your child

Your child will need specialist referral and advice, but there's a lot you can do as a parent. Your child needs a special diet that's high in protein and energy. He will be prescribed extra vitamins, as well as enzyme capsules to take before each meal.

To keep his lungs clear, breathing exercises and daily physiotherapy to bring up the sticky mucus from the lungs are a must. This helps to reduce infection and prevent lung damage. Once a physiotherapist has shown you how to do these, you can do them yourself for your child. Always get prompt treatment for any chest infections.

Make sure that your child has regular exercise, such as running or swimming, and any activities that involve stretching the trunk and arms. Your physiotherapist will be able to advise you what's best for your child.

Newer treatments for cystic fibrosis include lung transplantation, and soon gene therapy may be possible, too.

down syndrome

Down syndrome is a chromosomal condition. The usual number of chromosomes is 23 pairs, but in Down syndrome there's an extra chromosome number 21, or a rearrangement of chromosome 21 called a "translocation". It can be diagnosed before birth by amniocentesis or CVS (see page 21).

Encourage your child
Many children with Down syndrome can learn with patience and encouragement from a loving parent.

Symptoms

Children with Down syndrome have a round face, slanting eyes, and a wide nose. The mouth is usually small and the tongue relatively large, and the fingers and toes are often short. They usually have learning difficulties, which can be mild or severe. About half of all children with Down syndrome have either gut or heart problems so they can suffer recurrent infections or anaemia.

What to do for your child

Patience, love, and following your doctor's advice are the key to getting the best out of your child. Many children with Down syndrome are very affectionate, and can learn a lot with encouragement. You will need to work hard at this, and concentrate on the things that your child can do and enjoys. Some children with Down syndrome go to mainstream schools, and achieve a degree of independence.

autism

Autism is a disorder of development that affects a child's communication, social skills, and behaviour. It can be mild or severe, and the cause is unknown.

Symptoms

More boys than girls have autism, and it's usually diagnosed between eight months and three years of age. It can be hard to diagnose and needs specialist assessment. Babies may dislike cuddles and make little eye contact. Children with autism favour complicated rituals for even minor activities and throw tantrums if their routine alters. They may show repetitive behaviour, such as rocking back and forth. Their speech is immature and they remain aloof. Some have learning difficulties, although others have normal or even superior intelligence.

What to do for your child

Although there's no cure for autism, there are many therapies that you can carry out with your doctor's guidance. Massage and physiotherapy, for instance, can help, depending on your child's particular needs. He'll benefit from a structured and supportive environment and plenty of individual attention. With help, many children with autism can learn social skills and take part in society.

cerebral palsy

Cerebral palsy is a brain condition that causes muscle weakness. It's quite common and can be mild or severe. The cause isn't known, but it's likely that many cases arise before birth. Although the condition doesn't go away, it doesn't deteriorate either.

Symptoms
These vary according to the severity of the condition, and the child's age. Children with cerebral palsy often have normal intelligence, but weakness makes it hard to show this, especially if speech is impaired.

What to do for your child
Make the most of his abilities. Remember that he is capable of loving, thinking, and learning, but his physical limitations make this hard to convey. Stretching and physiotherapy techniques to do at home will keep his limbs mobile. Speech therapy is often needed, too. With help, your child may be able to attend a mainstream school.

Living with cerebral palsy
Cerebral palsy causes mild or severe muscle weakness, but a child's intelligence often remains unimpaired.

epilepsy

Epilepsy is a condition that causes recurrent seizures (or convulsions), during which electrical signals in the brain are disturbed. There are two main types – grand mal and petit mal – and, although there is no mental disability, both can interfere with learning if seizures are frequent.

Symptoms
In grand mal, the child's eyes may roll or he may cry out before losing consciousness. Then he'll clench his teeth, and his limbs may go stiff or jerk. He may froth at the mouth or lose control of his bladder. Afterwards, he'll feel dazed or tired. In petit mal, there's a short absence or trance-like moment lasting only a couple of seconds, during which the child won't be aware of anything.

What to do for your child
During a seizure, lay your child on his side, loosen tight clothing, and move any objects on which he could hurt himself. Otherwise, don't restrain him and stay with him until it ends. When it's over, lay him in the recovery position (see page 269) and get medical help. Let him rest until he feels like getting up.

There's no cure for epilepsy but regular medication can help prevent seizures. This is why it's important to give your child his medication as prescribed by your doctor. Do be aware of situations in which he might get injured if he has a seizure (such as swimming), but try not to be overprotective.

attention deficit disorder

Attention deficit disorder (ADD) covers a range of behaviour difficulties, including hyperactivity and attention deficit hyperactivity disorder (ADHD). It's most common in boys, and the exact cause isn't known, but both genetic and environmental factors are believed to play a role.

Symptoms
Your child will have an unusually short attention span and will often be very restless. He may be clumsy, impulsive, and disruptive. Although young children are all like this to some degree, in a child with ADD these characteristics are more pronounced.

What to do for your child
Your doctor will make the initial diagnosis. Sometimes ADD runs in families and, although there's no cure for it, there's plenty you can do to help your child.

Drugs can increase your child's attention span, but they're not the whole treatment. Consistent handling and a calm, loving atmosphere will help to bring out the best in your child. Be as positive as you can to build his self-esteem, and remember to always praise him when he's playing well. Be specific in your instructions to him and set him clear boundaries so that he knows what is acceptable behaviour.

A predictable daily routine will help to prevent his restlessness and improve his behaviour, which in turn will benefit the whole family.

safety

The best way to keep your baby or child safe as she grows up is to see the world from her point of view. There are many tempting things to explore, which she'll do without any awareness of danger. To avoid potential hazards, you'll have to stay one step ahead of her as she enters each new stage of development.

When your baby is small, you need to supervise her constantly, even taking her from room to room with you to keep her safe. As she grows into an inquisitive toddler, you'll have to be just as watchful, although you can keep a greater distance in particular situations, while she learns some independence.

Pressing dangers
Never attempt to do the ironing with your young child around. Sit her securely in her highchair or playpen, or, better still, leave it until she's sleeping.

Toys and playthings

There are many ways to ensure that your child's toys and playthings are safe.
◆ Toys should meet British Safety Institute (BS) standards or carry the CE mark.
◆ Follow the recommended ages on toy packages. They are given for safety reasons.
◆ Check the size of the toy and make sure there are no parts that can be swallowed.
◆ Read instructions before giving your child a toy and show her how it works.
◆ Remove strings or ribbons over 20cm (8in) long – they could strangle a baby.
◆ Children under age eight can choke or suffocate on deflated or broken balloons.
◆ Baby walkers are a common cause of accidents – use only on a level surface under the closest supervision or, better still, avoid using one altogether.

Babies on the move

Once your baby starts to roll, and then crawl, she faces many more potential risks.
◆ Put covers on electrical sockets. Turn off sockets after use and replace worn flexes.
◆ Cover low-level glass with safety film, or make sure it's safety glass.
◆ Consider corner covers for tables and other sharp areas, and perhaps remove heavy or fragile objects until she's older.
◆ Never iron near her. Put her in a playpen, or leave your ironing until she's asleep.
◆ Keep hot drinks well out of her reach.
◆ As your baby starts pulling herself up on the furniture, be aware of flimsy side tables, or shelves that may fall onto her.

Beware of stairs

Many injuries in the home happen on or around the stairs.
◆ Until she can climb up and down on her own, fix stair gates at both top and bottom.
◆ When your baby learns to crawl, show her how to come down backwards.
◆ Make sure your banisters are safe, with gaps of no more than 10cm (4in) between the spindles. Horizontal bars could become a ladder, so change them or board them in.
◆ Never leave things on or near the stairs.
◆ Ensure the latch on your front door is out of reach, or fit a bolt high up on the inside to stop her toddling into the street.

safe as **houses**

A general safety check around your home is always a good idea, but never more so than when there's a baby or young child in the house.

◆ Install window locks and cupboard locks where needed.

◆ Always keep matches, lighters, and firelighters well out of reach.

◆ Lock away chemicals and medicines.

◆ Fit a smoke alarm, test it regularly, and replace batteries as required.

◆ Consider a carbon monoxide alarm.

◆ Fix loose carpets and secure rugs.

◆ Ensure furniture is made of flame-retardant materials.

◆ Fix fire guards over open fires.

in the kitchen

The kitchen is the hub of the home, and where many dangers lurk. It's also where you are most likely to be distracted, making it harder to keep an eye on your child. If it's practical, keep her out of the kitchen when you're cooking. If not, make sure your safety measures are all in place.

♦ **Lock it away** Keep household cleaners and chemicals locked away. Knives and other sharp objects should be well out of reach in a locked drawer or cupboard. Make sure your child can't get at any plastic bags or wrap, which could be a suffocation hazard. Keep your waste bin where your child can't reach it. Fit child-resistant locks on cupboards and drawers, and perhaps on the fridge and freezer, too.

♦ **Prevent scalds** Fit a guard around the stove, and always turn saucepan handles towards the back when in use. Keep your child away from the oven as even the outside of the door can be very hot. Avoid trailing electrical cords – coiled or very short cords are better because your child is less likely to grab at them. Turn off all appliances, such as the washing machine, at the mains when not in use.

♦ **Guard against fire** Put matches out of reach. Keep a small fire extinguisher and a fire blanket handy. Learn how to put out small fires safely – for example, the correct way to put out a chip-pan fire is to cover it with a wet tea towel.

♦ **Out of harm's way** Always use a safety harness in your baby's highchair. As well

as eating in it, she can sit and play in it for a short time while you cook. You could put a playpen in the kitchen if there's space. Older children can sit at the table and draw or play with modelling clay if you're busy, but do supervise them. An alternative is a stairgate across the doorway of the kitchen, so that your child can play just outside it, where you can keep an eye on her while you cook.

♦ **Food and meal times** As you prepare food, wipe up spills straight away, to prevent slips and falls. Keep hot dishes in the middle of the table, so your child is less likely to reach them. Avoid having a tablecloth for now – a baby or child can tug it, bringing down anything that's on the table.

Safe seat
Always use a safety harness when your child is sitting in her highchair. Never leave her to eat unsupervised in case she chokes.

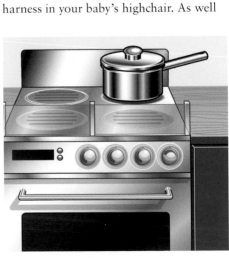

Around the oven
It's a good idea to fit a guard to the front of the stove and turn pan handles to the back to prevent your child reaching up and scalding herself.

Cupboards and drawers
Locks fitted to cupboards and drawers will deter little fingers from investigating their contents, but they're not completely child-proof so be alert.

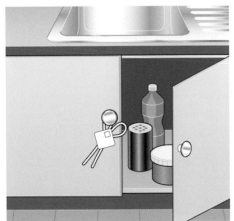

Dangerous substances
Household cleaners and chemicals should always be locked away. Seek urgent medical help if you suspect your child has swallowed something (see page 270).

in the bathroom

Many babies and children are fascinated by water, and bath time is an enjoyable, and necessary, part of their daily routine. As a parent, you will delight in your youngster's fun, but bathrooms can be dangerous places and drowning in particular is an obvious risk. So it's important to be aware of any potential accidents at bath time, and take steps to prevent them.

♦ **A watchful eye** A child can drown in less than 5cm (2in) of water, so never leave him unsupervised or even take your eyes off him while he's in the bath. Make sure you have everything you need before putting him in the bath – it's unsafe to leave him for even a moment. Ignore temptations to answer the door or the phone. Put on the answering machine at bath time, if you have one.

♦ **Get a grip** If your baby can't sit up yet, always support him behind his neck while he's in the water. Once he can sit up, a steadying hand on his arm is a good idea. Always use a non-slip mat on the bottom of the bath.

♦ **Hot tips** Run all the bath water before he gets in – cold water first, then the hot. If the tap is still hot, wrap a towel or

Splash happy
A non-slip rubber mat in the bath will help your child feel secure and prevent nasty bumps. Be particularly watchful when siblings are around.

face-cloth around it. Also cover or turn down any heated towel rails or radiators, as children tend to grab at these. Turn down the thermostat on the hot water supply if you can, to reduce the risk of

your child scalding himself if he plays with a tap and succeeds in turning it on.

♦ **Other hazards** Keep the toilet seat cover down until your child is ready for toilet training. All medicines, cleaners, razors, and even shampoos and mouthwashes need to be locked away safely. Remove keys and catches from the bathroom door to prevent a toddler accidentally locking himself in. Instead, place a bolt high up on the inside of the door, where your child can't reach.

in the bedroom

Your baby or child will spend a lot of time on his own in his bedroom, so you need to be confident that it's as safe as you can make it. To avoid the risks of overheating and suffocation, follow the advice on the prevention of cot death (see page 101).

♦ **Bedding** Duvets, cot bumpers, and sheepskins are not recommended for young babies because of the risk of overheating or suffocation. Make up your baby's cot so that his feet are to the foot of the cot and tuck in sheets and blankets securely. Don't give him a pillow before he's a year old.

♦ **Sleep tight** His cot should conform to BS safety standards. Position it away from the radiator and out of direct sunlight. Keep the cot side up until your toddler tries to climb out, then leave it down.

♦ **Cot toys** Don't put too many toys in your baby's cot, as they can make it hot and even suffocate him. Ideally, don't tie toys to the rails, but if you do, ensure the string is secure and less than 25cm (10in) long.

♦ **Changing stations** If you change him on a bed or changing table, keep your eye on him at all times. A mat on the floor is safest.

♦ **Secure windows** As he gets older, fit locks, and perhaps even bars, on windows.

♦ **Radiators** Turn down the thermostat on any radiators and cover them with towels.

Safe and warm
As well as turning down the thermostat, cover a radiator with a towel to prevent burns.

other people's homes

You and your family may have done everything possible to make your own home safe, but there will be times when you're visiting other people, who may not have the same approach to safety as you. Moreover, if they have no children, they're unlikely to have given much thought to child safety, or if their family's grown up, they may no longer have measures in place.

♦ **A close watch** In other people's houses, you need to be even more vigilant than in your own home. All the same, try to relax – you don't want anxiety to spoil your visit. Your child is bound to find things to explore safely. Just guide him in doing so.

♦ **Other children** If there are other children, be aware that they may not want to share everything, and that some of their toys may be unsuitable for your child.

♦ **Babysitting** If you plan to leave your child with someone else at their home for a couple of hours, talk about safety with them first. It's reasonable to brief them on what your child can, and does, get up to, and bring equipment, such as stairgates, if necessary. A childminder's home will have been vetted for safety by the local authority. She should be only too willing to discuss any safety issues around her home and put them right before caring for your child. But ultimately, if you're not convinced that the other adult is safety-conscious enough, don't entrust your child to her.

home **visits**

Try not to be embarrassed about talking about safety when you visit other people's homes – if you plan to leave your child there, it's vital.

♦ Scan the room for potential hazards, and be extra watchful as you may be distracted while chatting.

♦ Make sure others keep their mugs of tea or coffee out of reach.

♦ Be wary around any pets.

♦ Bring with you any equipment you may need and toys to keep your child out of mischief.

♦ Ask to close doors on rooms that may be particularly unsafe.

in the garden

It's great for children to have a chance to play outside in the fresh air. If you have access to a garden, there's a whole world for your child to explore and play in. But gardens also have their hazards. To help your child spend his time outdoors safely, spend a while planning how to reduce the risks.

♦ **Secure your garden** Ensure that your child can't get out into the street by locking gates securely and keeping fences maintained. Remember that a child can drown in as little as 5cm (2in) of water. So if you have a pond, for the time being either drain it and perhaps turn it into a sandpit, cover it with strong wire mesh or a trellis, or securely fence it off. Never leave your child unsupervised in a paddling pool and always empty it after use.

♦ **Poisonous plants** Many plants are poisonous, among them yew, foxgloves, lupins, lobelia, and lily of the valley. Dig them up if possible, or make sure your child doesn't play in them. Teach him from an early age not to eat berries or plants from the garden. Get rid of all toadstools and fungi as they appear.

♦ **Perfect pets** If you have a dog, make sure he doesn't relieve himself in the garden, or clear up immediately if he does. You can't prevent cats from doing so, but do teach your child not to put things in his mouth, especially soil.

♦ **Check equipment** Regularly check climbing frames and other garden toys for safety, and watch that little fingers can't be trapped in folding garden furniture. Use lawnmowers and other garden tools only when your child is not about. Keep equipment and chemicals locked away.

in the **park**

A trip to the park can be a fun outing that's good exercise for you and your child. Here's how to avoid accidents.

♦ Remember, there's no substitute for supervising your child.

♦ Use a play area that's properly fenced in, to prevent your child wandering off and to keep dogs out (see *Toxocara canis*, page 255).

♦ Swings should be right for your child's age. Under-ones need the box type. Don't let him run near swings.

♦ Climbing frames should be over a soft surface, not concrete.

♦ Take care on slides, especially if your child tries to slow down with his feet.

♦ Don't let your child step on or off moving roundabouts.

Pond risks
While your child is still young, cover your pond with a grid or strong netting, or put a secure fence around it. Alternatively, consider draining it and filling it in until he's older.

out and about

Whatever your child's age, you need to consider his safety when you're out and about. It can be a bit of a nuisance taking precautions when you're on a very short car journey, for instance, but accidents can happen anywhere and in a split second, so it's just as important to protect your child when you go around the corner as when you're heading farther away.

Buggies and pushchairs

◆ **Strap in** Always make sure your child's harness and lap belt are done up on every trip. If you do this from the very start, your child will have no trouble accepting it as part of the normal routine.

◆ **Well balanced** Keep the pushchair well maintained and never hang heavy shopping from the handles or it may tip up.

On foot

◆ **Road drill** As soon as your child is old enough to walk alongside you, start drilling into him how to cross the road safely. Even though at this stage you'll be holding his hand or his reins, you can usefully provide a running commentary.

Street wise
When you're out and about talk to your child about road safety from an early age. Always cross roads safely yourself to set a good example.

Tell him that you're finding a safe place to cross, that you're looking and listening before you cross and while you cross. Explain traffic lights to him. To establish good habits on pedestrian crossings, always wait for the sign saying that it's safe to cross even if the road is clear, and never run across the street.

In the car

◆ **Safe journey** Holding a baby or child in your arms in the car isn't safe, because in the event of an accident or sudden stop your weight could injure him. You must provide a special car seat for him. Always choose a car seat that meets BS safety standards, and buy it new, to avoid possible hazards such as worn fittings and straps or the possibility that it may have been in a car accident.

◆ **A good fit** Not all car seats suit all makes of car, so before buying check that the one you choose fits your particular car. The seat-belt buckle must never rest on the car seat frame because it could snap in a crash. When fitting the car seat, pull the seat belt tight – the car seat should sit firmly and not be able to be moved from side to side. If you're not sure, get professional help. NEVER put your child in a car seat on a passenger seat that has an airbag immediately in front of it – an inflated airbag can seriously harm or even kill a child. Check the car seat fit on every journey.

◆ **Correct choice** Ensure you have the right type of car seat for your child's size – his weight is a better guide than his age. Rear-facing seats are for babies from newborn up to about 10–13kg (22–28lb) weight. Depending on your baby's rate of growth, this will probably last nine months or so. Forward-facing car seats are for children weighing from 10kg (22lb) up to 25kg (55lb). Your child could be in this for

Adjust his safety harness to fit on every journey.

Car seat
You can fit your own car seat but follow instructions carefully. Seek professional advice, if needed.

several years, so choose a model that you'll be happy to use day in and day out. The ideal buckle is one that you can manage easily but that's too hard for your child to undo.

◆ **No distractions** Having got the seat, always use it. The harness must be adjusted and fastened securely on every trip, however short it may be. Babies often enjoy the car, but sometimes they cry from frustration, tiredness, or boredom. If this happens, stop the car as soon as you can. It's dangerous to drive with the distraction of a screaming baby or child. Toddlers sometimes try to undo their buckles. If your child succeeds, stop the car as soon as it's safe to do so. Secure the buckle again and tell him not to undo it. If he persists, stop the car again. It's a safety issue, so you mustn't give in however wilful your child may be. Be firm but try not to get angry. If you need to attend to your child for any reason during the journey, stop the car. It's dangerous to take your eyes off the road for even a fraction of a second.

on holiday

Travel has many benefits for your child. With a little forward planning, you can have a great time on holiday with your baby or young child. Try to choose a destination that will be relaxing for you as well as safe and hygienic for your child. The first couple of years you may not go far afield, but as time goes by you might like to become more adventurous.

Protective headgear
Babies and young children should always wear a sunhat. Choose one that has a wide brim and a flap to protect the back of the neck.

Going abroad

♦ **Immunizations** Your child's basic immunizations (see page 216) must be up to date. Depending on your destination, he may need other vaccinations or anti-malaria medicine. Ask your doctor or health visitor as you can't always rely on the information provided by travel agents.

♦ **Proper paperwork** Don't forget that your baby needs a ticket, his own passport, and other travel documents, according to current regulations. Check your travel insurance provides for all your medical needs abroad.

Travel by air

♦ **Flying high** Reserve your seats well in advance. If your child is under two, when you are booking ask for a seat where the cabin staff can install a sky-cot (bassinette) or a car safety seat. Pack plenty of nappies in your hand luggage, along with any milk or other feeds. Airlines can't always provide meals for youngsters but are usually happy to heat up food or milk that parents have brought with them.

travel sickness

Any time from 18 months or so, your child may develop motion sickness. Most children grow out of it by adolescence.

♦ Make sure that your child can see out of the window when you are travelling in a car, plane, or ship.

♦ Don't give him books to distract him – play games such as "I-Spy" instead.

♦ For longer journeys, consider travel sickness medication, or try acupressure bands from the chemist.

♦ Keep to hand a supply of bags, paper towels, and change of clothes for your child, just in case.

♦ **Air pressure** If you have a baby, give him a breast- or bottle-feed (or a dummy) during ascent and descent to avoid earache from pressure changes in the aircraft. A child can suck or chew a sweet, but supervise him in case he chokes. To prevent dehydration, give your child plenty to drink during the flight.

♦ **In-flight entertainment** Keep your child entertained with a selection of toys and books. Airlines often provide goody bags for youngsters, but he'll probably want the comfort of his favourite soft toy, too.

♦ **Jet lag** If you're travelling across several time zones, your child may be jet-lagged and unsettled for a day or two. Arrange meal times and bedtime around the new time as soon as possible. There's no harm in using a dose of your child's usual travel sickness medicine to make him drowsy before bed. See a doctor if he doesn't settle within a couple of days, in case he's ill.

Sun protection

♦ **Skin care** Because young skin is so much more sensitive than an adult's, your child needs careful protection from the sun to avoid getting burnt or overheated. For a baby under six months old, it's best to keep him out of direct sunlight. Use a parasol or sunshade on the pram or buggy, and put him in a wide-brimmed hat. Keep his arms and legs covered with clothes made of cool but closely woven fabric, such as cotton.

♦ **Block it out** Keep your child out of direct sun at the hottest time of day, usually 10am to 4pm depending on latitude. The sun is more likely to burn if you're near water, or at high altitude. Even so, you'll need to apply sunscreen. The sun protection factor (SPF) numbers refer to protection against UVB, while a star system from * to **** relates to protection against UVA. In practice, your child needs to be screened against both, and

the higher the number of SPF and stars, the greater the protection. All children should use a sunscreen of SPF 30. Apply half an hour before going outside. Many sunscreens are waterproof, but even these should be reapplied every three to four hours if your child spends a lot of time in the water. Check the label on the bottle.

♦ **Cooler climates** Even in cooler northern countries, a child can be seriously sunburnt, making him uncomfortable and increasing his risk of developing skin cancer later in life. So it's smart to carry sunscreen with you when you go outside with your child, at home or on holiday. A cool, cloudy start to the day can give way to sunshine later.

♦ **Drink plenty** To protect against the dehydrating effect of sun and warm weather, make sure your child always has plenty to drink. If you're breastfeeding, offer feeds more often. Bottle-fed babies can have extra drinks of plain water, or very dilute fruit juice.

Insect protection

♦ **Avoiding stings** Mosquitoes and other insects often love a child's tender skin, so cover up your baby's or child's arms and legs and smooth on some insect repellent (made for children) in the early evenings, when stinging insects are at their most active. In a malaria area, protection against mosquito bites with repellents and mosquito bed nets is as important as taking anti-malaria medicine.

first aid

Children are inquisitive and often unaware of dangers, so unintentional injuries are common. Thankfully, most are minor, but it's vital to know what to do in an emergency. Learn first aid before you need it, so you're prepared if the worst happens.

The first-aid procedures detailed in this section are those recommended by the British Red Cross. The guidance given in these pages is not, however, a substitute for an in-depth knowledge of first aid, so an even better way to protect your family is for you, your partner, and other carers to attend a recognized first-aid course. You are more likely to be able to save a child's life if you receive proper first-aid training and keep up to date with refresher courses every few years.

CONTENTS

ABC of resuscitation

For a baby (under one year old)

1 **Gently stimulate the baby:** tap her foot gently. If there's no response, shout for help, then carry on with the ABC of resuscitation. Never shake a baby.

2 **Open her airway:** on a flat surface, place your hand on her forehead and tilt her head back very gently. Pick out any *obvious* obstruction with your fingertips. Gently lift her chin with one finger.

Check for breathing with your ear close to her mouth.

3 **Check breathing:** put your ear close to her mouth and feel for breaths. Also, look for any chest movement. Check for 10 seconds.

4 **If your baby is breathing,** cradle her on her side, supporting her head lower than her body. Take her with you and **CALL AN AMBULANCE.** Check her breathing as you wait.

If your baby isn't breathing, send a helper to **CALL AN AMBULANCE** and begin Rescue Breathing. Put your baby on her back, breathe in, and seal your lips over her mouth and nose. Breathe out until you see her chest rise, then remove your mouth. Give two effective breaths. If her chest doesn't rise, tilt her head and try again up to five times to give two effective breaths. If you're alone, give Rescue Breathing and CPR (see right) for one minute then take her with you and **CALL AN AMBULANCE.**

5 **Check circulation:** look for moving, coughing, or breathing for no more than 10 seconds. If there are signs of circulation, give 20 rescue breaths, one every three seconds, then re-check circulation. **CALL AN AMBULANCE,** and continue this cycle until help comes.

IF YOUR CHILD IS UNCONSCIOUS, FOLLOW THE ABC OF RESUSCITATION:

A is for Airway **B** is for Breathing **C** is for Circulation.

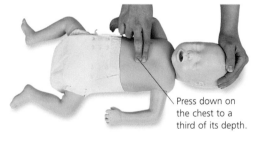

Press down on the chest to a third of its depth.

6 **If there are no signs of circulation,** start Chest Compression combined with Rescue Breathing (known as CPR). Place two fingers on the lower half of your baby's breastbone, about one finger's width below the nipple line and press down to one-third of the depth of her chest five times within a space of three seconds. Give one rescue breath. Continue for one minute, alternating five chest compressions with one rescue breath then, if you haven't already done so, **CALL AN AMBULANCE.** Continue CPR until help arrives.

For a child (over one year old):

1 **Check for a response**: call your child's name and gently tap her shoulder to see if she reacts. If there's no response, shout for help, then carry on with the ABC of resuscitation.

2 **Open her airway**: place one hand on her forehead and gently tilt her head back. Pick out any *obvious* obstruction from her mouth. Gently lift her chin.

As you breathe out the chest will rise.

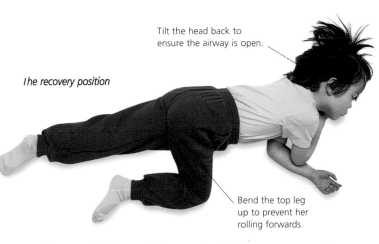

Listen for breathing and check if you can feel a breath on your face.

3 **Check breathing**: put your ear close to her mouth and feel for breaths. Also look at her chest and tummy for any movement. Check for 10 seconds.

If your child isn't breathing, send someone to **CALL AN AMBULANCE** and begin Rescue Breathing. Place her on her back, pinch her nostrils together, then take a fairly deep breath, and seal your lips around her mouth. Breathe out until you see her chest rise, then remove your mouth and watch it fall. Give two effective breaths, one breath every three seconds. If the chest doesn't rise, tilt her head farther back and try again up to five times to give two effective breaths.

5 **Check for signs of circulation**: look for moving, coughing, or breathing for no more than 10 seconds. If there are signs of circulation, give 20 rescue breaths, one every three seconds, then re-check circulation. **CALL AN AMBULANCE**. Continue this cycle until help arrives.

The recovery position

Tilt the head back to ensure the airway is open.

Bend the top leg up to prevent her rolling forwards.

Press down to a third of the depth of the chest.

4 **If your child is breathing**, put her in the recovery position. Place her on her side on a firm surface, with the uppermost arm and leg up. Tilt her head back to keep the airway open. **CALL AN AMBULANCE**. Keep checking her breathing until help arrives.

6 **If there's no sign of circulation**, start Chest Compression combined with Rescue Breathing (CPR). Place one finger on the lower tip of your child's breastbone, and put the heel of your other hand immediately above it. Press down with the heel of the hand to a third of the depth of her chest five times within a space of three seconds. Give one rescue breath. Continue for one minute, alternating five Chest Compressions with one rescue breath then, if you haven't already summoned help, **CALL AN AMBULANCE**. Continue CPR until help arrives.

CHOKING

If your baby or child is unconscious and you know he has choked (see page 270), go straight to CPR.

---

choking

Babies and young children put whatever they find into their mouths, so choking is a common emergency in the very young. It's caused by a piece of food, toy, or other object becoming lodged in the windpipe. You must dislodge the object quickly to allow your child to breathe properly.

What can I do?

For a child (over one year old):

♦ If your child can't cough the obstruction up, make him bend forwards and give five sharp slaps between the shoulder blades.

♦ Pick out any obvious blockages from his mouth with your fingertips.

♦ If your child's still choking, stand or kneel behind him. Make a fist and place it against the lower half of the breastbone.

♦ Grasp the fist with your other hand and pull inwards sharply (chest thrust). Do this five times. Check his mouth again.

♦ If this fails, give five upward abdominal thrusts by placing your fist in the middle of the upper abdomen below the rib cage. Check his mouth again.

♦ Repeat the cycle of back slaps, chest thrusts, and abdominal thrusts three times, then **CALL AN AMBULANCE**. Continue until help arrives or the child becomes unconscious (see ABC of resuscitation, page 269).

IN AN EMERGENCY!

CALL AN AMBULANCE if:

♦ your child stops breathing
♦ you cannot free the blockage
♦ your child continues to choke after the blockage has been freed
♦ your child becomes unconscious.

Place a fist just below the rib cage.

FOR A BABY (UNDER ONE YEAR OLD)

♦ Lay your baby face down along your forearm, use your hand to support him. For a bigger baby, you'll need to sit or kneel.

♦ Give him five blows between the shoulder blades with the heel of your hand.

♦ Turn him face up and check if the object has come up. Pick out any obvious blockages with your fingertips.

♦ If he is still choking, put two fingers on the lower half of his breastbone and give five downward thrusts. Check the mouth.

♦ Repeat the cycle of back slaps and chest thrusts three times, checking the mouth each time. Then take your baby with you and **CALL AN AMBULANCE**.

If your baby becomes unconscious, use the ABC of resuscitation (see page 268).

---

poisoning

Keep all poisons locked away, as babies and children are curious by nature. As well as alcohol, household chemicals, and medicines, be aware of poisonous plants. Poisons can also be breathed in or absorbed through the skin.

SYMPTOMS

Symptoms vary according to the type of poison, but you may notice any of the following:

♦ vomiting
♦ diarrhoea or stomach pain
♦ seizures
♦ drowsiness
♦ unconsciousness
♦ burns or discoloration around the mouth
♦ poisonous substance or container nearby.

What can I do?

♦ Try to identify the poison and how much was taken. If possible, ask your child what happened, and do not be angry with him. Remember that young children often put things in their mouths.

♦ Call the doctor or an ambulance, and if possible keep a sample of the poison or the container to show the doctor.

♦ If you think your child has swallowed a chemical product, wash his skin and lips with water. Don't give your child anything to drink unless it's on your doctor's advice.

♦ If your child vomits, keep a sample to show the doctor, but you should never make your child sick, as this can make his condition worse.

♦ If he is unconscious but breathing, place

IN AN EMERGENCY!

CALL AN AMBULANCE if:

♦ you think your child has swallowed poison: amounts of drugs, vitamins, and alcohol too small to affect an adult can have serious effects on babies and children. **DO NOT make your child vomit, as the regurgitated poison may cause damage on the way up.**

him in the recovery position (see page 269).

♦ If your child is unconscious and not breathing, follow the ABC of resuscitation (see pages 268–269). Before you begin Rescue Breathing, wipe his face with a damp cloth to prevent you from taking any of the poison.

electric shock

Even safe electrical appliances and sockets can turn into lethal objects if a child pokes wet fingers or metal implements into them. Electric shocks range from mild shocks that cause a brief tingling sensation, to burns and severe shocks that can even stop your child's breathing and heartbeat.

SYMPTOMS

♦ crying from fright
♦ deep burns, often small
♦ muscle spasm
♦ unconsciousness
♦ no breathing

What can I do?

♦ If your child is still in contact with the electricity, the first thing to do is to break the contact between him and the current. Switch the electricity off at the mains or pull the plug out.

♦ If you can't do this, stand on some insulating material, such as a pile of newspapers, a telephone directory, or a rubber car mat. Using a dry, non-conducting object, such as a wooden broom handle, push the electrical source away from your child.

♦ As a last resort, insulate your hand by wrapping it in a dry cloth or some newspaper, or put on a dry rubber glove, and drag your child away by his clothes. Do not touch your child's skin.

♦ If he is unconscious, check his breathing and start Rescue Breathing and CPR if necessary. **CALL AN AMBULANCE.**

♦ If you find any burns on your child, **CALL AN AMBULANCE.** Electrical burns can occur where your child touched the electrical source, but they can also appear on any part of the body that was in contact with the ground. These burns do not always appear serious at first glance, but they can be very deep and always require urgent medical attention.

IN AN EMERGENCY!

CALL AN AMBULANCE if:
♦ your child has lost consciousness, even for a few seconds
♦ your child has electrical burns.

burns and scalds

The aim is to cool the area as quickly as possible. A burn can be superficial, partial thickness, full thickness, or a combination. Young children often panic if they suffer a burn, and may run around and cry or scream.

A superficial burn involves the outermost layer of skin and is painful. It looks red, but heals well. A partial thickness burn involves the whole of the outer layer and is red, raw, and blistered. A full-thickness burn affects all the skin layers and can actually be painless, because nerve endings are damaged. It may lead to scarring later.

Burns are serious in a child as dehydration and shock can result. For all burns, seek medical help.

SYMPTOMS

♦ a superficial burn will be red, swollen, and tender
♦ a partial-thickness burn will be red, blistered, raw, and very painful
♦ a full-thickness burn often looks white or waxy, or dark and charred; it may be painless

What can I do?

♦ Cool the burn by running it under cold water for about 10 minutes. For burns on the trunk, put your child in the bath and use a shower, but don't let him get too cold because he could develop hypothermia (see page 275).

♦ Do not remove clothing that is stuck to the affected area. It doesn't matter if clothes get wet. If necessary, carefully cut around any clothing that is stuck to the skin.

♦ Cover the burn with a non-fluffy, sterile dressing. Alternatively, you can use kitchen film. Do not apply adhesive dressings, ointments, gels, butter, fats, etc.

♦ Get medical help.

IN AN EMERGENCY!

CALL AN AMBULANCE if:
♦ his clothing has caught fire
♦ he has a chemical or electrical burn
♦ he has a full-thickness burn (which may look white or waxy, or dark and charred).

TAKE YOUR CHILD TO HOSPITAL if:
♦ he has any other type of burn.
If you're unsure, call the doctor.

BURNING CLOTHES

♦ If your child's clothes catch fire, stop him moving. Don't let him run about even though he may want to.

♦ Lie him down so the flames cannot burn his face and airway.

♦ Dowse the flames with water.

♦ Alternatively, wrap him in a non-flammable (wool or cotton) coat or blanket and roll him along the ground to smother the flames.

Call an ambulance, even if your child seems well.

seizures

These are caused by temporary electrical over-activity or irregularity in the brain. In young children, the most common cause is a high fever (see pages 224 and 226–227); this causes seizures known as febrile seizures. Other causes of a seizure are a recent head injury, tumours, certain illnesses, poisoning, infection, or congenital brain defects. Seizures are usually isolated events, but epilepsy sufferers have repeated attacks (see page 261).

SYMPTOMS

♦ noisy breathing or breath holding
♦ sudden loss of consciousness
♦ rigid muscles, followed by jerking limbs
♦ temporary loss of control over bodily functions, for instance your child may wet or soil herself
♦ possible frothing at the mouth, blood-stained if she has bitten her tongue

What can I do?

DO NOT attempt to restrain your child in any way. Your initial reaction is often to try to prevent your child from flailing, but you must leave the seizure to run its course. The only reason for ever moving her during a seizure is to stop her getting hurt, for instance by moving her from the path of an oncoming car.

♦ Clear a space around your child to stop her hurting herself on surrounding objects.
♦ Note the seizure's start and finish time.
♦ Stay with your child to reassure her when the attack is over.
♦ If she has a fever, try to bring down her temperature as quickly as possible (see pages 224 and 226).
♦ If your child is unconscious after the seizure, check breathing. If she is breathing, put her in the recovery position (see page 269) and summon help. If she is not breathing, begin Rescue Breathing and CPR if necessary (see pages 268–269).

IN AN EMERGENCY!

CALL AN AMBULANCE if:
♦ your child has not had a seizure before
♦ she has had a recent head injury
♦ the attack lasts for more than 10 minutes.
If you are unsure what to do, call the doctor.

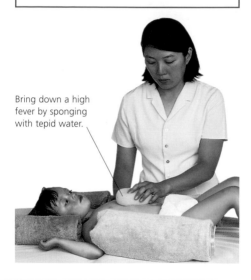

Bring down a high fever by sponging with tepid water.

anaphylactic shock

This is a rare, severe allergic reaction to particular stings, foods (especially nuts), or drugs causing constriction of the air passages. Symptoms may develop within a few minutes of the child ingesting the food or drug or being stung. The face and neck can swell during a reaction, and this increases the risk of suffocation.

SYMPTOMS

♦ red, blotchy rash all over the body
♦ puffy eyelids or face
♦ rapid, shallow breathing
♦ rapid or weak pulse
♦ clammy skin
♦ anxiety or confusion
♦ wheezing or difficulty breathing
♦ unconsciousness

What can I do?

First, **CALL AN AMBULANCE**.
♦ Help your child into the position that best enables her to breathe and loosen any tight clothing.

♦ Reassure her while you wait for the ambulance to arrive. Check her breathing and pulse every few minutes.
♦ If your child loses consciousness, assess her condition and check to see if she is breathing. If she is breathing, put her in the recovery position and wait for help.

♦ If she stops breathing, begin rescue breathing immediately (see pages 268–269).
♦ If your child has a known allergy, she may have medication to take in case of an attack: use this as soon as the attack starts, following the instructions carefully and, if possible, noting the time you gave it.

IN AN EMERGENCY!

CALL AN AMBULANCE if:
♦ you suspect your child is suffering an anaphylactic shock.

Put your child in the recovery position while you wait for the ambulance.

fractures, sprains, and dislocations

Young children have quite flexible bones, so broken bones are unusual in this age group. Until the diagnosis of a break, sprain, or dislocation has been confirmed by a doctor, you should treat the injury in the way described below. Partial breaks, known as greenstick fractures, mend easily. Sprains, where the ligaments are damaged, cause symptoms similar to a broken bone but usually less severe. If one or more bones slip out of place the joint is dislocated.

SYMPTOMS

♦ severe pain and tenderness
♦ swelling
♦ deformity of the affected area, for instance a limb may look misshapen or shorter than the other
♦ inability or reluctance to use the injured part

What can I do?

♦ Do not move your child unless absolutely necessary. Remove any clothing that is constricting the injured area.
♦ You can immobilize the injured limb by strapping it to an uninjured part of the body. You can support an injured arm in a sling, but do not attempt to bend an injured elbow. If you suspect a spine injury, DO NOT move the child. Support her head, place padding around her, and then **CALL AN AMBULANCE.**
♦ Do not give your child anything to eat or drink, as broken bones and dislocations may require an anaesthetic.

IN AN EMERGENCY!

CALL AN AMBULANCE if:
♦ you can't support the injured part while you take your child to the hospital yourself.
♦ you suspect an injury to the spine.

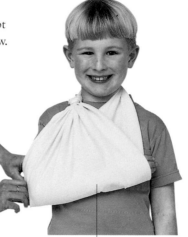

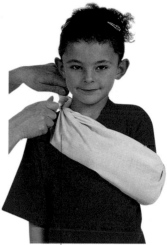

Arm slings support the arm or wrist, or take the weight off the shoulder.

Elevation slings are used to reduce bleeding, pain or swelling.

finger and toe injuries

Hold the fingers under running water to cool the injury.

Trapped or crushed fingers and toes are very common in small children. These injuries can be acutely painful, but are not usually dangerous. Severed digits are very serious, but with prompt action they can be repaired.

IN AN EMERGENCY!

CALL AN AMBULANCE if:
♦ a finger or toe is severed.
Put the severed part in a plastic bag and wrap the bag in a cloth for protection. Place the bag in a container filled with ice and label with the name of your child and the time of the incident. Apply pressure to the limb to stop the bleeding, but do not touch the raw part.

What can I do?

♦ Your child may be frightened and in pain, so stay with her and reassure her.
♦ Run cold water over the injured part or apply ice, wrapped in a clean cloth, or an ice pack to reduce the swelling.
♦ If the skin is broken, apply direct pressure over the wound and raise the limb. Apply a clean dressing.

head injury

Children often bump their heads, and fortunately most incidents are not serious. Any cut to the scalp or forehead will bleed profusely, which is distressing for both parent and child. Severe blows to the head can result in compression of the brain, the symptoms of which may not appear until several hours later, so it is important to be able to spot them.

What can I do?

♦ If your child's head is bruised, apply a cold compress to the bruised area. This can be a cloth wrung out in cold water or an ice pack wrapped in a clean, damp cloth.

♦ Keep checking the bruise. Remove the pad if you see a red patch with white centre.

♦ If there is bleeding, place a clean cloth over the injury and press on the wound.

♦ Check for any unusual symptoms for up to 24 hours (see *In an Emergency!*, right).

♦ If your child is unconscious or the bump is severe:
CALL AN AMBULANCE.

A cold compress can stop the injured area from swelling.

IN AN EMERGENCY!

CALL AN AMBULANCE if your child displays any unusual behaviour or any of the following symptoms up to 24 hours after receiving a head injury:
♦ unconsciousness (even if very brief)
♦ vomiting
♦ noisy breathing or unusual snoring
♦ double vision
♦ drowsiness or loss of coordination
♦ dislike of bright light or headache
♦ discharge from the nose or ear
♦ unusual crying.

UNCONSCIOUSNESS

If your child loses consciousness, check breathing. If he's not breathing, send a helper to call an ambulance and start Rescue Breathing. If he is breathing, put him in the recovery position, then call an ambulance.

drowning

Even very shallow water can be a hazard to babies and children, so never leave a young child alone in or near water. Drowning can kill because inhaled water stops air getting into the lungs. It can also stop breathing by causing spasm of the throat. In addition, cold water can bring on hypothermia (see opposite).

What can I do?

♦ If you can do so safely, pull your child out of the water. Be very careful if there is any chance that he might have injured his neck or back.

♦ Do not endanger your own life trying to rescue a child from drowning. If you cannot reach the child safely unaided, summon help.

♦ **If your child is conscious,** give him comfort and reassurance. He is at risk of hypothermia so keep him warm but don't heat him up too quickly.
CALL AN AMBULANCE.

♦ **If your child is unconscious but breathing** place him in the recovery position and **CALL AN AMBULANCE.** If he is coughing, choking, or vomiting, he is breathing. Cover your child with a blanket, towel, or coat to prevent hypothermia.

♦ **If your child is unconscious** and is not breathing, clear any debris, such as seaweed, from his mouth and begin Rescue Breathing and CPR if necessary (see pages 268–269). **CALL AN AMBULANCE** and continue CPR until help arrives or he begins breathing. If he begins breathing, put him in the recovery position and keep him warm.

IN AN EMERGENCY!

CALL AN AMBULANCE even if your child seems to have recovered now. This is because the airways can swell up later.

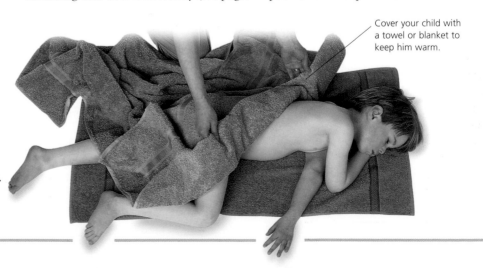

Cover your child with a towel or blanket to keep him warm.

hypothermia

This happens when the body temperature becomes dangerously low, causing body functions to slow down and eventually stop. Babies can develop it quite easily (see box right), but in older children it is most likely to occur after playing outside in very cold conditions or falling into cold water.

SYMPTOMS

♦ shivering
♦ very cold, pale skin
♦ weakening pulse
♦ listlessness
♦ slow, shallow breathing
♦ failing consciousness

What can I do?

♦ The most important thing is to warm your child gradually. Do not put a source of direct heat, such as a hot water bottle, next to your child's skin.

♦ Change his wet clothes for dry ones. Wrap him in warm towels or blankets, or dress him in warm clothes, including a hat, and put him to bed in a warm room.

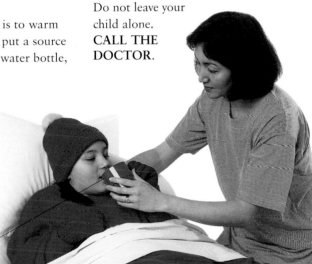

Help your child to sip a warm drink.

IN AN EMERGENCY!

CALL AN AMBULANCE if your child loses consciousness. Begin the ABC of resuscitation (see pages 268–269).

♦ Give him a warm drink and some high-energy food, such as chocolate. Do not leave your child alone.
CALL THE DOCTOR.

HYPOTHERMIA IN BABIES

Temperature regulation is not fully developed in the very young, so babies may lose warmth rapidly and can even develop hypothermia in a cold room.

Symptoms include:
♦ pink, healthy-looking skin that feels cold
♦ limp, unusually quiet baby
♦ refusal to feed.

Increase your baby's temperature GRADUALLY in a warm room:
♦ replace any wet or damp clothes
♦ put a hat on his head
♦ wrap him in a blanket
♦ use your body heat to warm him by cuddling him against your body.
CALL THE DOCTOR.

heat exhaustion and heatstroke

These happen when the body becomes severely overheated. Both heat exhaustion and heat stroke usually occur in hot weather. Heat exhaustion is due to loss of body salts and water due to excessive sweating. Heatstroke is a failure of the body's temperature control system.

SYMPTOMS

Heat exhaustion
♦ headache and dizziness
♦ cramp-like pains in limbs or abdomen
♦ pale, clammy skin and sweating
♦ rapid, weak pulse

Heatstroke
♦ hot, flushed dry skin
♦ temperature above 40°C (104°F)
♦ rapid loss of consciousness

What can I do?

For heat exhaustion
Lay your child down in a cool place and remove his outer clothing. Use a folded towel or pillow to raise his legs. Reassure your child and give him sips of water.

For heatstroke
Heatstroke strikes quickly and your child may lose consciousness. To help prevent this, lay him down somewhere cool and remove his clothes. Cover him with a cool,

IN AN EMERGENCY!

CALL AN AMBULANCE if:
♦ your child loses consciousness or fails to improve
♦ your baby is under a year old.
Open the airway, check breathing, and be ready to start Rescue Breathing (see pages 268–269). If he is breathing, put him in the recovery position.

wet sheet and fan him. Alternatively, you can sponge him down with tepid (not cold) water until his temperature drops to about 38°C (100.4°F) (see page 227).

insect bites and stings

These can be very upsetting and painful for a young child, but most bites and stings are not serious. Some people do develop a severe allergic reaction, known as anaphylactic shock, and while this is rare, it is important to be able to spot the warning signs (see page 272).

SYMPTOMS

♦ your child may be panicking or crying after a sting
♦ the area stung may be red, often with a central white area and a tiny hole, or punctum, showing the site of the sting
♦ alternatively, the sting may still be visible
♦ insect bites are usually bigger than stings, especially horse-fly bites, which are ragged

What can I do?

♦ Bites and stings can be frightening, so it is important to calm your child down and reassure her that she'll be all right.
♦ Keep her as still as possible so you can look at the sting or bite. If the sting is still in the skin, scrape it off using your fingernail or the back of a knife or a credit card.
♦ Hold a cloth wrung out in ice-cold water or a bag filled with ice-cubes and wrapped in a towel over the area to ease the pain and swelling. See the doctor if a sting or bite gets worse in a few hours or days.

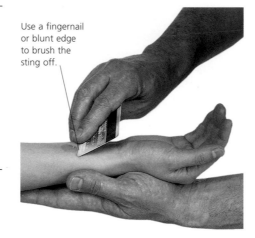

Use a fingernail or blunt edge to brush the sting off.

♦ If your child has been stung in the mouth, give her a cold drink or an ice-lolly to suck, then take her straight to hospital. If she has trouble breathing, don't give her anything to drink.
♦ If your child collapses, she may be suffering an allergic reaction to the sting (see *anaphylactic shock*, page 272).

IN AN EMERGENCY!

CALL AN AMBULANCE if:
♦ your child has difficulty breathing
♦ she has been stung in the mouth or throat
♦ she has been bitten by a snake, spider, or scorpion, or has a severe jellyfish sting
♦ she feels dizzy or faints
♦ she develops a widespread rash.

NETTLE RASH

Nettles cause itchy red bumps on the skin. Dab the rash with calamine lotion to soothe the itching or place a cold compress over the rash for about 10 minutes.

Dock leaves are a traditional remedy for nettle stings, so you may like to find a few leaves nearby and rub very gently onto the area stung by nettles.

If the rash is widespread, **CALL THE DOCTOR**.

cuts, grazes, and bleeding

Cuts and grazes are common in childhood and can usually be treated simply at home as long as they are not dirty or infected, but severe bleeding is serious and requires swift action.

What can I do?

Cuts and grazes
♦ Wash your hands. Rinse the wound under the tap or wipe around it with an antiseptic wipe, or cotton wool and warm water.
♦ Remove any particles of dirt or gravel. DO NOT remove any embedded objects.
♦ Put a plaster over the wound and change daily. DO NOT use antiseptic cream.
♦ See your doctor if it is tender and red.
Severe bleeding
♦ If there is severe bleeding, apply direct pressure to the wound and raise the limb above the level of your child's heart.

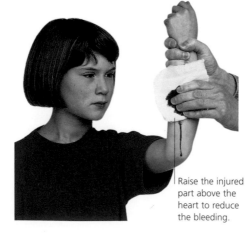

Raise the injured part above the heart to reduce the bleeding.

IN AN EMERGENCY!

GO TO HOSPITAL if:
♦ your child has a large, deep, or jagged cut
♦ she has severe bleeding
♦ she has a bad cut to the face
♦ she has a cut or graze that is very dirty
♦ she has a puncture wound caused by something dirty
♦ she has something embedded in the wound.

♦ Dress the wound with a clean, non-fluffy pad secured with a bandage.
♦ Lay your child down if you suspect shock, keeping the injured part raised, then **CALL AN AMBULANCE**.

foreign bodies in the ears, eyes, or nose

Young children often push items such as bits of food, small beads, and marbles into their ears or nose. It is very important that you supervise young children when they're eating and don't allow them to play with small items such as these until they are old enough to understand the danger they can pose.

What can I do?

♦ Reassure your child. She may be afraid that you'll be angry with her.

♦ If the object is in your child's nose, ask her to gently blow her nose (if she is old enough to understand). Otherwise, or if this does not work, calmly reassure your child, tell her to breathe through her mouth and then **GO TO HOSPITAL**.

♦ Do not attempt to remove the object yourself as you may inadvertently push it farther in.

♦ If the object is in her ear, do not attempt to remove it yourself. Try to find out what the object is. Reassure her and **GO TO HOSPITAL**.

GO TO HOSPITAL if:

♦ your child cannot remove a foreign object from her nose by blowing it

♦ your child has pushed an object into her ear

♦ you are unable to dislodge an object from her eye by washing it

♦ the object is on the coloured part of the eye

♦ the eye is bleeding.

FOREIGN OBJECT IN THE EYE

Particles of dirt and eyelashes often get into the eye, but they can usually be removed fairly easily.

♦ Pain, blurred vision, or a red, watering eye may indicate a foreign object lodged in the eye and your child may rub her eye.

♦ If the eye is irritated but you cannot actually see the object, take her to a doctor as she may have an eye infection, or the foreign object could be hidden under the eyelid.

♦ Reassure your child and try to stop her rubbing the eye.

♦ If you can see the object on the white of the eye, pour clean, cold water over the eye. Tilt her head and aim the water over the inner corner so that water will wash over the eye.

♦ If this does not work, try to remove the object using a clean cotton bud moistened with water.

♦ **DO NOT** touch the coloured part of the eye or the pupil; both of these are covered with a thin layer of cornea, which is very easily scratched, even with a tiny piece of cotton wool.

If you are still unable to dislodge the object or it is on the pupil or coloured part of the eye, **GO TO HOSPITAL**.

Aim the water over the inner corner so that it washes the eye.

nosebleeds

Nosebleeds are quite common in childhood and can be the result of rough play, nose-picking, or excessive nose blowing. Some children are prone to nosebleeds.

What can I do?

♦ Help your child to sit upright, leaning slightly forwards.

♦ Pinch the nostrils together below the bridge of the nose for 10 minutes. Don't release them during this time just to see if the bleeding has stopped.

♦ Encourage your child to breathe through her mouth and spit out the

Pinch the nostrils firmly together.

GET MEDICAL HELP if:

♦ your child's nose is still bleeding after 30 minutes.

blood rather than swallow it.

♦ If her nose is still bleeding after 10 minutes, re-apply pressure for two further periods of 10 minutes. If the nose is still bleeding, get medical help.

♦ Speak to your doctor if your child has frequent or very heavy nosebleeds.

useful addresses

pregnancy and birth

The Active Birth Centre
25 Bickerton Road
London N19 5JT
Tel: 020 7281 6760
Web: www.activebirthcentre.com
Information and classes on natural
active childbirth

AIMS (Association for Improvements in the Maternity Services)
5 Ann's Court
Grove Road
Surbiton
Surrey KT6 4BE
Tel: 0870 7651433
Web: www.aims.org.uk

APEC (Action on Pre-eclampsia)
84–88 Pinner Road
Harrow
Middlesex HA1 4HZ
Tel: 020 8427 4217
Web: www.apec.org.uk
National charity providing support,
information, and education on pre-eclampsia
(helpline open weekdays 10am–1pm)

ARC (Antenatal Results and Choices)
73 Charlotte Street
London W1T 4PN
Tel: 020 7631 0285 (office hours)
Web: www.arc-uk.org
Information and support around
antenatal screening and testing and for
when an abnormality has been diagnosed

Association for Post Natal Illness
145 Dawes Road
London SW6 7EB
Tel: 020 7386 0868
Web: www.apni.org
Advice for women with postnatal
illness and depression

BabycareTENS
108 George Lane
South Woodford
London E18 1AD
Tel: 020 8532 9595
Web: www.babycaretens.com
For the hire and purchase of
TENS machines

BLISS (Baby Life Support Systems)
1st Floor
68 South Lambeth Road
London SW8 1RL
Tel: 0500 618140 (9.30am to 5pm weekdays)
General enquiries: 0870 7700337
Web: www.bliss.org.uk
Helpline for parents of premature
and special needs babies

Caesarean Support Network
Yvonne Williams
55 Cooli Drive
Douglas
Isle of Man
Tel: 01624 661269 (after 6pm)
Support for women who have had a
Caesarean section

Foresight
28 The Paddock
Godalming
Surrey GU7 1XD
Tel: 01483 427839
Web: www.foresight-preconception.org.uk
Association for promotion of
pre-conceptual care for both parents

Independent Midwives' Association
1 The Great Quarry
Guildford
Surrey GU1 3XN
Tel: 01483 821104
Web: www.independentmidwives.org.uk

Issue (National Fertility Association)
114 Lichfield Street
Walsall
West Midlands WS1 1SZ
Tel: 01922 722888
Web: www.issue.co.uk
Advice and counselling on all
aspects of fertility

The Maternity Alliance
45 Beech Street
London EC2P 2LX
Tel: 020 7588 8582
Web: www.maternityalliance.org.uk
Advice and information about
maternity rights and benefits

Miscarriage Association
c/o Clayton Hospital
Northgate
Wakefield
West Yorkshire WF1 3JS
Tel: 01924 200799
Web: www.miscarriageassociation.org.uk
Advice and information on a national
network of miscarriage support groups

National Childbirth Trust
Alexandra House
Oldham Terrace
Acton
London W3 6NH
Tel: 0870 4448707
Web: www.nctpregnancyandbabycare.com
Antenatal classes and postnatal help

Promedics Ltd
Moorgate Street
Blackburn
Lancashire BB2 4PB
Tel: 0800 371614
Web: www.promedics.co.uk
For the hire and purchase of TENS
machines and other pregnancy aids

Quitline

211 Old Street
London EC1V 9NR
Tel: 0800 002200
Pregnancy smoking helpline: 0800 1699169
Web: www.quit.org.uk
Support to help stop smoking

Royal College of Midwives

15 Mansfield Street
London W1G 9NH
Tel: 020 7312 3535
Web: www.rcm.org.uk

SANDS (Stillbirth and Neonatal Death Society)

28 Portland Place
London W1B 1LY
Tel: 020 7436 5881
Web: www.uk-sands.org
National support network for bereaved parents

TAMBA (Twins and Multiple Birth Association)

2 The Willows
Gardner Road
Guildford
Surrey GU1 4PG
Tel: 0870 770 3305; helpline 01732 868000
Web: www.tamba.org.uk
Support and information for families of twins, triplets, and more

Vegetarian Society

Parkdale
Durham Road
Altrincham
Cheshire WA14 4QG
Tel: 0161 928 0793
Web: www.vegsoc.org
For information on vegetarian diets during pregnancy and for infants

baby and child care

Association of Breastfeeding Mothers

PO Box 207
Bridgwater TA6 7YT
Tel: 020 7813 1481
Web: home.clara.net/abm
Information, encouragement, and support for breastfeeding mothers, mothers-to-be, their families, and relevant health professions

Association for Post Natal Illness

145 Dawes Road
London SW6 7EB
Tel: 020 7386 0868
Web: www.apni.org
Advice on postnatal illness and depression

BLISS (Baby Life Support Systems)

1st Floor
68 South Lambeth Road
London SW8 1RL
Tel: 0500 618140 (9.30am to 5pm weekdays)
General enquiries: 0870 7700337
Web: www.bliss.org.uk
Helpline for parents of premature and special needs babies

CRY-SIS

BM CRY-SIS
London WC1N 3XX
Tel: 020 7404 5011
Advice on babies who cry excessively

Gingerbread

7 Sovereign Court
Sovereign Close
London E1W 3HW
Tel: 0800 018 4318
Web: www.gingerbread.org.uk
Advice and support for one-parent families

Health Visitors Association

40 Bermondsey Street
London SE1 3UD
Tel: 020 7939 7000
Web: www.msfcphva.org

Home-Start

2 Salisbury Road
Leicester LE1 7QR
Tel: 0116 2339955
Web: www.home-start.org.uk
Provides emotional and practical support to families with at least one child under the age of five years in their own homes

La Leche League

BM 3424
London WC1N 3XX
Tel: 020 7242 1278
Web: www.laleche.org.uk
Helpline for breastfeeding advice and information, open weekdays 9am–8pm

MAMA (Meet-a-Mum Association)

376 Bideford Green
Linslade
Leighton Buzzard
Bedfordshire LU7 2TY
Tel: 01761 433598; helpline: 020 8768 0123 open weekdays 7–10pm
Web: www.MAMA.org.uk
Advice and support for isolated and depressed mothers

National Childbirth Trust

Alexandra House
Oldham Terrace
Acton
London W3 6NH
Tel: 0870 4448707
Web: www.nctpregnancyandbabycare.com
Antenatal classes and postnatal help

National Childminding Association

8 Masons Hill
Bromley
Kent BR2 9EY
Tel: 020 8464 6164
Web: www.ncma.org.uk
Provides information on all aspects of childminding

National Council for One Parent Families

255 Kentish Town Road
London NW5 2LX
Tel: 0800 018 5026
Web: www.oneparentfamilies.org.uk
Information and advice for lone parents

National Stepfamily Association

(see Parentline Plus)

Parentline Plus

520 Highgate Studios
53–79 Highgate Road
London NW5 1TL
Tel: 0808 800 2222
Web: www.parentlineplus.org.uk
Support and information for parents

Parents at Work

45 Beech Street
London EC2Y 8AD
Tel: 020 7628 3565
Web: www.parentsatwork.org.uk
Helping working parents and their
employers find a better balance between
responsibilities at home and at work

TAMBA (Twins and Multiple Birth Association)

2 The Willows
Gardner Road
Guildford
Surrey GU1 4PG
Tel: 0870 770 3305; helpline 01732 868000
Web: www.tamba.org.uk
Support and information for families of
twins, triplets, and more

Vegetarian Society

Parkdale
Durham Road
Altrincham
Cheshire WA14 4QG
Tel: 0161 928 0793
Web: www.vegsoc.org
Information on vegetarian diets for infants

development

British Association for Early Childhood Education (Early Education)

136 Cavell Street
London E1 2JA
Tel: 020 7539 5400
Web: www.early-education.org.uk
Support, advice, and information for
everyone concerned with the education and
care of children from birth to eight years

Pre-school Learning Alliance

69 King's Cross Road
London WC1X 9LL
Tel: 020 7833 0991
Web: www.pre-school.org.uk
Supporting the work of
community pre-schools

TAMBA (Twins and Multiple Birth Association)

2 The Willows
Gardner Road
Guildford
Surrey GU1 4PG
Tel: 0870 770 3305: helpline 01732 868000
Web: www.tamba.org.uk
Support and information for families of
twins, triplets, and more

health

ASBAH (Association for Spina Bifida and Hydrocephalus)

42 Park Road
Peterborough PE1 2UQ
Tel: 01733 555988
Web: www.asbah.org

British Red Cross

9 Grosvenor Crescent
London SW1X 7EJ
Tel: 020 7235 5454
Web: www.redcross.org.uk

British Standards Institute

389 Chiswick High Road
London W4 4AL
Tel: 020 8996 9000
Web: www.bsi-global.com

Child Accident Prevention Trust

18–20 Farringdon Lane
London EC1R 3HA
Tel: 020 7608 3828
Web: www.capt.org.uk

Child Death Helpline

Open every evening 7–10pm and
Mondays, Wednesdays, and Fridays
10am–1pm
Tel: 0800 282986
For all those affected by the death
of a child

Contact-a-Family

209–211 City Road
London EC1V 1JN
Tel: 0808 808 3555 (weekdays 10am–4pm)
Web: www.cafamily.org.uk
Helping families who care for children
with any disability or special need

Council for Disabled Children

8 Wakely Street
London EC1V 7QE
Tel: 020 7843 6000
Web: www.ncb.org.uk

Cystic Fibrosis Trust

11 London Road
Bromley
Kent BR1 1BY
Tel: 020 8464 7211
Web: www.cftrust.org.uk

Diabetes UK

10 Parkway
London NW1 7AA
Tel: 020 7424 1000
Web: www.diabetes.org.uk

Down's Syndrome Association

155 Mitcham Road
London SW17 9PG
Tel: 020 8682 4001
Web: www.downs-syndrome.org.uk

Hyperactive Children's Support Group

71 Whyke Lane
Chichester
West Sussex PO19 7PD
Tel: 01243 551313
Web: www.hacsg.org.uk

MENCAP

123 Golden Lane
London EC1Y 0RT
Tel: 020 7454 0454
Web: www.mencap.org.uk

Meningitis Research Foundation

Midland Way
Thornbury
Bristol BS35 2BS
Tel: 01454 281811 (24-hour helpline:
080 8800 3344)
Web: www.meningitis.org

Meningitis Trust

Fern House
Bath Road
Stroud
Gloucestershire GL5 3TJ
Tel: 01453 768000
Web: www.meningitis-trust.org

National Asthma Campaign

Providence House
Providence Place
London N1 0NT
Tel: 020 7226 2260
Web: www.asthma.org.uk

National Autistic Society

393 City Road
London EC1V 1NG
Tel: 0870 6008585
Web: www.nas.org.uk

National Eczema Society

Hill House
Highgate Hill
London N19 5NA
Tel: 0870 2413604 (weekdays 1–4pm)
Web: www.eczema.org

National Deaf Children's Society

15 Dufferin Street
London EC1Y 8UR
Tel: 0808 8008880
Web: www.ndcs.org.uk

NHS Direct

Tel: 0845 4647
Web: www.nhsdirect.nhs.uk

Royal Society for Prevention of Accidents

Edgbaston Park
353 Bristol Road
Edgbaston
Birmingham B5 7ST
Tel: 0121 248 2000
Web: www.rospa.co.uk

Scope

6 Market Road
London N7 9PW
Tel: 020 7619 7100
Helpline: 0808 800 3333
Web: www.scope.org.uk

Sickle Cell Society

54 Station Road
Harlesden
London NW10 4UA
Tel: 020 8961 7795
Web: www.sicklecellsociety.org

St Andrew's Ambulance

48 Milton Street
Cowcaddans
Glasgow G4 0HR
Tel: 0141 332 4031
Web: www.firstaid.org.uk

St John Ambulance

27 St John's Lane
Clerkenwell
London EC1M 4BU
Tel: 020 7324 4000
Web: www.sja.org.uk

index

Page numbers in *bold italic* refer to illustrations and captions.

acknowledgements

Dr Carol Cooper would like to thank her agent Catherine Clarke, Anna Davidson and her team at DK, Alison Pottle of the cardiology department at Harefield Hospital, and Maria Buckingham of Chorleywood Health Centre.

Dorling Kindersley would like to thank the following writers:
Pregnancy: Joanna Moorhead
Baby and child care: Tracey Godridge
Development: 0–6 months Katy Holland, 6–12 months Tracey Godridge, 12–24 months and 24–36 months Harriet Griffey

Dorling Kindersley would also like to thank Viv Armstrong of the British Red Cross, Tracey Ward, Nicola Rodway, and Caroline Buckingham for their contributions to this book.

Illustrators Debbie Maizels and Philip Wilson
Indexer Dorothy Frame
Proofreader Alyson Lacewing
Models Whippersnappers Day Nursery, Felstead, Essex; Kasey Berhardsen and Simon Alpin with Lowell, Tracey Townsend, Mark, Sally, Harvey, and Sidney Barron; Arucha with Eya Choudhury, Esmari with Jeanri Burger, Fiona with Beatrice and Tabitha Ashley-Norman, Anne and Roland with Callum Nightingale, Danny with Violet Mermelstein, Mark and Lupia with Sasha Noor, Beej with Ria Shah, Chris Nunn and Julia Nicholls with Lauren, Erin with Gabriel Sorensen, Darren and Louise with Inca Rix, Alison with Leo and Evie Dolon, Julia Harris and Colin with Mari Short, Doug, Tali, Noa, Ella, and Gil Krikler, Joe Ejiofor and Anne Stenett with Lauren, Jeanette and Paul with Daisy Copperwaite, Famoush Bikdeli with Dara Adjudani, Lorna with Rhys and Bethan Holland, Mr and Mrs Stennett, Colin and Veronique with baby Bozunga, Beth and Biraj with Emma Parma, Sarah and baby Broome, Jo with Jade Salliger, Jason with Kasia Wall, Linda with Mackenzie Quick, Simon with Oban Murrell, Rachana with Arianna Shah, Penny with Anastasia Stephens, Thimmie with Emily Pickering, Andrea with Joel Peters, Rachel with Zoe Nayani, Rachel with baby Best, Isabelle with Carla Wicker-Jourdan, Alison with Phoebe Lee, Tali with Gil Krikler, Denise with Kymani and Kymarley Woodstock, Helen with Joseph Jack and Leo Stiles, Mulki with Wyse Ali, Janis and Maureen Lopatkin with Mia Lopatkin, Mr & Mrs Kiyomura with Eri, Michelle with Charlie Terras, Ivor with Ruby Baddiel, Rachel with Zoe Nayani, Maria with Jasmine Leitch, Lilian with Gregory Maya, Tracey with James Coleman-Ward, Faith Knight with her dad, Janis and Maureen Lopatkin with Mia Lopatkin, Mrs Sugiya with Nana and sister, Lina with Anna Maria Sheridan, Shelley with Sadie Goswell, Penny with Evie McCann, Kay with Ben Whiteley, Lynn with Esme Spencer, Carol with Hannah Tennant, Nicki with Max Riggall, Tina with Lewis Oakey, Fiona with Ellie Messer, Sarah with Phoebe Berman, Simon with Lauren Murrell, Deborah with Aaron Bright, Mr and Mrs Perez, George with Sophia Sirius, Tony with Christina and Louise Aquino, Sima and Tim with Danielle and Tal Randall, Gaynor with Oliver Benveniste, Sue with Anya Dziewulski, Deborah with Sadie Seitler, Meena with Shaun MacNamara, Jane with Luke Rimell, Cheryl and John with Yasmin Weekes, Orlean with Ethan Stennett, Sibel with Lara Peck, Teresa with Isabelle.
Hair and make-up Tracy Townsend

Picture researcher Samantha Nunn
Picture librarians Hayley Smith and Sarah Mills

Picture credits
Dorling Kindersley would like to thank the following for their kind permission to reproduce their photographs: (Abbreviations key: t=top, b=bottom, r=right, l=left, c=centre)
17: Stone/Getty Images (bl); 20: Mother & Baby Picture Library/emap esprit; 21: Mother & Baby Picture Library/emap esprit/Ian Hooton (tr); 29: Mother & Baby Picture Library/emap esprit (br); 33: Mother & Baby Picture Library/emap esprit (tl); 35: Stone/Getty Images (tr); 39: SPL (bl), SPL/Neil Bromhall/Genesis Films (tr); 43: SPL/Mike Bluestone (b); 47: SPL/Ruth Jenkinson/ Midirs (t); 49: SPL/Joseph Nettis (b); 51: SPL/Petit Format/Nestle (bl); 53: TCL/Getty Images (br); 63: Art Directors & TRIP/Helene Rogers (tr); 65: Mother & Baby Picture Library/emap esprit/Ruth Jenkinson; 73: Mother & Baby Picture Library/emap esprit (t); Mother & Baby Picture Library/emap esprit/Mampta Kapoor (bl); 75: Mother & Baby Picture Library/emap esprit/Frances Tout (b); 76: Mother & Baby Picture Library/emap esprit (bc), Mother & Baby Picture Library/emap esprit/Eddie Lawrence (br); 77: Mother & Baby Picture Library/emap esprit (bc), Mother & Baby Picture Library/emap esprit/Eddie Lawrence (bl), SPL/Joseph Nettis (tc); 91: Corbis Stock Market/Jon Feingersh; 114: Stone/Getty Images; 116: TCL/Getty Images; 117: Corbis Stock Market/David Raymer; 125: Art Directors & TRIP/Helene Rogers; 145: Stone/Getty Images; 149: Robert Harding Picture Library/Caroline Wood/Int'l Stock (b); 169: Corbis Stock Market/Steve Prezant (tr); 216: Stone/Getty Images; 219: SPL/Medical Illustration, St. Bartholomew's Hospital (tr); SPL/Tricia Reid (tl); 232: Stone/Getty Images; 234: Corbis Stock Market/LWA-Dann Tardif; 235: SPL/Antonia Reeve; 244: Meningitis Research Foundation (tr); 252: SPL/Dr P. Marazzi; 253: SPL/Dr P. Marazzi (cr); 257: SPL/Hattie Young; 258: The Image Bank/Getty Images; 259: SPL/Dr P. Marazzi (br); 260: SPL/Gary Parker (cr); 261: SPL/Will & Deni McIntyre (tr); 265: Garden Picture Library/Juliet Greene.
All other images © Dorling Kindersley.
For further information see: www.dkimages.com